Reconsidering Resilience in Education

Adeela ahmed Shafi · Tristan Middleton ·
Richard Millican · Sian Templeton
Editors

Reconsidering Resilience in Education

An Exploration using the Dynamic Interactive
Model of Resilience

 Springer

Editors
Adeela ahmed Shafi
School of Education and Humanities
University of Gloucestershire
Cheltenham, UK

Tristan Middleton
School of Education and Humanities
University of Gloucestershire
Cheltenham, UK

Richard Millican
School of Education and Humanities
University of Gloucestershire
Cheltenham, UK

Sian Templeton
School of Education and Humanities
University of Gloucestershire
Cheltenham, UK

ISBN 978-3-030-49235-9   ISBN 978-3-030-49236-6   (eBook)
https://doi.org/10.1007/978-3-030-49236-6

This Springer imprint is published by the registered company Springer Nature Switzerland AG
The registered company address is: Gewerbestrasse 11, 6330 Cham, Switzerland

Acknowledgments

The editors would like to thank all of those colleagues from our own institution and those from further afield with whom we have talked about our ideas, our past and present students and our friends and families.

In particular, we would like to extend our thanks to

Prof. Hazel Bryan for her support and encouragement in the early stages of the development of this book.

Dr. Jenny Hatley for her editorial advice and support.

Dr. Paul Vare for his contribution to the development of the Dynamic Interactive Model of Resilience (DIMoR).

Rebecca Pritchard for early contributions to the development of this book.

Augmented Reality (AR) Image of the Dynamic Interactive Model of Resilience

The editors would like to especially thank the hard work of the Creative Computing Team at the University of Gloucestershire in creating the cover diagram and associated webpages to a 3D Augmented Reality visualisation. This involved research students, ***Carl Green, Sam Lord*** and ***Toby Monks***, under the supervision of academic course leader, ***Zayd Abdullah Dawood***.

Contents

Editors and Contributors

About the Editors

Dr. Adeela ahmed Shafi, MBE, Associate Professor in Education University of Gloucestershire, School of Education and Humanities, Francis Close Hall, Swindon Road, Cheltenham, Glos. GL50 4AZ.

Adeela has a background in psychology and education and has been teaching in higher education for over 17 years. Her research draws on psychological theories to explore how to re-engage young offenders with formal education and learning in a secure custodial setting. Adeela's other research includes how to develop academic resilience and buoyancy in higher education students. She has also worked on international projects in Rwanda and Pakistan as well as an EU project on emotional education. Adeela has recently won two EU bids of 3 years duration, each running parallel. The first is on re-engaging young offenders with education and learning with three European partners. The second is a project designed to develop social and emotional competencies through active games in young people in conflict with the law. This is with ten partners across seven European partners. Adeela has an established publishing profile and leads the REF submission for Education at the University of Gloucestershire. Adeela is an active community worker and also stood for MP in 2010. e-mail: ashafi@glos.ac.uk.

Tristan Middleton, Senior Lecturer in Education University of Gloucestershire, School of Education and Humanities, Francis Close Hall, Swindon Road, Cheltenham, Glos. GL50 4AZ.

Tristan is Senior Lecturer in Education and Joint Course Leader for the MA Education suite at the University of Gloucestershire. Tristan is an experienced Primary School Class Teacher, Senior Leader, Special Educational Needs Coordinator and Designated Teacher for both Safeguarding and Looked-After Children. He also ran a Nurture Group for seven years. Tristan is Chair of Directors of Leading Learning for SEND CiC which oversees the work of the National SENCO Award Provider Partnership and also a member of NurtureUK's

Research, Evidence & Ethics Trustee Sub-Group and Associate Editor of the International Journal of Nurture in Education. He is currently a member of the Erasmus+ RENYO project team focusing on the re-engagement of young offenders with education and learning, with three European partners. He has recently published "Using an Inclusive Approach to Reduce School Exclusion: A Practitioner's Handbook" with Lynda Kay, published by Routledge and the book chapter "Teaching Assistants identifying key factors to their successful work with challenging children and finding a new discourse." In: H. R. Wright & M. E. Hoyen (Eds.) Discourses We Live By: Personal and professional perspectives on education. Open Book Publishers, Cambridge. e-mail: tmiddleton1@glos.ac.uk.

Richard Millican, Senior Lecturer in Education University of Gloucestershire, School of Education and Humanities, Francis Close Hall, Swindon Road, Cheltenham, Glos. GL50 4AZ.

Rick is a Senior Lecturer in Education and the Course Leader for the BA (Hons) Education at the University of Gloucestershire where he has worked for the past 10 years. Prior to that, he has a long history of working within education, but in different contexts and phases. These include as a Drama and Music teacher across age ranges, a teacher of learners with social and emotional difficulties aged 5–18, a teacher of English as a Foreign Language to children and adults and a teacher trainer. He has worked in various countries including Spain, Oman and Egypt and in schools, further education colleges and universities including Leeds and Birmingham.

His current interests are in social justice and sustainability and in the role of education in helping to create a fairer and sustainable world. He is currently working on an international research project, A Rounder Sense of Purpose, which is developing a framework of competences for educators of sustainable development linked to the Sustainable Development Goals. This has led to various recent publications alongside work into developing academic resilience and buoyancy with higher education students. e-mail: rmillican@glos.ac.uk.

Sian Templeton, Senior Lecturer in Education University of Gloucestershire, School of Education and Humanities, Francis Close Hall, Swindon Road, Cheltenham, Glos. GL50 4AZ.

Sian Templeton is a Senior Lecturer in Education at the University of Gloucestershire and a practicing Educational Psychologist working with teaching staff, children, young people and their families. She has worked in a variety of educational settings with a focus on supporting the social, emotional and cognitive needs of vulnerable learners to enable them to engage with education. She achieved this through working directly with the young people, with the families, teaching staff and a range of professionals from health and social care. In addition to direct work, she also believes in exploring more systemic opportunities for promoting and supporting access to education for all. She teaches on both Undergraduate and Postgraduate courses within her University role across a range of areas within education and leads on a number of psychology-based education modules. She is involved in ERASMUS + projects related to her areas of interest. Sian's research includes resilience, emotional education and supporting young offenders in re-engaging with education and she is just commencing her DEdPsy at University College London. e-mail: stempleton@glos.ac.uk

Contributors

Adeela ahmed Shafi School of Education and Humanities, University of Gloucestershire, Cheltenham, UK

Jenny Hatley Dept. Education & Inclusion, University of Worcester, Worcester, UK

Tristan Middleton School of Education and Humanities, University of Gloucestershire, Cheltenham, UK

Richard Millican School of Education and Humanities, University of Gloucestershire, Cheltenham, UK

Rebecca Pritchard School of Education and Humanities, University of Gloucestershire, Cheltenham, UK

Sian Templeton School of Education and Humanities, University of Gloucestershire, Cheltenham, UK

Paul Vare School of Education and Humanities, University of Gloucestershire, Cheltenham, UK

List of Figures

List of Tables

Part I
Resilience: Building a Model

Chapter 1
A Need for Resilience

Richard Millican and Tristan Middleton

Abstract This chapter begins by setting the context for the need for resilience. It explores some of the changes to societies that have occurred in recent years arguing that the accelerating pace of change leads to increased stresses on individuals and on society itself. This is placed in the context of a neoliberal political arena and a digital and globalised world. The argument that these issues have the danger of being toxic both to communities and to individuals and can lead to increased feelings of pressure and isolation will be considered. Mental health statistics and crime rates will be used to highlight the need for individuals (and societies) to develop resilience to help cope with the change and flux. The chapter will then proceed to discuss the impact of change on education and argue that parallel pressures exist. It will illustrate the view that neoliberalism has resulted in an instrumental approach to education and discuss how the increasing focus on targets, achievement, competition and marketisation has led to increased strain for teachers and learners alike. An argument will be made that educational contexts are a microcosm of wider society and suffer the same consequences by using statistics of rising mental health issues in learners and teachers and an increasing attrition rate. It is suggested that while educational reform is needed, there is a pressing and additional need for resilience.

This chapter makes the case for a reconsideration of the idea of resilience. It suggests that contemporary life has increased both stresses upon, and threats towards, individuals as well as organisations and society. It presents the view that, as a result, there is a need for the resilience to be able to deal with these stresses and threats, but also to resist them where desired. It makes the case for thinking about resilience as something that is dynamic and interactive whereby the relationship between actors and the structures around them are mutually interdependent so that whilst actions

R. Millican (✉) · T. Middleton
School of Education and Humanities, University of Gloucestershire, Francis Close Hall, Swindon Road, Cheltenham, Gloucestershire GL504AZ, UK
e-mail: rmillican@glos.ac.uk

T. Middleton
e-mail: tmiddleton1@glos.ac.uk

© Springer Nature Switzerland AG 2020
A. ahmed Shafi et al. (eds.), *Reconsidering Resilience in Education*,
https://doi.org/10.1007/978-3-030-49236-6_1

of individuals can strengthen or weaken the structures, so too can the actions of structures nurture or threaten the individuals within.

The chapter argues that the pace of change is ever increasing and that some of these changes have resulted in tensions and conflicts that put pressure on the individuals within society and also potentially between them and could even lead to threats to society itself. It goes on to suggest that some changes seem to imply a lack of congruence between stated aims of and rationale behind the change, and the reality of practice.

Using mental health and wellbeing metrics as indicators, this chapter proposes that current rates of change and the mismatch between rhetoric and reality have led to a growing number of stressors on both individuals and society and highlights the need for both to develop the resilience to be able to cope with, and respond to, contemporary life. It argues however, that this response need not be passive, but could be proactive and anticipatory ie agentic.

Using education as an example of a system within society, the chapter will suggest that, as with the broader context, the rate of change in recent years has increased with a plethora of structural, policy, pedagogical and administrative changes. It draws parallels with wider society, arguing that the result has been greater pressures on the actors within and tensions between them that, ultimately, could impact on the educational settings and even back on society itself. Again, it proposes that there are similar dissonances between stated purpose or 'mission', and practice within the system.

Considering indicators similar as those mentioned above in addition to attrition rates of educators, truancy levels of learners and failure rates of establishments, the need for resilience for all those involved is emphasised and, arguably, for the settings themselves. Moreover, it proposes that resilience should not infer simply a passive ability to cope and endure, but the potential to act and redirect change.

By considering the symbiotic relationship between society and individuals and then, by reflecting on the education system and its impact on the individuals within and how in turn they may react with the system and with wider society, the interdependency of these systems is highlighted.

Consequently, the case will be made for a need for resilience at all levels and a recognition that the actions and behaviours at any level have the potential to strengthen or weaken the resilience of systems around and within. Whilst examples used will predominantly draw on the UK context, issues presented and arguments made are applicable to other contexts.

Historical evidence shows that humans have always been social animals creating and living in social systems but, in common with systems in general, existing in a state of flux. Developments and changes to societies have occurred as a result of external factors like invasions from other groups, food and water supply fluctuations, and natural disasters; or internal developments like technological discovery, shifts in knowledge and understanding, and new ideological movements. While some of these factors have caused shocks to society which take time to recover from eg plague, war, drought and famine, others can be perceived as risks and as such cause stress and anxiety which can be met with resistance eg introduction of new religions, industrial revolution and artificial intelligence. If the pace and management of the change is appropriate, then usually the systems involved can adapt and evolve to accommodate them and survive. However, an important point to emphasise here is that usually this does involve adaptations. In other words, society and the individuals within it have not tended to remain the same, but have undergone a process of change towards something eg beliefs, values, structures, behaviours in order to survive—so new ways of being emerge in response to the factor that occurred. Nothing stays the same. Harari (2015, p. 78) states 'People are usually afraid of change because they fear the unknown. But the single greatest constant of history is that everything changes'.

In recent years, with ever increasing technological advances leading to a digital and globalised world, the pace of change is noticeably greater resulting in the need to evolve and adapt more rapidly (see for example Marsh, 2014). Much of this development is clearly positive as opportunities for people to travel and be more geographically mobile have increased; there are more choices and consumer goods at our disposal; new devices are constantly being invented; and novel and exciting opportunities for entertainment are being developed. Benefits for individuals and society are many as the ease of communication brings us closer and enables us to be more connected with obvious advantages for those with mobility issues; as much labour-intensive work is able to be undertaken by computers; as an increasing number of illnesses and conditions are able to be cured enabling us to live longer and more healthily and, theoretically at least, we have more leisure time at our disposal.

However, despite the obvious benefits brought by these developments, as society and the individuals within adapt to the changes, unforeseen pressures and tensions emerge not because of the technology itself, but due to the speed of introduction and the way it is sometimes used, demonstrating the need for resilience just to remain apace.

The rate of recent changes seems to be placing individuals under tension as they struggle to keep abreast of developments and deal with expectations created. For example, there is increased pressure to purchase and consume and to be financially able to do so. In addition, many feel the need to live what others might judge to be an exciting life that maximises the myriad opportunities available and to display evidence of doing so through social media (see for example Gaskell et al., 2016). In addition, recent research from America has suggested there are causal links between social media use and depression (see Lin et al., 2016).

Looking at statistics of social and individual wellbeing (Wilkinson & Pickett, 2010, 2018; Health at a Glance: Europe 2018) there is evidence that, for example, despite the increases in GDP and technology that were meant to make life easier and less labour intensive, rates of depression, suicide, murder, drug and alcohol addiction and isolation have all increased and that feelings of wellbeing are decreasing. Further, research from Hargreaves et al. (2018) found that the proportion of 4–24 year olds who have a longstanding mental health condition rose from 0.8% in 1995 to 4.8% in 2014.

Added to this, as technology shifts the way that things are done, working environments and practices change and, although governments might claim that employment rates are growing, much of that employment is in unstable, temporary, part time or zero-hour contract jobs (Grimshaw, Johnson, Keizer, & Rubery, 2017). These often lead to insecurities and poor rates of pay and a subsequent increase in the wealth gap with more families and children living in poverty. The richest 10% in Britain now hold 45% of wealth and the poorest 50% just 8.7% (see equalitytrust.org.uk). Those that are in work are frequently working long hours and in stressful conditions. They are left feeling inadequate or unvalued as they are subjected to challenging performance indicators and demanding targets without the security of tenured positions and with reducing trade union protection (see for example The Taylor Review, 2017 and DfBEIS, 2018). It would thus appear that these pressures and stresses on individuals are threatening the ability of many to cope.

Such technological developments are not only impacting on individual behaviours, but as we become more integrated and exposed through physical and virtual contact to different social groupings and practices, individual, local and national customs and cultures change. Indeed, Weinstein (2010, p. xvii) argues that, over the past few decades there has been 'rapid and accelerating rates of change in human relations, from the interpersonal to the international level' leading De La Sablonniere, in her typology of social change, to define 'dramatic social change' (2017) as that which, because of its pace, has the potential to rupture social and normative structures and threaten cultural identity. As the digital generation rewrites and redefines itself and society, some of the value systems and accepted institutions that have been regarded as constants in recent generations have been, and continue to be, challenged. This has led to, for example, reconceptualised understandings and definitions of family, gender, marriage, sexuality, disability, education and nationhood.

A dominant theme of many of these reconceptualisations has been to dismantle inequities and barriers within our systems and to work towards social justice. Suffragette movements to civil rights, anti-apartheid to equal rights, disability rights to gay pride are examples of civil protest movements that have helped tackle the hegemony of white, heterosexual male advantage and have assisted the shift of national discourses to those that recognise the rights of all to fair treatment and equal voice and representation. Whilst there have been some disruptions to this trajectory, gradually attitudes, language, culture and values are changing towards an acceptance of the need for a fairer world and this is, generally, reflected in legislation for example the Human Rights Act 1998, Employment Act of 2008 and Equality Act of 2010.

However, paradoxically, while we see these progressive shifts in mindset, legislation and discourse towards what should be a socially just, inclusive world, the reality is often of a different kind (Fukuyama, 2018). The move towards a digital society and recent political agendas have added to what appears to be the fragmentation of society with a rise in tribalism and individualism and we see increasing numbers of hate crimes towards members of minority groups (Home Office, 2019), continued stigmatism of LGBT members (Gordon, 2016) and underrepresentation of people with disabilities (Powell, 2019) and other minority groups in positions of power (see Home Office, 2018).

Furthermore, the pace of change whereby it is possible to see religious, cultural and family traditions that have been present for generations rejected and eschewed within a lifespan, can also lead to societal and intergenerational strife as older generations struggle to hold onto what is familiar and dear to them while younger generations adopt new and sometimes alien behaviours (Heath, 2014). Alongside this, societal change has meant that some of the support structures that used to exist have weakened or disappeared with fewer people engaged in community organisations such as faith groups, community centres, unions, clubs and societies (Seddon, 2011) and an increasing number of people existing in smaller, more fragmented and dissipated family units with, arguably, less support and protection (Knipe, 2017). These changes are causing further stress, but are also removing some of the supportive structures that help protect individuals and bind them together and help them to deal with the pressures involved.

Such tensions and inconsistencies will inevitably have an impact. There thus appears to be a disconnect, or a lack of congruence, between perhaps what was expected and what seems to be emerging, with the narrative of creating a more prosperous and socially just society and one which continues to show indicators of inequality, marginalisation and social and individual malaise (Wilkinson & Pickett, 2010). This tension seems to exist and to be placing stress at different levels; at the level of the individual as they struggle to cope, at that of the family and local community as they are potentially dissipated and fragmented and at that of wider society where reactions to differences in distribution of wealth and opportunity appear to be resulting in increased resentment and social division (Greitemeyer & Sagioglou, 2017).

Furthermore, recent changes through industrialisation to globalisation and digitisation have led to unexpected consequences beyond those that have occurred directly to individuals and societies and have extended to the environment itself. Many of the recent changes have been predicated on continued economic and material growth which is built on the extraction and use of the Earth's natural resources and on humankind's ability to control nature. However, recent research (eg IPCC 2018) reveals that this threatens the very structures that sustain life as the climate shows signs of change, sea levels rise, much biodiversity is lost and there is increasing evidence that we have entered the sixth mass extinction (the Anthropocene). Recent research from Radchuk et al. (2019) reveals that animals are failing to adapt their behaviours quickly enough to cope with the pace of climate change and that this threatens their existence. This will be discussed further in Chap. 3, but shows how our actions are threatening the resilience of the biosphere that protects us and enables us to survive which will in turn create increased risks and vulnerabilities to us as individuals and societies and is further evidence of how systems are interdependent (see also Bendell, 2018).

Viewing education as a microcosm of wider society, it is arguably possible to track similar patterns. Within England, since a government funded education system began in 1870, there has been a steady flow of policy changes affecting provision. However, in recent years the volume and pace of change has increased with structural changes as a result of, for example, academisation and free schools; content and practice changes, for example national curriculum and exams system revisions; and shifts in accountability through Ofsted, performance-related pay and league tables.

As with societal change mentioned earlier, such changes have ostensibly been made to improve standards, to provide more choice for parents and to break cycles of disadvantage. Successive governments have made alterations to the education system with the intention of creating a 'meritocratic society', to 'not leave anyone behind' and to 'widen participation' thus providing 'opportunity for all'. In other words, as part of an endeavour to create a fairer and socially just society.

Much has been achieved with education acts enabling education to be free at the point of delivery from the age of 4 to now 18, free pre-school education, equal educational opportunities for girls and boys, inclusive practice for those with learning difficulties and/or disabilities and for those of different national heritage or speakers of other languages. There has been a standardisation of the curriculum (Graham & Tytler, 2018) and moves towards more comprehensive and equitable provision and more people are progressing onto university education than ever before (Bolton, 2019).

However, these achievements appear to have had some detrimental impact on both the educators and the learners themselves. Teachers and head teachers find it increasingly difficult to deal with this constant raft of changes and there have been many reports of practitioners working evenings, weekends and throughout their holidays in order to keep abreast of the workload. Perhaps unsurprisingly, as a consequence, we find both an increasing attrition rate as teachers leave the profession and rising incidences of those off work with stress. Perryman and Calvert (2019) found that 40–50% of respondents surveyed had left or were considering leaving the profession within 10 years of starting citing workload (71%) and target driven culture (57%) as reasons, along with wanting to improve work/life balance (75%). In addition, Patalay and Gage (2019) showed that symptoms of depression rose from 9% to 14.8% and self-harm from 11.8% to 14.4% from 2005 to 2015 among young people and recent research from the National Education Union (2019) revealed that 83% of respondents said that mental health of pupils had deteriorated over the past two years with rising reports of anxiety, self-harm and even cases of suicide. It appears again, that people are finding it difficult to cope.

An implication of recent changes is that they have been underpinned by a neo-liberal ideology that is based on the premise that, in order to improve standards and increase efficiency, it is beneficial to create a market that generates choice for users and competition between the providers (Lynch, 2006; Molesworth, Scullion & Nixon, 2010). As mentioned above this has, arguably, been advantageous for the users. Educational standards have seemingly improved and parents and students have more choice and say regarding educational provision. However, it has also meant that the previous settlement and established structures and ways of working have been altered and some of the protective factors such as local authority professional development courses and advisory teachers that used to exist within the education system are under pressure. The formation of academies, multi academy trusts and free schools mean that collaboration between local authority schools and the support structures provided by the council are disappearing; the pressures of the National Curriculum and the English Baccalaureate mean that the opportunity for learners to find space and pathways within the curriculum to follow their own interests and passions is reducing; and league tables based on exam performance and Ofsted data mean that pressures for institutions to conform and follow standardised and established procedures are increasing (Brill, Grayson, Kuhn, & O'Donnell, 2018). This has the potential to increase stresses on individuals within the system, but also on the institutions and structures contained as they struggle to adapt to, and survive within, marketised environments.

It also appears that there is a parallel disconnect or tension between the stated intention of the system eg inclusive, equal opportunity and social justice and the reality on the ground of a system that shows indicators of inequality, increasing stress and narrowing opportunities. Signs of shifting focus from existing as a public service to one that is product and consumer focused are evident, with the over-riding instrumentalist vision of preparing learners for employment, meeting the needs of business and thus growing the economy (see, for example, DfE vision statement 2019). Gaps still exist, for example, between attainment 8 achievement rates and subsequently life chances of learners from different social economic statuses (free school meals 34.4%, others 48.3%), SEN (27.2%, not SEN 49.8%) (DfE Key Stage 4 statistics 2018) and between those learners who attend private schools and those that do not (proportion of private school pupils achieving A*s and As at A level 48%, national average 26%, achieving A of grade 7 at GCSE 63% compared to 23%—Kynaston & Green, 2019). This disconnect between stated intention of achieving a fair system and the reality of the system can again lead to tensions and frustrations and threaten the wellbeing of stakeholders involved.

There is also growing tension between an arts-based, liberal education and one that is employment focused where rewards are not to be found intrinsically, but are increasingly monetised (see for example employability rankings for universities and their courses).

This instrumentalist view of education whereby the focus and purpose are increasingly narrowed and targeted towards employment and ultimately a contribution to economic growth, can also have an impact beyond the immediate actors within the system and on the environment itself. The predominant assumption within much of education appears to be that the world will largely remain as it is and the status quo will continue unchallenged. Consequently, the damage that our actions and behaviours are causing the planet and each other remains generally unquestioned and unchecked and there is a need for an education that encourages us to look critically at the world and to develop what Freire (in Apple, 2018) terms conscientisation, or a rounder sense of purpose (see Vare, Millican & de Vries, 2018 and Chap. 13).

Once again this shows interdependency within the system and how changes to education to improve standards and, ostensibly, to improve opportunities for all, appear to be continuing to harbour inequalities, be adding stress to individuals and the structures within, but how they are also potentially contributing to global and environmental stress, thus demonstrating a need for resilience at all levels.

A functionalist perspective might suggest that such is the natural order of things. That inequalities are not only inevitable, but desirable and that they help society to function and that part of education's role is to help differentiate between the skills and abilities of individuals and to assist each to find their role in society. It might also suggest that there is a need for an understanding and acceptance of difference in strengths and interests that will result in differing levels of achievement and career pathways and that, whilst all roles are vital to the smooth running of society, not all will return similar rewards.

While individuals have the belief that should they wish to, through their own hard work, determination and merit, they too could achieve and become more successful, this acceptance and consensus might remain. However, as the world becomes more digitised, interconnected and globalised and people become more aware of disparities in opportunities and wealth, there are signs of discomfort with this perspective (Bloodworth, 2016) as indicated through, for example, the Occupy Movement (Addley, 2011).

Part of the problem is that, where there are winners, there are also losers. Despite some positive initiatives recently encouraging corporations to adopt ethical and sustainable practices, markets do not tend to have a social responsibility and, consequently, organisations and individuals within them usually exist and work for their own benefit rather than that of others (Amankwah-Amoah, Antwi-Agyei & Zhang, 2017). Hence the success of one company, will normally be at the expense of another, the success of one individual will mean they have beaten others and the success of one school or university will likewise mean the relative failure of other institutions (Dorling, 2016).

Whilst support structures are in place to pick up and encourage the losers and people feel that opportunities are fair, success has been deserved and based on merit and when the difference between being a winner or a loser is not too great, then this may be perceived as acceptable. However, as suggested earlier, many of these structures and networks have themselves been threatened, as families, social networks, support groups, local authority provisions and even national allegiances become fragmented, weakened, or are dismantled.

Moreover, it can be seen that the flow of capital is such that wealth and opportunity appear to be concentrating in the hands of a few. This can be evidenced on a macro level with the wealthy and powerful countries of the north becoming more so at the expense of poorer countries of the south. Similarly, on a micro level where privileged individuals benefit from economic, social and cultural capital providing significant advantages which are used to further themselves rather than to support and develop others.

Such circumstances show potential to lead towards increasing individualism and protectionism. This can play out in political arenas as populistic, nationalistic and intolerant of those of difference, or who do not obviously conform to the norm and contribute to the economy. In the corporate and social worlds it can manifest as short-termist and profit-driven. These disparities in distribution of wealth and opportunity and shifts towards individualism are increasing the risks to individuals and societies and are potentially making them more vulnerable, thus threatening their resilience.

It can be seen that such attitudes are potentially detrimental to the environment too as, while short term political, personal and economic gain remain the dominant driver, there is a danger that the profit motive will override any immediate social or environmental concerns.

From a conflict perspective then, one might be cynical about the way society has been evolving and possibly question whether some of the structures that exist deliberately advantage certain groups eg white, 'Christian', middle-class males whilst consistently marginalising and disadvantaging others. One might reflect on the concentrations of wealth and poverty and the gaps between them and wonder whether structural injustices exist and whether society is as meritocratic as some might suggest.

Such thoughts might lead to dissatisfaction and unease with the way that society has evolved, is structured and is heading. It could clash with sensibilities and values and could feel unfair and unsustainable. These feelings of injustice can themselves be a source of stress and anxiety and can lead to either a feeling of impotence and frustration, or an active desire to make change.

There is therefore, arguably, a need for a critical perspective whereby, if we are sincere about a commitment to social justice and equal rights, we are collectively and individually aware and critical of society and strive to work towards congruence between what we say and what we do. In other words, we seek to remain true to our values and to ease the tensions and conflicts within ourselves, education and within broader society and in so doing, strengthen ourselves as individuals and the institutions and societies in which we live and work.

However, this is not an easy position to take and necessitates strength to analyse self, others and society at large, to reflect on values and the meaning of social justice and sustainability and to actively work towards a fairer world, resisting developments that are unfair, unjust and unsustainable and that as a result cause stress, anxiety and add risk and vulnerability.

There is therefore a need for resilience. But a concept of resilience that does not consider an individual, institution or society as a separate entity to be made resilient and strong. Such a perspective might believe that resilience is found within and that it is possible to provide a fix eg a strategy, a pill, a protective wall or an aggressive marketing campaign that will give strength and protect. Rather, a concept of resilience is needed that recognises that resilience is not within the system and fixed, but something that changes with time and context and is the result of the interactions within and between the system itself and other systems. A concept of resilience that acknowledges the interplay between individuals and other individuals, between individuals, groups and structures and between structures, wider society and the environment. In other words, one that takes a systems perspective and takes account of the interaction between systems and recognises that there are times when there is a need to cope, to adapt and to be flexible, but other times when there is a need to resist and even to be the instigator of change. Thus, a concept of resilience that accepts that systems have agency and thus some control over direction of travel and over response. An understanding of resilience that recognises that it is something that is dynamic and contextual and that emerges from interactions between systems, affecting simultaneously all systems involved in those interactions.

Such a concept of resilience could help shift mindsets. An acceptance that resilience is not within a system eg individual, institution, society, but that it is something that changes and is caused by interactions between systems can assist with this change. It can help with an analysis of individuals, institutions and societies to look at protective factors and causes of stress, risk and vulnerability such as those mentioned above. In other words to look at things more holistically and, if we are serious about striving for a fair world, rather than trying to fix individual systems, strive to create conditions that are nurturing, supportive and protective of all systems at all levels eg that of individual, institution and society and of the environment and thereby create the conditions for resilience—for all to flourish.

This chapter has attempted to show that while change is constant, recent societal and technological advances have meant that the pace of change has increased and has led to a range of stresses and tensions at different system levels from individual, to society and on to the environment as they adapt to these changes. It suggests too, that these system changes have a symbiotic relationship with other systems causing further impact. It acknowledges that many of the changes are positive, but that some will result in unforeseen and unwanted consequences which then create further stresses and tensions in what could become a feedback loop of stress. The chapter indicates that a by-product of the change has been the dismantling of some of the protective factors that were in place that helped enable systems to cope. It makes the case for resilience:

(a) To be able to cope with, and adapt to, ongoing changes and deal with the increasing pace of change
(b) To be able to deal with the tensions and conflicts that exist caused by differences in rhetoric and reality and hegemonic and personal values
(c) To be able to, if so desired, resist pressures and direction of travel and to actively work towards a different way of behaving and living, that on an individual, group, or larger scale might be more congruent in claims of fairness, social justice and sustainability and the way that this is acted out.

However, it stresses that resilience is not something found within, but that it is something that emerges as a result of interactions between systems and, consequently, needs a holistic approach and a mindset that recognises interdependence. Such a mindset would accept that it is in the interests of all to nurture and protect and strive for a socially just and sustainable world and, in so doing, create conditions for resilience for all.

To this end, this book offers a new consideration of resilience and presents a model—The Dynamic, Interactive Model of Resilience (ahmed Shafi et al., 2020) in Chap. 2. This model conceptualises resilience as a quality that emerges as a result of interactions between systems and acknowledges system agency. It also recognises the role of protective and risk factors and system vulnerabilities and invulnerabilities.

Chapter 3 considers resilience above and beyond the individual and highlights the connections between individuals, society and the environment. It stresses the need to view the world and our activity within it more holistically and shows how the DIMoR (ahmed Shafi et al., 2020) can assist with this and help move towards sustainable and thereby resilient societies and individuals.

Chapters 4 and 5 turn attention towards education with Chap. 4 questioning the current system and whether it is helping resilience or hindering it, and 5 critiquing approaches to the teaching of resilience suggesting that it needs to be through a systemic approach rather than through targeted resilience building programmes.

Chapter 6 offers an example of this by looking at the Early Years Foundation Stage and the opportunities provided therein for facilitating the building of resilience.

Chapter 7 uses the DIMoR (ahmed Shafi et al., 2020) to make links between mental health and wellbeing and resilience and thereafter to consider the role of education in meeting needs.

Subsequent chapters focus on UK or European-based research projects within education that have explored aspects of education linked to resilience and illustrate the value of the DIMoR (ahmed Shafi et al., 2020) through various applications. Whilst the nature of these examples are based on the UK or European context, the principles of DIMoR (ahmed Shafi et al., 2020) can be applied to different contexts.

Chapter 8 reports on research into the impact of assessment feedback on student emotional state and uses the DIMoR (ahmed Shafi et al., 2020) to analyse context to identify other risks and protective factors.

Chapter 9 discusses research into practitioner resilience whilst working on nurture groups in the field of SEND. Again findings are analysed using the lens of the DIMoR (ahmed Shafi et al., 2020).

Chapter 10 uses the DIMoR (ahmed Shafi et al., 2020) to analyse the results of a European research project into the creation and implementation of an emotional education programme for school pupils.

The next Chap. 11, is based on research conducted in a young offenders institution that explored the complexities of re-engaging those incarcerated with education and uses the DIMoR (ahmed Shafi et al., 2020) to help structure the experiences and contexts of the young people involved.

Chapter 12 draws links between emergent learning through the use of the internet and Self-Organising Learning Environments (SOLE) and the emergence of resilience and offers suggestions for a pedagogy that helps the emergence and development of both.

Chapter 13 returns to a consideration of broader systems and reflects on the current climate crisis, suggesting that there is a need for a different approach to education that has sustainability at its heart. It presents findings from a European research project that developed a set of competences for educators of education for sustainable development and uses the DIMoR (ahmed Shafi et al., 2020) to show how these can help lead to sustainability and resilience at all levels, from individuals to the environment.

Chapter 14 is a concluding chapter that provides an overview of each, attempting to bring out salient themes towards an overall summary of lessons learnt.

References

Addle, E. (2011). *Occupy movement: From local action to a global howl of protest*. The Guardian, 18 October 2011. Retrieved November 13, 2019, from https://www.theguardian.com/world/2011/oct/17/occupy-movement-global-protest.

ahmed Shafi, A., Templeton, S., Middleton, T., Millican, R., Vare, P., Pritchard, R. et al. (2020). Towards a dynamic interactive model of resilience (DIMoR) for education and learning contexts. *Emotional and Behavioural Difficulties, 25*(2), 183–198. https://doi.org/10.1080/136 32752.2020.1771923.

Amankwah-Amoah, J., Antwi-Agyei, I., & Zhang, H. (2017). Integrating the dark side of competition into explanations of business failures: Evidence from a developing economy. *The Journal of The European Academy of Management, 15*(1), 97–109.

Apple, M. W. (2018). *The struggle for democracy in education: Lessons from social realities*. Milton: Taylor and Francis.

Bendell, J. (2018). Deep adaptation: A map for navigating climate tragedy. IFLAS Occasional Paper 2. www.iflas.info.

Bloodworth, J. (2016). *The myth of meritocracy: Why working class kids still get working class jobs*. London: Biteback Publishing.

Bolton, P. (2019). *Higher education student numbers*. Briefing Paper, No 7857. House of Commons Library.

Brill, F., Grayson, H., Kuhn, L., & O'Donnell, S. (2018). *What impact does accountability have on curriculum, standards and engagement in education? A literature review*. Slough: NFER.

Department for Education. (2019). *About us*. Retrieved November 13, 2019, from https://www.gov.uk/government/organisations/department-for-education/about.

Department for Business, Energy & Industrial Strategy Trade Union Membership. (2017). Retrieved May, 2018, from https://assets.publishing.service.gov.uk/government/uploads/system/uploads/attachment_data/file/712543/TU_membership_bulletin.pdf.

Dorling, D. (2016.) England's schools make us the extremists of Europe. The Guardian, February 23rd, http://www.theguardian.com/education/2016/feb/23/england-schools-extremist seurope-tests-excludes-elitism.

Fukuyama, F. (2018). Against identity politics: The new tribalism and the crisis of democracy. *Foreign Affairs, 97*(5), 90–114, 23p.

Gaskell, G., Veltri, G., Theben, A., Folkford, F., Bonatti, L., Bogliacino, F., Codagnone, C., et al. (2016). Study on the impact of marketing through social media, online games and mobile applications on children's behaviour: Final report. Luxembourg: Publications Office. https://doi.org/10.2818/917506.

Gordon, P. (2016). Bullying, suicide, and social ghosting in recent LGBT narratives. *The Journal of Popular Culture, 49*(6).

Graham, D., & Tytler, D. (2018). *A lesson for us all: The making of the national curriculum*. London: Routledge.

Greitemeyer, T., & Sagioglou, C. (2017). Increasing wealth inequality may increase interpersonal hostility: The relationship between personal relative deprivation and aggression. *The Journal of Social Psychology, 157*(6), 766–776. https://doi.org/10.1080/00224545.2017.1288078

Grimshaw, D., Johnson, M., Keizer, A., & Rubery, J. (2017). The governance of employment protection in the UK: How the state and employers are undermining decent standards. In A. Piasna & M. Myant (Eds.), *Myths of employment deregulation: How it neither creates jobs nor reduces labour market segmentation*, Chapter 11. Brussels: ETUI.

Harari, Y. N. (2015). Homo Deus 2015. London: Vintages.

Hargreaves, D., Pitchforth, J., Fahy, K., Ford, T. Wolpert, M., & Viner, R. (2018). Mental health and well-being trends among children and young people in the UK, 1995–2014. Psychological Medicine. https://doi.org/10.1017/S0033291718001757.

Heath, A. (2014). Introduction: Patterns of generational change: Convergent, reactive or emergent? *Ethnic and Racial Studies, 37*(1), 19. https://dx.doi.org/10.1080/01419870.2014.844845.

Home Office. (2018). Hate crime, England and Wales 2017/18. https://assets.publishing.service. gov.uk/government/uploads/system/uploads/attachment_data/file/748598/hate-crime-1718-hos b2018.pdf.

Home Office. (2019). Hate crime, England and Wales, 2018/19 Home Office Statistical Bulletin 24/19. Retrieved October 29, 2019, from https://assets.publishing.service.gov.uk/government/upl oads/system/uploads/attachment_data/file/839172/hate-crime-1819-hosb2419.pdf.

IPCC. (2018). *Global warming of 1.5°C. An IPCC Special Report on the impacts of global warming of 1.5°C above pre-industrial levels and related global greenhouse gas emission pathways, in the context of strengthening the global response to the threat of climate change, sustainable development, and efforts to eradicate poverty* [V. Masson-Delmotte, P. Zhai, H. O. Pörtner, D. Roberts, J. Skea, P.R. Shukla, A. Pirani, W. Moufouma-Okia, C. Péan, R. Pidcock, S. Connors, J. B. R. Matthews, Y. Chen, X. Zhou, M. I. Gomis, E. Lonnoy, T. Maycock, M. Tignor, T. Waterfield (eds.)]. In Press.

Knipe, E. (2017). Families and households: 2017 Office for national statistics.

Kynaston, D., & Green, F. (2019). *Engines of privilege: Britain's private school problem*. London: Bloomsbury.

Lin, L., Sidani, J., Shensa, A., Radovic, A., Miller, E., Colditz, J., et al. (2016). Association between social media use and depression among US Young Adults, Depression and Anxiety 22:323–331. *Wiley Periodicals*. https://doi.org/10.1002/da.22466

Lynch, K. (2006). Neo-liberalism and marketisation: The Implications for higher education. *European Educational Research Journal, 5*(1), 1–17.

Marsh, P. (2014). The world struggles to keep up with the pace of change in science and technology. Retrieved August 29, 2018, from https://www.ft.com/content/b1da2ef0-eccd-11e3-a57e-00144f eabdc0.

Molesworth, M., Scullion, R., & Nixon, E. (2010). *The martketisation of higher education and the student as consumer*. London: Routledge.

OECD/EU. (2018). Health at a glance: Europe 2018: State of Health in the EU Cycle. *OECD Publishing, Paris*. https://doi.org/10.1787/health_glance_eur-2018-en

Patalay, P. & Gage, S.H. (2019). Changes in millennial adolescent mental health and health-related behaviours over 10 years: A population cohort comparison study. *International Journal of Epidemiology, 48*(5), 1650–1664

Perryman, J., & Calvert, G. (2019). what motivates people to teach, and why do they leave? *Accountability, performativity and teacher retention, British Journal of Educational Studies*. https://doi. org/10.1080/00071005.2019.1589417

Powell, A. (2019). People with disabilities in employment. Briefing Paper No 7540. House of Commons Library.

Radchuk, V., Reed, T., Teplitsky, C., et al. (2019). Adaptive responses of animals to climate change are most likely insufficient. *Nature Communications, 10*, Article number: 3109.

De la Sablonnière, R. (2017). Toward a Psychology of social change: A typology of social change. *Frontiers in Psychology, 8*, 397. https://doi.org/10.3389/fpsyg.2017.00397

Seddon, C. (2011). Lifestyles and social participation. Office for National Statistics; Social Trends 41.

Taylor, M. (2017). Good work: The Taylor review of modern working practices. Department for Business, Energy & Industrial Strategy. Retrieved August 29, 2018, from https://www.gov.uk/ government/publications/good-work-the-taylor-review-of-modern-working-practices.

The Equality Trust. (2019). Retrieved November 13, 2019, from https://www.equalitytrust.org.uk/ scale-economic-inequality-uk.

Vare P, Millican R, de Vries G (2018) 'A Rounder Sense of Purpose: towards a pedagogy for transformation' Research in Action Special Issue (4) TEESNet August 2018 pp.18–22 https://www. hope.ac.uk/departmentsandfaculties/facultyofeducation/researchinthefaculty/researchinaction/

Weinstein, J. (2010). *Social change* (3rd ed.). Lanham, MD: Roman and Littlefield.

Wilkinson, R., & Pickett, K. (2018). *The inner level: How more equal societies reduce stress*. Restore Sanity and Improve Everyone's Well-being: Penguin.

Wilkinson, R., & Pickett, K. (2010). The spirit level: Why equality is better for everyone. Penguin.

Richard Millican is a Senior Lecturer in Education and the Course Leader for the BA (Hons) Education at the University of Gloucestershire where he has worked for the past 10 years. Prior to that he has a long history of working within education, but in different contexts and phases. These include as a Drama and Music teacher across age ranges, a teacher of learners with social and emotional difficulties 5–18, a teacher of English as a Foreign Language to children and adults and a teacher trainer. He has worked in various countries including Spain, Oman and Egypt and in schools, further education colleges and universities including Leeds and Birmingham.

His current interests are in social justice and sustainability and in the role of education in helping to create a fairer and sustainable world. He is currently working on an international research project, A Rounder Sense of Purpose, which is developing a framework of competences for educators of sustainable development linked to the Sustainable Development Goals. This has led to various recent publications alongside work into developing academic resilience and buoyancy with higher education students.

Tristan Middleton is Senior Lecturer in Education and Joint Course Leader for the MA Education suite at the University of Gloucestershire. Tristan is an experienced primary school class teacher, Senior Leader, Special Educational Needs Coordinator and Designated teacher for both Safeguarding and Looked-After Children. He also ran a Nurture Group for seven years. Tristan is Chair of Directors of Leading Learning for SEND CiC which oversees the work of the National SENCO Award Provider Partnership and also a member of NurtureUK's Research, Evidence & Ethics Trustee Sub-Group and Associate Editor of the International Journal of Nurture in Education. He is currently a member of the Erasmus+ RENYO project team focusing on the re-engagement of young offenders with education and learning, with three European partners. He has recently published "Using an Inclusive Approach to Reduce School Exclusion: A Practitioner's Handbook" with Lynda Kay, published by Routledge and the book chapter "Teaching Assistants identifying key factors to their successful work with challenging children and finding a new discourse." In: H.R. Wright & M.E. Hoyen (Eds.) Discourses We Live By: Personal and professional perspectives on education. Open Book Publishers, Cambridge.

Chapter 2
Towards a Dynamic Interactive Model of Resilience

Adeela ahmed Shafi and Sian Templeton

Abstract This Chapter explores a range of theoretical models of resilience and human development to understand the concept of resilience as it has developed over time and how it is understood today. These include both classic and contemporary ideas such as those of Bronfenbrenner, Masten, Rutter and more recently, Ungar and Downes. In doing so, the chapter presents a new model of resilience built by taking the key elements of established theories to offer a dynamic and interactive model of resilience that recognises individual agency and its complex reciprocal interactions both with other individuals but also with the wider system within which the individual unit is situated. This chapter positions the DIMoR as an important contribution to this book in understanding resilience for learning in a range of educational contexts.

Introduction

Resilience originates from the Latin word 'resiliens' and broadly encapsulates the concepts of recoil and rebound. Originating within the field of structural engineering focusing on how our physical infrastructures survive natural disasters such as hurricanes, floods etc., resilience has since burgeoned into a variety of domains including community development, ecosystems and public services. In the 20th Century developmental psychologists started to utilise the term for individuals who had suffered from trauma and 'survived' despite these adverse circumstances.

This chapter explores how resilience has been conceptualised during the 20th Century in the psychological and human development literatures. It will consider how the primary focus within the literature has previously been on individual resilience and does not necessarily consider how the individual also impacts on others.

A. ahmed Shafi (✉) · S. Templeton
School of Education and Humanities, University of Gloucestershire, Francis Close Hall, Swindon Road, Cheltenham GL50 4AZ, UK
e-mail: ashafi@glos.ac.uk

S. Templeton
e-mail: stempleton@glos.ac.uk

© Springer Nature Switzerland AG 2020
A. ahmed Shafi et al. (eds.), *Reconsidering Resilience in Education*,
https://doi.org/10.1007/978-3-030-49236-6_2

A critique of this reductionist approach to resilience will be developed by questioning the validity of generalising these findings to more preventative and proactive approaches. The discussion assesses the contribution that the models of Daniel, Wassell, & Gilligan (1999), Bronfenbrenner (1979) and Ungar (2013) contribute to the understanding of resilience. The chapter will end with the new and adapted model of resilience; the DIMoR proposed by ahmed Shafi et al. (2020), which takes the key ideas of existing models but draws on systems thinking and complexity theory to present a model which recognises the socio-ecologically embedded nature of the individual which acknowledges individual agency as they journey through life encountering many other such systems.

Early Resilience Research

There are many definitions of resilience which have contributed to our understanding of the concept over the last few decades. Within this chapter, we will highlight some of the key definitions as they both demonstrate the development of our conceptualisation of resilience later in this chapter and provide the evidence base for our proposal of more dynamic interactive definition of resilience, which then helps to frame the discussion held in the rest of this book.

Whilst there are many definitions of resilience across a variety of disciplines; there is however, some commonality between them: adaptability in the face of adversity, a focus on positive qualities and strengths, coping with trauma and the appreciation that resilience is not fixed, but an unstable construct that fluctuates over time. There is also more recently the recognition that resilience is a dynamic process, which involves behavioural and cognitive components alongside emotional psychological components that interact with the individual and their surrounding systems. Kaplan (2014) suggests that we proceed with caution however when coming to a definition or focus point for assessing and understanding resilience however in his argument that "Although it is conceivable that the term might usefully be applied to interpersonal as well as individual-level systems, the context for usage should be clarified in each instance." p. 40. Therefore, as a broad definition, this book will focus on the ideas portrayed by Masten (2015), p. 9 where she states the focus on resilience as arising as a result of adaptation and survival of systems after adverse circumstances which at times involves 'successful transformation to a stable new functional state'.

In her seminal book 'Ordinary Magic' (2015), Ann Masten has helped shape our understanding of this evolving understanding of resilience which has developed during the last couple of decades. She has described this as '4 waves' of theoretical and evidence-based perspectives about resilience providing a guiding framework for a broader conceptualisation of resilience.

This chapter will go on to explore the multi-systemic possibilities that can open up the debate and discussion around the concept of resilience even further. Within Wave 1 behavioural psychologists tended to reconstruct the events that led to school failure, delinquency and crime, and serious mental health problems by studying the history of individuals in whom such problems surfaced. Long (2000) argued that this retrospective approach can create the impression that a poor developmental outcome is inevitable if an individual is exposed to adversity since it examines only the lives of 'casualties' not the lives of the survivors. Ideas from Positive Psychology and the work of Martin Seligman et al. (2005) focuses on a strengths-based approach through the exploration of factors which can contribute to the sustainability of individuals and communities. The research on resilience has therefore explored factors that contribute to the lives of survivors in order to establish *how* they have survived despite adversity and individual risk factors. Three main groups were initially identified by Masten et al. (1990) as the focus from which to provide a lens to explore these survivors who recovered and prospered despite significant factors which could interfere with healthy development:

1. Individuals who thrive despite their high-risk status (such as birth defects);
2. Children who develop coping strategies in the face of adversity (such as children of parents/carers who misuse alcohol and/or drugs);
3. Those who have suffered extreme trauma (such as sudden bereavement, abuse, natural disasters or war).

In recognition of the variable contexts and qualities that might influence resilience, Werner & Smith (1982) advocated the importance of developing a lifespan approach to understanding resilience. In light of the above considerations, Wang, Haertal, & Walberg (1997) suggested that resilience develops where individuals succeed despite personal vulnerabilities that have arisen as a result of events and conditions within their environmental context. The focus in these ideas is very much on the individual and the skills and traits that they bring to the task of lifespan development.

This early research focus led to an initial conceptualisation of resilience as an 'individual invulnerability' with a focus on the individual qualities of resilient children (Cefai, 2007; Gilligan, 2004). This approach implied that resilience was absolute and unchanging; more of a character 'trait' rather than contextualising resilience within a broader sphere. The idea of resilience being a 'character trait' was further perpetuated through ideas put forward by Daniel et al. (1999) in their model which explored resilience as being on a spectrum of resilience and vulnerability. We will explore their model in more detail later in this chapter, however, a key factor in this model is proposed by Daniel (2003) in his highlighting of the resilience dimension as referring to the intrinsic qualities of the individual. Although there was a growing interest in understanding resilience, not all research at the time was focusing on this 'trait' nature of resilience. Even before Daniel, Wassell & Gilligan's model was developed, Masten (1994) cautioned against using the term 'resiliency' because of the association with personality traits. The potential danger of this association was an acceptance that some individuals had the 'ability' to be resilient whilst others did not which is contrary to the strengths-based understanding within the field of resilience. Masten advocated to instead use the term 'resilience' more flexibly to describe positive adjustment when experiencing disruption. Gilligan (2004) also recognised the potential limitation of perpetuating the 'fixed' idea of a trait-based understanding of resilience and suggested that instead we need to recognise the variable quality of resilience and the role of reciprocal relationships and interactions between an individual and their personal context as being key rather than an individual's personality.

In recognition of the potential of personal context to contribute to the healthy development of an individual's resilience, Kaplan (1999) posited that resilience was an integrative theory of adaptation of life stress. In this definition, Kaplan recognised that adaptability is key in that there are individual differences in both the *development of resilience* and *response to stressful life events*. For example, in the face of bereavement, no two individuals will respond in the same way; their response will depend upon (amongst others); culture, faith, prior experience, personal factors etc. It is also important to note here that responding in a resilient manner does not equate to (in the case of bereavement) supressing the emotional response and behaving as if there has been no change in the individual's life circumstances. Dent & Cameron's (2003) discussion of resilience as the ability to 'bounce back' from adversity perpetuates the expectation that individuals should just 'move on' from extremely challenging life events. There is a danger in this conceptualisation of resilience as 'bouncing back' because this can minimise the impact of adversity on individuals, thus promoting the expectation that we, as humans, should just be able to 'get over it' despite circumstances which challenge that. Relating to this, it is also important in terms of engendering a resilient approach to be able to manage difficult feelings and recognise that they are valid. This construct of moving on instead of recognising impact could be potentially contributing to the increasing prevalence of mental health needs within our population and is discussed in more detail in Chap. 7.

The development of resilience in children and young people could be viewed as being compromised by the notion that resilience is founded upon risk factors and promotors. This challenge is well illustrated through the consideration of Adverse Childhood Experiences (ACEs), situations where children do not have access to the typical human adaptive systems and are instead in situations of threat beyond the bounds of their capacity (Masten, 2015, p. 286). The ACE Study (Felitti et al., 1998) identified seven categories of adverse experiences, later increased to nine (Bellis et al., 2013) and then ten categories (McEwen & Gregerson, 2019). Felitti et al.'s (1998) research identified a correlation between the number of Adverse Childhood Experiences (ACEs) and later challenges in life. Whilst there is considerable statistical evidence to support the view that ACEs are risk factors which impact negatively throughout a person's later life, there is the risk of giving too great a focus upon risk factors and considering that young people who have experienced a high number of risk factors have a pre-determined negative outcome in later life. The reality is illustrated recently by author Kerry Hudson (2019), who scored eight out of ten on the ACE's measure of childhood trauma, having attended nine primary schools and five secondaries, lived in council flats and Bed & Breakfast accommodation with her single mother, amongst other experiences, and is now a successful novelist. It is interesting to note that many of the characteristics are of families and communities rather than individual children thus re-affirming the potential impact of exploring resilience at a wider systemic rather than individual level.

The research now sought to identify protective forces which set those resilient children apart from those who did not adjust so successfully. From the field of Social Work and as a result of his work with children and young people in the looked after system, Gilligan (2004) summarises this change in thinking about the construct of resilience "… while resilience may previously have been seen as residing in the person as a fixed trait, it is now more usefully considered as a variable quality that derives from a process of repeated interactions between a person and favourable features of the surrounding context in a person's life." p. 94 As a result of this recognition of the potential for external factors to the individual to influence their development trajectory, the idea of 'protective factors' being able to 'balance out' the risk factors; the analogy of a 'see-saw' (Fig. 2.1) is often used to exemplify this. Werner & Smith (1982) go on to argue that protective factors have a stronger impact on a child's developmental pathway than risk factors. This led to a focus on how educators and others within an individual's ecology could support the development of resilience through a focus upon protective factors (Fig. 2.2).

A key theme within the protective factors literature is around the importance of relationships either within the family or externally (Werner & Smith, 2001; Rutter, 2013). Werner's research as far back as 1993 identified stable care and 'appropriate attention' during the first year of life as particularly powerful protective factors

> Wave 1: This wave was broadly 'descriptive' and focused on developing an understanding of the concept in its own right.
>
> Wave 2: Focused on an exploration of processes leading to resilience and introduced the idea of 'protective factors' with an emphasis on exploring how protective factors work and how do individuals survive when exposed to risk within their environment. Research in this wave explored notions of proximal and distal factors influencing the development of resilience.
>
> Wave 3: Concentrated on the promotion of resilience through interventions and continued to explore risk and protective factors in more depth. This wave recognised the potential for individuals and settings to make a difference to outcomes for individuals and focused on exploring what could be done to optimise these outcomes. This led to a continued exploration of risk and protective factors in more depth.
>
> Wave 4: This wave, largely initiated by the work of Michael Ungar (2013) in his recognition of the importance of analysing the interactions between individuals and their contexts and individual differences. There is also currently a growing discussion around the possibility of genetic influences on outcomes and how these might interact with the individual and their environment (Rutter 2013).

Fig. 2.1 The waves of resilience research

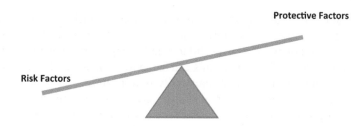

Fig. 2.2 Balance between risk and protective factors

or through a recognition of the opportunities for relationships with others within the wider system of the individual, (such as school teachers). There is a danger of an overly simplistic interpretation of these findings though, as Werner (1993) acknowledged the nuance of the dynamic within the parent/child in her findings within the famous Kauai Longitudinal study. This study was the first study to explore the impact of biological, psychological and adverse life events from birth to mid-life on a cohort which included individuals from a range of ethnic, social and economic backgrounds. The study identified the importance of the dynamic nature of resilience and highlighted the importance of families in contributing to this; considering them to be a 'protective factor' in the development of resilience. However, within this study Werner found that those babies who were socially active with helpful sleeping and feeding habits tended to elicit more positive responses from carers and other adults therefore highlighting the complexity of the dynamic.

In addition to the importance of families demonstrated by the Kauai study, a variety of other protective factors have also been identified within the wider literature through research with survivors of adversity. These are grouped into three broad categories:

- **'Within person' focused** such as: personality traits; cognitive ability and scholastic competence (Condly, 2006); social competence (including eliciting positive response from others, Bernard, 1991); agency (Bohle, Etzold & Keck, 2009); problem solving skills (Bernard, 1991)
- **Relationship focused** such as: relationships with schools' staff (Catalano et al., 2004), Sense of community and social support (Luthar et al., 2000)
- **Context focused** such as: Participation in religious organisations (Ungar, Ghazinour, & Richter, 2013), Staying in school (Ungar et al., 2013).

An understanding of protective factors can help us to conceptualise resilience as a framework from which we can develop an understanding of what is going on (for the individual, the setting, the family). A futures pathway can then be formulated which mitigates these absences and thus optimises the developmental pathway of an individual. For example, a child who lives within a disrupted family environment might have a key person who supports them in the school setting which helps to mitigate against less available care and support in the home setting. Alternatively, an example might be a neighbourhood where there are high levels of youth violence and disruption offers opportunities for youths to proactively engage in problem-solving the difficulties and suggesting and implementing potential solutions. The potential in understanding the range of protective factors provides us with the opportunity to target interventions with an evidence base; focusing on what works and what has gone well previously thus optimising the potential for the optimisation of developmental pathways.

As discussed earlier, interventions have focused on building an individual's resilience through a focus on the above areas. Examples of this in educational practice include the Young Minds Interactive Resilience Framework (Young Minds, 2012) which provides an explanation and evidence base of the protective factors identified and ideas for how educators might develop these factors within a school environment. However, although it is very useful for educators to be able to access resources such as that of the Resilience Framework, we need to be cautious about drawing causal links. This is because it is difficult to identify whether someone who appears to be well-adapted and has lots of protective factors in place are not just coping because they haven't had the exposure to significant risk factors such as those described by Werner yet.

In an attempt to recognise the interactive nature of risk and protective factors and the links between resilience and vulnerability, Daniel et al. (1999) developed the model shown in the Fig. 2.3.

The resilience dimension is used to refer to intrinsic qualities of an individual; these are personal qualities of the individual or the 'nature of the person' such as their

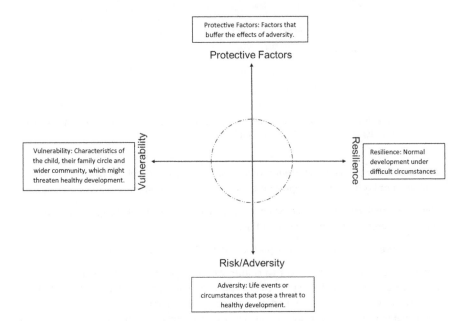

Fig. 2.3 A spectrum of resilience and vulnerability Daniel et al. (1999), p. 61

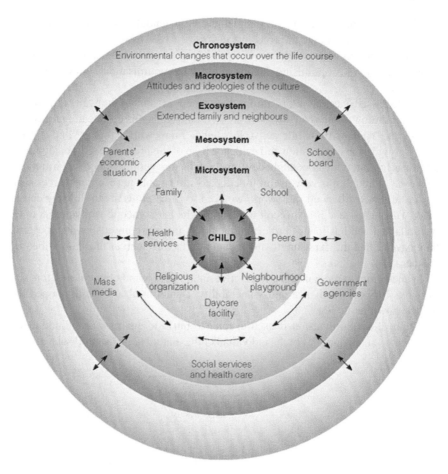

Fig. 2.4 Bronfenbrenner's bio-psych-social-ecological model of human development. Source: http://msnaeemsclass.weebly.com/developmental-theories.html

An example of equifinality in the education arena for a teenager could be when the school environment becomes more important than the home environment.

The differential impact could be when the protective factor of belonging to a group of friends has greater impact than that of the parents.

Similarly, the cultural moderation aspect would determine how this played out.

For example, if the child belongs to a culture where family and community has greater importance, which would affect the child's appraisal of a negative situation at school. In essence, Ungar's model attempted to enhance Bronfenbrenner's model with these additional principles and are drawn from his own social-ecological model of resilience.

Fig. 2.5 Example of equifinality, differential impact and cultural moderation

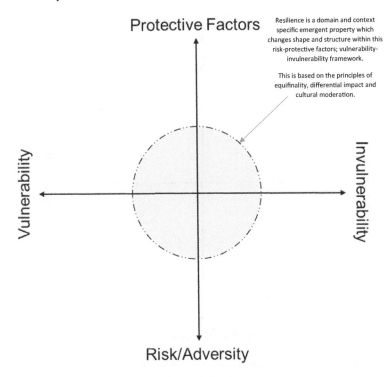

Fig. 2.6 The adapted Daniel et al. (1999) model of resilience

personal traits and behaviours; having a secure attachment; well-developed intrapersonal and interpersonal skills; being socially included and problem-solving skills amongst others. Goldstein & Brooks (2014) highlight the importance of individuals being aware of these intrinsic qualities through: self-cognition (individuals cognitive evaluative response to these traits, behaviour and experiences); self-evaluative (linking to Carl Rogers ideas of congruence between our actual and ideal self (see Rogers, 1959 for more on the ideas of congruence)); and finally self-feelings (contiguity of individuals actual and ideal self which in turn reduces negative self-feelings and maximizes the probably of more positive self-feelings). Through this self-awareness and evaluation an individual is therefore more likely to be situated towards the 'resilience' pole of this dimension.

The vulnerability dimension is defined by 'susceptibility to negative developmental outcomes after exposure to risk factors such as perinatal stress, poverty, parental psychopathology, and disruptions of their family unit.' (Werner, 1993, p. 503). It therefore refers to the more immediate systems around the child which might threaten optimal development such as having an isolated parent, lack of community support and poor housing. The final dimension identified for the understanding of individual differences is that of protective, (such as a positive school experience), and adverse (i.e. parental depression, domestic violence) environments.

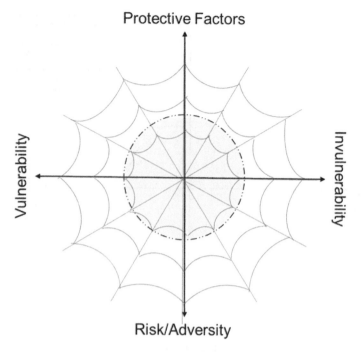

Fig. 2.7 Our developing model of Daniel et al. (1999) and Bronfenbrenner

For example, the wider system could be a particular school, its organisational structure, the physical structure of school buildings/layout, its policies, rules, location, the culture. Within this wider system are all the individual systems such as other pupils, teachers or support staff all of whom reciprocally interact with the wider system and its own structure, reflecting Morin's notion of complexity.

Fig. 2.8 Example of a wider system

This dimension covers extrinsic factors and is therefore located at the outer ecological levels of family and wider community. When considered together Daniel, Wassell & Gilligan argued that these dimensions provide a framework for the assessment of adverse and positive factors at all ecological levels of a child's socio-emotional environment. The two dimensions will interact: an increase in protective factors will help to boost a child's individual resilience. They refer to their model as providing a framework for assessment, however, individual differences which have been acknowledged by a range of authors highlights issues such as; how do we measure what is risk for one person as being a risk for another person? How do we measure comparable impacts of different risky situations? An additional concern is around the use of 'poles' to differentiate between the concepts included on the model, for example—is resilience the opposite of vulnerability; some individuals may appear invulnerable due to the perception that they have not yet experienced adversity. They therefore may not have had the opportunity to demonstrate either vulnerability or resilience as their internal resources have yet to be tested; should we instead be recognising a subtler, less polarised notion of resilience? Considerations such as these will be explored later in the chapter when we adapt the model to encompass a framework extends our understanding of resilience.

Moving towards this is Luthar, Chichetti, & Beckers' (2000) definition which suggests that resilience is "a dynamic process encompassing positive adaptation within the context of significant adversity" (p. 543). This leads us to a conceptual-isation of resilience as that of competence and success despite adversity and disad-vantage which is a less polarised view than the Daniel et al. model. This definition is important in the development of our understanding of the concept of resilience in that it highlighted at the time that resilience was not about just coping with every day knock backs, but that the true test of resilience occurred in the face of significant adversity which interfere with an individual's life course development. This also highlights again that not all challenging life experiences are experienced equally, but that there is a recognition that when risk factors and stressful events outweigh protective factors then even the most resilient of individuals can develop problems.

Resilience as Dynamic and Interactive

More recently, the interactive and dynamic nature of resilience has been the focus of discussion in the wider literature. Rutter (2013) proposes that "resilience is an inter-active phenomenon... indicating that some individuals have relatively good outcome despite having experienced serious stresses or adversities" (p. 474). This definition still appears to place the emphasis on resilience as an individual construct although it differs from earlier definitions in its acknowledgement of the dynamic nature of this construct and individual differences within it. Ungar (2013) adds to this, focusing on resilience as more of a *process,* (rather than individual phenomenon), which can optimise an individual's ability to cope when facing significant adversity. This defi-nition from Ungar recognises the potential for other factors outside of the individual to influence the coping mechanisms of individuals, particularly in relation to his emphasis on the *quality* of the multiple systems that an individual interacts with and how the *quality* of these systems accounts for most of the individuals developmental success under negative stress. This recognition of the wider influences on individ-uals as systems is reinforced through Masten (2016) in her suggestion that resilience is "the capacity of a system for successful adaptation to disturbances that threaten system function, viability or development" (p. 298). The idea of successful adapta-tion recognises the range of, and variability in, influences on optimal development. It also highlights the need for exposure to risk in order to develop resilience; we need to be able to develop strategies to help us to 'cope' in stressful and challenging situ-ations, but we can only develop those strategies after exposure to challenge and risk. In his 2013 paper reviewing the literature on resilience, Michael Rutter illustrated this using the analogy of immunisations; we develop a resistance to the disease as a result of being exposed to the disease in the first place, not from completely avoiding contact. Rutter (2013) called this the 'steeling effect' because this has a strengthening effect with regards to later adversity. In this paper, he also introduces the idea of 'bidi-rectional effects', which recognises the reciprocal interactive nature of relationships. This can be illustrated through the example of how a parent might respond to a child refusing to go to school because of being bullied and how the child then responds to that parent, compared to how a parent responds to child refusing to go to school because they have not completed their homework. These 'bidirectional effects' are key to a deeper understanding of resilience and will be explored in more detail later in this chapter.

Until this point, the literature described has focused primarily upon within child factors which may/may not contribute to the development of resilience. This construc-tion as a consequence of this is also is in danger of blaming the individual when things go wrong or they fail to adapt to adverse situations and events. This approach has the potential to limit individuals and does not provide a platform from which to explore the potential for further development. In line with Masten's (2015) ideas described above and presented as part of Wave 4, this chapter will now move on to presenting the need for a more systems-based approach to exploring and analysing resilience, recognising the range of systems an individual is situated within.

Resilience from a (Complex) Systems Approach

Systems thinking emerged from a critique of the reductionist approach of researching phenomena by breaking it down into its constituent parts in order to understand it. By contrast, systems thinking seeks to explore a phenomenon either as a system or as part of a system. For example, exploring resilience as a characteristic of just the individual would not be sufficient, rather it is better to explore resilience within the individual in a way that recognises and acknowledges that the individual is a system within other systems. This includes how the individual is situated within a family, community and a society. Resilience research came to recognise this as discussed earlier but referred to these other systems as proximal or distal factors that interacted with and predicted risk or protection. Such models came to be known as social-ecological approaches.

Ungar and colleagues (2013) made the connection between Bronfenbrenner's (1979) seminal ecological model of human development and the parallel advances centred around a social-ecological interpretation of resilience. Bronfenbrenner later updated this model to emphasise the importance of proximal processes of Person, Place, Context and Time (PPCT) as being at the heart of human development which resulted in a re-labelling of the model to a bio-ecological theory; a fuller explana-tion of this updated model can be found in Bronfenbrenner & Morris (2007). The basic principles of Bronfenbrenner's bio-ecological model emphasised the impor-tance of context on human development. Its major feature included the concept of a range of nested systems centring around any individual or organism. These are the microsystem, mesosystem, macrosystem (and a later added chronosystem). In terms of education, the microsystem is concerned with the immediate (social) environment in which a child is situated. Those in the microsystem have the most direct impact or influence on the child and would include the parents, siblings, friends, teachers, extended family—all those with whom the child has immediate, direct and day-to-day interactions. The mesosystem involves the interaction between those actors who are in the microsystem but the interactions may not necessarily involve the child directly, but still have an influence on them. The macrosystem is further away from the individual child and includes the wider community, such as the school, church, community, local authorities—some would also include socioeconomic status, ethnicity, culture and other features of the wider environment that have an influence on the meso and microsystems. The child is not likely to have direct interaction with the macrosystem. The chronosystem refers to the time and historical era within which a child is living and how that impacts on their life. For example, the impact of technology in current times very much shapes the child's interactions at the micro, meso and macro levels.

Underpinning this is the idea that the individuals own repertoire of characteristics interact in idiosyncratic and dynamic ways shaping their world and in turn shaping their own ongoing development. This is where the aspects of Person, Place, Context and Time become essential elements within Bronfenbrenner's ideas. Place focuses more around the mesosystem and the importance of people and objects and their influence on human development with Person encapsulating the individual's bio-psychological characteristics such as disposition, bioecological resources and demand characteristics. Context encompasses the number of connections and nature and quality of these connections; this might include closer influences such as those systems within the mesosystem but also those more distal factors from within the exosystem such as decisions made by social institutions (i.e. whether or not a school might introduce an after-school club or a parents work place adopting flexi time to allow parents to leave work in time for school pick ups) and also incorporating the macrosystem such as government policy decisions etc. Finally, Time refers to continuities and changes over time which can be internal (such as aging/disease) and consider an individual's lifecourse or through successive generations.

These ideas moved the debate and research on resilience from a focus on the individual to the individual as a system within wider dynamic and interactive systems—all of which influence an individual's resilience following adversity. However, as pointed out earlier, there has been less focus on exploring the multiple and simultaneous interactions between systems such as individuals, family, school, rather than just dual interactions of, for example, individual-family, individual-school, family-school. Instead, it is necessary to explore the multiple interactions between these mesosystems and the other systems in order to explore resilience in a more nuanced way (ahmed Shafi et al., 2020).

Bronfenbrenner himself acknowledged that his representation of the bio-psycho-social-ecological system appeared to reduce interactions into a necessary order rather than the complexity as described above. Ungar made the links between Bronfen-brenner's ideas and resilience in a number of papers of which the Ungar et al. (2013) was a significant contribution. In this review of the research they found that there were additional features which contributed to our understanding of resilience: the more that a child is exposed to adversity, the more a child's resilience depends on the quality of the environment, (rather than their personal qualities), and the resources available to nurture and sustain well-being. They emphasised that access to these resources that nurture well-being were shaped by negotiations between individuals or groups (such as families and communities), and those such as schools and local governments who act as the gatekeepers to the resources. How successful these negotiations were and the extent to which they were 'constrained' or 'facilitated' either optimised, or was detrimental to, the efficacy of the individual and the group. These factors can operate between many of the different systems highlighted in Bronfenbrenner's original model with Ungar et al. (2013) re-emphasising Bronfenbrenner's original argument that no one system has supremacy over any other system; instead system interactions across levels are understood to be complex and the boundaries between these different levels flexible. Ungar's (2013) social ecological model attempt to respond to this and posited three principles of resilience: *equifinality, differential impact* and *cultural moderation. Equifinality* referred to how in particular circum-stances, one system or another can become more influential to the outcome, where in certain circumstances, the environment is more important than individual charac-teristics and sometimes, individual characteristics are more significant. The *differ-ential impact* notion suggests that protective factors can have a differential impact in different contexts and time. This differential impact results from both an individual's perception of resources available and the structures which are in place to make it more or less possible to fully exploit the available and accessible resources; this concept leads to a significant point of divergence between positive psychology and the study of resilience. If, for example, there was an intervention focusing on the development of self-efficacy such as assigning a mentor for an individual, this may have a small positive effect on the individual and others involved in the mentoring programme. The mentoring may have a small positive effect across the population involved in the mentoring programme. However, there may be no effect, or a much larger effect than expected when mentoring is provided for an individual facing high levels of adversity; thus, helping to explain complexity rather than homogeneity in the way that humans in different contexts respond to adversity. This leads on to *cultural moderation*, which, although implicit in the principles of equifinality and differential impact, brings to the fore the cultural impact on an individual's appraisal of a situation and the extent to which this influences resilience and suggests that how individuals explore and negotiate for resources is influenced by culture (Chen & Rubin, 2011).

In their discussion around equifinality, differential impact and cultural moderation, Ungar et al. (2013) suggest that the environment is therefore often more important that the individual, however, we would argue that this ignores that role of indi-vidual agency. In 2017, Paul Downes also recognised this and proposed a further model of resilience, which attempted to reconceptualise foundational assumptions of resilience, by proposing a cross-cultural, spatial systems domain that took account of individual agency in resilience trajectories. Downes drew upon both Bronfenbrenner and Ungar's models of resilience and, builds on a re-interpretation of Lévi-Strauss & Weightman (1973) ideas of cross-cultural observations of contrasts between concentric and diametric spatial systems. A diametric spatial structure may be visualised as a rectangle split in half, whereas concentric spatial structure is a circle with another inside it, essentially sharing a common central point.

Both these structures exist together as part of a system of relations and are mutually interactive. However, in diametric space, both oppositional realms can be detached whereas in a concentric space, there is an assumed connection. Downes uses this notion of space as an application of self to other in his phenomenological account of resilience. Particularly, how individual agency interacts with various aspects of their contextual and spatial systems to challenge the notion of 'bouncing back'—because bouncing back assumes a return to the same place. Downes' approach recognised that resilience and how an individual's agency interacts in the concentric and diametric spaces of relation means that a person does not 'return' to a previous place before adversity, but actually moves along in time and space, depending on their phenomenology. This offers an explanation that brings individual agency and interpretation into sharper focus more so than previous models, which have objectified the individual as having intrinsic qualities, such as intelligence, calm manner and other such factors that impact resilience. Biesta (2016) develops this further with his comments around the role of agency and his emphasis on the need for us as humans to develop within an action orientated framework where we rely "on the activities of others to take up our beginnings, yet others will always do so in their own, unpredictable ways… we can only be free when we act." (p. 92). However, only Downes has really focused on this in relation to resilience, offering a phenomenological focus within his suggestion that 'individual experience is a system of concentric and diametric spatial relations in interplay'. This thereby further exemplifies the complexity of resilience and how not only does the individual reside within spatial systems, but there is agency and lived experiences which can shape the trajectory of resilience.

Thus, a range of systems models have emerged and several of these have been useful in resilience research. However, Morin (2008) argued that whilst systems thinking recognises the existence of an entity within a network of systems, it still takes a 'reductionist type' approach by presenting the system as a whole. Systems thinking does not fully appreciate the emergent qualities of an interaction between the parts and the whole. Morin called for a paradigmatic shift in thinking which acknowledges the complexity of systems thinking, suggesting that:

Life is a cluster of emergent qualities resulting from the process of interaction and organization between the parts and the whole, a cluster which itself retroactively affects the parts, the interactions, and the partial and global processes that produced it. (p. 374)

This summarises what Morin referred to as complexity theory. Through the continual and dynamic interaction between the parts and the whole, the processes and products that bring the phenomenon back to its original state in a loop, demonstrate how neither can be separated. For example, individuals produce society, which then produces individuals. Systems, however, have to operate in certain ways to ensure that they maintain themselves as separate systems that are not subsumed into the wider system of which they are a part. For example, in order to maintain one's identity as a distinct being (or system) there are times when a person needs to close themselves off from threats or disruptions (in the form of adversity) from the wider system/s. An open system organises to "close itself off from the outside world to maintain its structures and its internal environment" (Morin, 2008, p. 374) in order to keep itself integrated and steady. In the case of adversity, such as parental neglect, a child can close themselves off from other adults in order to protect, and thus maintain itself as a distinct system. This may be interpreted as becoming 'hardened' or 'streetwise' or tough'. Thus, resilience is the process by which the system adapts in order to respond to disruption in its environment but also to protect itself as a system.

Complexity theory enables us to bring forth both individual aspects of resilience but locate them within the wider systems of which they are a part. It recognises that systems interact in a way that is responsive, agentic and impacts on the overall system, moving from the potentially reductionist view of systems to a recognition that we are interacting with complex adaptive systems in which each component part feeds back to change the system of which it is a part (Levin et al., 2015). That which emerges is dynamic and interactive and calls for a more dynamic and interactive model of resilience that accepts the proactivity and agency of the individual in a system.

The Dynamic Interactive Model of Resilience

Given the contributions of these models, each of which have added to and built our understanding of resilience in contexts, we present a new model, the Dynamic Interactive Model of Resilience (DIMoR) (ahmed Shafi et al., 2020) which draws on complexity theory, to build on Daniel et al., Bronfenbrenner's, Ungar's and Downes' existing models of resilience. This DIMoR is devised to be a more complete representation of resilience that considers both individual agency as well as the range of complex systems that the individual is a part of (see Fig. 2.9). The range of (reciprocal) interacting systems is likely to reflect the particular context, domain and temporal conditions of the individual system, as suggested by Ungar through his concepts of *equifinality, differential impact* and *cultural moderation*. This is because the context and conditions will interact with the individual and shape their resilience at that time and in that space.

In building this model, ahmed Shafi et al. (2020) began by adapting Gilligan's model by replacing his notion of resilience on the x-axis of their spectra (see Fig. 2.3 of Gilligan's model) with vulnerability at one end and invulnerability at the other. This is because resilience was not believed to be at one end of a spectrum, rather that resilience is the emergent property of the range of dynamic and reciprocal interactions between the individual and contextual systems. ahmed Shafi et al. (2020) thus

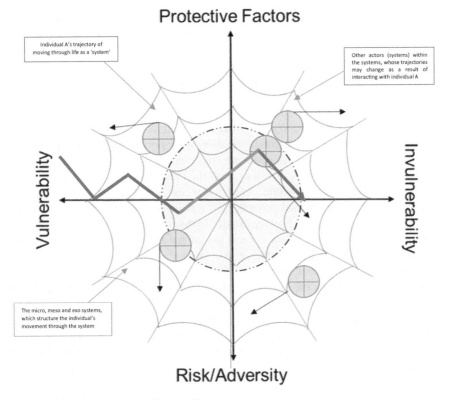

Fig. 2.9 The dynamic interactive model of resilience (DIMoR)

proposed the following adaptation of Gilligan's model (see Fig. 2.6) which placed vulnerability at the other end of the scale. Resilience at the opposite end of the scale to vulnerability suggests that if you are invulnerable then you must be resilient. However, this leaves no room for vulnerability and indicates that resilience is quite simplistic. Evidence suggests that for learning to occur, there needs to be an optimum space where there is some vulnerability which creates an 'openness to learning' rather than an invulnerable 'rigidness' which can prevent learning (Deakin-Crick et al., 2017). Resilience is an emergent property of risk-protective, vulnerability-invulnerability and for this reason, it is presented by ahmed Shafi et al. (2020) as coming out of the cross-roads of these factors. Resilience is also context and domain specific, based on Ungar's principles of equifinality, differential impact and cultural moderation as well as Downes' notion of agency.

ahmed Shafi et al. (2020) then proposed an adapted ecological model which retained the idea of the range of nested systems of Bronfenbrenner, but which recognised the interaction of these systems and the interconnectivity of structures that shape the system. These include, for example, the State, laws, policies and even physical structures, such as location or communities that can structure experiences. This is presented as a web-like structure in the Fig. 2.7, but retains the concentric circles. Having a web-like structure connects the concentric circles from Bronfenbrenner's model to indicate the structural nature of the micro, meso, exo and macro systems which shape experience. These are dependent on the principles of equifinality, differential impact and cultural moderation as well as the individual's agency within relational contexts. The adaptation of Gilligan's model as described in the Fig. 2.6 is then super-imposed on top of the web-like structure, thereby taking account of both the (structural) systems around the individual as well as the individual's own risk-protective/vulnerability-invulnerability matrix. An interaction of all these is what shapes the emergent property of resilience (represented by the dotted lines).

The next part of the model building took the individual system in the Fig. 2.7, 'zooming out' and placing it within a much wider context (system) that illustrated the range of other such 'individual systems' that are also situated within a much wider contextual system of society, itself embedded in the systems of the Earth's biosphere (Folke, 2016). This wider system features the same web-like structure and the same risk-protective/vulnerability-invulnerability matrix that would be present within any individual system or organisation.

The result is the Dynamic Interactive Model of Resilience (DIMoR), represented below. The smaller 'systems' (orbs) added to the DIMoR Fig. 2.8 represent the individual systems as they navigate any given wider system. For example, the individual pupil navigating the school system whilst reciprocally interacting both with other pupils and teachers as well as the school as a system. The school itself can be further zoomed out as part of the education system, and further again to society, to global society and so on.

The DIMoR, as a theoretical model, shows how individual systems (A) are agentic actors moving through life navigating containing other such individual systems within the wider web-like system of society. Dynamic and reciprocal interactions with all of these systems can influence the trajectory of those individual systems. This illuminates our understanding of resilience being less about the individual alone. Rather resilience is a domain and context specific emergent property of the interactions between the individual and their contexts. Consequently, resilience cannot simply be an individual trait, but rather is a responsive feature which changes shape and structure within its own risk-protective, vulnerability-invulnerability framework (Fig. 2.2) as well as that of the system within which the individual is situated. It is important to note that the individual could be any unit, such as a school, an organisation, a business, a community and so on.

This model thus builds on the existing models of Daniel et al., Ungar and Bronfenbrenner, draws on complexity theory and, like Downes, acknowledges individual agency, but most importantly forefronts the reciprocal interactions which shape resilience in the individual which can in turn shape the resilience of society (and vice versa). This model represents the dynamic nature of resilience that is context, domain and even relationships specific which, although alluded to in previous models has not been fully expressed in one model.

Conclusion

This Chapter has sought to explore the concept of resilience and assess the contribution of a range of seminal models to our understanding of it. In so doing we have highlighted how each model presents a different dimension of the picture, all of which present a different aspect of resilience. In the DIMoR model we have tried to build on all these models and present a complete picture of resilience without reducing it to its parts, nor build a holistic model that then loses the role of the parts. In so doing we retain the complexity of the nature of resilience in humans that is both dynamic and interactive.

References

ahmed Shafi, A., Templeton, S., Middleton, T., Millican, R., Vare, P., Pritchard, R. et al. (2020). Towards a dynamic interactive model of resilience (DIMoR) for education and learning contexts. *Emotional and Behavioural Difficulties, 25*(2), 183–198. https://doi.org/10.1080/136 32752.2020.1771923.

Bellis, M. A., Lowey, H., Leckenby, N., Hughes, K. & Harrison, D. (2013). Adverse childhood experiences: retrospective study to determine their impact on adult health behaviours and health outcomes in a UK population. *Journal of Public Health, 36*(1), 81–91.

Benard, B. (1991). *Fostering resiliency in kids: Protective factors in the family, school, and community.* Portland, OR: Western Center for Drug-Free Schools and Communities.

Biesta, G. J. J. (2016). *Beyond learning: Democratic education for a human future Abingdon.* Oxon: Routledge.

Bohle, H. G., Etzold, B., & Keck, M. (2009). Resilience as agency. *IHDP Update, 2,* 8–13.

Bronfenbrenner, U. (1979). *The ecology of human development.* Harvard University Press.

Bronfenbrenner, U., & Morris, P. A. (2007). The bioecological model of human development. In: W. Damon, R. M. Lerner, & R. M. Lerner (Eds.) *Handbook of child psychology* (Chapter 14). https://doi.org/10.1002/9780470147658.chpsy0114.

Catalano, R., Haggerty, K., Oesterles, S., Fleming, C., & Hawkins, D. (2004). The importance of bonding to school for healthy development: Findings from the social development research group. *Journal of School Health, 74*(7), 252–261.

Cefai, C. (2007). Educational resilience. *Journal of Emotional and Behaviour Difficulties, 12*(2), 87–89.

Chen, X., & Rubin, K. H. (2011). *Socioemotional development in cultural context.* New York: The Guilford Press.

Condly, S. J. (2006). Resilience in children: A review of literature with implications for education. *Urban Education, 41*(3), 211–236.

Crick, R. D., Barr, S., Green, H., & Pedder, D. (2017). Evaluating the wider outcomes of schools: Complex systems modelling for leadership decisioning. *Educational Management Administration & Leadership, 45*(4), 719–743.

Daniel, B. (2003). The value of resilience as a concept for practice in residential settings. *Scottish Journal of Residential Child Care, 2*(1), 1–15.

Daniel, B., Wassell, S., & Gilligan, R. (1999). *Child development for child care and protection workers.* London: Jessica Kingsley Publishers.

Dent, R., & Cameron, R. (2003). Developing resilience in children who are in public care: The educational psychology perspective. *Educational Psychology in Practice, 19*(1), 3–19.

Downes, P. (2017). Extended paper: Reconceptualising foundational assumptions of resilience: A cross-cultural, spatial systems domain of relevance for agency and phenomenology in resilience. *International Journal of Emotional Education, 9*(1), 99–120.

Felitti, V., Anda, R., Nordenberg, D., Williamson, D., Spitz, A., Edwards, V., et al. (1998). The relationship of adult health status to childhood abuse and household dysfunction. *American Journal of Preventive Medicine, 14,* 245–258.

Folke, C. (2016). Resilience (Republished). *Ecology and Society, 21*(4), 44. https://doi.org/10.5751/ES-09088-210444.

Gilligan, R. (2004). Promoting resilience in child and family social work: issues for social work practice, education and policy. *Social Work Education: The International Journal, 23*(1), 93–204.

Goldstein, S., & Brooks, R. (2014). *Handbook of resilience in children.* New York: Springer.

Hudson, K. (2019). I was taken into care at two years old—what really happened? *The Guardian.* Available at https://www.theguardian.com/lifeandstyle/2019/may/04/taken-into-care-at-two-years-old-what-really-happened. Accessed 1 Oct 2019.

Kaplan, H. B. (1999). Toward an understanding of resilience: A critical review of definitions and models. In M. D. Glantz & J. L. Johnson (Eds.), *Resilience and development* (pp. 17–83). New York: Kluwer Academic/Plenum.

Kaplan, H. B. (2014). Reconceputalizing Resilience. In: S. Goldstein & R. Brooks, *Handbook of resilience in children* (pp 39–55). New York: Springer.

Levin, P. S., Williams, G. D., Rehr, A., Norman, K. C., & Harvey, C. J. (2015). Developing conservation targets in social-ecological systems. *Ecology and Society, 20*(4).

Lévi-Strauss, C., & Weightman, J. (1973). *From honey to ashes.* New York: Harper & Row.

Long, R. (2000). *Making sense of behaviour: Supporting pupils with emotional and behavioural difficulties through consistency.* London: Routledge.

Luthar, S., Cicchetti, D., & Becker, B. (2000). The construct of resilience: A critical evaluation and guidelines for future work. *Child Development, 71*(3), 543–562.

Masten, A. S. (1994). Resilience in individual development: Successful adaptation despite risk and adversity: Challenges and prospects. In: *Educational resilience in inner city America: Challenges and prospects* (pp. 3–25). Lawrence Erlbaum.

Masten, A. S. (2015). *Ordinary magic.* New York: Guilford Press.

Masten, A. S. (2016). Resilience in developing systems: the promise of integrated approaches. *European Journal of Developmental Psychology, 13*(3), 297–312.

Masten, A. S., Best, K. M., & Garmezy, N. (1990). Resilience and development: Contributions from the study of children who overcome adversity. *Development and Psychopathology, 2*(4), 425–444.

McEwen, C. A., & Gregerson, S. F. (2019). A critical assessment of the adverse childhood experiences study at 20 years. *American Journal of Preventive Medicine, 56*(6), 790–794.

Young Minds. (2012). Interactive resilience framework. Available at https://www.boingboing.org.uk/interactive-resilience-framework/. Accessed 11 Oct 2019.

Morin, E. (2008). *On complexity.* Cresskill: Hampton Press.

Rogers, C. (1959). A theory of therapy, personality and interpersonal relationships as developed in the client-centered framework. In: S. Koch (Ed.), *Psychology: A study of a science. Vol. 3: Formulations of the person and the social context.* New York: McGraw Hill.

Rutter, M. (2013). Annual research review: Resilience–clinical implications. *Journal of Child Psychology and Psychiatry, 54*(4), 474–487.

Seligman, M. E., Steen, T. A., Park, N., & Peterson, C. (2005). Positive psychology progress: empirical validation of interventions. *American Psychologist, 60*(5), 410.

Ungar, M. (2013). Resilience, trauma, context, and culture. *Trauma, Violence, & Abuse, 14*(3), 255–266.

Ungar, M., Ghazinour, M., & Richter, J. (2013). Annual research review: What is resilience within the social ecology of human development? *Journal of Child Psychology and Psychiatry, 54*(4), 348–366.

Wang, M., Haertal, G., & Walberg, J. (1997). Fostering educaitonal resilience in inner-city schools. http://www.temple.edu/LSS. Accessed 23 Sep 2018.

Werner, E.E. (1993). Risk, resilience, and recovery: Perspectives from the kauai longitudinal study. *Development and Psychopathology, 5*(04), 503–515.

Werner, E., & Smith, R. S. (1982). *Vulnerable but invincible: a longitudinal study of children and youth.* New York: McGraw-Hill.

Werner, E. E., & Smith, R. S. (2001). *Journeys from childhood to midlife: Risk, resilience, and recovery.* Ithaca, NY: Cornell University Press.

Adeela ahmed Shafi is an Associate Professor in Education at the University of Gloucestershire. She has a background in psychology and education and has been teaching in higher education for over 17 years. Her research draws on psychological theories to explore how to re-engage young offenders with formal education and learning in a secure custodial setting. Adeela's other research includes how to develop academic resilience and buoyancy in higher education students. She has also worked on international projects in Rwanda and Pakistan as well as an EU project on emotional education. Adeela has recently won two EU bids of 3 years duration, each running parallel. The first is on re-engaging young offenders with education and learning with three European partners. The second is a project designed to develop social and emotional competencies through active games in young people in conflict with the law. This is with ten partner across seven European partners. Adeela has an established publishing profile and leads the REF submission for Education at the University of Gloucestershire. Adeela is an active community worker and also stood for MP in 2010.

Sian Templeton is a Senior Lecturer in Education at the University of Gloucestershire and a practicing Educational Psychologist working with teaching staff, children, young people and their families. She has worked in a variety of educational settings with a focus on supporting the social, emotional and cognitive needs of vulnerable learners to enable them to engage with education. She achieved this through working directly with the young people, with the families, teaching staff and a range of professionals from health and social care. In addition to direct work, she also believes in exploring more systemic opportunities for promoting and supporting access to education for all. She teaches on both Undergraduate and Postgraduate courses within her University role across a range of areas within education and leads on a number of psychology-based education modules. She is involved in ERASMUS + projects related to her areas of interest. Sian's research includes resilience, emotional education and supporting young offenders in re-engaging with education and she is just commencing her DEdPsy at University College London.

Chapter 3
Resilience and Society

Paul Vare

Abstract The focus of this chapter is wider than that of other chapters in this book because its focus is the environmental 'web' of the Dynamic Interactive Model of Resilience (ahmed Shafi et al., 2020). The environment is characterised as a multi-dimensional, complex adaptive system. Guattari's notion of different ecological registers (environment, social relations and human subjectivity) is introduced with the addition of technology as proposed by Pringle (The ecosystem is an apparatus: From machinic ecology to the politics of resilience. In: Pringle T, Koch G, Stiegler B (Eds) Machine. Meson Press, Lüneburg, 2019). This leads to a *socio-material* stance being taken in understanding how resilience is enhanced at society level. Three examples of research into social resilience building illustrate, among other things, the importance of boundary-crossing—a process of pro-actively linking different actors or social sectors. Consideration is given to the question of measurement and assessment of social resilience before concluding that learning is a central feature of any resilient building process and that this in turn is enhanced by openness and the sharing of power.

Introduction

It may seem unnecessary to dedicate a discrete chapter to resilience and society when in the preceding chapter we have characterised our Dynamic Interactive Model of Resilience (DIMoR) (ahmed Shafi et al., 2020) as a process already embedded in social-ecological systems. It is the nature of this embeddedness however that begs further exploration as does its implications for the way in which we set about securing societal level resilience.

Earlier in this volume we established that our notion of resilience extends well beyond narrow definitions of 'bouncing back' after a disturbance. Definitions of resilient societies are discussed below but at this stage it is enough to say that

P. Vare (✉)
School of Education and Humanities, University of Gloucestershire, Francis Close Hall, Swindon Road, Cheltenham GL50 4AZ, UK
e-mail: pvare@glos.ac.uk

© Springer Nature Switzerland AG 2020
A. ahmed Shafi et al. (eds.), *Reconsidering Resilience in Education*,
https://doi.org/10.1007/978-3-030-49236-6_3

resilience should be understood more broadly than as a quality that one either has or lacks entirely. Taking this a step further, Vandana Shiva (Arguello Sanjuan et al., 2016) equates resilience with survivability, arguing that a resilient system:

> … should, like all living systems, have the capacity to self-organise and to self-heal—to repair from within. (Ibid, p. 2)

That is to say, to *be* is to have some degree of resilience. Our concern therefore is the extent to which this quality can be enhanced, expanded and even enjoyed.

Society as System

As discussed in Chap. 2, an individual human subject moving through life will constantly encounter other entities, each one a system in their own right, that will act upon the individual just as the individual acts reciprocally on them. This emergentist view is similar to that proposed by Arendt (1958) who recognises how each individual's trajectory is frustrated by those of others in an apparently haphazard process of becoming. This understanding of human subjectivity is described succinctly by Osberg & Biesta (2008) who go on to show how learners' horizons can be limited by traditional educational approaches that aim to maximise homogeneity among students rather than promoting diversity. In terms of resilience, it should not be surprising that increasing diversity among individuals is seen as a promising strategy given that high biological diversity is widely understood to enhance the resilience of ecological systems. Away from the classroom, social capital, or our network of 'relationships of mutual acquaintance and recognition' (Bourdieu, 1997, p. 51), is likely to be one of many determinants of resilience levels among both individuals and societies as are interactions with our multi-faceted environment.

Turning then to this complex environmental web, we include not only the biophysical world, fundamental though that is, but also human society, its technology and the cultural patterns of thought and action that guide each of us and to which we each contribute. For example, in a prescient awareness of the seriousness of the threats to our natural environment, Guattari (1989) recognises that technical solutions alone will be inadequate. Drawing on what he terms *ecosophy*, Guattari calls instead for an 'ethico-political' approach that pays equal attention to three 'ecological registers': The environment, social relations and human subjectivity (Guattari, 1989, p. 28).

Thinking of the environment as systemic registers can help us to grasp the importance of each aspect while taking care not to lose sight of the complex whole. Diverse authors accord a special role to each of these dimensions with many calling for a re-grounding in nature in the first instance (Naess, 2005; Wilson, 1984; Louv, 2005). Bonnett (2017) highlights the strength to be drawn from attentiveness towards our environment and how, for example, a strong sense of place can sustain us. Nature has a significant role to play here. If we are not attentive to our environment, particularly to the myriad relationships in the natural world around us:

... we enter ontological free fall: Our lives untouched and unsustained by a world that we pass through but do not inhabit. (Bonnett, 2017, p. 83)

This speaks simultaneously to our individual resilience as well as our connectedness to the wider world. Bonnet contrasts a purely scientific, reductionist understanding of nature with a phenomenological appreciation of relationships in nature that help to create unique places and the interplays between this and our own cultural lives. In this way we not only value the *otherness* of nature but draw strength from the way in which it becomes a part of us.

In our hunter-gatherer past, as in some indigenous societies today, this may be a taken-for-granted assumption. For a variety of cultural and historical reasons[1] we struggle today to recognise this oneness with our environment. This is not simply a function of our experiences of nature being mediated by modern technology, although that must also be a concern, rather it is a more deep-seated failure to recognise how our own human subjectivity is created through all the dimensions that comprise our environment. Pringle (2019) builds on Guattari's *Three Ecologies* making a strong case for including machines in our foundational understanding of ecology itself. Without even considering the implications of artificial intelligence and technologically enhanced humans, we can already observe the way in which machines, from national grids to microchips, are deeply embedded in our social, cultural and physical environment.

Machines, by magnitude, complexity, availability, or mass production, are inherently social devices. They never leave us alone. (Pringle, 2019, p. 51)

While making the case for the ubiquity of machines, Pringle shows how the boundaries between the physical and social elements of our environment are blurred to the extent of becoming indistinguishable.

While in humanist education research there is a long tradition of including the role of the material as something used by people, a post-humanist stance, such as that taken by Sørensen (2009), places humans not above materials but *among* them:

These materials may be used by humans, but they may also use the humans and influence and change the educational practice, which then is no longer particularly human; instead it is *socio-material."* (Sørensen, 2009, p. 2)

The concept of *sociomaterial* research in education is adopted by Fenwick et al. (2011) as an umbrella term for approaches that explore human development through our integrated physical and social spheres. Appropriately these approaches include complexity research as well as Actor Network Theory (Latour, 2005) and Cultural-historical Activity Theory (Engeström, 2001).

The latter is derived from work initiated in Soviet Russia where Lev Vygotsky expanded psychological models of learning by highlighting the role of cultural artefacts, chiefly language, in the learning process.

---

[1] The 'blame' for this human-environment separation in Western culture has been placed variously on Plato, Christianity, the Enlightenment (with a special mention for Cartesian dualism) and the capitalist economy.

The insertion of cultural artefacts into human actions was revolutionary in that the basic unit of analysis now overcame the split between the Cartesian individual and the untouchable societal structure. The individual could no longer be understood without his or her cultural means; and the society could no longer be understood without the agency of individuals who use and produce artefacts. (Engeström, 2001, p. 134)

This understanding of learning as a social rather than an individual process, underpins Cultural-historical Activity Theory, which takes as its basic unit of analysis an *activity system* comprising a subject acting on an object using mediating artefacts and having its own rules and division of labour (Engeström, 1987). While Vygotsky's original iteration of Activity Theory focused on the individual, his follower, Leont'ev, extended this to include collective activity with the understanding that systems can learn as well as the people within them (Engeström, 2001).

If systems of activity can learn, then why not whole societies? While Vygotsky identified language as critical in passing on cultural knowledge between generations, more recently we have come to understand that our cultural learning predates even our first words. This is achieved through what Lent (2017) describes as a pruning process whereby a child's neural pathways are strengthened (or left to wither) depending on their pattern of use as they learn to follow behaviours, speech acts and other cultural norms in the society into which they are born. In this way Lent sees culture 'sculpting' our human subjectivity through a network of meanings accumulated over generations. This cultural understanding of self in relation to society is implicated by Butler (1993) as the process by which we are all gendered far sooner in life than was realised hitherto; for Butler there is no 'self' preceding or outside a gendered self:

… gendering is, among other things, the differentiating relations by which speaking subjects come into being… the 'I' neither precedes nor follows the process of this gendering, but emerges only within the matrix of gender relations themselves." (Butler, 1993, p. 7)

Whom we become therefore, both as an individual and as a society, is a function not only of our biology and our lived experience but also the thought and culture of so many who have gone before us. And so to our multi-layered environment we must add what Gregory Bateson (1972) calls the 'ecology of ideas' that extends beyond the boundaries of individual minds to establish a wider system of thought. Crucially, Bateson observes how this can work for good and ill noting that there is "an ecology of bad ideas, just as there is an ecology of weeds." (Bateson cited in Guattari, 1989, p. 27). Just as environmental conditions can sustain us or render us vulnerable and our own machines can serve us or harm us, so our ideas, and the cultural outcomes that they generate, will require judicious navigation between their risk-laden and protective features. At the societal level this is often a political undertaking, a point I return to below.

The environmental web in our model of resilience (DIMoR ahmed Shafi et al., 2020) is thus understood as being simultaneously social, cultural, historical and physical while each dimension is interrelated with the others thus increasing the complexity of the whole and rendering it impossible to understand in terms of simple linear causalities. As Folke (2016) reminds us, complex adaptive systems are characterised by agents that interact in unpredictable and unplanned ways. New properties emerge when interacting elements feed back on the system to create a new phenomenon. Such complexity leads Folke to conclude that:

> The resilience of individuals, groups, and communities is tightly coupled to this interplay and the emergent properties of the whole. (Folke, 2016, p. 6)

Compared to linear modes of thought, unpredictable emergence seems unworldly; indeed, in a review of the conceptual foundations of emergence theory, Clayton and Davies (2006) explain that the motivation for emergentist thinking was originally metaphysical. Empirical studies have since demonstrated the real world presence of emergent properties, with life and mind often cited as familiar cases, i.e. they are genuinely novel properties that are not predictable from a study of the components from which they emerged yet they are irreducible to any of those components. In providing a social example of emergence, Pueyo (2014) cites economic recessions as a recurring feature that cannot be explained in terms of microeconomics, 'hence, recessions are an emergent property of capitalism' (Ibid, p. 3434). This is not to suggest that we adopt a fatalist stance towards our situation, characterised as it is by an enduring inscrutability, rather it impels us to better prepare for the unexpected while striving to understand the sources of that unpredictability so that we might extend our horizon of forewarning.

All of which serves to illustrate the complex nature of the web device that forms the background of the DIMoR (ahmed Shafi et al., 2020) heuristic, it also underscores the dynamic nature of the agents that move within the model. There are of course limitations in constructing any static heuristic device whose function is to make visible a complex and dynamic theoretical construct. While each dimension of the environment is partially constituent of the other, it would be a mistake to suggest that any of this is fixed particularly given that an essential characteristic of complex adaptive systems is their unpredictability. Equally, just as the concentric rings in Bronfenbrenner's heuristic modelling are not intended to be seen as hierarchical (Ungar et al., 2013), so we should not attempt to propose a hierarchy among these environmental factors—while accepting that the biophysical environment pre-exists and continues to support every aspect of our experience. It is critical to remain cognisant of the *context* in which these interactions are played out, for this will determine the relative importance of each dimension. The key issue is to avoid giving an a priori emphasis to a single approach in the assumption that it can more assuredly confer resilience in any given context. Furthermore, as Guattari proposes, it is essential to work *transversally* that is, across the mutually impacting dimensions of biophysical nature, social relations, cultural and technological artefacts and human subjectivity.

What Is a Resilient Society?

Before going further, we should not forget the broad definition offered above by Shiva of resilience as life (Commonwealth Foundation, 2015), i.e. a quality that all living beings have to some degree. By insisting on this broad definition Shiva aims to avoid "dominant and hegemonic interpretations of resilience" (Ibid, p. 2) that can compound the vulnerability of poorer communities in the global South. Those who strive for a definition often do so in order to facilitate measurement as discussed below. While this may appear reasonable, measurement is by nature reductionist and can be readily incorporated into systems of control.

With this caution in mind, there are a number of definitions that can be applied to resilience in relation to social-ecological systems. Quinlan et al. (2015) describe no less than eight, ranging from the narrow engineering definition of an ability to recover from perturbations, through the formal ecological notion of achieving coherence while absorbing disturbances and adapting to them, to the idea of social systems that can learn and even benefit from exogenous stress. In a quest to move towards a more encompassing concept, Benedikter & Fathi (2017) identify four 'lead concepts' of a resilient society:

1. Disaster preparedness as exemplified by the *Sendai Framework for Disaster Risk Reduction* (UNDRR, 2015). A principle player here is the Government of Japan, reflecting that country's proneness to natural disasters. The Disaster Risk Reduction (DRR) approach provides a framework for international cooperation to enhance disaster preparedness and reduce the impact of hazards on social and physical infrastructure and has been closely aligned with education for sustainable development, which is seen as a principal means of implementation (Shaw & Uitto, 2016).
2. An innovative, multidisciplinary approach that focuses on risk adjustment and disaster transformation rather than preparing for and minimizing risks. Lead agencies include the Stockholm Resilience Centre while locally based approaches include the Transition Towns Movement (Transition Towns, 2019).
3. A systematic multi-sector stocktaking approach pioneered by the German Pestel Institut in an effort to define levels of risk and preparedness across developed societies.
4. Technology-based networks centred on 'liberation technology', which aims to ensure everyone has access to the internet, and 'participatory technological innovation' that disperses and democratises the production of knowledge away from established centres such as governments, universities and corporations. This opens the possibility of an eternal practice-theory-practice cycle, termed the 'Multiversity', with the aim of building social resilience.

Given the foregoing discussion on the complex and adaptive nature of social-ecological systems, it is perhaps surprising that only the first two examples make explicit connections to social, economic and environmental interactions that are commonly associated with popular notions of *sustainable development*, which, in common with resilience, focuses across spatial and temporal scales. The last two examples also stand apart as they have a specific provenance with the third being tied to a German institute while the fourth remains closely associated with California's Silicon Valley.

Direct linkages to sustainable development require some caution given that the task of defining this term has grown increasingly problematic over time, indeed the Worldwatch Institute (2013) declared, with some exasperation, that sustainability had become a *sustainababble*. The concept of sustainable development has nature conservation roots appearing initially in the *World Conservation Strategy* (IUCN-WWF-UNEP, 1980) as an environmental policy concept while it was first used in the UK Parliament in relation to rainforest conservation (Hansard, 1986). By the time it was re-defined in 'The Brundtland Report' (WCED, 1987), the wording had become an uneasy compromise between the economists and environmentalists within the privileged drafting group (Sauvé in Scott & Gough, 2003). The familiar Brundtland definition: "development that meets the needs of the present without compromising the ability of future generations to meet their own needs" (WCED, 1987, Chap. 2, paragraph 1) is followed immediately with a clarification of 'needs' that highlights global inequality. Thus the definition emphasises the three pillars of environmental, economic and social development as well as a futures orientation. As Folke (2016) observes, sustainability science has direct relevance to notions of resilience because core sustainability concerns such as biodiversity loss, climate change and gross inequality among people all render us vulnerable. The overlap between resilience and sustainable development may not be exact but it does help us to recognise a wide range of activities, from local to global in scale, which can be seen as efforts to enhance the resilience of societies.

Developing Social Resilience—Some Examples

While accepting that some degree of resilience is being exhibited by simply existing, no society lives in an unchanging vacuum so there is always more to be done to enhance its adaptive capacity and thus its sustainability. Technological developments will play a part of course for, as Pringle (2019) has demonstrated, machines have become an integral part of our ecology. However, any vision of a resilient society depends on a process of *social learning*, as Benedikter & Fathi (2017) observe:

> All things considered, crucial factors for future societies such as sustainable environment and social planning design will not be able to offer adequate tools to deal with upcoming challenges without improving knowledge of resilience in a networked and interconnected multi-level governance approach … (Benedikter & Fathi, 2017, p. 5)

Given the inherent complexity of society, enhancing resilience is unlikely to be a straightforward issue. These are generally complex problems, often paying no respect to geographical or bureaucratic boundaries and having no clear-cut solutions. They are obdurate or 'wicked problems', a concept borrowed from design and systems planning (Bore & Wright, 2009) and applicable to the DIMoR (ahmed Shafi et al., 2020) concept of resilience. Such issues demand ways of working that are variously inter- (between), multi- (among several) and trans- (overarching/holistic) disciplinary. Experience in international conservation and development contexts (Vare, 2007) certainly involves all of these combinations and involves *boundary crossing* or working across disciplines and social sectors. This is by no means a straightforward task as there will be different conceptual frameworks in play among the various stakeholders. Meanwhile, Meadows (2008) reminds us that reductionist thinking remains vital as there will always be a need for discipline-based expertise even though some highly credentialed experts may lack the skills or inclination to engage with a broad range of stakeholders.

The model in Fig. 3.1 illustrates the way in which different forms of expertise may be linked in addressing a multi-faceted sustainable development issue. In this model, even the relatively isolated experts to the right of the diagram are brought into the process through pro-active boundary crossing by a trans-disciplinary worker whose own expertise lies primarily in facilitation rather than a specific technical area linked to the issue at the centre. Such boundary crossing roles can be found in large corporations, particularly in corporate social responsibility teams that seek to link the expertise present across a company. They may also be evident in higher education institutions where cross-cutting issues such as sustainability are seen as strategic priorities for the institution. Such roles are frequently trans-disciplinary in that they can extend to engagement with wider 'non-expert' society, often with a focus on specific communities, which may be geographically based or identified as communities of interest or circumstance.

In reviewing theories and strategies that attempt to improve linkages between research-based knowledge and action in the context of sustainability, van Kerkhoff & Labell (2006) find that research-based knowledge building falls into four broad categories: *Participation, integration, learning, and negotiation.* In this order they form a hierarchy of deepening engagement. They also suggest that:

> … the relationships between research-based knowledge and action can be better understood as arenas of shared responsibility, embedded within larger systems of power and knowledge that evolve and change over time. (van Kerkhoff & Labell, 2006, p. 445)

That said, the depth of engagement in these 'arenas of shared responsibility' cannot be assumed simply by the presence of a multi-agency approach as shown in the first of the following four examples of different activities focused on developing a more resilient society.

Firstly, in line with the DRR concept, the UK's *Community Resilience Development Framework* (HM Government, 2019) acknowledges the strength of adopting a participatory approach to emergency management and integrating this with community led action. It does not, however, appear to provide space for listening to—or learning from—communities. On the one hand this may be justified because this is about emergency planning yet it could also be argued that the more serious the situation, the more important it is to learn in all directions, albeit quickly. In this case, roles

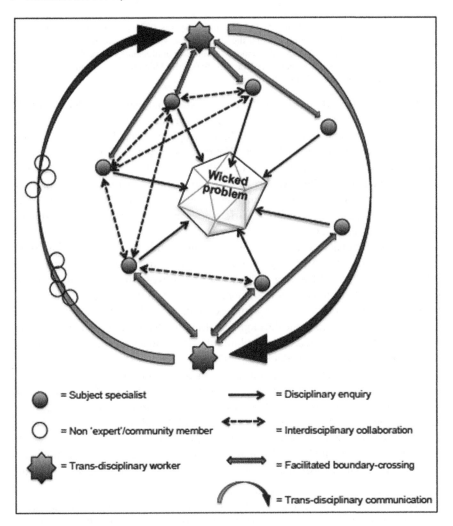

Fig. 3.1 Building resilience: Inter-, multi- and trans-disciplinary working on a 'wicked problem'

and responsibilities are to be clearly defined by the Government's responder agencies; neither the word 'negotiation' nor 'negotiate' appear anywhere in the 17-page document. The emphasis here is on preparedness rather than learning.

A second UK example also features a multi-agency approach, this time at local government level. A multi-agency risk assessment conference (MARAC), is a collaborative approach initially instigated by local police forces to tackle domestic abuse; it has since been extended to include the wider community in order to tackle anti-social behaviour (ASB). This community or C-MARAC approach has brought several benefits, not least the constructive engagement of voluntary groups, which has encouraged creativity and innovation, and the clarification of risks from multiple perspectives:

... they quickly secured the involvement of many organisations and departments which had previously been reluctant to attend meetings. Those who had seen ASB panels only as a means to justify the use of enforcement action soon appreciated this problem-solving approach could successfully manage risk present on behalf of both the victim and perpetrator across a variety of cases. (Dunn, 2018, p. 1)

In this case the Metropolitan Police, realising that being 'in charge' as the responder agency was insufficient, worked with private sector contractors as joint facilitators to initiate boundary crossing between agencies and the wider community in one local area (borough) of London. The process of engagement appears to have included all four of van Kerkhoff & Labell's (2006) categories from participation through to negotiation. Positive results have led to the adoption of the C-MARAC approach across London while maintaining governance at the borough level. In this way the approach exemplifies polycentric governance, a key principle of resilience building (Biggs et al., 2015).

In another national level example, albeit within a tightly bounded sector, the South African Qualifications Authority (SAQA) working with researchers from Rhodes University investigated learning pathways for progression in work-based learning in the context of sustainable development. Environmental sustainability became a focus for this project because of its complex, multi-faceted nature and the fact that it underpins social and economic development. Importantly, from the perspective of an analysis of resilience, researchers explored the social-material context of workers' learning pathways (Lotz-Sisitka et al., 2017) to identify how specific mechanisms and practices were blocking the translation of policy into practice. This revealed specific issues such as 'switchpoints' between different levels of qualification as well as wider systemic issues such as poverty that impeded progress at the level of basic qualifications. As the foregoing discussion of the DIMoR (ahmed Shafi et al., 2020) environment makes clear, a simple policy analysis or a series of workplace case studies alone would be insufficient to reveal the absences or the cross-boundary practices needed to resolve this complex set of issues. As the researchers conclude:

The case data show ... that it is the social-material *actualisation* of these policies that is important. Hence, we place a high emphasis on the *boundary crossing practices* that are needed to traverse the boundaries created by the social-material boundary making factors and processes. This we argue, ought to be a key focus of any articulation/learning pathways research programme or articulation implementation initiative. (Lotz-Sisitka et al., 2017, p. 179)

The findings of this approach led to both specific and systemic recommendations and crucially an awareness of the need to *negotiate* and cross the boundaries encountered by learners on their pathway to useful qualifications.

The fourth example comprises a study of different social resilience building processes across a global network of protected areas known as *biosphere reserves*. In 1973 the UNESCO Man and Biosphere Programme proposed a global network of designated areas to address the pressing question of how to "reconcile the conservation of biodiversity, the quest for economic and social development and the maintenance of associated cultural values" (UNESCO, 1995, p. 3). There are now 669 biosphere reserves in 120 countries. In a study underpinned by the concept of resilience Shultz et al. (2018) examined community-based learning, sustainability policy and governance around a sample of eleven biosphere reserves in an effort to explore the 'concept-reality gap'. Space does not permit a full account of their results but they do reveal, perhaps inevitably, a wide variety of approaches and challenges across a diverse range of social-ecological conditions. Given the complex nature of these contexts, learning assumes central importance with examples ranging from those with authority learning to facilitate, to local communities rediscovering their connection to an environment from which they had become isolated owing to draconian attempts to 'protect' it. Above all it is the position of biosphere reserves as an 'in between' space, involving all sectors of society as well as conflicting social, ecological and economic goals, that generates so much need for learning. The results of the study highlight:

- The importance of politics and power in learning for sustainability
- The role of intermediaries and bridging organisations in multi-level governance
- The need for reflexivity and knowledge-action relationships.

These results not only highlight the need for learning but they point to the multi-dimensional and multi-directional nature of that learning. As mentioned in relation to Bateson's (1972) 'ecology of ideas', there is an essential political dimension to all of this. Knowledge is not only equated with power but sharing power is seen to generate learning, which in turn has the potential to build resilience. Boundary crossing practices are made explicit in the second bullet point. The issue of knowledge-action relationships echoes the concept of praxis that goes beyond simply linking theory and practice but demands that we make critical judgements about how we act and consider the implications for others (Carr & Kemmis, 1986). This is of particularly significance to the DIMoR (ahmed Shafi et al., 2020) where reflexivity is an explicit feature of the model. In complex adaptive systems, where we cannot be certain of the outcome of our actions, we can at least try to be clear about the values that underpin them.

Assessment and Measurement

Any consideration of social resilience would be incomplete without some reflection on how we might know whether we are becoming more or less resilient as a society. Such considerations will of course depend on what we mean by resilience. The DRR approach, for example, may include a degree of stock-taking in terms of supplies, trained personnel and so forth while Benedikter & Fathi's (2017) 'Multiversity' example will emphasise the numbers of connections, the diversity of knowledge sources and the potential to further grow these features.

Firstly, we should differentiate between measurement and assessment. Quinlan et al. (2015) point out that while measurement may be more specific, it necessarily involves a degree of simplification and carries the danger of offering a fragmentary understanding of the whole system. Measuring resilience is a fraught process even at the individual level. For societies, such measurements will involve a range of technical judgements on *what* can be measured coupled with value judgements on *why* one measure or indicator should be rated more highly than another.

Resilience *assessments* aim for a deeper understanding of whole system dynamics, as such they may include measurements but it is the assemblage of these that is important as it will be based on a theoretical understanding of the context as well as agreed definitions of resilience. Quinlan et al. (2015) identify a range of approaches to measuring resilience and echo the DIMoR (ahmed Shafi et al., 2020) view of resilience when discussing the strengths of holistic assessment approaches:

> By identifying which aspects of resilience are most relevant to different cases, the assessment approach recognizes that resilience is a dynamic property shaped by many different processes as well as the larger context in which a system is embedded. (Quinlan et al., 2015, p. 681)

Resilience assessments will be shaped therefore by understandings from different disciplines as well as (potentially) community-based perspectives and should take account of changes over time, as well as rates of change, and across space, as well as at different scales. These dimensions are reflected in the seven principles or strategies for sustaining and enhancing resilience proposed by Biggs et al. (2015):

- Maintain diversity and redundancy
- Manage connectivity
- Manage slow variables and feedbacks
- Foster complex adaptive systems thinking
- Encourage learning
- Broaden participation; and
- Promote polycentric governance.

Reflecting on the DIMoR (ahmed Shafi et al., 2020), this list can be seen to be seen to be overlapping and/or mutually reinforcing. The web within the DIMoR highlights the likely inadequacy of highly centralised governance structures, instead it would suggest the need for proactive efforts to enhance connectivity, which may in turn demand boundary crossing activity. The principle of fostering complex adaptive systems thinking also highlights the need to encourage learning across any social-ecological system.

To guide resilience assessments these seven principles have been arranged by Quinlan et al. (2015) along two axes: A vertical axis, with management and gover-nance at one end and analysis at the other, and a horizontal axis running between system structure and system dynamics. The resulting chart below offers a range of metrics that might be considered in a comprehensive assessment of resilience. The vertical axis in particular helps to highlight a valuable distinction between measure-ments that consider the system itself (e.g. an ecological survey) and a focus on the way in which the system is governed (e.g. the investigation by Lotz-Sisitka et al. (2017) of the South African Qualifications Agency) (Fig. 3.2).

Whether devising measurements or broader assessments, both will be bounded by technical possibilities and value judgements; the value dimension cannot be avoided, no matter how 'scientific' the data appear to be. However, we theorise resilience,

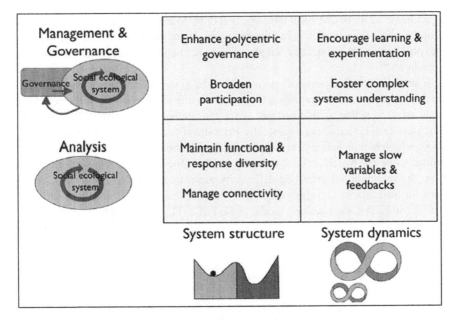

Fig. 3.2 Strategies for enhancing resilience (Biggs et al., 2015) arranged on two axes. *Source* Quinlan et al. (2015), p. 684

the long term health of any social-ecological system will be underpinned by the hard realities of the biophysical environment, indeed Folke (2016) insists that the "biosphere connection is a central observation of resilience thinking" (Ibid, p. 13). Yet even this aspect of resilience is subject to value judgements, especially where exact measurements are unachievable.

In their well-renowned assessment of ecological planetary boundaries, Rockström et al. (2009) propose a range of indices for measuring issues as diverse as ozone depletion and ocean acidification. By remaining within these boundaries, which if transgressed, could have catastrophic consequences, humanity should continue to find that Earth is a safe place to live. Out of nine planetary boundaries identified, Rockström's team estimates that humanity has already crossed three of them: Climate change, biodiversity loss and changes to the global nitrogen cycle. They admit that defining a boundary for the last of these three is not straightforward. Human fixation of nitrogen for agricultural purposes is the mechanism by which additional nitrogen is released into the environment. They envisage this mechanism as a giant 'valve' controlling the flow of nitrogen and so they propose the following:

> As a first guess, we suggest that this valve should contain the flow of new reactive nitrogen to 25% of its current value, or about 35 million tonnes of nitrogen per year. Given the implications of trying to reach this target, much more research and synthesis of information is required to determine a more informed boundary. (Rockström et al., 2009 np)

Phrases such as 'at first guess' can open up spaces for informed debate but they can also be seized upon by vested interests (one might imagine these coming from the agricultural sector or chemical industries) in order to undermine the science where it counters short-term interests. In this way political and economic values are brought into play despite the existential dangers of overshooting this and other environmental boundaries.

If environmental aspects of social-ecological systems are open to value judgements, the problems are magnified when considering the social side of the equation. In an effort to define a 'safe and just space for humanity' Raworth (2012) uses the nine planetary boundaries proposed by Rockström et al. (2009) to form a 'ceiling' above which human activity should not rise. To this she adds a 'floor' of eleven social indicators below which humanity should not fall. The social dimensions are drawn from the international priorities defined by governments at the 2012 UN Conference on Sustainable Development (Rio + 20). By arranging these boundaries in concentric circles, the resulting model in the Fig. 3.3 forms a doughnut shape, hence

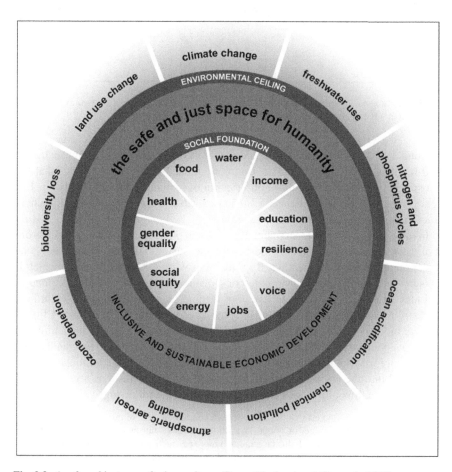

Fig. 3.3 A safe and just space for humanity or 'Raworth's doughnut' (Raworth, 2012)

Raworth branded her subsequent work in this area as 'doughnut economics'. Interestingly Raworth includes resilience as a category within her social foundation and relates this specifically to "climate-change adaptation, disaster-risk reduction, and well-designed social protection schemes." (Raworth, 2012, p. 9) No measures are available for resilience although Raworth suggests looking at multiple dimensions of poverty as an example of how this might be measured.

Clearly the 'floor' of the model is socially constructed and therefore open to debate, as are those environmental indicators which, although based on proposed absolute values, have yet be defined with precision. Assessing this space of resilience will demand negotiation on the one hand and refined scientific observation on the other, all of which has implications for education, which may have a key role—or not—in informing this debate.

Assessment of resilience is thus a political undertaking. It could be argued, for example, that the neoliberal turn in the late Twentieth Century (Harvey, 2005) has protected millions from overbearing state governments while driving technological innovation that has in turn enhanced our adaptive capacity and reduced our vulnerability. Against this, one might highlight the way in which a diminution of state controls, twinned with the pursuit of narrow economic goals, has greatly increased the risk of environmental catastrophe while the widening gap between 'haves' and 'have nots' has loosened the social ties that any model of resilience would identify as critical protective factors. Perhaps the greatest risk is that this does *not* become a matter of political deliberation. For Lazzarato (2009) *depoliticization* is a key characteristic of neoliberalism. By citing various forms of governmentality, that is social mechanisms that lead us to conform in certain ways, Lazzarato shows how the logic of competition and individualism are reproduced without any alternative approaches being apparent. This narrows our latitude for making decisions around what we might perceive to be risky endeavours such as radical deregulation (something that may be presented as simply removing burdensome red tape) and protective factors such as a functioning welfare system (that may be framed as the moral hazard of rewarding idle citizens with tax payers' money). Such framing is by no means unique to neoliberals. Totalitarian governments, from those of the Soviet Union to Nazi Germany, have by definition practiced their own form of depoliticization, ultimately leading their citizens down paths of least resilience.

Towards an Educational Response

Insofar as the complex nature of the social-ecological system underpinning our Dynamic, Interactive Model of Resilience underscores the central place of learning, so it also has fundamental implications for the way in which we pursue formal education. Indeed the pages of this volume introduce a number of educational responses to this concept of resilience.

The interactive nature of our coming into being and its impact on personal resilience points to the value of facilitating a diversity of encounters and potential relationships both within the classroom (Osberg & Biesta, 2008) and beyond. To this we might add a more critical awareness of the diverse layers or registers that comprise our environments such that the richness of our ecological endowment can be better explored, enjoyed and ultimately become a source of inner fortitude. This has perhaps never been a more vital than in the present age of accelerating ecological destruction globally while in the UK and elsewhere, young people are experiencing rising levels of mental health issues; the two are likely to be inseparable.

For Bowers (2002), the appropriate educational response to our unsustainability is to develop an *eco-justice pedagogy* based on the root metaphor of ecology. This would, Bowers claims:

- Highlight discriminatory environmental politics such as the dumping of toxic wastes on the poor
- Reclaim the non-commodified aspects of community life such as relationships, self-reliance, the arts and cultural traditions
- Be mindful of our responsibility to future generations, something which critical pedagogy alone overlooks.

Eco-justice pedagogy is underpinned by a systemic understanding of ecology, one that draws on complexity theory so it has the feel of an appropriate prescription. Bowers does not, however, make explicit our debt to the past or ascribe any particular value to the technological strands that have become embedded in our ecology (Pringle, 2019). That said, it is based on a democratic vision of society, which as we have seen, is likely to be a critical component of a truly resilient society.

A more open-ended version of this pedagogy would avoid the early identification of a single, preferred value framework, rather it would be sensitive to the values that emerge from the engagement of learners with real world situations—and each other. In this way educators avoid imposing their own cultural norms on others. Sen's (1999) definition of human development rests on people having the freedom to lead lives that *they* have reason to value—not lives that others, such as educators, have reason to value on their behalf, no matter how unshakeable the educator's moral conviction. For some time there have been calls within the education for sustainability literature for education to present self-evidently useful and appropriate skills, knowledge and attitudes while simultaneously developing the capacities of learners to navigate complex and controversial social-ecological issues (Vare & Scott, 2007). Similarly, there has been a shift away from sustainability being seen as a prescription with an indistinct goal to becoming "a capacity for critical thinking, reflexivity, and transformation" (Wals, 2017, p. 19) within education. All of which will require appropriate competences on the part of educators (see Chap. 13).

Conclusion

This review of social resilience informed by the DIMoR (ahmed Shafi et al., 2020) has raised a number of issues in terms of the integrated composition of our environment in the Twenty-first Century as well exploring some of the questions that the DIMoR raises in relation to social resilience.

Having introduced the complex nature of the environment underpinning our model of resilience, I have sought to introduce various definitions of resilient societies while remaining cognisant of the power relations that any definition implies. The diversity of settings in which resilience is pursued demonstrates the elasticity of the term while identifying the central importance of learning, whatever the definition. Just as the contexts for resilience-focused activity vary markedly, so do the means by which resilience is measured. These include a focus on social-ecological systems themselves as well as the governance structures that seek to manage these systems.

The social context in which all this takes place cannot be assumed to be benign nor is the long-term habitability of our planet assured by any means. Achieving a sustainable path for humanity will require a degree of social transformation at many levels; this is essentially a political project that is necessarily underpinned by values. Without being prescriptive about which values should prevail, our understanding of resilience as a quality sustained in a complex adaptive social-ecological environment suggests that social arrangements characterised by openness and power-sharing are likely to prove more resilient than others. This will require contributions from a wide range of disciplines and social sectors, including civil society, which in turn calls for a cadre of boundary-crossing organisations and individuals working proactively to open lines of communication so that systems—and societies—can learn more effectively, thereby enhancing their own resilience.

References

ahmed Shafi, A., Templeton, S., Middleton, T., Millican, R., Vare, P., Pritchard, R. et al. (2020). Towards a dynamic interactive model of resilience (DIMoR) for education and learning contexts. *Emotional and Behavioural Difficulties, 25*(2), 183–198. https://doi.org/10.1080/136 32752.2020.1771923.

Arguello Sanjuan, R., Cooper, G. & D'Cruz, M. (eds) (2016). *What makes societies resilient? Commonwealth People's Forum Insight Series.* London: The Commonwealth Foundation.

Arendt, H. (1958). *The human condition.* Chicago: University of Chicago Press.

Bateson, G. (1972). *Steps to an ecology of mind.* Chicago: University of Chicago Press.

Benedikter, R., & Fathi, K. (2017) What is a resilient society? Accessed at https://intpolicydigest. org/2017/09/17/what-is-a-resilient-society.

Biggs, R., Schlüter, M., & Schoon, M. L. (2015). *Principles for building resilience: Sustaining ecosystem services in social-ecological systems.* Cambridge: Cambridge University Press.

Bonnet, M. (2017). Sustainability and human Being: Towards the hidden centre of authentic education. In B. Jickling & S. Sterling (Eds.), *Post-sustainability and environmental education: Remaking education for the future.* Palgrave Pivot: Cham, Switzerland.

Bore, A., & Wright, N. (2009). The wicked and complex in education: developing a transdisciplinary perspective for policy formulation, implementation and professional practice. *Journal of Education for Teaching: International Research and Pedagogy, 35*(3), 241–256.

Bourdieu, P. (1997). The forms of capital. In: A. Halsey, H. Lauder, P. Brown, & A. Wells (Eds.), *Education, culture, economy, society* (pp. 46–58). Oxford, UK: Oxford University Press.

Bowers, C. (2002). Toward an eco-justice pedagogy. *Environmental Education Research, 8*(1), 21–34.

Butler, J. (1993). *Bodies that matter.* New York: Routledge.

Carr, W., & Kemmis, S. (1986). *Becoming critical. Education, knowledge and action research.* Lewes: Falmer.

Clayton and Davies. (2006). *The re-emergence of emergence: The emergentist hypothesis from science to religion.* Oxford: Oxford University Press.

Commonwealth Foundation. (2015). *What makes societies resilient?* Commonwealth Insights CPF 2015 Series.

Dunn, P. (2018). *Community multi-agency risk assessment conferences: Dealing more effectively with high risk and complex ASB Cases.* London: Capsticks.

Engeström, Y. (1987). Learning by expanding: An activity—theoretical approach to developmental research. Helsinki: The Laboratory of Comparative Human Cognition. Accessed at http://lchc.ucsd.edu/mca/Paper/Engestrom/expanding.

Engeström, Y. (2001). Expansive learning at work: toward an activity theoretical reconceptualization. *Journal of Education and Work, 14,* 1.

Fenwick, T., Edwards, R., & Sawchuk, P. (2011). *Emerging approaches to educational research: Tracing the socio-material.* London: Routledge.

Folke, C. (2016). Resilience (Republished). *Ecology and Society, 21*(4), 44. Accessed at https://doi.org/10.5751/ES-09088-210444.

Guattari, F. (1989). *The three ecologies, translated by Ian Pindar and Paul Sutton.* London: The Athlone Press.

Hansard. (1986). Written question by Reginald Freeson MP. Accessed at http://hansard.millbanksystems.com/written_answers/1986/jun/09/rain-forests.

Harvey, D. (2005). *A brief history of neoliberalism.* Oxford: OUP.

HM Government. (2019). *Community resilience development framework.* London: Cabinet Office.

IUCN-WWF-UNEP. (1980). *The world conservation strategy.* Gland, Switzerland: IUCN, UNEP and WWF.

Latour, B. (2005). *Reassembling the social: An introduction to actor-network-theory.* Oxford: OUP.

Lazzarato, M. (2009). Neoliberalism in action, theory, culture & society. 26(6), 109–133.

Lent, J. (2017). *The patterning instinct: A cultural history of humanity's search for meaning.* Amherst, New York: Prometheus Books.

Lotz-Sisitka, H., Mohanoe, N., Ramsarup, P., & Olvitt, L. (2017). Boundary making and boundary crossing in learning pathways access and progression: Voices from the workplace in SAQA (2017). Learning pathways for sustainable development, the national qualifications framework (NQF), and lifelong learning in South Africa. South African Qualifications Authority (SAQA). *Bulletin, 17,* 1.

Louv, R. (2005). *Last child in the woods: Saving our children from nature-deficit disorder.* London: Atlantic Books.

Meadows. D. (2008). *Thinking in systems: A primer* (D. Wright, Ed.). London: Earthscan.

Naess, A. (2005). The shallow and the deep, long-range ecology movement: A summary. In A. Drengson (Ed.), *The selected works of arne naess.* Dordrecht: Springer.

Osberg, D., & Biesta, G. (2008). The emergent curriculum: navigating a complex course between unguided learning and planned enculturation. *Journal of Curriculum Studies, 40*(3), 313–328.

Pringle, T. (2019). The ecosystem is an apparatus: From machinic ecology to the politics of resilience. In: T, Pringle, G, Koch, & Stiegler B (Eds.) *Machine.* Lüneburg: Meson Press.

Pueyo, S. (2014). Ecological econophysics for degrowth. *Sustainability, 6,* 3431–3483. https://doi.org/10.3390/su6063431.

Quinlan, A. E., Berbes-Blazquez, M., Haider, L. J., & Peterson, G. D. (2015). Measuring and assessing resilience: broadening understanding through multiple disciplinary perspectives. *Journal of Applied Ecology, 53,* 677–687. https://doi.org/10.1111/1365-2664.12550.

Raworth K (2012) *A safe and just space for humanity: Oxfam Discussion Paper.* Oxford: Oxfam.

Rockström, J., Steffan, W., Noone, K., Persson, Å., Chapin, F. S., Lambin, E. F. et al. (2009). Planetary boundaries: Exploring the safe operating space for humanity. *Ecology and Society, 14*(2), 32. Accessed at http://www.ecologyandsociety.org/vol14/iss2/art32.

Scott, W. A. H., & Gough, S. R. (2003). *Key issues in sustainable development and learning*. London: Routledge, Falmer.

Sen, A. (1999). *Development as Freedom*. Oxford: Oxford University Press.

Shaw, R., & Uitto, J. I. (Eds.). (2016). *Education for sustainable development and disaster risk reduction*. Tokyo: Springer Japan.

Shultz, L., West, S., Juárez Bourke, A., d'Armengol, L., Torrents, P., Hardardottir, H., et al. (2018). Learning to live with social-ecological complexity: An interpretive analysis of learning in 11 UNESCO biosphere reserves. *Global Environmental Change, 50*, 75–87.

Sørensen, E. (2009). *The materiality of learning: Technology and knowledge in educational practice*. Cambridge: Cambridge University Press.

Transition Towns. (2019). Accessed at https://transitionnetwork.org.

UNDRR. (2015). *Sendai framework for disaster risk reduction 2015–2030*. Geneva: United Nations Office for Disaster Risk Reduction.

UNESCO. (1995). *Biosphere reserves. The seville strategy and the statutory framework of the world network*. Paris: UNESCO. Accessed at https://unesdoc.unesco.org/ark:/48223/pf0000103849.

Ungar, M., Ghazinour, M., & Richter, J. (2013). Annual research review: What is resilience within the social ecology of human development? *Journal of Child Psychology and Psychiatry, 54*(4), 348–366.

van Kerkhoff, L., & Labell, L. (2006). Linking knowledge and action for sustainable development. *Annual Review of Environment and Resources, 31*, 445–477.

Vare, P. (2007). From practice to theory: Participation as learning in the context of sustainable development projects. In A. D. Reid, B. B. Jensen, J. Nikel, & V. Simovska (Eds.), *Participation and Learning: Perspectives on education and the environment, health and sustainability*. Dordrecht: Springer Press.

Vare, P., & Scott, W. A. H. (2007). Learning for a change: Exploring the relationship between education and sustainable development. *Journal of Education for Sustainable Development, 1*(2), 191–198.

Wals, A. E. J. (2017). Transformative social learning for socio-ecological sustainability at the interface of science and society: A forward-looking retrospective. In G. Michelsen & P. J. Wells (Eds.), *A decade of progress on education for sustainable development reflections from the UNESCO chairs programme*. Paris: UNESCO.

WCED. (1987). *Our common future: The brundtland report*. Oxford: OUP.

Wilson, E. O. (1984). *Biophilia: The human bond with other species*. Cambridge, MA: Harvard University Press.

Worldwatch Institute (2013). *State of the world 2013: Is sustainability still possible?* Washington: Island Press

Paul Vare is Postgraduate Research Lead and Course Leader for the Doctor of Education at the University of Gloucestershire's School of Education. Before joining the University in 2013, Paul worked for over 35 years in environmental education and education for sustainable development in the UK and on international development projects, chiefly in sub-Saharan Africa. For over a decade Paul represented European ECO Forum, a coalition of citizens' organisations, on various expert groups of the United Nations Economic Commission for Europe (UNECE) where he assisted in drafting the UNECE Strategy for Education for Sustainable Development. He is currently leading an international research project, A Rounder Sense of Purpose, which is developing a framework of competences for educators of sustainable development. Paul has a Masters of Philosophy Degree from Bristol University and a Doctor of Education from the University of Bath. Recently he co-authored a book with Prof. Bill Scott (University of Bath) called The World We'll Leave Behind: grasping the sustainability challenge that introduces a wide range of issues, concepts and strategies related to sustainable development. Paul's lifelong passion for the environment has been expressed through research, habitat management, drawing, painting, or simply walking in all weathers.

Chapter 4
Resilience in Education: Hindrance and Opportunity

Adeela ahmed Shafi

Abstract Education and schools have long been cited in the resilience literature as being a key protective factor for resilience. This Chapter begins by taking an historical and philosophical approach to how education systems themselves may have become an adversity through which people must pass as part of their preparation for society. This is, in part, due to the measurement, standards and marketization of education having an impact on not only young peoples' mental health and well-being, but also that of teachers. It has meant that its quality as a protective factor for developing resilience is challenged. The chapter goes on to consider how resilience can still be developed through education if there is an acute recognition of the range of often competing factors within any given (education) setting/system. In doing so, interventions or approaches designed to develop resilience through education have a greater chance to be successful.

Introduction—The Complexity of Resilience and the Complexity of Education

Resilience as a concept has been the focus of research in a range of disciplines for the last five decades. It may be defined as 'the positive pole of the ubiquitous phenomenon of individual differences in people's responses to stress and adversity' (Rutter, 1990, p. 181). With regards to children and young people in education, resilience refers to a quality that enables them to succeed in educational endeavours despite adversity in their lives, such as mental health, drugs, poverty or other such adverse circumstances and which has come to be known as educational resilience (Wang, Heartal, & Walberg, 1997). As discussed in Chap. 2, the discourse on resilience shifted from an individual deficit and risk model to one of a strengths-based approach, which focused on protective factors that could mitigate against the risks (Zimmerman & Arunkumar,

A. ahmed Shafi (✉)
School of Education and Humanities, University of Gloucestershire, Francis Close Hall, Swindon Road, Cheltenham GL50 4AZ, UK
e-mail: ashafi@glos.ac.uk

© Springer Nature Switzerland AG 2020
A. ahmed Shafi et al. (eds.), *Reconsidering Resilience in Education*,
https://doi.org/10.1007/978-3-030-49236-6_4

1994). This shift meant that the research began to focus on the environmental conditions that could support children at risk and help develop individual competencies such as problem-solving, social skills or autonomy as protective factors and components of resilience (Mandleco, 2000a, 2000b). The research showed that families, schools and communities had a part to play in this (e.g. Gilligan, 2000; Luthar, Cicchetti, & Becker, 2000). Indeed, the research found schools were a key protective factor for children at risk and that children who had a good sense of belonging to their school (Masten, 2001; Garmezy, 1993) with positive relations with teachers meant that they were more resilient to stress and adversity and more likely to succeed in education (Werner & Smith, 1982).

In recent times, education and schools as places which provide education have become to be viewed as a key site for developing resilience and the competencies, which can act as protective factors (e.g. Donaldson et al., 2015; Paterson et al., 2014). This has resulted in rafts of interventions designed to 'support resilience'. However, many of these tend to be discrete interventions that have no wider policy initiatives (Ager, 2013) and in many ways simplified resilience as something that can be developed through individual interventions. However, for resilience initiatives to be effective, the approach needs to be considered in a much more deliberate and whole system (Ager and Metzler, 2017; ahmed Shafi, Templeton, Huang & Pritchard, under review) way which takes account of the many modern complexities of the education system and the schools within it (as highlighted in Chap. 3).

In modern times, education and schools have evolved to become a very institutionalised, sophisticated and complex machinery, playing an important role in the economy as well shaping the social fabric of society. Education is considered an engine for empowering and advancing individuals and society—but at the same time, it paradoxically mirrors and reproduces the inequalities and injustices within society. This complex and contradictory relationship that education as an institution has with society has not come without its own emergent and inbuilt problems. The drive for improving standards in education has led to a standardisation of education (through national curriculums), a measurement culture (through incessant national and international tests), a surveillance approach (though e.g. OFSTED), all combined with a rapidly changing society means that young people need to be resilient just to navigate the systems and structures of a formal education system. This chapter will explore these issues as well as how resilience can be developed *through* education and also how it is needed *for* education.

In doing so we can develop a new generation that can lead the way in dismantling what has become the 'formulaic nature of education' and modernise it to foster the development of individuals, communities and societies to steer and positively adapt to change. Until children and young people develop the skills to cope with the existing structures, only then will they be in a position to change them. We propose the use of the Dynamic Interactive Model of Resilience (DIMoR) (ahmed Shafi et al., 2020) within the educational arena as one way to do this. The model demonstrates the complexity of schools and educational settings and how they interact both with the individual and the communities and society they are situated within. Employing such a model for resilience in education is more likely to have positive and lasting benefits that go beyond the confines of formal education and schools can indeed be the place where resilience is fostered.

The 'Purposes' of Education

For many societies, education and schooling is a means through which children are prepared for entering the labour market (Carnoy, 2017). This kind of education and schooling emerged in the 19th Century from the needs of a growing industrialised economy that needed specialised labour and skills. With the industrial revolution in full swing, formal schooling was seen as the turning point for a modern conception of childhood. Children (including poor children) were removed from factories and streets and put into schools to be educated (Stearns, 2016). Despite the raft of education legislation that has followed since the 1870 Education Act, many would argue that the education provision of today does not deviate too much from this original model for compulsory education in England of that time (e.g. Roderick & Stephens, 2016; Simmons, Thompson, & Russell, 2014).

However, we are now in the midst of another revolution - the technological and information revolution. This new revolution has, and is, occurring at a much faster pace than any other in history (Collins & Halverson, 2018). It demands a different kind of education, one that fosters and facilitates change, one that prepares children for a world that is not yet known, for jobs that may not yet have been created. We now require another turning point: one which prepares individuals with the skills and aptitude to respond positively to change, including the challenges, uncertainty and setbacks that characterise change, in order to find opportunities that may lie within such conditions. The discourse around developing 'non-cognitive skills', such as grit, perseverance and resilience (Gutman & Schoon, 2012; Garcia, 2016) to respond to a 21st Century which demands transferable and renewable skills needed for an ever changing world (Short & Keller-Bell, 2019) is gaining traction. In essence, education needs to develop resilient individuals to develop resilient communities and societies.

Philosophical Approaches to Education

To propose a refocus of the debate about the purpose/s of education, it is useful to go back to basics and consider what is meant by education, schooling and learning. These terms have become so intertwined and interchangeable and people have come to think of them as the same. Education has been the subject of contemplation since at least the times of Socrates 469–499 BC. Using what is now known as the 'socrative method' Socrates used dialogue and the posing of questions to stimulate debate to further knowledge about the world. Socrates believed that knowledge starts from self-knowledge and criticality because it informs our critical examination of society and the wider world. However, as we know Socrates was sentenced to death for corrupting the youth and disrupting society. Plato, Socrates' disciple, took a more 'functionalist' model of education whereby he thought education should produce citizens competent in meeting the needs of the state. However, he also believed that pupils should be educated according to their capacities and interests. In this way, he believed you produce citizens who we might today call 'self-actualised', but also useful to the state and society. This view does not feel too different to today in that schools prepare young people for jobs useful to society and that they are rewarded by salary and status depending on their 'usefulness'. Plato and Socrates have been key to questions regarding the state's role in education, aims of education and the curriculum. Today we see the role of states as central in how education systems are set up and shaped across the world (Dale, 2017).

Aristotle introduced the idea of morals in education, again emerging from the idea of the citizen's responsibility towards the state and the state to community. He advocated how education was about instilling moral character in childhood. Rousseau (1712–1778), often referred to as the philosopher of freedom, believed that humans were born free and good, but that society was the corrupting factor (Rousseau & May, 2002). He believed education could play a role in preserving the natural goodness of the human whilst having a sense of civic duty. Rousseau believed that through education it would be possible to enable the child to explore and experience the world and facilitate what they were interested in, which could then contribute to society. It is possible to see echoes of Rousseau in John Dewey's (1859–1952), relatively more recent, writings on education concerning timing and readiness of learning new things. Their main point of similarity is that they believe in the child's own motivation and direct action in the educational process. We also see this in the writings of other educationalists such as Piaget (1896–1980) and Vygotsky (1896–1934) who place the child at the centre of education. Philosophers and educationalists from Socrates to Dewey and Piaget have all spoken in some way about the role of experience, curiosity and contribution to society or state as key purposes of education. It suggests that preparation for society has been considered a purpose of education for some time. In the last two centuries, education has become synonymous with school as formal sites of providing education. In many ways, education, learning and schools have become terms that are used interchangeably.

Education, Learning and Schools

Education and learning need to be distinguished because they are not necessarily one and the same thing (Biesta, 2009). According to Robinson and Aronica (2016), education refers to *programs of learning*—for learning that is unlikely to happen unless it was deliberate, for skills such as learning to read and write. Like others, (e.g. Biesta, 2015), Robinson, distinguishes between learning and education. Many things that are learned are not specifically taught through programs of learning, but are the result of natural development (e.g. walking or talking) and natural human curiosity, such as exploring the world around you. Learning refers to the process of acquiring new skills and knowledge and is a mechanism through which education is acquired. Learning is this not a product or an end, but the process through which a person becomes educated. In this way education and learning are inter-related but distinct concepts. Schools, according to Robinson have become the primary vehicles in which to deliver organised programs of learning, programs that help equip young people with the knowledge and skills required for living in the society into which they are born. Robinson insists that schools can be any site where people come to learn and need not necessarily be a school building in what has become the traditional (and formal) sense.

The aims and purpose of education for Robinson is 'to enable students to understand the world around them and the talents within them so that they can become fulfilled individuals and active compassionate citizens' (p. xvi). This definition continues to make the connection between the individual and their talents and, how understanding the world round them can help students to connect those talents to becoming active and compassionate citizens. In doing, so they can become fulfilled individuals. Inherent in this is the interconnection between the individual and society. Nevertheless, the education system (at least in England and Wales) has come to resemble a very institutionalised form (May, 1973) and the following sections consider how these have evolved and have impacted on the individual.

The Modern Education System

Within the modern educational arena, the fusion of education, schooling and learning has led to a standardisation of education. High stakes testing and assessments have become a means to do this by purporting to be a reflection of the learner's skills, knowledge and talents. The situation has such emerged that the tests themselves have become the end. Not meeting one's own and others expectations in these assessments and standards have had an impact on young people and their ability to cope and/or prepare for their futures (Banks & Smyth, 2015). One of the purposes of these assessments in schools is to determine who is best suited to work in which industry, so it could be argued that the aim to become active citizens which fit into society remains. However, the now traditional school model has become very intertwined with the idea of a production of a workforce to feed into the economy and has become a vehicle for filtering people into particular stratums of society (as discussed in Chap. 1). This way of thinking about the purpose of education means a narrow view of what education is for (Ball, 2017) where the individual has been subsumed. This purpose has permeated the thinking of students, parents, schools, policy makers, employers, economists, politicians and the state (Biesta, 2015) where the tests are the measure of success. An outcome of this approach to education, school and learning is that young people are taught to the test and learn to the test, which has an impact on motivation, creativity and innovation (Harlen & Deakin-Crick, 2010). It means that young people have had less opportunity to deviate from the standardisation and its measurement—in effect, they struggle when something does not fit the accustomed form of learning and are thus less resilient to change or novel situations (Deakin Crick, 2012). Whereas education thinkers (Socrates, Plato, Aristotle, Dewey, Vygotsky, Piaget, Robinson) have always placed the individual at the centre with responsibilities to state and society, somewhere along the way, we have lost the individual within this discourse. The 'standards movement'—as it has come to be labelled—has played a role in this and has had an impact on the individuals going through the education system.

A 'Measurement Culture'

The rise of measurement in education has become pronounced in the last 20 years (Biesta, 2015) and has shaped education to become removed from many of the original purposes of education. In this section, it is argued that the measurement of education has led to a formulaic form of education. This has not only negated the role of education in developing individuals who are resilient and able to navigate setback, challenge or adversity, but has actually contributed to *becoming* one of the setbacks, challenges or adversities that have to be faced by young people in education.

The global focus on measurement has led to the development of international and comparative measures of educational success through, for example the Programme for International Student Assessment (PISA) and Trends in International Mathematics and Science Study (TIMSS). National and international league tables and the 'race to the top' of these league tables has emerged as way of unproblematically raising standards in education. Many have argued (e.g. Tomlinson, 1997; Nicolaidou & Ainscow, 2005; Hess, 2005; Klemenčič & Mirazchiyski, 2018) that this approach makes assumptions about equality of opportunity in terms of race, gender, socioeconomic status and that all engaging in the 'race' have the same starting points. Despite such challenges, politicians and policy-makers alike have played a significant role in promoting this 'evidence- based discourse, including and encouraging the use of, randomised control trials in education. This has had the effect of turning teaching and learning into a 'cause and effect' and 'what works' kind of model.

This has in many ways contributed to the reducing of education to set of solutions for what works for improving standards. The field of school effectiveness and school improvement research from the 1970s has played a role in narrowing the debate into a set of (testable) variables (Biesta, 2009), despite their original noble intention of improving the quality of education. However, this measurement agenda has led to a profound effect not only on education policies but also teacher activity and their own resilience within schools (Altrichter & Kemethofer, 2015). In essence, the measurement outcomes have become the overall aim of education and the purpose of schools. Pupils are merely producers of the data that is to be measured. Whilst this has focused the debate of quality education to be based on facts rather than vague concepts (Biesta, 2015) and it has improved education standards (Altrichter & Kemethofer, 2015), it has also come to dominate, rather than lend support to the argument. In essence, education as a means to develop the individual has diminished and actually become an issue itself. Not 'measuring up' in such a 'measurement culture' has played a role in contributing to contributed to some of the mental health and well-being issues that are now emerging in recent literature and which is discussed in a later section of this chapter.

The measurement culture has also led to what Biesta (2009) termed 'learnification' or the development of a language of learning that is focused solely on process. This has since shaped debate and discourse around education and contributed to reducing it to 'learning as process' and measures that assess this process. The debate about what education is actually for, or the purpose, has become lost in learnification. Biesta argues that learning is an individualistic process, necessary for education to happen. Education, though, is about a relationship between the individual and the world around them. The new language of learning (learnification) has prevented the asking of broader questions and instead has focused debate on the processes of learning. For example, we speak about learners not pupils, learning not education.

Biesta (2009) suggests a framework for asking questions about the purpose of education, which incorporates broader elements in order to extend this debate back out. These are *qualification, socialisation* and *subjectification.* Qualification refers to skills and knowledge that people need to perform and contribute to society and one of the main reasons for having a formal education system. Socialisation refers to becoming a citizen of society through education, through the development of shared norms and values. Subjectification is the opposite of socialisation and refers to the gaining of independence and autonomy or, the development of the individual. These purposes of education do not seem entirely distinct to the purposes of education outlined by the earliest of philosophers discussed earlier in this Chapter. However, the focus on measurement and standards has meant that the subjectification aspect of education has been side-lined, in favour or a more 'formulaic nature of education'. This has had consequences for the young people and teachers in the system.

Resilience *for* Education

We are currently situated within a time when young people in the UK (and many other Western societies) are the least happy (The Good Childhood Report, 2018), young people and children's mental health and well-being is at an all-time low (Sadler et al., 2018, NHS Digital, 2018). The causes are copious and while neither the scope nor purpose of this chapter is to discuss them, mentioning a few of the causes (in no particular order) is worthwhile in order to understand the current context within which children and young people are situated. These include the pressures of continual assessment and exams (Putwain, 2009; Banks & Smyth, 2015), the impact of social media on mental health (Andreassen et al., 2016), social isolation (Weinstein et al., 2015) and loneliness (Enez Darcin et al., 2016), insecurity in the school-to-work transition (Saks, 2018), family worries (Yap, Pilkington, Ryan, & Jorm, 2014) or the financial pressures of higher education (Harrison, Chudry, Waller, & Hatt, 2015). This suggests a there is a mismatch between what is happening in schools and the preparing of individuals for a changing society.

'Formulaic Nature of Education'

A 'formulaic nature of education', driven by the need to reach the top of league tables, improve standards, as shown by measurement instruments, all encased within a context of accountability and competition in the education arena (Biesta, 2015; Rustique-Forrester, 2017) has meant that education (at least in the UK) has become linear, fixed and unmovable (Cullingford & Oliver, 2017). The impact on and consequences for pupils and children who deviate from it (deliberately or other) are pronounced. This impact comes in a variety of forms, including on the mental health and well-being of young people in the UK or deviation (in the form of absenteeism, failing exams, delinquency, disengagement, not taking employment, education or training [NEETs]) is not an option as there are fixed ways for success. That success is measured in terms of achieving learning outcomes, exam results or a well-paid job (Riley & Nuttall, 2017). This linearity and a risk averse culture has left children and young people fearful of uncertainty and unprepared for disruption (see Chap. 12). Those who deviate from it risk marginalisation (Cornish, 2017). Not allowing children to fail not only thwarts the development of resilience mechanisms to cope with failure, but also means that at the school level, head teachers take measures to ensure that their 'data' is not affected by deviance (or failure). For example, schools may resort to suspensions or expulsion of students who do not fit the behaviour model of their school in a sort of 'zero-tolerance' approach (Rustique-Forrester, 2017; Monahan, VanDerhei, Bechtold, & Cauffman, 2014)—a practice recently termed 'off-rolling' (Hughes, 2018; Long & Danechi, 2019). It is also not unusual for schools to 'perform' for Office for Standards in Education (OFSTED) inspections (Perryman, Maguire, Braun, & Ball, 2018) or for disruptive pupils to be coaxed into good behaviour in preparation for an imminent OFSTED visit (Ouston, Earley & Fidler, 2017).

This suggests that pupils who do not fit the model may be at risk of being marginalised in society (Simmons, Thompson, & Russell, 2014), which can have other longer-term negative outcomes (Rodwell et al., 2018). The ones who do become part of the system can succeed whilst in it because they have learned how to do so, but can ultimately be fragile, vulnerable and dependent when outside the system without the 'safety-net' of the measures they are used to (Deakin Crick et al, 2015). In this way, education, schooling and learning with this measurement and assessment culture is not preparing children with the autonomy and agency needed for responding to the change and flux that characterises 21st Century living (Ryan & Deci, 2016) (see Chap. 12). Instead, we have some unintended consequences of high stakes testing (Jones, 2007) which has impacted on the well-being of young people (Bonell et al., 2014). These include the risk of people who are not resilient to change, unable to respond positively and adapt to challenge and/or adversity or turn it into an opportunity. By creating a very formulaic education system, we have unwittingly created individuals who only know who to live in a structured and 'formulaic' way (Jones, 2007; Berliner, 2011).

However, the evidence suggests the world young people are entering is indeed the complete opposite. We are hurtling towards a world in which uncertainty, innovation and novel scenarios are the norm (Barnett, 2012; Scharmer, 2009). Where transferable skills are essential, where problem solving and solution focused attributes are not only desirable, but necessary. Education has to return to some of its original purposes, which is to enable individuals to recognise their own strengths and abilities to prepare them to contribute to society and achieve their potential. But this is not happening as we see with the alarming declines in mental health and well-being in young people in the UK. This all suggests limited resilience to the challenges and adversities that young people may be facing in their lives.

It would be inappropriate to blame all this on the assessments, competition, standards and accountability in education. However, combine this with the sheer speed of technological and societal changes, which have included an explosion in social media and an information highway where we are both consumers and co-creators, all play in presenting challenges to individuals. However, what we can say is that education has not adequately presented the space and opportunity to prepare for or respond to these. Education has been one of the slowest sites for responding to the challenges and opportunities that such advances bring (Herold, 2015), for example, education and schools are still only using technology for its use as tools to do what they have done before. What has yet to happen is for education to utilise technology to reach new ways of knowing and new knowledge that could only be known or facilitated through technology (e.g. see the work of Siemens (2017) on the theory of connectivism) (see Chap. 12). Thus, whilst education may be part of the problem, it is also represents part of the solution. Developing resilience to persevere and succeed despite the challenges is possible through education. However, this requires a different approach.

Resilience *Through* Education

This chapter has taken a very quick tour through historical philosophical discussions on the purpose of education to the contemporary context of education as a highly sophisticated, structured and outcomes based global 'education industry' (Verger, Lubienski, & Steiner-Khamsi, 2016) to make the argument that the education system itself can be an adverse environment. Whilst much of the resilience literature has referred to how an individual recovers from severe or extreme adversity (see Chap. 2), the literature is also beginning to talk about adjustment and adaptability to everyday setbacks and challenges (e.g. Gillham et al., 2013). This could be in the education arena (ahmed Shafi et al., 2018) or in terms of general well-being (CASEL, 2003; Luthar et al., 2000). These fields have dedicated and separate literature bases, but is relevant because going through education would be considered an 'everyday activity' and being able to adjust and adapt would require some resilience.

We can discuss this idea in the context of Biesta's framework for education and in particular how the 'learnification' (Biesta, 2009) of education has in some ways distorted and deviated the debate of the purpose of education into the process(es) of learning. This is because such discourse has contributed to the everyday education environment. Reframing the debate within the ideas of qualification, socialisation and subjectification offers the ability to retain the current qualification and socialisation driven agenda, but critique how the notion of subjectification has been side-lined. The fixation with qualification i.e. the obtaining of knowledge and skills has become the business of education. Further, the socialisation aspect that assimilates the individual into the norms and values of society so that they become an active member have also dominated in the sense that the attainment driven agenda narrows education into the measurable. The opportunity, space and support to develop the resilience in order to navigate the challenges of the education system or beyond has not been an explicit focus of education.

As this is a book on resilience, we posit that developing resilient individuals is one way in which to prepare for a society and world that is in continual flux. It is a way in which subjectification can be realised. As the Dynamic Interactive Model of Resilience (DIMoR) (ahmed Shafi et al., 2020) in Chap. 2 indicates, the individual is a system within a system, itself consisting of a range of other interacting systems all of which are moving in a range of directions. This dynamic representation of the individual system within wider systems (communities and society) moving and interacting with all the other individual systems makes for a complex lived experience. This suggests that education needs to prepare people for agentic movement through this complexity whereas philosophers and educationalists claim that education should develop children as individuals so that they can contribute to society in ways that are fulfilling. In some ways this can be used as an explanation for the 'challenges' that young people are facing with the growth of mental health issues, a hindrance in autonomy of thinking (Ryan & Deci, 2016) as well as to the challenges of democracy. As Noddings (2013) argues education is essential to an effective democracy. These issues could all be said to be symptomatic of the lack of subjectification in the education system where individuals are not encouraged in the principles of subjectification and so are not able to emancipate themselves by responding to challenges or effecting change. We consequently see a focus on quantification as if this is the ultimate aim of education and instead ignore the composite dimensions, which constitute the purpose of education.

It has resulted in a generation of young people less able to cope with and respond to the adversities of complex, modern living in multiple and dynamic systems (Dekker, 2016). This is likely to have an impact on society in which the individuals must live and contribute. As discussed in Chap. 3, resilient individuals make resilient communities, which make resilient societies. If we are to have sustainable and resilient societies, then it needs to be addressed at an individual level and through education in the earlier parts of an individual's life. It is well documented in the resilience literature that schools are a key protective factor, thus, the importance of schools in developing resilience needs more specific attention.

Resilience for Learning

It should also be noted how research on resilience in education is not only good for preparation for life, but also for the process of learning itself. It has been shown that there is an optimum level of resilience and is indeed a scale, where at one end sits the risk of vulnerability and dependence and at the other the risk of being rigid and brittle (Deakin Crick et al., 2015). For learning it is vital that the individual is situated somewhere between these two pole ends where there is an openness to learning. Being open to learning means a sense of vulnerability and dependence on perhaps a mentor, but it also means a level of being able to respect one's existing knowledge base. Hence, learning can only occur there is a healthy balance of vulnerability, staidness and openness. Resilient qualities can enable the individual to manage these (often) competing demands. It is for this reason that the development of resilient qualities need to be nurtured in the educational arena as part of individual development which will support the other purposes of education as discussed in this Chapter. Learning opportunities within a supportive educational context can present the amount of risk needed in order for learning to occur and it is this what makes school a protective factor.

Educational settings have been making efforts to develop resilience within pupils. For example, the use of the 'growth mind-set' concept (Dweck, 2010; Yeager & Dweck, 2012) has been used to help students recognise that failing is part of learning. Also, work by Morrison & Allen (2007) which outlined how resilience can be promoted in a variety of ways within the school context, taking account of individual and family factors. There are also a range of programs focused on developing social and emotional competences (e.g. CASEL, 2003, 2007; SEAL programs). However, many of these programs, whilst recognising that a systems approach is desirable, do not take account of the complexity of the dynamic interactions between the individual and all the other systems as identified in the DIMoR.

Resilience—A 'Buzz Word'?

The use of the term 'resilience' across so many disciplines in a multitude of ways suggests that it could be currently considered to have 'buzzword' status (see Brown, 2015). Its flexibility and malleability has invited critics to suggest a conceptual haziness and a temporary fashionableness, which has lent support to those who argue that the word has come to mean everything, but nothing. This is problematic because it means that the actual meaning of resilience, and what it entails, is itself at risk of becoming diluted and lost due to its perceived 'in vogue' status. We therefore propose that resilience in this book is used to refer to resilient qualities, as outlined in Chap. 2, and play an important function in how an individual navigates and positively adapts to the adversity and challenges in life. However, resilience is also by no means a silver bullet—it cannot solve problems but it can help provide the environment for solutions to prosper.

There are those who advocate that if resilience is becoming the ultimate way in which to deal with educational challenges as those mentioned earlier in this Chapter, is it not more appropriate to reconsider the challenges and whether that is where our efforts for change and adaptability should lie (Webster & Rivers, 2018)? In many ways, it is difficult to challenge this view, especially when considered against the discussions in Chap. 1, however whilst changing the education priorities and a revisiting of its purpose is necessary, it would be naïve to believe that all would then be resolved. For example, the issues which are beyond the educational arena will still be there, such as competition for jobs, resources, sustainability, technology. Thus, resilience in education is not just to 'survive' the education system, but more broadly about adapting positively to the challenges or adversity and be in apposition to change them. Again, it could be argued that the neoliberal agenda is driving such societal challenges and that is what needs to change rather than developing resilience at an individual level (Webster & Rivers, 2018). This is not a view this Chapter disagrees with, however in order to effect change in society we need resilient individuals, able to respond and adapt positively to the fast paces of change. Resilient individuals are needed even to change the systems causing the adversities.

Developing Resilience: An Integrated Systems Model for Education

The above section discussed why education is a good place to develop resilience and the DIMoR model put forward by ahmed Shafi et al. (2020) is useful in understanding how this might work in practice. This is particularly given the dynamic, interactive and complex systems that schools are, and the dynamic interactive systems of communities that schools themselves are situated mean. A model which recognises this is essential if resilience is to be developed in the school environment. The DIMoR offers a new way of looking at (educational) systems and illuminates the elements which may present as a hindrance or an opportunity.

As pointed out throughout this chapter, the resilience literature has long cited school as an educational setting to be a protective factor for resilience (e.g. Gilligan, 2000; Luthar, Cicchetti, & Becker, 2000). Schools can engender a sense of belonging (Masten, 2001; Garmezy, 1993), enable the development of positive relationships and provide the stability, which can mitigate the effects of other risk factors (Zimmerman & Arunkumar, 1994). Even the literature on resilience following major natural disasters or conflicts have shown the importance of setting up schools and educational settings as a means of recovery (Kia-Keating & Ellis, 2007). This is because they present the opportunity for a sense of stability or normality, which is essential following adversity. However, the literature has yet to fully explore the potential role of education in *developing* resilience that goes beyond discrete interventions.

Schools can be more than just a protective factor and need to play a more proactive role in developing resilient qualities for general mental health and well-being.

Drawing on the DIMoR model, it is important to consider that whilst education has a role to play in developing resilience, this is by no means a simplistic feat. One of the reasons is the complex nature of the child as an individual system and how the educational setting too, is a complex system with many other actors (systems) within it. The educational setting is itself situated within a wider complex societal system. As the ahmed Shafi et al's. (2020) DIMoR model suggests, all these systems interact in a dynamic and complex way. Recognising this is an essential part of developing resilience in educational settings because there is a danger that educational settings may 'teach resilience' in a seemingly unproblematic way and assume that this will develop resilience (Ager & Metzler, 2017) (see Chap. 5). However, given that educational settings are such a complex system it would be essential to develop a resilience culture that permeates throughout the systems, not just in a didactic form of teaching. This would involve a whole school system which in itself is not a new idea (see e.g. Gillham et al., 2013; Ager, 2013) but what is new is a recognition of the complexity of educational settings and the wider systems they sit within in order for any initiatives to be successful and more importantly, sustainable. The DIMoR Fig. 4.1 represents a school system which takes account of the individual systems within it. The full rationale of how this model was built is described in Chap. 2. However, in summary, ahmed Shafi et al's. (2020) DIMoR model combines the important contributions of Daniel, Wassell, & Gilligan (1999) risk/protective-vulnerability/resilience model,

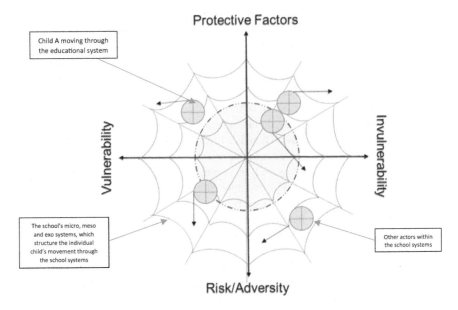

Fig. 4.1 The DIMoR as applied to a school setting

Bronfenbrenner (1979) bioecological model of human development, Ungar, Ghazinour, & Richter (2013) social-ecological model of resilience and Downes (2017) systems models of resilience present a dynamic and interactive model of resilience.

Child A represents an individual child navigating the educational system, interacting with other actors (children, teachers etc) within that system. Child A's experiences are likely to be structured and shaped by the school's systems, which include internal factors, such as the school rules, class compositions, teachers, the physical space as well as external factors, such as wider policy, that impacts on what happens within the school, the local community, other schools, its physical location, parents etc. These micro, meso and macrosystems of the school itself will shape the individual child's experience, including that of resilience development. Understanding how an individual is situated within such dynamic and interactive systems emphasises the importance of ensuring that any resilience development permeates throughout the educational system. It would highlight how developing resilience only within the classroom setting would quickly get lost within the range of dynamic interactions inherent in such systems. The DIMoR model would therefore support the notion of a system-wide cultural approach to developing resilience for it to be effective.

The role of education in developing resilience has overlaps with social and emotional learning (CASEL, 2003) as well as the development of 'positive character' (Elias et al., 2015) and other 'non-cognitive skills', also known as 'soft skills' (Gutman and Schoon, 2012). However, resilience extends these because it is concerned with enabling the individual to recover following adversity, but also enables the individual to learn from the adversity and become better prepared for the next. In this way, social and emotional learning, positive character and non-cognitive skills all contribute towards developing a resilient individual that can navigate the challenges, adversities and uncertainties of life in school and then beyond. However, these can only be developed whilst adopting a system-wide approach. Gillham et al. (2013) posit two main approaches to resilience, firstly, through explicit teaching of skills, curricula and/or coaching. Secondly, through promoting a resilient culture in schools through policies, school goals and aspirations, the development of support networks and increased collaborations and connections with parents and wider community organisations. There is a broad literature base which indicates that initiatives which seek to promote resilience in schools has positive effects on students' mental health and well-being as well as positive effects on academic performance (Christenson & Havsy, 2004). For example, students are more likely to be engaged and motivated at school which in turn promotes better school outcomes (Muenks, Yang, & Wigfield, 2017). People who feel equipped to deal with challenges and uncertainties and feel supported are more likely to take risks in learning and more likely to be creative and innovative in seeking solutions to problems (Moore & Westley, 2011). Nodding (2018) outlines how educational questions over time have both remained the same but also changed based on the society and time they are asked. Nodding, like Biesta (2015) argues that it is necessary to challenge the use of language and discourse in order to stimulate new ways of thinking about the same questions to illuminate new possibilities. Developing resilient individuals fosters the ability to take risks in challenging such notions of language and discourse.

We propose that taking a whole complex systems approach will have greater gains for developing individual resilience, which then develops school resilience, translating into community resilience and so on. In essence, resilience begets resilience. If education can take a greater and more deliberate role in developing resilient pupils, this is likely to have a long lasting effect on them throughout life (Gillham et al., 2013). Given that the individual is a dynamic, interactive system, the opportunities to interact with other systems is inherent and therefore work done in the educational arena is likely to filter into other community networks.

Conclusion

This chapter has explored how the purpose of education has, in recent decades, become very concerned with a narrow focus on a 'formulaic form of education' that is designed to measure learning outcomes and produce good results from students so that they may enter the workforce. However, this has had an impact on students, teachers and the nature of education. We propose that education needs to refocus itself to some of the earliest discussions on the purpose of education, which refer to fulfilled individuals who can contribute to and respond to the needs of society. Given the current fast paced change of modern society combined with education-specific issues, this has had an impact on young people's mental health and well-being which can have profound challenges for societies facing yet further flux, challenge and uncertainty. We believe education should play a key role in developing resilience both within individuals and, within the dynamic interactive systems of which they are a part. The ahmed Shafi et al. (2020) DIMoR has provided a useful framework through which to assess the range of reciprocal and interacting systems which could enable practitioners and policy makers to consider a much wider range of factors that affect the shaping of resilience for individuals and organisations. In so doing, education can help develop resilient individuals preparing them for addressing the challenges of life. Developing resilient individuals supports the development of resilient communities prepared for innovation and creativity, ready to deal with ever-new challenges and uncertainties that we cannot 'qualify' them for in advance. Resilience can help them not only weather such a future but shape such a future.

References

Ager, A. (2013). Annual research review: Resilience and child well-being–public policy implications. *Journal of Child Psychology and Psychiatry, 54*(4), 488–500.

Ager, A., & Metzler, J. (2017). Where there is no intervention: Insights into processes of resilience supporting war-affected children. *Peace and Conflict: Journal of Peace Psychology, 23*(1), 67.

ahmed Shafi, A., Hatley, J., Middleton, T., Millican, R., & Templeton, S. (2018). The role of assessment feedback in developing academic buoyancy. *Assessment & Evaluation in Higher Education, 43*(3), 415–427.

ahmed Shafi, A., Templeton, S., Middleton, T., Millican, R., Vare, P., Pritchard, R. et al. (2020). Towards a dynamic interactive model of resilience (DIMoR) for education and learning contexts. *Emotional and Behavioural Difficulties, 25*(2), 183–198. https://doi.org/10.1080/136 32752.2020.1771923.

ahmed Shafi, A., Templeton, S., Huang, S., & Pritchard, R. (under review). Educator conceptualisations of emotional education in six partner organisation countries across in Europe. *European Journal of Teacher Education.*

Altrichter, H., & Kemethofer, D. (2015). Does accountability pressure through school inspections promote school improvement? *School Effectiveness and School Improvement, 26*(1), 32–56. https://doi.org/10.1080/09243453.2014.927369.

Andreassen, C. S., Billieux, J., Griffiths, M. D., Kuss, D. J., Demetrovics, Z., Mazzoni, E., et al. (2016). The relationship between addictive use of social media and video games and symptoms of psychiatric disorders: A large-scale cross-sectional study. *Psychology of Addictive Behaviors, 30*(2), 252–262. https://doi.org/10.1037/adb0000160.

Ball, S. J. (2017). *The education debate.* Policy Press.

Banks, J., & Smyth, E. (2015). Your whole life depends on it: academic stress and high-stakes testing in Ireland. *Journal of Youth Studies, 18*(5), 598–616. https://doi.org/10.1080/13676261. 2014.992317.

Barnett, R. (2012). Learning for an unknown future. *Higher Education Research & Development, 31*(1), 65–77.

Berliner, D. (2011). Rational responses to high stakes testing: The case of curriculum narrowing and the harm that follows. *Cambridge Journal of Education, 41*(3), 287–302.

Biesta, G. (2009). Good education in an age of measurement: On the need to reconnect with the question of purpose in education. *Educational Assessment, Evaluation and Accountability (Formerly: Journal of Personnel Evaluation in Education), 21*(1), 33–46.

Biesta, G. J. (2015). *Good education in an age of measurement: Ethics, politics, democracy.* Routledge.

Bonell, C., Humphrey, N., Fletcher, A., Moore, L., Anderson, R., & Campbell, R. (2014). *Why schools should promote students' health and wellbeing.* British Medical Journal Publishing Group.

Bronfenbrenner, U. (1979). Contexts of child rearing: Problems and prospects. *American Psychologist, 34*(10), 844.

Brown, K. (2015). *Resilience.* Development and Global Change: Routledge.

Carnoy, M. (2017). Education, economy and the state. In: *Cultural and economic reproduction in education* (pp. 79–126). Routledge.

CASEL. Collaborative for Academic, Social, and Emotional Learning. (2003). *Safe and sound: An educational leader's guide to evidence-based social and emotional learning programs.* Chicago: Author.

Christenson, S. L., & Havsy, L. H. (2004). Family-school-peer relationships: Significance for social, emotional, and academic learning. Building academic success on social and emotional learning: What does the research say. 59–75.

Collins, A., & Halverson, R. (2018). *Rethinking education in the age of technology: The digital revolution and schooling in America.* Teachers College Press.

Cornish, C. (2017). Educated or warehoused?": The educational experiences of former NEET and so-called disengaged youth in a Further Education (FE) College in England. *European Journal of Multidisciplinary Studies, 2(6)*, 318–324. https://doi.org/10.26417/ejms.v6i1.p318-324.

Crick, R. D. (2012). Deep engagement as a complex system: Identity, learning power and authentic enquiry. In: *Handbook of research on student engagement* (pp. 675–694). Boston, MA: Springer.

Cullingford, C., & Oliver, P. (2017). *The national curriculum and its effects*. Routledge.

Dale, R. (2017). Education and the capitalist State: Contributions and contradictions. In: *Cultural and economic reproduction in education* (pp. 127–161). Routledge.

Daniel, B., Wassell, S., & Gilligan, R. (1999). *Child development for child care and protection workers*. London: Jessica Kingsley Publishers.

Deakin Crick, R., Huang, S., ahmed Shafi, A., & Goldspink, C. (2015). Developing resilient agency in learning: The internal structure of learning power. *British Journal of Educational Studies, 63*(2), 121–160.

Dekker, S. (2016). *Drift into failure: From hunting broken components to understanding complex systems*. CRC Press.

NHS Digital (2018) Mental Health of Children and Young People in England, 2017 [PAS]. Retrieved December 24, 2018, from https://digital.nhs.uk/data-and-information/publications/statistical/mental-health-of-children-and-young-people-in-england/2017/2017.

Donaldson, S. I., Dollwet, M., & Rao, M. A. (2015). Happiness, excellence, and optimal human functioning revisited: Examining the peer-reviewed literature linked to positive psychology. *The Journal of Positive Psychology, 10*(3), 185–195.

Downes, P. (2017). Extended paper: Reconceptualising foundational assumptions of resilience: A cross-cultural, spatial systems domain of relevance for agency and phenomenology in resilience. *International Journal of Emotional Education, 9*(1), 99–120.

Dweck, C. S. (2010). Even geniuses work hard. *Educational Leadership, 68*(1), 16–20.

Elias, M. J., Leverett, L., Duffell, J. C., Humphrey, N., Stepney, C., & Ferrito, J. (2015). Integrating SEL with related prevention and youth development approaches. In J. A. Durlak, C. E. Domitrovich, R. P. Weissberg, T. P. Gullotta, (Eds.) (2017) *Handbook of social and emotional learning: research and practice*. Paperback edn. (pp. 33–49). New York: Guilford Press.

Enez Darcin, A., Kose, S., Noyan, C. O., Nurmedov, S., Yılmaz, O., & Dilbaz, N. (2016). Smartphone addiction and its relationship with social anxiety and loneliness. *Behaviour & Information Technology, 35*(7), 520–525.

Garcia, E. (2016). The need to address non-cognitive skills in the education policy agenda1. In: *Non-cognitive skills and factors in educational attainment* (pp. 31–64). Springer.

Garmezy, N. (1993). Children in poverty: Resilience despite risk. *Psychiatry, 56*(1), 127–136.

Gillham, J. E., Abenavoli, R. M., Brunwasser, S. M., Linkins, M., Reivich, K. J., & Seligman, M. E. (2013). *Resilience education*. Oxford: Oxford Handbook of Happiness.

Gilligan, R. (2000). Adversity, resilience and young people: The protective value of positive school and spare time experiences. *Children and Society, 14*(1), 37–47.

Gutman, L. M., & Schoon, I. (2012). Correlates and consequences of uncertainty in career aspirations: Gender differences among adolescents in England. *Journal of Vocational Behavior, 80*(3), 608–618.

Harlen, W., & Deakin-Crick, R. (2010). Testing, motivation and learning. Readings for learning to teach in the secondary school: A companion to M level study, 276.

Harrison, N., Chudry, F., Waller, R., & Hatt, S. (2015). Towards a typology of debt attitudes among contemporary young UK undergraduates. *Journal of Further and Higher Education, 39*(1), 85–107.

Herold, B. (2015). Why ed tech is not transforming how teachers teach. *Education Week, 34*(35), 8.

Hess, F. M. (Ed.). (2005). *With the best of intentions: How philanthropy is reshaping K-12 education*. Harvard Education Press.

Hughes, R. (2018). Illegal off-rolling of students: Yet more evidence emerges. *Seced, 2018*(25), 1–1.

Jones, B. D. (2007). The unintended outcomes of high-stakes testing. *Journal of Applied School Psychology, 23*(2), 65–86.

Kia-Keating, M., & Ellis, B. H. (2007). Belonging and connection to school in resettlement: Young refugees, school belonging, and psychosocial adjustment. *Clinical Child Psychology and Psychiatry, 12*(1), 29–43.

Klemenčič, E., & Mirazchiyski, P. V. (2018). League tables in educational evidence-based policy-making: Can we stop the horse race, please? *Comparative Education, 54*(3), 309–324.

Long, R., & Danechi, S. (2019). House of commons library: Briefing paper: Number 08444, 20 February 2019. *Off-rolling in English schools.*

Luthar, S. S., Cicchetti, D., & Becker, B. (2000). The construct of resilience: A critical evaluation and guidelines for future work. *Child Development, 71*(3), 543–562.

Mandleco, B. L. (2000b). An organizational framework for conceptualizing resilience in children. *Journal of Child and Adolescent Psychiatric Nursing, 13(3)*, 99–112. https://doi.org/10.1111/j.1744-6171.2000.tb00086.x.

Mandleco. (2000a). An organizational framework for conceptualizing Re.pdf. Retrieved from https://onlinelibrary.wiley.com/doi/pdf/10.1111/j.1744-6171.2000.tb00086.x.

Masten, A. S. (2001). Ordinary magic: Resilience processes in development. *American Psychologist, 56*(3), 227.

May, M. (1973). Innocence and experience: the evolution of the concept of juvenile delinquency in the mid-nineteenth century. *Victorian Studies, 17*(1), 7–29.

Monahan, K. C., VanDerhei, S., Bechtold, J., & Cauffman, E. (2014). From the school yard to the squad car: school discipline, truancy, and arrest. *Journal of Youth and Adolescence, 43*(7), 1110–1122. https://doi.org/10.1007/s10964-014-0103-1.

Moore, M. L., & Westley, F. (2011). Surmountable chasms: Networks and social innovation for resilient systems. *Ecology and Society, 16*(1).

Morrison, G. M., & Allen, M. R. (2007). Promoting student resilience in school contexts. *Theory into Practice, 46*(2), 162–169.

Muenks, K., Yang, J. S., & Wigfield, A. (2017). Associations between grit, motivation, and achievement in high school students.

Nicolaidou, M., & Ainscow, M. (2005). Understanding failing schools: Perspectives from the inside. *School Effectiveness and School Improvement, 16*(3), 229–248.

Noddings, N. (2013). *Education and democracy in the 21st century.* Teachers College Press.

Noddings, N. (2018). *Philosophy of education.* Routledge.

Ouston, J., Earley, P., & Fidler, B. (2017). *OFSTED inspections: The early experience.* Routledge.

Paterson, C., Tyler, C., & Lexmond, J. (2014). *Character and resilience manifesto. Allparty parliamentary group on social mobility.* Retrieved from http://www.educationengland.org.uk/documents/pdfs/2014-appg-social-mobility.pdf.

Perryman, J., Maguire, M., Braun, A., & Ball, S. (2018). Surveillance, Governmentality and moving the goalposts: The influence of ofsted on the work of schools in a post-panoptic era. *British Journal of Educational Studies, 66*(2), 145–163. https://doi.org/10.1080/00071005.2017.1372560.

Putwain, D. W. (2009). Assessment and examination stress in key stage 4. *British Educational Research Journal, 35*(3), 391–411.

Riley, K. A., & Nuttall, D. L. (2017). *Measuring quality: Education indicators: United Kingdom and international perspectives.* Routledge.

Robinson, K., & Aronica, L. (2016). *Creative schools: The grassroots revolution that's transforming education.* Penguin books.

Roderick, G., & Stephens, M. (2016). *Where did we go wrong?: Industrial performance, education and the economy in victorian britain.* Routledge.

Rodwell, L., Romaniuk, H., Nilsen, W., Carlin, J. B., Lee, K. J., & Patton, G. C. (2018). Adolescent mental health and behavioural predictors of being NEET: a prospective study of young adults not in employment, education, or training. *Psychological Medicine, 48*(5), 861–871.

Rousseau, J. J., & May, G. (2002). *The social contract: And, the first and second discourses.* Yale University Press.

Rustique-Forrester, E. (2017). Exploring the policy influence of England's national curriculum on school exclusion: A dilemma of intended entitlement and unintended exclusion? In: *The national curriculum and its effects* (pp. 121–150). Routledge.

Rutter, M. (1990). Psychosocial resilience and protective mechanisms. In: J. Rolf, A. Masten, D. Cicchetti, K. Nuechterlein, & S. Weintraub (Eds.) *Risk and protective factors in the development of psychopathology*. New York: Cambridge University Press.

Ryan, R. M., & Deci, E. L. (2016). Facilitating and hindering motivation, learning, and well-being in schools: Research and observations from self-determination theory. *Handbook on Motivation at Schools,* 96–119.

Sadler, K., Vizard, T., Ford, T., Marchesell, F., Pearce, N., Mandalia, D. et al. (2018). Mental health of children and young people in England, 2017. NHS Digital. https://dera.ioe.ac.uk/32622/1/MHCYP%202017%20Summary.pdf.

Saks, A. M. (2018). Job search and the school-to-work transition. *The Oxford Handbook of Job Loss and Job Search*. https://doi.org/10.1093/oxfordhb/9780199764921.013.008.

Scharmer, C. O. (2009). *Theory U: Learning from the future as it emerges*. Berrett-Koehler Publishers.

Short, M. N., & Keller-Bell, Y. (2019). Essential skills for the 21st century workforce. In: *Handbook of research on promoting higher-order skills and global competencies in life and work* (pp. 134–147). IGI Global.

Siemens, G. (2017). *Connectivism*. Foundations of Learning and Instructional Design Technology.

Simmons, R., Thompson, R., & Russell, L. (2014). *Education, work and social change: Young people and marginalization in post-industrial Britain*. Springer.

Stearns, P. N. (2016). *Childhood in world history*. Routledge.

The Good Childhood Report 2018. (2018). https://www.childrenssociety.org.uk/good-childhood-report. Retrieved 24 Dec 2018.

Tomlinson, S. (1997). Diversity, choice and ethnicity: the effects of educational markets on ethnic minorities. *Oxford Review of Education, 23*(1), 63–76.

Ungar, M., Ghazinour, M., & Richter, J. (2013). Annual research review: What is resilience within the social ecology of human development? *Journal of child psychology and Psychiatry, 54*(4), 348–366.

Verger, A., Lubienski, C., & Steiner-Khamsi, G. (2016). The emergence and structuring of the global education industry: Towards an analytical framework. In: *World yearbook of education* 2016 (pp. 23–44). Routledge.

Wang, M., Heartal, G., & Walberg, J. (1997). *Fostering educational resilience in inner-city schools*. http://www.temple.edu/LSS. Accessed 23 Sep 2018.

Webster, D., & Rivers, N. (2018). Resisting resilience: Disrupting discourses of self-efficacy. *Pedagogy, Culture & Society,* 1–13. https://doi.org/10.1080/14681366.2018.1534261.

Weinstein, A., Dorani, D., Elhadif, R., Bukovza, Y., Yarmulnik, A., & Dannon, P. (2015). Internet addiction is associated with social anxiety in young adults. *Annals of Clinical Psychiatry, 27*(1), 4–9.

Werner, E., & Smith, R. S. (1982). *Vulnerable but invincible: A longitudinal study of children and youth*. New York: McGraw-Hill.

Yap, M. B. H., Pilkington, P. D., Ryan, S. M., & Jorm, A. F. (2014). Parental factors associated with depression and anxiety in young people: A systematic review and meta-analysis. *Journal of Affective Disorders, 156,* 8–23.

Yeager, D. S., & Dweck, C. S. (2012). Mindsets that promote resilience: When students believe that personal characteristics can be developed. *Educational Psychologist, 47*(4), 302–314.

Zimmerman, M. A., & Arunkumar, R. (1994). Resiliency research: Implications for schools and policy. *Social Policy Report, 8*(4), 1–18.

Adeela ahmed Shafi is Associate Professor in Education at the University of Gloucestershire. She has a background in psychology and education and has been teaching in higher education for over 17 years. Her research draws on psychological theories to explore how to re-engage young offenders with formal education and learning in a secure custodial setting. Adeela's other research includes how to develop academic resilience and buoyancy in higher education students. She has also worked on international projects in Rwanda and Pakistan as well as an EU project on emotional education. Adeela has recently won two EU bids of 3 years duration, each running parallel. The first is on re-engaging young offenders with education and learning with three European partners. The second is a project designed to develop social and emotional competencies through active games in young people in conflict with the law. This is with ten partner across seven European partners. Adeela has an established publishing profile and leads the REF submission for Education at the University of Gloucestershire. Adeela is an active community worker and also stood for MP in 2010.

Chapter 5
'Teaching' Resilience: Systems, Pedagogies and Programmes

Tristan Middleton and Richard Millican

Abstract Beginning from the premise that educational settings are well placed to impact positively on the resilience of children and young people, this chapter addresses some of the key issues for consideration when attempting to promote resilience through educational settings using the DIMoR (ahmed Shafi et al. in Emotional and Behavioural Difficulties 25, 2020) as a lens. The implications of educational settings being complex systems which interact with individuals, as systems themselves is explored. The discussion then continues to address the implications for pedagogical approaches before moving on to critique the use of specific programmes designed to promote learner resilience. In conclusion some recommendations for education for resilience are proposed.

Introduction

This chapter uses the DIMoR as a starting point for understanding the concept of resilience. The DIMoR identifies resilience as a process and not fixed position (ahmed Shafi et al., 2020). This definition of resilience reflects the way in which a system navigates a direction of travel in the face of risk, protective factors, vulnerabilities and invulnerabilities within its encounters with other systems. The factors of Person, Place, Context and Time (PPCT) (Bronfenbrenner & Morris, 2007) influence this navigation within the framework of the perception and expectations of the system. The individual is identified as a system itself (Clarke & Crossland, 1985), co-existing alongside and within other systems, which may be, for example, individuals, organisations, cultures and temporal systems. As systems interact, disruption occurs as expectations are challenged. Where these challenges are significant for the system,

T. Middleton (✉) · R. Millican
School of Education and Humanities, University of Gloucestershire, Francis Close Hall, Swindon Road, Cheltenham, Gloucestershire GL504AZ, UK
e-mail: tmiddleton1@glos.ac.uk

R. Millican
e-mail: rmillican@glos.ac.uk

© Springer Nature Switzerland AG 2020
A. ahmed Shafi et al. (eds.), *Reconsidering Resilience in Education*,
https://doi.org/10.1007/978-3-030-49236-6_5

the ability to navigate towards a desired outcome is the area where resilience can support the resolution of the disruption.

Through the use of the DIMoR (ahmed Shafi et al., 2020) the authors will identify three levels through which the development of resilience in education settings can be analysed and will consider the difficulties presented in taking a programme-based approach to the teaching of resilience. It will conclude by proposing some ways forward for education settings that wish to support the development of resilience for their learners.

Educational settings such as schools, further education and higher education settings, are highly developed institutions, influenced by national and local policies and operating within a context of active directorships and leadership groups. This situation of policy and leadership, where there is a focus on the improvement of schools, provides a context of educational institutions where there is regular dialogue around how best to adapt and develop the institutions in order to prepare children and young people for a role in society (Meyer, 2007, p. 115). As such, educational institutions can be identified as being ideally positioned as places to work to support and develop attributes of children and young people (Eccles & Roeser, 2012; Noble & McGrath, 2018), and in particular upon the areas of health, wellbeing and resilience (Banerjee, McLaughlin, Cotney, Roberts, & Peereboom, 2016). Where a school focus is taken, we can reflect that for the majority of children and young people a significant period of time is spent in school and schools present a system, which would be described by Bronfenbrenner (1979) as a meso-system, where there is an ability to consciously implement changes to the environment with the purpose of promoting resilience (Henderson & Milstein, 2003). Furthermore, the location of schools, situated between the community and families, provides the opportunity for the development of "family-school-community partnerships" (Wang, Haertel & Walberg, 1997, p. 134) to address co-occurring risks to resilience which exist across these interacting systems. A number of more recent reports and studies, linked to challenges faced by education systems and the children and young people within these systems, include recommendations about linking communities, families and schools. A recent English example is the Timpson Review of School Exclusions (Timpson, 2019) which includes a recommendation for the development of multi-disciplinary teams focussed on vulnerable children and young people, built around schools. The majority of English Local Authorities publish guidance on Early Help and Team Around the Family approaches to support the needs of vulnerable children and young people.

Many educational practitioners may respond with the view that highlighting the collaborative nature of schools, families and communities expresses an ideal view and that, despite efforts to connect more widely, schools often work as isolated oases in the interests of learners (Roeser, Midgley & Urdan, 1996). Within this context it is possible to view the school as a lifeline for the promotion of resilience in children and young people, in the face of challenges in their families and communities such as Adverse Childhood Experiences (ACE) (Felitti et al., 1998), socio-economic challenges and cultural differences, as well as the challenges presented by encountering new learning situations.

Chapter 4 has given the underpinning rationale of the appropriateness of addressing resilience within educational settings and how the DIMoR (ahmed Shafi et al., 2020) can facilitate thinking about this. This leads the authors to consider how educational settings can best address resilience. Through consideration of educational settings as systems, this chapter proposes that the development of resilience and teaching resiliency should be considered on 3 different levels within educational contexts.

At one level, the educational systems and structures, arrangements and expectations need to be considered. The impact of these systemic factors on group and individual resilience should be considered alongside the opportunities available to adapt them according to the outcome the changes may have.

The second level is that of the pedagogy which guides practice, both at an institutional and individual level. The authors will explore the implications for pedagogy when using the DIMoR (ahmed Shafi et al., 2020) as a lens through which to consider the development of resilience in educational settings.

The third level is based on the understanding that, for education practitioners, operationalising an approach to develop resilience is often considered through the use of explicit programmes. The authors will consider the use of published programmes as a tool to develop learner resilience.

A Systems Perspective

Educational institutions are systems which are, to a greater or lesser extent, purposefully constructed, according to a particular perspective, around the purpose and role of education within society. When considering the role of schools in promoting resilience through the DIMoR, taking a systems perspective (ahmed Shafi et al., 2020) prompts some key issues. These include, how the system interacts with the learners as groups and individuals, how it allows navigation, engenders expectations, provides and allows for protective and risk factors and the impact upon resilience. Masten (2015) points out that whilst schools have the potential to act as positive influencers upon the protective resilience factors, they can also have a negative impact and increase risk factors, because, as Masten suggests, a number are, "poorly suited to the needs of their students" (p. 222). It is therefore important to consider how educational institutions, including schools, further education and higher education settings, can act as systems which effectively support the development of the resilience of their learners.

If we understand that an individual's resilience is a relational concept between the individual's expectation and their experience when they encounter other systems, it can then be possible to have a positive impact on resilience by altering the nature of the systems they encounter. Therefore, by changing aspects of the school system, we can impact on this dynamic relationship (Lerner et al., 2013) and the resilience factors which emerge. A key component that does influence educational institutions are the leaders. Leadership can be considered as a significant point of interface between the individual learner and the educations system, in that leaders make positive decisions and take actions to alter the education system with the explicit intention of impacting on the learners. In a literature review conducted by Leithwood, Louis, Anderson, and Wahlstrom (2004) the significance of leadership actions upon learning was identified as being highly significant and only second to classroom instruction.

However, another perspective identifies that systems may not react in a linear, cause and effect, way and that it is not possible to take a reductionist view of the way in which school systems evolve. In other words, that it may not be possible to design a system which promotes resilience through specific actions or which can be successful in creating a specified chosen impact. Instead, it can be suggested that systems are self-organising organisms (Kelly & Allison, 1999), which change as a result of their engagement and interaction with other systems. This analysis of systems, aligned to complexity theory (Morrison, 2002) makes it more challenging to identify successful approaches or actions which can be taken by school leaders. These two perspectives are, however, not necessarily contradictory. Whether we view the leader in a school as a guiding decision-maker, able to implement an approach with specific aims or the leader as one system which is interacting within the school system in an organic and complex way, both of these perspectives acknowledge the impact of the leader on the school system. The difference highlighted by these perspectives accentuates that within both, there is a significant role for the interacting systems to play. The self-perpetuating nature, or autopoiesis (Wheatley, 1992, p. 20), character of protective resilience factors means that if the relational interactions can happen within the context of protective resilient factors, the impact on the individual is likely to be the development of more protective resilient factors. The extent to which the presence of the protective resilient factors in the educational system will impact on the individual who interacts with that system is open to debate. The argument of inter-subjectivity (Hart, Blincow, & Thomas, 2008, p. 132) highlights the substantial range of contextual factors with which the meeting systems will also interact and therefore the significance of each interaction may be diluted, or indeed enhanced. For example, a pupil in a school in one week may interact with 15–20 teachers, over 100 students and many more individuals online, however if each individual is also interacting with similar numbers, then the inter-subjective influence can be extremely large. In addition to this, the individual idiosyncratic characteristics of each learner and the dynamic nature of the influences of PPCT (Bronfenbrenner & Morris, 2007) also mean that design of educational institutions should not be made with the expectation of particular levels of impact upon learner resilience. What this systems perspective does however imply, is that it is desirable within the school system to have a balance of protective and risk factors which is weighted in favour of the protective. This will act as an enabling basis to provide the child or young person with the opportunity to learn the necessary skills for resilience (Cohen, 2013) through experiencing conflict or adversity whilst maintaining a direction of travel. This perspective leads us to consider the second perspective to understand the pedagogical approaches that might be best suited to facilitate and engender protective resilience factors.

A Pedagogical Perspective

The DIMoR presents resilience as a dynamic and multi-levelled emergent quality (ahmed Shafi et al., 2020), and as such there are clear implications for pedagogy. Resilience, as a form of learning, is seen as existing in the context of the interaction of systems, where there is a co-evolution as a result of these interactions (Morrison, 2008, pp. 26–27). The importance of resilience as a factor in learning, for which the case has been made in previous chapters, raises significant questions with regards to the employment of a didactic pedagogy based upon the transmission of a fixed body of knowledge or that of a learner moving towards a single normative outcome (see Chap. 4). Instead, when resilience is the focus, as the resource which enables children or young people to be ready to interact with a rapidly changing world, which their teachers are unable to predict (Claxton, 2002), particular pedagogical theories and approaches are implied. Pedagogies which empower children and young people to make informed decisions are needed. Higher order thinking skills such as applying, including interpretation and implementations, analysing, including questioning, comparing and contrasting, and evaluating, including critiquing, appraising and judging (Bloom et al., 1956), are needed to enable learners to develop the ability to navigate change, uncertainty, surprise and adversity. These are approaches which recognise the importance of contextual factors including environment, relationships, and individual character and perceptions. The pedagogical approaches of constructivism (Piaget, Vygotsky), discovery learning (Bruner) and experiential learning (Kolb) are approaches which enable this development. These pedagogical approaches align with the DIMoR in that the agentic interaction of the learner with other systems (individuals, groups and wider systems) are recognised as significant factors in emergent learning outcomes (ahmed Shafi et al., 2020). The fact that the DIMoR places significance on the individual, as a system, navigating their way through learning, with the autonomy to make choices about the direction of their learning, yet being influenced by other systems they encounter, supports the argument that Early Years pedagogical approaches need to be expanded to learners of a much wider age range. The Early Years learning environment, with a person-centred approach, positions the pedagogue as a facilitator of learning, scaffolding learning through their interactions and resourcing. It uses language aligned with coaching approaches to support the child to explore the world and other people, around them. The importance of pedagogies which support person centred and learner-led activities is also encompassed in literature about play. This literature recognises play, an open and outcome-free activity, as a primary learning behaviour which serves to develop resilience (Lester & Russell, 2008). Such pedagogical principles are aligned with the DIMoR (ahmed Shafi et al., 2020) and could be effectively integrated with systems, interventions and approaches which are in school settings (Banerjee et al., 2016) and beyond. The consideration of Early Years pedagogies for developing residence in education settings will be further discussed in Chap. 6.

Where a particular pedagogical approach is taken there are consequent implications for the taught curriculum. In the case of using the DIMoR (ahmed Shafi et al., 2020) through which to frame the development of resilience in learners, we have argued that there are implications of socially situated and person-centred pedagogies. This pedagogical approach challenges approaches to curricula which are focused on the didactic transmission of desirable knowledge. Instead it implies a curriculum which may be skills-based and where learning outcomes are wide and adaptable according to context and to the individual learner. Key skills such as mastering the contextual languages to understand and communicate will be important, as will the development of thinking skills. The use of the DIMoR (ahmed Shafi et al., 2020) identifies that resilience is needed to help the learner navigate through the consequences of the individual interacting with another system and their expectations being challenged. In order for an individual to understand and have some ability to manage expectations the curriculum will also need to have psychological elements which promote attributes of self-understanding and self-awareness. Metacognition is described by Grigg and Lewis (2019, p. 16) as, "the beliefs and knowledge individuals hold about their cognitive processes and their ability to manage these processes". These metacognitive skills are also a desirable aspect of the curriculum to promote the learner's ability to be adaptive. The pedagogical perspective therefore implies a curriculum aimed at developing the individual and their ability to understand and adapt to and/or change the environment they encounter. Claxton (2018) describes the outcomes of such a pedagogy as creating epistemic character. What is far less important or relevant within a curriculum where the pedagogy is focused on developing resilience, as defined by the DIMoR (ahmed Shafi et al., 2020), is the acquisition of knowledge and/or facts and the instrumental approach of ensuring these things are learnt and tested.

If practitioners are to teach for resilience, they may be likely to experience a clash of pedagogies. Where practitioners focus on resilience as an important factor in education they will be moved to consider the ways in which they teach. As has been argued above, the DIMoR (ahmed Shafi et al., 2020) implies a pedagogy which is context related and focussed on individual needs (Masten, 2015). The pedagogical approaches for developing resilience are likely to conflict with the dominant discourse and values system guiding policy in UK education (see Chap. 1). This has been described as being underpinned by a 'commodification of education' (Johnston and Bradford, 2019, p. 19), where competition and hierarchical structures are embodied (Tomlinson, 2017). Some consider that this managerial approach of audit and examination is reducing the opportunity for teachers to practice pedagogy (Allen & Goddard, 2017) through imposing regulation and unmanageable workload by de-professionalising teachers through a discourse of deficit (Ball, 2016). The emerging picture is one of a highly regulated education system with a focus on didactic teaching approaches. This context presents a significant challenge for the teacher who seeks to teach for resilience through a flexible and socially constructed pedagogy.

Webster and Rivers (2018) challenge the validity of aiming to teach or develop resilience in learners, putting forward the view that this approach is a way of papering over the negative impacts of an education system which is not appropriate for the learners involved. Whilst there may well be merit in developing a more user-friendly system, in which the learner is empowered to have control over the way in which their educational experience promotes positive changes in their lives (Freire, 1996), it is unrealistic to aim to eliminate all adversity in systems. Rutter (2013) also suggests that a manageable level of challenge and stress may foster aspects of resilience. Within the DIMoR, when two systems meet, the encounter may change the direction of both systems, however this is not always perceived as adversity and the outcomes and adaptations may be positive. If educational environments are changed in such a way that learners are shielded or protected from risk (Wang et al., 1997) or protective factors are imposed, as a way of promoting "wellness" and "success" (Doll, 2013, p. 400), this may result in learners becoming scared of risk or adversity as a result of limited experience. Furthermore, through the reduction of risk, choice for learners can be limited and diversity restricted. Rather than a hegemonic aim of reducing difference in pursuit of more user-friendly educational settings, we may need to aim for more diversity within our institutions and focus on enabling learners to make their own informed choices in consideration of their particular contexts, within a nurturing and enabling environment (Masten & Barnes, 2018).

A Programme-Based Perspective

The third level of thinking which needs to be considered is that of how educators can operationalise teaching for resilience. If both a systemic approach and a particular pedagogic approach is taken, there is still the need to plan for and lead educational experiences for the learners. Decisions need to be made around curriculum design, programmes and interventions and how these may best develop resilient children and young people. In short, this is the question; 'what is the best way to teach for resilience?'.

In considering the potential for a curriculum for resilience, questions relating to the existence of core skills relating to resilience are raised, as well as whether these skills may be formed into a taxonomy. Furthermore, if there are core skills, whether these skills are able to be taught or learnt, or whether the complexity of systems encountering each other means that the development of resilience is not suited to a focused, curriculum-led or programmed approach.

There are a number of interventions and approaches to teaching children and young people skills associated with resilience. Banerjee et al. (2016) point out that schools often link health and wellbeing to resilience, and as such, wide ranging approaches may be deemed by schools to be developing resilience. The "Resilience Framework" (www.boingboing.org.uk), which is based upon Resilient Therapy (Hart et al., 2008) offers a focused approach to developing resilience, providing educators with outcomes and approaches. Another example is "*The Resilient Classroom: A Resource Pack for Tutor Groups and Pastoral School Staff*" (Taylor & Hart, 2016), which offers a range of short activities for educators in schools to use to promote resilience.

It is important to acknowledge the positive impact that such programmes can have for individual learners and that there is some research evidence to support the positive outcomes of such programmes (Hart et al. 2016; Noble & McGrath, 2018), although the tension around this evidence is discussed later in this chapter. However, whilst approaches such as these offer schools a clear approach to developing learner resilience, with outcomes and approaches which can fit comfortably into lesson plan formats, the use of such programmes can be flawed when adapted or misunderstood by practitioners. The programme-based approach could be considered as taking a reductionist approach to developing resilience. There is a risk that if resilience is presented as a list of key attributes and skills, then schools may be tempted to consider that they can teach those skills and then, in a reductionist way, believe that they have addressed resilience in their curriculum. They may also be at risk of over emphasising particular attributes or skills and pushing learners to be 'over-resilient' by way of displaying particular attributes or skills, whilst not actually being able to employ them in context. This possibility of the over-teaching of isolated skills or particular strategies relating to resilience could also be considered to lead to the negation or reduction of emotions. For example, practitioners could use the "Resilience Framework" (www.boingboing.org.uk) as a checklist of skills, rather than a set of ideas and prompts. In this situation, educators might attempt to develop an inflated sense of hope, braveness or responsibilities, leading to negative impact on the learner. This approach of focusing on particular attributes or skills could also lead to a false sense of safety on the part of the children and young people. If they perceive that they have been provided with the protective factors necessary to make them resilient, it is possible that they may become risk-unaware, believing that they are resilient, whilst actually not having the understanding or skills to navigate the context. Therefore, rather than being able to adapt to the particular context and have a level of agency through which to be able to make decisions about appropriate adaptations to situations, they may be limited to making choices from the skills they have been taught. It is also possible that a perception of being resilient may prompt risk-seeking behaviours, as a result of a false sense of safety, and compromise the actual safety of children or young people.

The operationalisation of the promotion of resilience through teaching skills and attributes is founded upon the conceptualisation of resilience as a set of internal and individualised factors. This approach risks neglecting the importance of contextual factors and complex relationships and development, in a similar way that considering someone to be healthy and unlikely to need medical services neglects a range of influences and interactions (Masten, 2015, p. 300). It also risks the teaching of resilience becoming assimilated into the audit and examination approach to education discussed above.

The *Child and Youth Resilience Measure* (Resilience Research Centre, 2016) is an example of an attempt to assess resilience levels in individuals. This developing resource is careful to acknowledge contextual influences, with the suggestion that when the administration is undertaken an initial set of contextual, site-specific questions is devised and administered. There is, however, a significant risk that practitioners take the 28 questions as a checklist of resilience indicators.

Banerjee et al. (2016) identify a lack of clear research evidence to support particular operational [programme] approaches to the development of resilience within school settings. Hart and Heaver (2013, p. 47) also point to many approaches being "Vague and conceptually weak" in their definition and use of the term resilience. Furthermore, when we conceptualise resilience as the dynamic emergence of properties of interrelated systems, as opposed to individual intrinsic qualities (Roisman, Padrón Sroufe, & Egeland, 2002), challenges are presented to providing generalisable research evidence.

Evaluation of the impact of approaches to developing resilience are often measured through observable behaviours within the school context, including levels of engagement, academic achievement or the ability to return to a previous state of being, following a traumatic event. These factors may be relevant as protective factors within the DIMoR, and therefore indicators towards resilience (ahmed Shafi et al., 2020), however are not likely to be enough to evaluate the effectiveness of approaches to develop resilience within the context of PPCT (Bronfenbrenner & Morris, 2007). This raises questions and implications for the approaches used to evaluate programmes aiming to promote resilience in education settings. In particular there may be particular challenges to the pervasive expectation that experimental and Randomised Control Trial approaches to evaluation will be the best approach. Positivist approaches to research evidence are likely to be challenged by the wide range of contexts and 'variables' which may influence the development of the individual. Furthermore, the indicators used to evidence resilient learners may well be conflated with narrow curriculum related successes (Agasisti & Longobardi, 2017), such as exam results (see Chap. 4). Researchers may need to consider more qualitative and creative approaches which capture inter-relationships, context and changes over time.

Developing resilient learners risks becoming perceived as a silver bullet, with skilled marketeers and providers of professional development courses offering a simplified, tick-box approach, presenting resilience as a static state of internal attributes or skills.

Suggestions

The DIMoR (Ahmed Shafi et al., 2020) provides a lens through which to consider the development of resilience in children and young people in school settings. This lens moves the focus away from operational considerations, focused upon interventions aiming to develop particular characteristics in individuals. Instead, the focus needs to be towards a systems-based and holistic view of individual learners interacting with others and within a range of systems. This needs to take into account individual relationships, organisational relationships and wider systems relationships, in an inter-related and dynamic context.

Some recent moves towards reconceptualising the school curriculum which take a wider systemic view are evident in some international contexts. Some clear examples include the "Framework for 21st Century Competencies" (MoE Singapore, 2019) and the remodelled core curriculum created by the Finish National Agency for Education (2016), around Transversal competences. These curriculum statements reframe the conceptual aims of the curriculum away from narrow academic performance targets towards competencies for learning, world awareness and social engagement.

The focus of developing a school environment (Cohen, 2013) which allows for the promotion of factors related to resilience is an approach which is recommended as a way of encompassing contextual and systemic differences. Within this focus is the need for practitioners to focus on their own understanding of resilience and the interactions they have which can impact positively on the resilience of children and young people (Morrison & Allen, 2007). Rather than attempting to construct a set of consistent curriculum outcomes and targets, leaders in schools need to take account of the complexity of the systems and relationships influencing the learners in their settings. Consideration of a range of psychological, relational and organisational systems needs to be undertaken. The understanding that all of these systems change in an organic way as a result of interactions means that a blueprint, or set approach based on cause and effect, may not be an effective way attempting to construct or direct the school setting. Instead it may be more effective to aim to influence the school environment towards a congruence of ideas, values and practice through nurturing the positive aspects of the systems as a collective strengths-based approach through developing systems which emphasise collaboration and flexibility of approaches and outcomes. As such the emphasis for developing resilience may need to be on doing things differently and also doing different things.

References

Agasisti, T., & Longobardi, S. (2017). Equality of educational opportunities, schools' characteristics and resilient students: An empirical study of Eu-15 countries using Oecd-Pisa 2009 data. *Social Indicators Research, 134*(3), 917–953.

ahmed Shafi, A., Templeton, S., Middleton, T., Millican, R., Vare, P., Pritchard, R. et al. (2020). Towards a dynamic interactive model of resilience (DIMoR) for education and learning contexts. *Emotional and Behavioural Difficulties, 25*(2), 183–198. https://doi.org/10.1080/136 32752.2020.1771923.

Allen, A., & Goddard, R. (2017). *Education & philosophy: An introduction.* Los Angeles: SAGE.

Ball, S. J. (2016). Neoliberal education? Confronting the slouching beast. *Policy Futures in Education, 14*(8), 1046–1059.

Banerjee, R., McLaughlin, C., Cotney, J., Roberts, L., & Peereboom, C. (2016). *Promoting emotional health, well-being and resilience in primary schools.* Public Policy Institute Wales.

Bloom, B.S. (Ed.). Engelhart, M. D., Furst, E. J., Hill, W. H., & Krathwohl, D. R. (1956). *Taxonomy of educational objectives, handbook I: The cognitive domain.* New York: David McKay Co Inc.

Bronfenbrenner, U. (1979). *The ecology of human development.* Cambridge, MA.: Harvard University Press.

Bronfenbrenner, U., & Morris, P. A. (2007). The bioecological model of human development. In: W. Damon, R. M. Lerner, & R. M. Lerner (Eds.), *Handbook of child psychology* (Chapter 14). doi.org/10.1002/9780470147658.chpsy0114.

Clarke, D., & Crossland, J. (1985). *Action systems: An introduction to the analysis of complex behaviour.* London: Methuen.

Claxton, G. (2002). *Building learning power: Helping young people become better learners.* Bristol: TLO.

Claxton, G. (2018). *The learning power approach: Teaching learners to teach themselves* (p. 2018). Miami May: ICOT conference.

Cohen, J. (2013). Creating a positive school climate: A foundation for resilience. In S. Goldstein & R. B. Brooks (Eds.), *Handbook of resilience in children* (2nd ed., pp. 411–423). New York: Springer.

Doll, B. (2013). Enhancing resilience in classrooms. In S. Goldstein & R. B. Brooks (Eds.), *Handbook of resilience in children* (2nd ed., pp. 399–410). New York: Springer.

Eccles, J. S., & Roeser, R. W. (2012). School influences on human development. In L. C. Mayes & M. Lewis (Eds.), *The Cambridge handbook of environment in human development* (pp. 259–283). New York: Cambridge University Press.

Felitti, V. J., Anda, R. F., Nordenberg, D., Williamson, D. F., Spitz, A. M., Edwards, V., et al. (1998). Relationship of childhood abuse and household dysfunction to many of the leading causes of death in adults. *American Journal of Preventive Medicine, 14*(4), 245–258.

Finish National Agency for Education. (2016). *New national core curriculum for basic education.* Retrieved May 15, 2019, from www.oph.fi/english/curricula_and_qualifications/basic_edu cation/curricula_2014#Transversal%2520competences%2520as%2520part%2520of%2520ev ery%2520subject.

Freire, P. (1996). *Pedagogy of the oppressed* (New rev. ed.). London: Penguin.

Grigg, R., & Lewis, H. (2019). *Teaching creative and critical thinking in schools.* London: Sage.

Hart, A., Blincow, D., & Thomas, H. (2008). Resilient therapy: Strategic therapeutic engagement with children in crisis. *Child Care in Practice, 14*(2), 131–145.

Hart, A., & Heaver, B. (2013). Evaluating resilience-based programs for schools using a systematic consultative review. *Journal of Child and Youth Development, 1*(1), 27–53.

Hart, A., Gagnon, E., Eryigit-Madzwamuse, S., Cameron, J., Aranda, K., Rathbone, A., & Heaver, B. (2016). Uniting resilience research and practice with an inequalities approach. *Sage Open, 6*(4). 2158244016682477.

Henderson, N., & Milstein, M. M. (2003). *Resiliency in schools: Making it happen for students and educators.* Thousand Oaks, California: Corwin Press.

Johnston, C., & Bradford, S. (2019). Alternative spaces of failure. Disabled 'bad Boys' in alternative further education provision. *Disability & Society, 34*(9–10), 1548–1572.

Kelly, S., & Allison, M. A. (1999). *The complexity advantage: How the science of complexity can help your business achieve peak performance* . New York: McGraw-Hill.

Leithwood, K., Louis, K. S., Anderson, S., & Wahlstrom, K. (2004). *How leadership influences student learning.* Minneapolis, MN.: Center for Applied Research and Educational Improvement, University of Minnesota.

Lerner, R. M., Agans, J. P., Arbeit, M. R., Chase, P. A., Weiner, M. B., Schmid, K. L., & Warren, A. E. A. (2013). Resilience and positive youth development: A relational developmental systems model. In S. Goldstein & R. B. Brooks (Eds.), *Handbook of resilience in children* (2nd ed., pp. 293–308). Dordrecht: Springer.

Lester, S., & Russell, W. (2008). *Play for a change: Play policy and practice: Review of contemporary perspectives.* London: National Children's Bureau.

Masten, A. S. (2015). *Ordinary magic: Resilience in development.* New York: Guilford Press.

Masten, A. S., & Barnes, A. J. (2018). Resilience in children: Developmental perspectives. *Children (Basel, Switzerland), 5*(7). 10.3390/children5070098.

Meyer, J. W. (2007). The effects of education as an institution. In A. R. Sadovnik (Eds.), *Sociology of education: A critical reader* (pp. 115–130). Abingdon, Oxon: Routledge.

MoE Singapore. (2019). *21st century competencies.* Retrieved May 15, 2019, from www.moe.gov. sg/education/education-system/21st-century-competencies.

Morrison, G. M., & Allen, M. R. (2007). Promoting student resilience in school contexts. *Theory Into Practice, 46*(2), 162–169.

Morrison, K. (2002). *School leadership and complexity theory.* London: Routledge Falmer.

Morrison, K. (2008). Educational philosophy and the challenge of complexity theory. *Educational Philosophy & Theory, 40*(1), 19–34.

Noble, T., & McGrath, H. (2018). Making it real and making it last! Sustainability of teacher implementation of a whole-school resilience programme. In M. Wosnitza, F. Peixoto, S. Beltman,

& C. F. Mansfield (Eds.), *Resilience in education: Concepts, contexts and connections* (pp.289–312). Cham, Switzerland: Springer.

Resilience Research Centre. (2016). *Child and youth resilience measure.* Retrieved April 11, 2019, from https://cyrm.resilienceresearch.org/.

Roeser, R. W., Midgley, C., & Urdan, T. C. (1996). Perceptions of the school psychological environment and early adolescents' psychological and behavioral functioning in school: The mediating role of goals and belonging. *Journal of Educational Psychology, 88*(3), 408.

Roisman, G. I., Padrón, E., Sroufe, L. A., & Egeland, B. (2002). Earned-secure attachment status in retrospect and prospect. *Child Development, 73*(4), 1204–1219.

Rutter, M. (2013). Annual research review: Resilience—Clinical implications. *Journal of Child Psychology and Psychiatry, 54*(4), 474–487.

Taylor, S., & Hart, A. (2016). *The resilient classroom: A resource pack for tutor groups and pastoral school staff.* Retrieved April 11, 2019, from https://youngminds.org.uk/media/1463/the_resilient_classroom-2016.pdf.

Timpson, E. (2019). *Timpson review of school exclusion.* London: HMSO.

Tomlinson, S. (2017). *A sociology of special and inclusive education: Exploring the manufacture of inability.* Abingdon, Oxon: Routledge.

Wang, M. C., Haertel, G. D., & Walberg, H. J. (1997). Fostering educational resilience in inner-city schools. *Issues In Children's And Families' Lives, 7,* 119–140.

Webster, D., & Rivers, N. (2018). Resisting resilience: Disrupting discourses of self-efficacy. *Pedagogy, Culture & Society.* https://doi.org/10.1080/14681366.2018.1534261

Wheatley, M. J. (1992). *Leadership and the new science: Learning about organizations from an orderly universe.* San Francisco: Berett-Koehler.

Tristan Middleton is Senior Lecturer in Education and Joint Course Leader for the MA Education suite at the University of Gloucestershire. Tristan is an experienced primary school class teacher, Senior Leader, Special Educational Needs Coordinator and Designated teacher for both Safeguarding and Looked-After Children. He also ran a Nurture Group for seven years. Tristan is Chair of Directors of Leading Learning for SEND CiC which oversees the work of the National SENCO Award Provider Partnership and also a member of NurtureUK's Research, Evidence & Ethics Trustee Sub-Group and Associate Editor of the International Journal of Nurture in Education. He is currently a member of the Erasmus+ RENYO project team focusing on the re-engagement of young offenders with education and learning, with three European partners. He has recently published "Using an Inclusive Approach to Reduce School Exclusion: A Practitioner's Handbook" with Lynda Kay, published by Routledge and the book chapter "Teaching Assistants identifying key factors to their successful work with challenging children and finding a new discourse." In: H.R. Wright & M.E. Hoyen (Eds.) Discourses We Live By: Personal and professional perspectives on education. Open Book Publishers, Cambridge.

Richard Millican is a Senior Lecturer in Education and the Course Leader for the BA (Hons) Education at the University of Gloucestershire where he has worked for the past 10 years. Prior to that he has a long history of working within education, but in different contexts and phases. These include as a Drama and Music teacher across age ranges, a teacher of learners with social and emotional difficulties 5-18, a teacher of English as a Foreign Language to children and adults and a teacher trainer. He has worked in various countries including Spain, Oman and Egypt and in schools, further education colleges and universities including Leeds and Birmingham.

His current interests are in social justice and sustainability and in the role of education helping to create a fairer and sustainable world. He is currently working on an international research project, A Rounder Sense of Purpose, which is developing a framework of competences for educators of sustainable development linked to the Sustainable Development Goals. This has led to various recent publications alongside work into developing resilience and bouyancy with higher education students.

Part II
Exploring Resilience in Educational: Practice

Chapter 6
Resilience in the Early Years

Rebecca Pritchard

Abstract This chapter explores the development of a context within early years practice which provides a crucial opportunity for supporting children's resilience. It seeks to emphasise the importance of intervening early in order to encourage the emergent path of resilience, supported through neuroscientific research. Connections are made between the curriculum, values and community, in seeking to take a more systemic approach to understanding and meeting the needs of children. Explicit understanding and support for children to take risks and seek challenge, within the context of a key person relationship, is advocated to build the foundations of resilience. It is suggested that this early years approach provides a basis to not only influence the trajectory for resilience in children but to serve as a model for broader educational practice.

Introduction

Creating 'a healthy context for development' (Masten, 2001) within the early years can be considered a starting point for our children's trajectory in developing resilience. This is no small undertaking and recent lobbying from a range of organisations, research foundations and political movements emphasise how crucial the early years are in laying the foundations for resilience (Leach, 2017; Mathers, Eisenstadt, Sylva, Soukakou, & Ereky-Stevens, 2014). Arguably supporting the development of children's resilience is the greatest gift that we can provide for our children, and one that we have been aware of for some time, as illustrated by Frederick Douglass's famous quote, "it is easier to build strong children than repair broken men" (cited in Greenberg, 1998). Article 6 of The United Nations Convention for the Rights of Children (Gov.uk 2010) refers to children having the right to survive and reach their full potential and what has become increasingly apparent is that the early years context can significantly influence whether that potential is realised in subsequent years. More recently it has become possible to evidence the significance of developing

R. Pritchard (✉)
School of Education and Humanities, University of Gloucestershire, Francis Close Hall, Swindon Road, Cheltenham, Gloucestershire GL50 4AZ, UK
e-mail: insighteps@gmail.com

© Springer Nature Switzerland AG 2020
A. ahmed Shafi et al. (eds.), *Reconsidering Resilience in Education*,
https://doi.org/10.1007/978-3-030-49236-6_6

resilience for future life outcomes through the fields of psychology and neuro-science (Clarke & McLaughlin, 2018; Siegel, 2015).

Recent publications revealing the correlation between Adverse Childhood Experiences (ACE's) and poor health outcomes, ranging from obesity and mental illness to heart conditions and ultimately early death, are stark reminders of the impact that early life experiences have on our subsequent development (Felliti et al., 2019). Understanding how these adverse experiences influence our development has been illuminated through developments in neuroscience. The Harvard Centre for the Developing Child presents clear research evidence that depicts how brain growth is directly influenced by an infants' surroundings and how they interact with their environment (2016). The complex developing dance between nature and nurture has been possible to choreograph in much more depth and detail so that we can appreciate the subtle but vital processes that influence successful growth.

This chapter proposes that resilience can be fostered as a core concept within early years practice, explored within the broad structure of the bio-psycho-social model (Bronfenbrenner, 1994) with further consideration given to highlight the factors that contribute to the complexity that exists, exemplifying the Dynamic Interactive Model of Resilience (DIMoR). Initially, consideration is given to the wider cultural landscape in which resilience transcends as a common language with which we seek to support future generations, before moving on to explore the specific contexts driving early years practice in England. A closer focus on the early years statutory framework and curriculum seeks to illustrate how fostering resilience can be located as the essence of effective practice.

The Early Years Cultural Landscape

Anthropological studies depict the cultural influences on communities supporting the transition within adulthood to parenting (Weisner, 2010). Indeed the measure of a successful society is how it manages to care for the future generation, responding to the vulnerable and dependant nature of the species to ensure survival. It would be naive to suggest culture alone provides a set of protective resources, when links between psychosocial and structural resilience are required (Panter-Brick & Eggerman, 2012). However, it is proposed that strong links with cultural traditions are associated with having some control over personal circumstances and more developed self-regulation skills (McDonald, Kehler, Bayrampour, Fraser-Lee, & Tough, 2016). Although further study is needed to explore the impact of cultural connectedness (McDonald et al., 2016), Ungar's suggestion of the importance of cultural moderation within his principles of resilience support consideration of the impact of the community of parenting practice (2013). Within our diverse society the range of perspectives, values and beliefs provide an opportunity to consider the individual differences and strengths that can be offered within our interactions. The presence of a shared value system is considered to be a protective factor, offering safety, understanding, and a more predictable context and sense of belonging (Werner, 2000).

The presence of protective factors can however have differential impact in different contexts and time, reflecting the complexity of these interacting factors. As families navigate their way through the challenges of parenting this complexity can present vulnerability and risk. Parents are required to interact with others, including health and early years professionals. Aside from the direct family unit, the early years provide the first experience of care and education of their children outside the family and with this comes a variety of challenges, questions and experiences. This relates to Ungar's principle of equifinality in which these different systems can be more or less influential on the outcomes for children (2013). From the start, parents, children, siblings (families) exist within a complex 'early years' system. A system which over the course of time has become increasingly subject to policy change and monitoring arrangements to endeavour to seek an equal and universal service for families to reduce social inequality through welfare reform.

It is evident that we are facing new challenges within our fast pace changing environment. This places greater pressure on our need to be able to adapt and respond flexibly, whilst meeting the needs of our children to enable them to have the foundations to manage and cope with future challenges. Previous chapters have focused on some of these challenges; sustainability, the role of the internet, the education system, youth offending and mental health. Amongst this ever evolving world, the constant essential need for relationships remains, yet this critical component is so easily disrupted. Relationships are the root through which we learn who we are and the mirrors that reflect our developing identity. We are experience-dependant from birth, reliant on those around us to support our inbuilt drivers for growth. Nursery rhymes reveal the fragile nature and disturbing realities that speak of the challenges faced alongside the joy and wonder of the earliest years. Bowlby sought to emphasise his theory of attachment through the use of the William James quotation, the "greatest source of terror in infancy is solitude" (Howe, 2011). The need for an attachment(s) is a defining feature of being human, consistent across culture and is cited as a protective factor in the development of resilience (Werner, 2000). How we seek to develop and maintain these attachments may differ, but we are all reliant on our relationships—not to merely survive, but thrive.

Recognising these varied influencing factors and principles within the wider family system and community, the specific context of early years provision within England can be explored to illustrate how the nature of practice has been influenced through social policy and initiatives within education.

The Early Years Context

Whilst education has been regarded as the mechanism through which social mobility can be achieved, research has not reflected notable success with this ambition (Bertram & Pascal, 2001). Despite universal access to education, not all children have benefitted and the challenge of removing social inequality continues. Encouraging results from interventions in America such as the High Scope Perry Pre-school

Program (Schweinhart & Weikart, 1997) illustrate that investment in both the social and educational provision for pre-school children was worthwhile in the long term. Early intervention was recognised as providing children with a solid foundation leading to success in life (Sylva, 1994). Further research by Reynolds (1998) identified eight key principles to enable successful early intervention, principles either seeking to address risk factors or promote protective factors in the early years (Table 6.1).

The economic argument for investment in the early years has been politically persuasive and by enhancing provision in the early years this also provided opportunities for parents to return to work. Curriculum guidance was developed to establish desirable learning outcomes for children. Significant developments under the Labour government saw free pre-school education roll out in addition to the Sure Start Programme (1998) that became further enhanced as part of the Every Child Matters Strategy (DfES, 2003), a mechanism that facilitated the reality of multi-agency working. Early Years settings were required to follow a new curriculum, the Early Years Foundation Stage (EYFS) (DfES, 2007), designed to ensure equal access to quality early years education and a focus on preparing children for school. Working in practice during this time there was a strong sense of feeling empowered to provide a support service for all families, addressing the first 4 principles of Reynolds successful early intervention. The Supporting Families in the Foundation Years document (DoE, DoHSC, 2011), echoed the principles outlined by Reynolds, those deemed to be influential in intervening early are recognised. Although developing resilience is not explicitly referred to, there are clear intentions to focus on areas that make a difference to families.

Following mixed reviews on the impact of Sure Start, responsibility for its continued provision rests with Local Authorities (Bate & Foster, 2015) and this has resulted in controversy over the apparent reduction in support and services across the country. There are numerous risk factors that many children and families face and these are not limited to the most vulnerable. The varying practices across Local Authorities therefore speak to the challenges currently being faced in delivering an equitable service to families and children, despite the implementation of universal and

Table 6.1 Eight principles for successful intervention (Reynolds, 1998)

(1) Target children and families at highest risk of educational underachievement
(2) Begin participation early during the pre-school period and continue into the school period
(3) Provide comprehensive child-development services
(4) Encourage active parental involvement in educational and care provision
(5) Adopt a child-centred, structured approach to the pre- and primary school curriculum
(6) Ensure small class sizes and teacher/child ratios
(7) Offer regular staff development and in-service training for qualified teachers
(8) Undertake systematic evaluation and monitoring

tiered services designed to be responsive to need (Allen, 2011). Funding reductions have meant the 'early intervention' allocation has fallen by 64% between 2010/11 and 2017/18, increasing demands and a changing policy landscape have prompted a shift in focus (National guidance on the 'core purpose' of children's centres in 2013) to targeting 'high need' families, rather than open access to universal services (Delivering Children's Centre Services, 2018; Smith, Sylva, Sammons, Smith, & Omonigho, 2018). This more reactive stance to work in the Early Years suggests a move away from early intervention. Critics have also argued that policy developments over time have led to a 'schoolification' of the early years, that the focus is on the needs of the political, social and economic constructs of early childhood and education rather than the views of children and families at the centre (Faulkner & Coates, 2013). Whilst further consideration needs to be given to developing a more sustainable model for delivering support services in the early years, attention will be given to the nature of the microsystem supporting all children, specifically, the universal opportunities that lie within early years settings.

The Early Years Curriculum

The Statutory framework for the Early Years Foundation Stage (EYFS) (DfE, 2017) and Development Matters for the EYFS (Early Education, 2012) outline the approach to delivering a developmental curriculum from birth to age 5. Early learning goals are identified for children which then have implications for assessment. An incongruence exists between the clear aim for educative outcomes or 'school readiness' and the nurturing approaches advocated within a developmental curriculum. Within the structure of the curriculum, four key themes and principles underpin the guidance. These themes reflect a supportive context for children to develop, as depicted within Bronfenbrenner's, ecological systems theory (Fig. 6.1).

The characteristics of effective learning suggest that children cultivate agency when, engaged (playing and exploring), motivated (active learning) and developing their thought processes (creating and thinking critically). Child development theory has supported our understanding of how children learn through creating meaning from their experiences, with the appreciation that this crucially takes place within an environment of relationships. Within the early years, there is an imperative to intervene early and identify what might be or could be done, that would benefit children and their families. It could be argued that the very notion of trying to 'help' or 'intervene' undermines a resilient approach to support. However, this misses the key concept of resilience as an enabling tool and one in which the autonomy and strengths of the individual and context are sought. Grotberg (1995, p. 11) seeks to summarise the sources of resilience as 'I have, I am, and I can'. Simply put to highlight promoting a sense of self, developing self-esteem, self-efficacy and autonomy. As outlined within the Table 6.2, these sources of resilience, framed within a psychosocial context, directly correlate with the three aspects within Personal, Social and Emotional Development (PSED), prime area of learning within the EYFS.

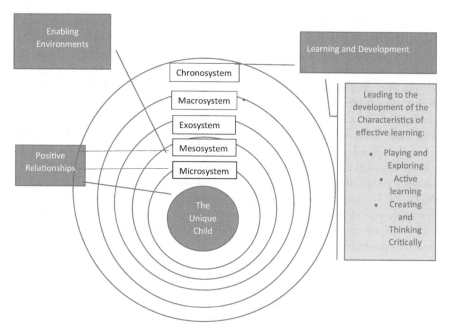

Fig. 6.1 Bronfenbrenner's bio-psycho-social-ecological model of human development annotated with themes from development matters in the EYFS (Early Education, 2012)

Table 6.2 Connections between sources of resilience with aspects of Personal, Social and Emotional Development (EYFS)

Source of resilience	Description	Aspect of PSED (development matters in the EYFS)
I have	People who; love me, set limits for me to protect me, want me to be able to do things by myself	Making relationships
I am	Loveable, concerned for others, able to take responsibility for my actions, hopeful about the future	Self-confidence and self-awareness
I can	Communicate my needs, problem solve, self-regulate	Managing feelings and behaviour

The EYFS curriculum guidance recognises the central role that the early years has in supporting the development of children's resilience. Although this concept is not named, it places the importance of children's PSED as a prime area of learning, identifying this as a priority. The significance of such an aspect of development is established within theory surrounding the importance of the executive functions of emotional intelligence and self-cognition (Goleman, 2011; Goldstein & Brooks, 2013). The focus on PSED advocates for the individual needs of the child, seeking to understand and be responsive in order to meet these needs. It is only through children experiencing the dependant and trusting relationship of another that they are able to feel safe and secure, and become more independent. The reliability of this attachment experienced through intimate interactions, provides a protective factor that can support the development of self and future relationships, forming a positive internal working model (Cowie, 2018) that reflects the sources of resilience as outlined by Grotberg (1995).

The Early Years: Relationships

It is proposed that the mechanism for these relationships to develop is through the key person approach (Elfer, 2013), not key worker—a substituted term which places incorrect emphasis on the administrative role within early years. The interactions that occur between individuals have been demonstrated to activate neural pathways that aid brain growth and development (Shonkoff, 2017). This fundamental connection between carer and child has been explored in depth, referred to as the 'serve and return', the ability to respond in an attuned way to children has a significant impact, highlighting the importance of how affection shapes a baby's brain and enables attachments to develop (Gerhardt, 2014). This key person's role, or always available adult (AAA) (McDonald et al., 2016), is to build a relationship through sensitive responses and in doing so provide a protective factor that supports the development of resilience. It is not to try and ensure that the child is never distressed or unhappy, much as we instinctively seek to protect our children and achieve emotional balance. The importance of emotional equilibrium is to develop an awareness of how feelings change, their purpose is to unsettle and notice if contexts are unsafe or potentially dangerous. Children need to know that uncomfortable feelings are manageable which is different to not experiencing uncomfortable feelings. Beginning to develop this tool of self-regulation is one that is initially managed by those caring for children, a life-long skill we seek to accomplish, 'Self-regulation, which is like an ongoing inner conversation, is the component of emotional intelligence that frees us from being prisoners of our feelings' (Goleman, 1998: 98).

Within children's development there is a cultural tradition and expectation that relationships support the mastery of skills leading to self-regulation. This level of executive function moves what begins as a reactive impulse to a behavioural response that is proactive and goal directed (Centre for the Developing Child Harvard University, 2016). It is important to acknowledge that the role of the key person as an attachment figure is skillful, being required to provide balance, relied upon when necessary and enabling children to be able to cope with uncomfortable feelings at times of distress. The Centre for the Developing Child identify different types of stress that are we are biologically programmed to respond to, to ensure our survival. A positive stress response is typically relatively short lived, promoting some physiological changes in heart rate and hormone levels and can be associated with moments such as beginning nursery. A tolerable stress response is longer lasting and in response to a significant event such as fear-provoking injury or bereavement. Within the context of supportive relationships the duration and impact of this stress can be buffered. Toxic stress refers to contexts that trigger prolonged activation of the stress response system which can result in significant alterations in the developing brain and it is these contexts that are connected with the research on adverse childhood experiences (ACEs) that result in poor life outcomes (Felitti et al., 2019). When children experience a stress response they are reliant on others to enable them to manage. A response that seeks to provide a child with the ability to regulate and mediate their stress response system will serve not only to provide physiological and psychological relief at the time, but also support as a guide for managing future stressors, thus becoming more resilient. These responses and factors that impact on them influence the trajectory of children in developing resilience.

As outlined in Chap. 2, Daniel, Wassell, and Gilligan's model of resilience (1999) can be used to further depict the dynamic and interactive nature of resilience, recognising the complexity of how children adapt to their surroundings and experiences. Supported by studies of risk and resilient factors following potential traumatic events, the cumulative nature of factors are identified (Bonnano & Diminich, 2013). In the case of protective factors, these build over time through experience and therefore have the capacity as a tool to transform stress from potentially being toxic to tolerable. This additive nature of layering of experience can be applied using Ungar's principles of equifinality, differential impact and cultural moderation to explore the trajectory of children in relation to their contexts (2013). In the DIMoR, (ahmed Shafi et al., 2020), children do not 'bounce back' from these challenging experiences but move on a trajectory of emerging resilience (Bonnano & Diminich, 2013).

The Early Years: Risk

The process of developing resilience can therefore not take place without some degree of challenge and potential vulnerability. When children are emotionally secure through the relationships they develop it is possible to explore, provide flexibility and compromise, and give enough room for choices and decisions where children can 'feel the edges of their autonomous interdependent self' (Manning-Morton, 2013, p. 61). Küenzlen, Bekkhus, Thorpe, and Borge identified that children exhibited an increase in pro-social behaviour following potentially traumatic events (2016). Within this study questions followed regarding the possible social mechanisms underlying resilience, suggesting an adaptive response in which children seek connections with other children. The study also recognised that in Norway there is greater emphasis on the physical environment allowing children to learn by taking risks. The importance of outdoor play to support physical, intellectual and social development has long been recognised (Little & Wyver, 2008), but the approach to supporting children in engaging with challenge and risk has been questioned. McClintic and Petty (2015) identified that practitioner's beliefs and approaches to outdoor play valued the role in children's development, yet focused on the role of supervision with adherence to rules, reminiscent of the 'bubble wrap generation' (Malone, 2007).

The EYFS statutory framework includes guidance on how settings need to ensure the safety of children and also manage risks, by 'making reasonable adjustments to ensure that staff and children are not exposed to risks' (DfE, 2017: 31), although understandably the application of this guidance is open to interpretation. Whilst the use of play and the outdoor environment is actively promoted within the early years guidance, the reality of what children experience is variable. The explicit message that "playing is the ability to take risks that would otherwise be too dangerous" (Hendricks, 2017, p. 5), to thereby foster sources of resilience, is not recognised broadly enough in practice. The development of play for children has seen a reduction in freedom and connection with the natural world and their ability to explore and challenge. The growth of forest school approaches and the desire to build practice in this area suggests that there is real interest and recognition of the need to support children's personal, social and emotional development. An approach to supporting resilience is more than following guidance or curriculum, it is about what is valued and believed to be important. Brock's review of professionalism from a practitioner perspective, recognises the importance not just of knowledge, skills and training (these are vital) but those of ethics and values and feeling empowered to act with professional judgement (2013).

Conclusion

This chapter has positioned the early years as a crucial opportunity to support emerging resilience for children, suggesting that this can be positively influenced and supported through the key person approach and the development of sensitive and attuned relationships. The early years statutory guidance and curriculum (DfE, 2017) supports and recognises the importance of children's personal, social and emotional development, yet does not make the significance of resilience explicit. There needs to be a clear message that resilience gives the possibility of well-being, but this does not necessarily equate with well-being. Practitioners can be reassured in recognising the role of discomfort, challenge and potential stress in supporting a developmental process which we are all biologically designed to respond and adapt to, in order to progress (Küenzlen et al., 2016).

It is acknowledged that the focus of this discussion has not been on the negative implications of disruption, but rather the prosocial development and growth that build the foundations of resilience (Shonkoff et al., 2015). Implementing this approach faces a number of potential barriers, of which there are too many to explore within the scope of this chapter. The importance of resilience as a value, a process and tool to aiding positive longer term outcomes for children warrants further attention. The DIMoR (ahmed Shafi et al., 2020), offers a conceptual rationalisation of how the trajectory of resilience is dynamic, interactive and heavily influenced by context and there is the opportunity to influence this beginning in the early years. This prospect can be extended; not only 'setting the scene' for later educational experience, but influencing what takes place in the wider educational system. These principles in practice for building resilience are not exclusive, and should be influencing our education of children across the age ranges.

References

ahmed Shafi, A., Templeton, S., Middleton, T., Millican, R., Vare, P., Pritchard, R. et al. (2020). Towards a dynamic interactive model of resilience (DIMoR) for education and learning contexts. *Emotional and Behavioural Difficulties, 25*(2), 183–198. https://doi.org/10.1080/136 32752.2020.1771923.

Allen, G. (2011). *Early intervention: the next steps, an independent report to Her Majesty's government by Graham Allen MP.* The Stationery Office.

Bate, A., & Foster, D. (2015). Sure Start (England) Briefing Paper Number 7257. Bonanno, G. A., & Diminich, E. D. (2013). Annual research review: Positive adjustment to adversity—Trajectories of minimal-impact resilience and emergent resilience. *Journal of Child Psychology and Psychiatry, 54*(4), 378–401.

Bertram, T., & Pascal, C. (2001). *The OECD thematic review of early childhood education and care: Background report for the United Kingdom.* Centre for Research in Early Childhood, University College Worcester.

Bonanno, G. A., & Diminich, E. D. (2013). Annual research review: Positive adjustment to adversity–trajectories of minimal–impact resilience and emergent resilience. *Journal of child psychology and psychiatry, 54*(4), 378–401.

Brock, A. (2013). Building a model of early years professionalism from practitioners' perspectives. *Journal of Early Childhood Research, 11*(1), 27–44.

Bronfenbrenner, U. (1994). Ecological models of human development. *Readings on the development of children, 2*(1), 37–43.

Center on the Developing Child at Harvard University. (2016). Building Core Capabilities for Life: The Science Behind the Skills Adults Need to Succeed in Parenting and in the Workplace.

Clarke, L., & McLaughlin, T. (2018). What do teachers need to know? Brain development and high quality early learning environments. *Early Education, 64,* 12.

Cowie, H. (2018). *Handbook of attachment: Theory, research, and clinical applications.*

Daniel, B., Wassell, S., & Gilligan, R. (1999). *Child development for child care and protection workers.* London: Jessica Kingsley Publishers.

Delivering Children's Centre Services. (2018). Local Government Association.

Department for Education and Skills. (2003). *Every child matters.* London: Department for Education and Skills.

Department for Education and Skills. (2007). *Practice guidance for the early years foundation stage.* Nottingham: DfES Publications.

Department for Education & Department of Health and Social Care. (2011). *Supporting Families in Foundation Years.* Government Publication. Available at: https://www.gov.uk/government/pub lications/supporting-families-in-the-foundation-years [Accessed 03.07.2020].

Department for Education. (2017). *Statutory Framework for the Early Years Foundation Stage Framework.* Available at: https://assets.publishing.service.gov.uk/government/uploads/sys tem/uploads/attachment_data/file/596629/EYFS_STATUTORY_FRAMEWORK_2017.pdf [Accessed 03.07.2020].

Early Education. (2012). *Development Matters in the Early Years Foundation Stage.* Available at: https://www.early-education.org.uk/development-matters [Accessed on 03.07.2020].

Elfer, P. (2013). *Key persons in the nursery: Building relationships for quality provision.* David Fulton Publishers.

Faulkner, D., & Coates, E. A. (2013). Early childhood policy and practice in England: Twenty years of change. *International Journal of Early Years Education, 21*(2–3), 244–263.

Felitti, V. J., Anda, R. F., Nordenberg, D., Williamson, D. F., Spitz, A. M., Edwards, V., ... Marks, J. S. (2019). Relationship of childhood abuse and household dysfunction to many of the leading causes of death in adults: The Adverse Childhood Experiences (ACE) study. *American Journal of Preventive Medicine, 56*(6), 774–786.

Gerhardt, S. (2014). *Why love matters: How affection shapes a baby's brain.* Routledge.

Goldstein, S., & Brooks, R. B. (2013). Why study resilience? In *Handbook of resilience in children* (pp. 3–14). Boston, MA: Springer.

Goleman, D. (1998). *Working with emotional intelligence.* Bantam.

Goleman, D. (2011). The brain and emotional intelligence: New insights. *Regional Business, 94.*

Gov.uk. (2010). *United Nations Convention On The Rights Of The Child (UNCRC): How Legislation Underpins Implementation In England.* Publications - GOV.UK. [online] Available at: https://assets.publishing.service.gov.uk/government/uploads/system/uploads/attachment_data/file/296368/uncrc_how_legislation_underpins_implementation_in_england_march_2010.pdf [Accessed 03.07.2020].

Greenberg, P. (1998, July). Some thoughts about phonics, feelings, Don Quixote, diversity, and democracy: Teaching young children to read, write, and spell part 1. *Young Children, 53*(4), 72–83. Harris, F. (2017). The nature of learning at forest school: Practitioners' perspectives. *Education 3–13, 45*(2), 272–291.

Grotberg, E. H. (1995). *A guide to promoting resilience in children: Strengthening the human spirit.*

Hendricks, B. E. (2017). *Designing for play.* Routledge.

Howe, D. (2011). *Attachment across the lifecourse: A brief introduction.* Macmillan International Higher Education.

Küenzlen, H., Bekkhus, M., Thorpe, K., & Borge, A. I. (2016). Potential traumatic events in early childhood and behavioural resilience: A longitudinal case control study. *European Journal of Developmental Psychology, 13*(3), 394–406.

Leach, P. (Ed.). (2017). *Transforming infant wellbeing: Research, policy and practice for the first 1001 critical days.* Routledge.

Little, H., & Wyver, S. (2008). Outdoor play: Does avoiding the risks reduce the benefits? *Australasian Journal of Early Childhood, 33*(2), 33–40.

Malone, K. (2007). The bubble-wrap generation: Children growing up in walled gardens. *Environmental Education Research, 13*(4), 513–527.

Manning-Morton, J. (2013). *Exploring Wellbeing in the Early Years.* McGraw-Hill Education (UK).

Masten, A. S. (2001). Ordinary magic: Resilience processes in development. *American Psychologist, 56*(3), 227.

Mathers, S., Eisenstadt, N., Sylva, K., Soukakou, E., & Ereky-Stevens, K. (2014). *Sound foundations: A review of the research evidence on quality of early childhood education and care for children under three. Implications for policy and practice.* Sutton Trust.

McClintic, S., & Petty, K. (2015). Exploring early childhood teachers' beliefs and practices about preschool outdoor play: A qualitative study. *Journal of Early Childhood Teacher Education, 36*(1), 24–43.

McDonald, S., Kehler, H., Bayrampour, H., Fraser-Lee, N., & Tough, S. (2016). Risk and protective factors in early child development: Results from the All Our Babies (AOB) pregnancy cohort. *Research in Developmental Disabilities, 58,* 20–30.

Panter-Brick, C., & Eggerman, M. (2012). Understanding culture, resilience, and mental health: The production of hope. In *The social ecology of resilience* (pp. 369–386). New York, NY: Springer.

Reynolds, A. J. (1998). Developing early childhood programs for children and families at risk: Research-based principles to promote long-term effectiveness. *Children and Youth Services Review, 20*(6), 503–523.

Schweinhart, L. J., & Weikart, D. P. (1997). *Lasting differences: The high/scope preschool curriculum comparison study through age 23. Monographs of the high/scope educational research foundation, number twelve.* Monograph Series, High/Scope Foundation, 600 North River Street, Ypsilanti, MI 48198-2898.

Siegel, D. J. (2015). *The developing mind: How relationships and the brain interact to shape who we are.* Guilford Publications.

Shonkoff, J., Levitt, P., Bunge, S., Cameron, J., Duncan, G., Fisher, P., & Nox, N. (2015). *Supportive relationships and active skill-building strengthen the foundations of resilience: Working paper 13.* Cambridge, UK: National Scientific Council on the Developing Child.

Shonkoff, J. P. (2017). Breakthrough impacts: What science tells us about supporting early childhood development. *YC Young Children, 72*(2), 8–16.

Smith, G., Sylva, K., Sammons, P., Smith, T., & Omonigho, A. (2018). Stop Start.

Sylva, K. (1994). The impact of early learning on children's later development. In C. Ball (Ed.), *Start right: The importance of early learning.* Lesley James, Royal Society for the Encouragement of Arts, Manufactures and Commerce, 8 John Adam Street, London, WC2N 6EZ, England, United Kingdom (15 British pounds).

Ungar, M. (2013). Resilience, trauma, context, and culture. *Trauma, Violence, & Abuse, 14*(3), 255–266.

Weisner, T. S. (2010). John and Beatrice Whiting's contributions to the cross-cultural study of human development: Their values, goals, norms, and practices. *Journal of Cross-Cultural Psychology, 41*(4), 499–509.

Werner, E. E. (2000). Protective factors and individual resilience. *Handbook of Early Childhood Intervention, 2,* 115–132.

Rebecca Pritchard Rebecca is a practicing Educational Psychologist who has also undertaken a Senior Lecturer role in Education at the University of Gloucestershire. She has worked in numerous settings encompassing early years through secondary education including specialist provision. She has been fortunate to develop a career that has enabled a focus on her particular interests of early years, resilience, autism and mental health through both local authority provision and private practice. Research interests have included a European study on emotional education and she is beginning her DEdPsy at the University College London. From supporting individuals and families with specific needs to the design and provision of training for professionals, teaching on Undergraduate and Postgraduate courses, Rebecca continues to develop her understanding and expertise across this fascinating subject.

Chapter 7
Resilience, Well-Being and Mental Health: The Role of Education Settings

Sian Templeton and Rebecca Pritchard

Abstract This chapter explores the rising profile of mental health and wellbeing within the school population. It tries to make sense of variables within defining mental health and wellbeing and the interaction between these definitions, schools, individuals within schools and the wider policy context. Some of the challenges for meeting the mental health needs of the student population are discussed with consideration of the impact of competing priorities on teacher ability to meet these needs. The link between mental health and well-being and resilience is considered with discussion using the DIMoR (ahmed Shafi et al., 2020), as an opportunity to understand wider influences on mental health and well-being. The chapter highlights links between expectations, teacher efficacy and the nature of taking a more systemic approach to understanding and meeting need across all levels within a system is highlighted and ideas for future research and approaches are suggested.

Introduction

The focus on mental health and well-being is a relatively recent phenomenon, (Pilgrim, 2017) Historically, there has been more of an approach of exclusion of those experiencing 'mental illness' using terms such as 'lunacy' and 'asylums' with an approach aligned with the medical model of disability whereby patients were treated with quasi-medical interventions or admitted to asylums as the rest of society did not know how to manage or tolerate mental illness. More recently, there has been a recognition that there is more of a continuum between mental illness and mental health and wellbeing with some arguing for a dual definition separating mental illness from mental health and wellbeing. Part of the argument for this dual definition centres around the idea that mental health and wellbeing does not have to be commensurate

S. Templeton (✉) · R. Pritchard
School of Education and Humanities, University of Gloucestershire, Francis Close Hall, Swindon Road, Cheltenham, Gloucestershire GL50 4AZ, UK
e-mail: stempleton@glos.ac.uk

R. Pritchard
e-mail: insighteps@gmail.com

© Springer Nature Switzerland AG 2020
A. ahmed Shafi et al. (eds.), *Reconsidering Resilience in Education*,
https://doi.org/10.1007/978-3-030-49236-6_7

with mental 'ill-health' and the deficit model but can also be about being mentally 'healthy'.

The more recent focus on mental health promotion has also made links to resilience as a concept. This connection between mental health promotion and resilience is made by both charities, such as The Mental Health Foundation offering practical guidance on promoting resilience as part of an integrated health and wellbeing programme, alongside academic research such as the meta-analysis conducted by Davydov, Stewart, Ritchie, and Chaudieu (2010) which found clear links between interventions for positive mental health and resilience. This idea has also been developed more specifically focusing on children and young people with Noble, McGrath, Wyatt, Carbines, and Robb (2008, p. 8) stating that "...in the context of school and educational settings, optimal student wellbeing is defined as a sustained state of positive emotions and attitude, resilience, and satisfaction with self, as well as with relationships and experiences at school." A number of these themes identified by Noble et al. will be explored within this chapter.

This chapter will therefore explore definitions of mental health and wellbeing and the need to distinguish this term from 'mental illness'. The current policy context and associated discourse is explored alongside and the inter-related nature of the current perceived 'crisis' within the mental health of our child and youth population and the relevant external sources which may contribute to this. How this discourse links to education in the broadest sense then focusing in on the various players within this system, (such as teachers, students and school leaders), and the bidirectional impact of these relationships is discussed with consideration as to how the DIMoR (ahmed Shafi et al., 2020) helps with both understanding and intervening to optimise outcomes for all.

Definition

The World Health Organization (2004, p. 10) defines mental health as being "a state of well-being in which the individual realizes his or her own abilities, can cope with the normal stresses of life, can work productively and fruitfully, and is able to make a contribution to his or her community." This definition makes the distinction that mental health is not focused upon a deficit model of something being wrong or the absence of mental illness, but also to be a full and active participant in daily life events. The conceptual and practical overlap between promoting well-being and preventing mental ill-health is reflected in the media with the potential to confuse. It has been suggested that the factors that influence mental illness are the reverse of those associated with well-being, i.e. working on a continuum. This appears to be the case in relation to some specific factors, such as; single parent family and school connectedness, identified in Patalay and Fitzsimons 'correlates of mental illness and well-being' (2016). However not all factors appeared to work in this way, such that an increase in mental ill-health results in a decrease in well-being or vice versa, this was identified with factors including; cognitive ability, health factors, and parent health. The continuum model has therefore been questioned, the two constructs, mental illness and well-being representing the domains of mental health on a single spectrum, are not influenced by the same factors at different ends of the spectrum (Patalay & Fitzsimons, 2016). Within this study the millennium cohort data evidence indicate that the determinants of well-being in many instances were different from the determinants of mental illness. For example whilst there were similar variables such as; "family structure, sibling bullying, peer problems", correlating with both mental illness and well-being, these were different in other areas such as; "family income, perceived socioeconomic status, cognitive ability, health status and neighbourhood safety". These outcomes provide clarity in using key terms, with a sharper focus for supporting the prevention and intervention of broader developmental drivers that contribute to mental illness in addition to addressing and improving areas that are likely to impact on children's well-being. Of the variables indicated in the study; school connectedness, being bullied, friendships, and perceptions of safe neighbourhood were strongly correlated with wellbeing. These findings can support the move within educational environments to promote well-being, enabling children and young people to achieve their potential and cope with the stressors in life. This latter aspect of the WHO definition, resonates with the concept of resilience, recognising that mental health is more than the absence of mental illness (Patalay & Fitzsimons, 2016). This suggests that well-being is a useful concept to connect the development of resilience, using protective factors to further support mental health (Roffey, 2016). The term well-being also infers the need to account for broader contextual factors (Weare & Gray, 2003; Watson & Emery, 2012) which incorporates ecological models of interaction supporting children and young people's development in line with dynamic nature of interacting systems within the DIMoR (ahmed Shafi et al., 2020).

In light of an approach that seeks to promote mental health, it is of great concern that recent self-report data indicates that young people's well-being is at an all-time low (Good Childhood Report, 2017; Prince's Trust Macquarie, 2018). More specifically, Pienaar and Johnston (2017) estimate that one in ten children and young people have a diagnosable mental health condition. Understanding what appears to be an alarming shift in the well-being of children and young people is crucial in developing a supportive response.

Current Context: Policy

The 'crisis' facing the mental health needs of children is well publicised with government figures citing that one in ten children need support for mental health difficulties, (DoH & NHS England, 2015). A 'perfect storm' has been developing in which the combined effect of the increased demand for mental health services for children and young people as well as significant financial pressures on the NHS service have resulted in reduced access to support (Thorley, 2016). Lessof, Ross, Brind, Bell, and

Newton's (2016) longitudinal study highlights specifically the increases in psychological distress among adolescent girls in comparison with their earlier study in 2005. In addition to this, an increase in internalising mental health problems in adolescents and young adults has been identified by Bor, Dean, Najman, and Hayatbakhsh (2014) with a substantial increase in hospital admission episodes where self-harm is recorded as the cause (Burt, 2016). In addition to this, a high prevalence of depressive symptoms has been identified as being recorded in 14 yr olds: 24% girls and 9% boys by Patalay and Fitzsimmonds (2016). However, Patalay and Fitzsimmonds go on to suggest that despite these alarming statistics, it still needs to be acknowledged that the majority of 3–14 yr olds in the UK are not suffering from 'mental ill health'; instead there is a substantial proportion of this population who are experience instead more general mental health and well-being difficulties.

The NSPCC childline review identified that 1 in 3 of their counselling sessions related to mental health and wellbeing issues (2016), of these 87% who reported difficulties were able to access local support services. Nevertheless, a national discrepancy exists within service provision with the Children's Commissioner (2016) reporting 79% of Child and Adolescent Mental Health services (CAMHS) imposing restrictions and thresholds to access their service which results in a national inequality in access to appropriate services with professionals trained to understand and meet the needs of our school-age population with ever increasing waiting lists resulting. Khan (2016) reports on the 'decade of delay' between the first signs of needing support and receiving help from mental health services. The reported cuts to CAMHS services (House of Commons Health Committee, 2014) as a service that meets the needs of children and young people with the more severe needs would suggest that perhaps there needs to be more of a focus on early intervention as a way of reducing the demand on this service. However the value of the early intervention allocation for local authorities dropped by 55% over the past 3 financial years (Thorley, 2016). Whilst there is a lack of clarity surrounding the statistical picture there are concerning trends facing our your people with girls reporting lower levels of life satisfaction than boys and higher symptoms of stress (Brooks et al., 2017).

The economic and social vision for the nation to transform outcomes for young people's mental health and well-being is clearly outlined in Future in Mind (2015). Key to the principles of this approach are the connectedness of mental health workers and school staff working in collaboration and support of one another. This call for multiagency working (Cooper, Evans, & Pybis, 2016), is not new and yet the history of developing policy and guidance illustrates the detached nature of practice within Education and Health.

Every Child Matters (DfES, 2003) was one of the first policies which considered emotional health and wellbeing more specifically relating to education. This policy outlined the importance of supporting foundations for children and with the first of five key outcomes for children as 'being healthy' which included mental health. Healthy lives, Healthy people (DoHSC, 2010) estimated that tackling poor mental health could reduce the overall disease burden by nearly a quarter, emphasising a strategy that gave equal weight to mental and physical health needs and for local solutions to address this public health issue. An approach that was echoed within

Achieving Equity and Excellence for children (DoH, 2011) to improve services for children. No Health without Mental Health (Gov, 2011) moved towards a set of shared objectives in which mental health is described as 'a priority across government' driven by sub-committee. The Health and Social Care Act (2012) sought to enable change through commissioning groups and a focus on public health across the life course designed to meet specific need although arguably emphasising national disparities. Awareness of early intervention and prevention has been supported with the implementation of the Early Years Framework and developments to the Early Years Foundation Stage (EYFS) curriculum (DfE, 2008) emphasising PSED as a prime area of development, an implicit focus on supporting children's mental health (Soni, 2012) aligned to supporting foundations for life, health and learning (Tickell, 2011).

The social shift in conceptualising mental health as everyone's responsibility (Future in Mind 2015) is reflected in terminology changes within key education policy documents such as the SEND Code of Practice to 'social, emotional and mental health difficulties' (DfE, 2015). The published 'Mental health and behaviour in schools' (DfE, 2016) and 'Counselling in schools: a blueprint for the future' (2016) which seek to clarify the responsibilities of schools and advise on whole school approaches to supporting mental health and well-being. Transforming children and young people's mental health provision (DoH & DfE, 2017) is a collaborative development which has the potential to move towards a reality of the Future in Mind vision (2015).

Factors Influencing MH

As previously outlined, a focus on mental health is proposed, rather than illness to move away from a deficit model, (Rogers & Pilgrim, 2014). Explanations of the widely socially accepted view of an increase in mental health difficulties, and portrayal of mental health difficulties in children and young people has provided debate surrounding possible causal factors which are challenging to substantiate within a clear evidence base (Deighton et al., 2019). The complexity of influencing factors on mental health has been the focus of Patalay and Fitzsimons study (2016). Of note, they identified that whilst the social gradient for mental illness is observed within children and young people, this is not the case for well-being. This indicates that social deprivation has not impacted on young children's subjective reports of well-being. Therefore the focus on supporting children's education and development is justified in promoting and impacting on their well-being. By providing additional protective factors within the opportunities that education provides can further the development of children's resilience.

The development of behaviours associated with social media suggest that there is a clear desire to engage in this discussion. The need to belong within social groups is a strong predictor of well-being for children, this need for perceived social acceptance, in order to achieve the protective factors of safety, described by Maslow, continue to be relevant in significantly influencing children's self-perception and emotional well-being (Bland & DeRobertis, 2017). The role of peer relationships is well documented and recognised as potential risk or support for well-being (Apland, Lawrence, Mesie, & Yarrow, 2017). The way in which children initially develop their relationships, are accepted and socialised, is heavily influenced by their carers. It is possible to identify tensions between expectations for social and cultural norms and potentially distressing experiences or actions that deviate from these (Rogers & Pilgrim, 2014). This resonates with Ungar's concepts of *equifinality, differential impact* and *cultural moderation* and the way in which these influence the trajectory of resilience. It is evident that parents report differently to children on their perceptions of well-being (Sixsmith, Nic Gabhainn, Fleming, & O'Higgins, 2007). Rogers and Pilgrim highlight the importance of acknowledging a potentially adult-centric view and the impact this may have on underlying approaches (2014). Seeking the views of children and engaging them in an appreciation of the factors that influence their well-being serves to develop a psychoeducational approach to building protective factors.

Over a third of UK 15 year olds in the UK are described as 'extensive users of social media' (Frith, 2017), with an increasing trend for younger children to be 'on-line' (Livingston & Hadden, 2009), with 27.6%, six years or younger when first using the internet. The Office for National Statistics has found a "clear association" between longer time spent on social media and mental health problems, with each additional hour spent online associated with a negative impact on life satisfaction (Frith, 2017). One factor that may contribute to this, identified within the PISA Wellbeing study, is the suggestion that 'extreme internet users' (defined by the OECD as a student who uses the internet for more than six hours outside of school on a typical weekend day), were more likely to report bullying than moderate internet users (PISA 2015). This group of extreme internet users, also reported poorer life satisfaction scores, suggesting a correlation between time spent on social media and well-being. However the way in which children and young people interact with social media is constantly evolving and there is potential to develop protective factors, being able to; "increase social connections, develop identity and seek help" in addition to other educative opportunities (Frith, 2017). Detailed discussion seeking to highlight how self-organised learning environments (SOLE) can support the development of resilience have been outlined within Chap. 12. What appears to be the most significant measure within recent studies is the proportion of time spent, "excessive use" is deemed to pose a risk with the potential to; "share too much, cyber bullying, influence body image, and be the source of potential harmful content or advice". Findings suggest that the self-regulation of social media use is a key skill that children and young-people need to develop. Feeling a sense of belonging is not purely achieved through peer relationships, the notion of school connectedness has also been directly attributed to pupil –teacher relationships. This 'key protective health asset' based on a caring relationship features repeatedly in children's feedback (Apland et al., 2017; Garcia-Moya, Brooks, Morgan, & Moreno, 2014). Overall, 80% of young people (79% of boys and 81% of girls) reported that they have at least one teacher they can go to if they have a problem (Brooks et al., 2017, HBSC report). The emphasis on the importance of this relationship has broader implications for the educator's role.

Role of the Educator in Supporting MH

Having outlined the current context of children and young people's mental health and the prevalence of those who are currently not receiving support, estimated at 40% (Weeks, Hill, & Owen, 2017), the role of schools has been identified as having a crucial opportunity in both identifying and supporting children and young people with mental health needs, DfES (2003), DCSF (2008, 2010) and DfE (2014a, 2014b). This echo's the WHO (2004) suggestion that mental health is 'everyone's business' and that 'neither mental nor physical health can exist alone' (p. 11). Alongside statutory duties to keep children safe (DfE, 2015, 2018), the UK Government's green paper about mental health, (DoHSC and DfE, 2017) further reinforces this shared responsibility for mental health. This first ever joint publication about the state of provision to support mental health problems, focuses on earlier intervention and prevention, emphasising the role of the school and educators in supporting children and young people.

School professionals thus find themselves in the position where they have the opportunity to have a positive impact on both recognising and supporting their students mental health needs (Graetz, 2016; Johnson, Eva, Johnson, and Walker 2011; Pienaar & Johnston, 2017; Thorley, 2016). One of the significant challenges in engaging vulnerable children and young people in support, is the need for them to meet professionals and attend clinic appointments, when often the very difficulties they are experiencing present barriers to accessing this external support. The opportunity to "bring support to them", rather than placing the emphasis on them needing to find it, would seem beneficial (Weeks et al., 2017). However, despite this opportune placing, Dods (2016) found that early career teachers have reported feeling underprepared in their 'mental health literacy' in order to act upon and support student mental health, with Graham, Phelps, Maddison, and Fitzgerald (2011) suggesting variability in teachers self-efficacy with regard to meeting the mental health population of their students. The Government is clear that is does not expect teachers to become mental health workers and yet it is very difficult to distinguish between these potentially overlapping roles. Vulnerable children and young people's testimony frequently illustrates the crucial role of individual teachers in making a significance difference. Often cited as the person that listened to them, the connection with a trusted adult (educational professional) has been demonstrated nationally and internationally to be a key protective factor (Garcia-Moya et al. 2014). This is not to suggest that this relationship is uni-directional (Roffey, 2012). Teachers have reported that one of the most significant factors that contributes to job satisfaction, a source of motivation and enjoyment, is the relationships they have with their students (Baumeister & Leary, 1995; Hargreaves, 2000). The importance of an enabling environment to support the development of relationships should therefore not be underestimated or undervalued. Teachers report that they view supporting student mental health as part of their role, though expressed concerns about their perceived competence (Mazzer & Rickwood, 2015). Previous research has demonstrated that non mental health professionals can be effectively trained to deliver support interventions such as Cognitive Behavioural Therapy (e.g., Ginsburg et al. 2008; Westbrook et al. 2008). However, this requires investment in staff training and where complexity exists, such as children and young people with neuro-developmental conditions, this is insufficient. Staff need to feel confident and equipped to support their students, the mismatch between feeling responsible and being able to support, given the time constraints within school settings, being cited as a significant contributor to teacher stress (Ekornes, 2017).

Supporting the Educator in Supporting MH

With Teacher stress and mental health issues increasingly hitting newspapers with headlines such as: "Teachers are at breaking point. It's time to push wellbeing up the agenda, (The Guardian, April 2018); "Nearly half of teachers struggle with mental health, suggests survey, (Hepburn, 2017); 'Epidemic of stress' blamed for 3,750 teachers on long-term sick leave, (The Guardian, January 2018) it is essential that the importance of educator voice and needs is kept central to the discussion around meeting mental health needs. Issues cited within these articles included the widely acknowledged work-load expectations, but also issues such as the "heavy burden' of guilt about the educational experience [offered to pupils]' (Asthana, 2018). This wider systemic impact is not isolated to just teaching staff, but the senior leaders in schools as well as teaching assistants and administrators (The Guardian, April 2018). These newspaper headlines are also featured within the wider research literature including the finding from Evans et al. (2018) which argues that teaching professionals are at an increased risk of common mental health disorders compared with other occupations.

This concern about the mental health of teachers is further underlined by the findings from the Teacher wellbeing index (2018) which is commissioned by the Education Support Partnership. This report found 67% of education professionals describe themselves as stressed with 76% having experienced behavioural, psychological or physical symptoms of their work and 43% of the professionals completing the survey experiencing symptoms which could meet the criteria for a diagnosis of anxiety. Despite these statistics, a significant proportion of respondents were working within the education profession because of the desire to make a difference, and to work with children and young people. This indicates that there is a potential dissonance between their expectations in entering the profession and their actual experience which has led to these worrying statistics. Evidence suggests that a mismatch between expectations and reality, (incongruence), particularly within the professional domain is negatively associated with symptoms of depression (Paloma, Garcia-Ramirez, & Camacho, 2014). This, alongside the finding from Spilt, Koomen, and Thijs (2011) that teacher's relational experiences with individual students are predictive of their wellbeing, suggests the interactions within the smaller sub-systems of the students

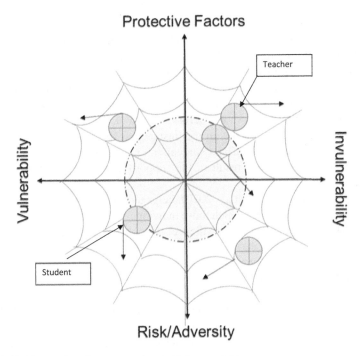

Protective Factors

Vulnerability

Invulnerability

Teacher

Student

Risk/Adversity

Fig. 7.1 Teachers and students as a system in their own right

and the teachers are crucial for optimising the wellbeing of both students and professionals working in schools. The DIMoR, (ahmed Shafi et al., 2020), can help to illustrate this in Fig. 7.1 whereby the smaller 'orbs' can represent both students and teachers carrying their various sub-systems, (which influence their beliefs, affect and behaviour), which then interact/ 'bounce' off each other thereby influencing the developmental trajectory of both sub-systems (in this case students and teachers).

There is much literature which emphasises the link between teacher and student mental health and wellbeing, (Johnson et al., 2011; Roffey, 2012). This runs concurrently with the growing expectation that schools, and therefore teachers, respond to the mental health needs of their student population in order to help the more traditional mental health services cope with the increasing demands on their resources as detailed in the opening of this chapter. It has been identified by Ford, Hamilton, Meltzer, and Goodman (2007), (amongst others), that teachers are the professionals most likely to have routine contact with students in regard to their mental health and thus an increasing number of interventions to intervene with difficulties in student mental health thereby becoming the responsibility of teaching professionals. However, poor teacher wellbeing can reduce teachers' belief in their ability to support students, (Sisask et al., 2013) with this problem being compounded by a lack of training in how to effectively do so, the cycle is then repeated as the associated feelings contributing to a lack of efficacy and thus a negative impact on teacher health and well-being. This therefore indicates that, in order to improve mental health of learners, we need to work towards improved mental health and wellbeing of teaching staff. This inter-related nature of the wellbeing of students and teachers is emphasised by Roffey (2012) in her article which found that schools who valued their teacher well-being obtained better outcomes for their students and also incidentally for the wider finances of the schools due to increased retention rates. This optimisation of outcomes occurred in schools where there was a whole-school ethos with a focus on relationships which were overtly discussed and promoted across the school. The DIMoR, (ahmed Shafi et al., 2020), would recognise this in this instance as the school being wider web with teachers, other school staff and students moving as the orbs and interacting, developing and adapting as a result of the support and challenge of this positive wider school ethos.

The DIMoR, (ahmed Shafi et al., 2020), helps to illustrate how both individuals, and the various systems within which those individuals reside interact in both protective and 'risky' ways to impact on resilience. If teachers are considered a system in their own right and the students are a different system then these interactions are critical in their impact on resilience; both for the teacher and the learner (see Fig. 7.1). Teacher well-being will impact on student well-being through their interactions and through the learning environment that they create within the wider 'web' of the DIMoR, (ahmed Shafi et al., 2020), and this interaction will be reciprocal. Therefore, in order to enhance teacher, and thus student well-being, there needs to be a climate, wider system, (in this case the wider web), which promotes openness and fosters mutually trusting relationships between, staff, students and the wider school community.

Role of the Setting in Supporting MH

As discussed in Chap. 5, there is a growing recognition of the opportunity that schools present in their key role in being able to impact on the mental health and wellbeing with Greenberg (2010) positing that they are the only real universal provision for children which is acknowledged within the government green paper, (DoHSC & DfE, 2017). Within the wider context of the mental health debate, (as discussed earlier), there is a wide recognition of the importance of early intervention (Humphrey & Wigelsworth, 2016; Parsonage, Khan, & Saunders, 2014) with Davies (2013) suggesting that a focus on prevention rather than a more reactive approach of dealing with mental illness is more cost effective (DoH & NHS England, 2015; Layard, 2005). The Department of Health and NHS England (2015) highlight the prevalence of the onset of mental health difficulties with their finding that 75% of adult mental health problems originate under the age of 18, whilst children and young people are still at school and posit that schools are one of the universal services which play a key role in the prevention of mental health problems. Thorley (2016) reinforces this focus arguing that early intervention mental health services for children and young people must be rejuvenated and goes on to suggest that secondary schools should play a central role in this. This is further developed by Stallard (2013) in his research where he advocates the potential of early intervention programmes and activities having a significant impact on psychosocial and academic performance with teachers not just in secondary schools, but across the age ranges being well-placed to support this.

As professionals who come into daily contact with parents, teachers are finding themselves increasingly utilised as a sources of support when parents are worried and concerned about the mental health of their children with Ford et al. (2007) finding that parents contacted teachers as mental health experts more than any other professional. There is a recognition however that teaching staff do not necessarily have the understanding and skill set to be able to both recognise and meet the mental health needs of children and young people. Ford et al. (2007) argued that this highlights the need for all professionals working with children, including teachers, to acquire basic skills in identification and management of minor difficulties and knowledge of how to access more specialised services. Foxcroft (2014) would support this, arguing that informational prevention can have a positive impact on reducing the prevalence of poor mental health. This would hold true for both parents and teachers in supporting their understanding of the causes and contributory factors of presenting mental health needs within children and young people. There is evidence that an understanding of concepts helps with teacher efficacy of practice (Ingvarson, Meiers, & Beavis, 2005). The House of Commons Health Committee (2014: 12) recommend that the Department for Education looks into including a core module within all Initial Teacher Training which focuses on mental health and that further modules should be provided for both teaching and support staff as part of the schools CPD provision. This recommendation arose out of the committee's finding that, according to reports from young people, the understanding amongst school staff was sporadic with some teachers and schools provide excellent support whilst some are less well trained and even seem 'scared' of discussing mental health issues. As teachers social and emotional competence can be seen a source of safety and security (Jennings & Greenberg, 2009) and supportive teacher-student relationships can enable a child or young person feels they belong to a wider community, then an increase in understanding which helps to develop prosocial competence in teachers would potentially help to further facilitate this sense of 'belonging'.

Schools are recognised as being well placed to make a very significant contribution to the emotional well-being of children which has positive implications for mental health, (Geddes, 2006). For children and young people who experience mental health difficulties as a result of their attachment relationships, schools and school communities can be construed as places of safety (Golding et al., 2012). This links to the ideas presented in Chap. 2 around the importance of relationships and community membership as protective factors in developing resilience. Banerjee, Weare and Farr's (2014) finding that a socially and emotionally literature school ethos impacts positively on pupil attendance, and then academic attainment reiterates the potential of schools to act as a protective mechanism for learners who may be experiencing difficulties outside of their school life. School settings are therefore key here due to their ability to create and sustain a sense of belonging for children and young people through both the formal and informal aspects of their curriculum as part of a broader ethos rather than simply relying on specific programmes designed to develop specific skills.

There is a growing argument that rather than focusing on 'discrete' programmes which respond to presenting mental health need that the focus instead should be on prevention and more of a whole school and wider systemic approach (Roffey, 2012; Sisask et al., 2013). Therefore, individualised packages would appear not to be sufficient to respond to the growing mental health needs within our student population discussed earlier in this chapter. The DIMoR would support this, recognising the bi-directional nature of interactions between individuals within the system (i.e. students and teachers), individuals and the system itself (i.e. students/teachers and the school), and various systems interactions with other systems (i.e. schools, CAMHs and government agencies). A more practical example of this is illustrated by the findings of Cooper et al. (2016) who analysed factors that help with longer term positive mental health outcomes included interagency understanding co-ordinated by a key named link person. This model of shared responsibility and understanding helps to reduce pressure and individual expectation, but also enables a more holistic vision of need. Noble et al. (2008) provide a useful framework for supporting this more holistic systemic approach in their analysis of effective approaches to supporting student wellbeing. There are clear links between their identified 'seven pathways' (see Table 7.1) to informing student wellbeing and the ideas from the resilience literature outlined in Chap. 2 as to the components that help optimise the resilience of learners.

The opportunity for a more joined up approach based on shared values within a setting which enacts a value system for staff well-being as well as student well-being as part of a wider systemic response has the potential to make a positive impact on not only student health and wellbeing but also that of staff within the setting too.

Conclusion

It would seem that schools now have a sharper focus on the need to support mental health needs in order to promote a mentally healthy and supportive school ethos. The recognition of the personal, social and economic impact of increasing teacher attrition highlights the need for a more holistic and mutually supportive approach to understanding and supporting the rising mental health difficulties reported in both our student and teacher populations. The DIMoR, (ahmed Shafi et al., 2020), offers an analytical tool to explore how, why and what can be implemented and changed at various levels, (individual, systemic and systems within systems) in order to optimise the longer-term outcomes through the development of protective factors to promote mental health and resilience within our school populations. More research is now needed to explore what works at each level with a view to developing more of a

Table 7.1 Pathways (Noble et al., 2008, pp. 9–10)

Pathway	School-based practices
A supportive, caring and inclusive school community	A community that fosters school connectedness, positive teacher-student relationships and parental involvement
Pro-social values	Values such as respect, honesty, compassion, acceptance of difference, fairness, responsibility are directly taught and indirectly encouraged
Physical and emotional safety	Via anti-bullying and anti-violence strategies, policies, procedures and programs
Social and emotional learning	Coping skills, self-awareness, emotional regulation skills, empathy, goal achievement skills, relationship skills
A strengths-based approach	Schools focusing on identifying and developing students' intellectual strengths (eg using a multiple Intelligences model) and character strengths
A sense of meaning and purpose	Through one or more of: spirituality, community service, participation in school clubs and teams, peer support, collaborative and authentic group projects etc
A healthy lifestyle	Good nutrition, exercise, avoidance of illegal drugs and alcohol

https://docs.education.gov.au/system/files/doc/other/scoping_study_into_approaches_to_student_wellbeing_final_report.pdf

holistic and multi-faceted approach to supporting mental health. This focus could consider aspects such as training, specific interventions, raising the profile of learner and teacher voice, psycho-education and policy change in order to become more responsive to the changing needs and risks present within society.

References

ahmed Shafi, A., Templeton, S., Middleton, T., Millican, R., Vare, P., Pritchard, R. et al. (2020). Towards a dynamic interactive model of resilience (DIMoR) for education and learning contexts. *Emotional and Behavioural Difficulties, 25*(2), 183–198. https://doi.org/10.1080/136 32752.2020.1771923.

Apland, K., Lawrence, H., Mesie, J. & Yarrow, E. (2017). *Children's voice: A review of the evidence on the subjective wellbeing of children excluded from school and in alternative provision in England.* London: Children's Commissioner for England.

Asthana, A. (2018, January 11). *Epidemic of stress'* blamed for 3,750 teachers on long-term sick leave. The Guardian. Retrieved October 8, 2019, from https://www.theguardian.com/education/2018/jan/11/epidemic-of-stress-blamed-for-3750-teachers-on-longterm-sick-leave.

118

S. Templeton and R. Pritchard

Banerjee, R., Weare, K., & Farr, W. (2014). Working with 'Social and Emotional Aspects of Learning' (SEAL): Associations with school ethos, pupil social experiences, attendance, and attainment. *British Educational Research Journal, 40*(4), 718–742.

Baumeister, R. F., & Leary, M. R. (1995). The need to belong: Desire for interpersonal attachments as a fundamental human motivation. *Psychological Bulletin, 117*(3), 497–529. https://doi.org/10.1037/0033-2909.117.3.497

Bland, A. M., & DeRobertis, E. M. (2017). Maslow's unacknowledged contributions to developmental psychology. *Journal of Humanistic Psychology*, https://doi.org/10.1177/0022167817739732.

Bor, W., Dean, A., Najman, J., & Hayatbakhsh, R. (2014). Are child and adolescent mental health problems increasing in the 21st century? A systematic review. *Australian & New Zealand Journal of Psychiatry, 48*(7), 606–616.

Brooks, F., Chester, K., Klemera, E. & Magnusson, J. (2017). *Cyberbullying: An analysis of data from the Health Behaviour in School-aged Children (HSBC) survey for England, 2014.* London: Public Health England.

Burt, A. (2016, January 21). *Self harm: Children: Department of Health written question.* Retrieved October 4, 2017, from https://www.theyworkforyou.com/wrans/?id=2016-01-18.22945.h.

Children's Commissioner. (2016). *Lightening review: Access to child and adolescent mental health services.* Retrieved October 4, 2016, from https://www.childrenscommissioner.gov.uk/wp-content/uploads/2017/06/Childrens-Commissioners-Mental-Health-Lightning-Review.pdf.

Cooper, M., Evans, Y., & Pybis, J. (2016). Interagency collaboration in children and young people's mental health: A systematic review of outcomes, facilitating factors and inhibiting factors. *Child: Care Health and Development Review.* https://doi.org/10.1111/cch.12322.

Davies, S. D. (2013). *Annual report of the Chief Medical Officer 2013: Public mental health priorities: Investing in the evidence.* London: Department of Health. www.gov.uk/government/publications/chief-medical-officer-cmo-annual-report-public-mental-health.

Davydov, D., Stewart, R., Ritchie, K., & Chaudie, I. (2010). Resilience and mental health. *Clinical Psychology Review, 30*(5), 479–495.

Deighton, J., Lereya, S. T., Casey, P., Patalay, P., Humphrey, N., & Wolpert, M. (2019). Prevalence of mental health problems in schools: Poverty and other risk factors among 28 000 adolescents in England. *The British Journal of Psychiatry,* 1–3.

Department for Children, Schools and Families (DCSF). (2008). *Targeted Mental Health in Schools (TaMHS) project.* London: DCSF Publications.

Department for Children, Schools and Families (DCSF). (2010). *Change in wellbeing from childhood to adolescence: Risk and resilience.* London: DCSF Publications.

Department for Education (DfE). (2008, 2016). *Early years foundation stage statutory framework (EYFS).* London: Her Majesty's Government Publications.

Department for Education (DfE). (2014a). *Mental health and behaviour in schools.* London: DfE Publications.

Department for Education (DfE). (2014b). *Special Educational Needs and Disability (SEND) code of practice.* London: DfE Publications.

Department of Health and Social Care (DoHSC). (2010). *Healthy Lives, Healthy People: our strategy for public health in England.* London: Her Majesty's Government Publications.

DfE, M. (2015). *Working together to safeguard children.*

DfE. (2018). *Keeping children safe in education: Statutory guidance for schools and colleges.*

Department for Education and Skills (DfES). (2003). *Every child matters: Change for children.* London: DfES Publications.

Department of Health (DoH). (2008). *Children and young people in mind: The final report of the national CAMHS review.* Retrieved February 16, 2012, from https://www.dh.gov.uk/en/Publicationsandstatistics/Publications/PublicationsPolicyAndGuidance/DH_090399.

Department of Health (DoH). (2011a). *No health without mental health: A cross-government mental health outcomes strategy for people of all ages. Supporting document—The economic case for improving efficiency and quality in mental health.* Retrieved May 9, 2012, from https://www.dh.gov.uk/prod_consum_dh/groups/dh_digitalassets/documents/digitalasset/dh_123993.pdf.

Department of Health (DoH). (2011). *No health without mental health: A cross-government mental health outcomes strategy for people of all ages.* London: Her Majesty's Government Publications.

Department of Health (DoH). (2014). *Closing the gap: Priorities for essential change in mental health.* London: Her Majesty's Government Publications.

Department of Health and NHS England (DOH & NHS England). (2015). *Future in mind: Promoting, protecting and improving our children and young people's mental health and wellbeing.* London: Her Majesty's Government Publications.

Department of Health and Social Care and Department for Education (DoHSC & DfE). (2017). *Transforming children and young people's mental health provision: A green paper.* London: Her Majesty's Government Publications.

Dods, J. (2016). Teacher candidate mental health and mental health literacy. *Exceptionality Education International, 26*(2), 42–61.

Education Support Partnership. (2018). *Teacher wellbeing index.* Retrieved October 8, 2019, from https://www.educationsupportpartnership.org.uk/sites/default/files/resources/teacher_well being_index_2018.pdf.

Ekornes, S. (2017). Teacher stress related to student mental health promotion: The match between perceived demands and competence to help students with mental health problems. *Scandinavian Journal of Educational Research, 61*(3), 333–353.

Evans, R., Brockman, R., Grey, J., Bell, S., Harding, S., Gunnell, D., Campbell, R., Murphy, S., Ford, T., Hollingworth, W., Tilling, K., Morris, R., Kadir, B., Araya, R., Kidger, J. (2018). A cluster randomised controlled trial of the Wellbeing in Secondary Education (WISE) Project – an intervention to improve the mental health support and training available to secondary school teachers: protocol for an integrated process evaluation. *Trials, 19*(1).

Ford, T., Hamilton, H., Meltzer, H., & Goodman, R. (2007). Child mental health is everybody's business: The prevalence of contact with public sector services by type of disorder among British school children in a three-year period. *Child and Adolescent Mental Health, 12*(1), 13–20.

Frith, E. (2017). *Social media and children's mental health: A review of the evidence.* Education Policy Institute.

Garcia-Moya, I., Brooks, F., Morgan, A., & Moreno, C. (2014). Subjective well-being in adolescence and teacher connectedness: A health asset analysis. *Health Education Journal.*

Geddes, H. (2006). *Attachment in the classroom: The links between children's early experience, emotional well-being and performance in school.* London: Worth Pub.

Ginsburg, G. S., Becker, K. D., Kingery, J. N., Nichols, T. (2008). Transporting CBT for Childhood Anxiety Disorders into Inner-City School-Based Mental Health Clinics. *Cognitive and Behavioral Practice, 15*(2), 148–158.

Golding, K., Durrant, E., Fain, J., Frost, A., Mills, C., Roberts, N., … Worrall, H. (2012). *Observing children with attachment difficulties in school.* London: Jessica Kingsley Publishers.

Graetz, B. (2016). Student mental health programs: Current challenges and future opportunities. In R. Shute & P. Slee (Eds.), *Mental health and wellbeing through schools.* Oxon: Routledge.

Graham, A., Phelps, R., Maddison, C., & Fitzgerald, R. (2011). Supporting children's mental health in schools: Teacher views. *Teachers and Teaching: Theory and Practice, 17*(4), 479–496.

Greenberg, M. T. (2010). School-based prevention: Current status and future challenges. *Effective Education, 2,* 27–52.

Hargreaves, A. (2000). Mixed emotions: teachers' perceptions of their interactions with students. *Teaching and Teacher Education, 16*(8), 811–826.

Hepburn, H. (2017, February 27). *Nearly half of teachers struggling with mental health, suggests survey.* TES 27/02/2017. Retrieved October 8, 2019, from https://www.tes.com/news/nearly-half-teachers-struggling-mental-health-suggests-survey.

House of Commons Health Committee. (2014). *Children's and adolescents' mental health and CAMHS: Third report of session 2014–2015.* Retrieved October 4, 2017, from https://publicati ons.parliament.uk/pa/cm201415/cmselect/cmhealth/342/342.pdf.

Humphrey, N. & Wigelsworth, M. (2016). Making the case for universal school-based mental health screening. *Emotional and Behavioural Difficulties, 21*(1), 22–42.

Ingvarson, L., Meiers, M., & Beavis, A. (2005). Factors affecting the impact of professional development programs on teachers' knowledge, practice, student outcomes and efficacy. *Education Policy Analysis Archives, 13*(10), 1–28.

Jennings, P. A., & Greenberg, M. T. (2009). The prosocial classroom: Teacher social and emotional competence in relation to student and classroom outcomes. *Review of Educational Research, 79*(1), 491–525.

Johnson, C., Eva, A., Johnson, L., & Walker, B. (2011). Don't turn away: Empowering teachers to support students' mental health. *The Clearing House: A Journal of Educational Strategies, Issues and Ideas, 84*(1), 9–14.

Khan, L. (2016). *Missed opportunities: A review of recent evidence into children and young people's mental health.* Centre for Mental Health.

Layard, R. (2005). Originally presented at "Mental health: Britain's biggest social problem?", 20th January 2005, *Strategy Unit Seminar on Mental Health.*

Lessof, C., Ross, A., Brind, R., Bell, E., & Newton, S. (2016). *Longitudinal study of young people in England cohort 2: health and wellbeing at wave 2.* DfE research report.

Mazzer, K. R., & Rickwood, D. J. (2015). Teachers' role breadth and perceived efficacy in supporting student mental health. *Advances in School Mental Health Promotion, 8*(1), 29–41.

Noble, T., McGrath, H., Wyatt, T., Carbines, R., & Robb, L. (2008, November). *Scoping study into approaches to student wellbeing: Final report.* Report to the Department of Education, Employment and Workplace Relations, PRN 18219. Retrieved October 8, 2019, from https://docs.education.gov.au/system/files/doc/other/scoping_study_into_approaches_to_student_wellbeing_final_report.pdf.

NSPCC. (2016). *Childline annual review 2015–16: It turned out someone did care: What children are contacting Childline about.* Retrieved October 4, 2017, from https://www.nspcc.org.uk/services-and-resources/research-and-resources/2016/childline-annual-review-2015-16-turned-out-someone-did-care/.

Paloma, V., García-Ramírez, M., & Camacho, C. (2014). Well-being and social justice among Moroccan migrants in Southern Spain. *American Journal of Community Psychology, 54*(1–2), 1–11.

Parsonage, M., Khan, L. & Saunders, A. (2014). *Building a better future: The lifetime costs of childhood behavioural problems and the benefits of early intervention.* London: Centre for Mental Health.

Patalay, P., & Fitzsimons, E. (2016). Correlates of mental illness and wellbeing in children: Are they the same? Results from the UK Millennium Cohort Study (MCS). *Journal of the American Academy of Child and Adolescent Psychiatry, 55*(9), 771–783.

Pienaar, F., & Johnston, P. (2017). In the eye of the 'perfect storm'. *Every Child Journal,* 6.3 & 6.4, 52–56.

Pilgrim, D. (2017). *Key concepts in mental health* (4th ed.). London: SAGE.

Prince's Trust Macquarie. (2018). *Youth Index 2018.* Retrieved May 16, 2019, from https://www.princes-trust.org.uk/about-the-trust/news-views/macquarie-youth-index-2018-annual-report.

Roffey, S. (2012). Pupil wellbeing—Teacher wellbeing: Two sides of the same coin?. *Educational and Child Psychology, 29*(4), 8. Retrieved from https://www.aber.ac.uk/en/media/departmental/sell/pdf/wellbeinghealth/Pupil-wellbeing---Teacher-wellbeing--Two-sides-of-the-same-coin-(2012).pdf.

Roffey, S. (2016). Building a case for whole-child, whole-school wellbeing in challenging contexts. *Educational & Child Psychology, 33*(2), 30–42.

Rogers, A., & Pilgrim, D. (2014). *A sociology of mental health and illness.* Berkshire: Open University Press.

Sisask, M., Varnik, P., Varnik, A., Apter, A., Balazs, J., Balint, M., … Danuta, W. (2013). Teachers satisfaction with school and psychological well-being affects their readiness to help children with

mental health problems. *Health Education Journal, 73*(4), 382–393. https://doi.org/10.1177/001
7896913485742.

Sixsmith, J., Nic Gabhainn, S., Fleming, C., & O'Higgins, S. (2007). Childrens', parents' and
teachers' perceptions of child wellbeing. *Health education, 107*(6), 511–523.

Soni, A. (2012). *Promoting emotional well-being or mental health in England?* (p. 172). Debates on
Early Childhood Policies and Practices: Global snapshots of pedagogical thinking and encounters.

Spilt, J. L., Koomen, H. M., & Thijs, J. T. (2011). Teacher wellbeing: The importance of teacher–
student relationships. *Educational Psychology Review, 23*(4), 457–477. https://doi.org/10.1007/
s10648-011-9170-y.

Stallard, P. (2013). School-based interventions for depression and anxiety in children and
adolescents. *Evidence-Based Mental Health, 16*(3), 60–61. https://doi.org/10.1136/eb-2013-
101242.

Stanley, J. (2018, April 10). *Teachers are at breaking point. It's time to push wellbeing up the
agenda.* The Guardian. Retrieved October 8, 2019, from https://www.theguardian.com/teacher-
network/2018/apr/10/teachers-are-at-breaking-point-its-time-to-push-wellbeing-up-the-agenda.

Thorley, C. (2016). Education, education, mental health: Supporting secondary schools to play a
central role in early intervention mental health services, IPPR. Retrieved October 4, 2019, from
https://www.ippr.org/publications/education-education-mental-health.

Tickell, C. (2011). *Tickell review of the early years foundation stage: A review into the impact of
the early years foundation stage (EYFS) on children's learning and development, and early years
practitioners.* London: Her Majesty's Government Publications.

Watson, D., & Emery, C. (2012). *Children's social and emotional wellbeing in schools: A critical
perspective.* Policy Press.

Weare, K., & Gray, G. (2003). *What works in developing children's emotional and social competence
and wellbeing?* London: Department for Education and Skills.

Westbrook, D., Kennerley, H., Kirk, J. (2008). *An Introduction to Cognitive Behavior Therapy:
Skills and Applications.* Oxford: SAGE.

Weeks, C., Hill, V., & Owen, C. (2017). Changing thoughts, changing practice: Examining the
delivery of a group CBT-based intervention in a school setting. *Educational Psychology in
Practice, 33*(1), 1–15.

World Health Organization. (2004). *Promoting mental health: Concepts, emerging evidence,
practice. Summary Report.* Geneva: World Health Organization.

Sian Templeton is a Senior Lecturer in Education at the University of Gloucestershire and a
practicing Educational Psychologist working with teaching staff, children, young people and their
families. She has worked in a variety of educational settings with a focus on supporting the social,
emotional and cognitive needs of vulnerable learners to enable them to engage with education. She
achieved this through working directly with the young people, with the families, teaching staff and
a range of professionals from health and social care. In addition to direct work, she also believes
in exploring more systemic opportunities for promoting and supporting access to education for all.
She teaches on both Undergraduate and Postgraduate courses within her University role across a
range of areas within education and leads on a number of psychology-based education modules.
She is involved in ERASMUS + projects related to her areas of interest. Sian's research includes
resilience, emotional education and supporting young offenders in re-engaging with education and
she is just commencing her DEdPsy at University College London.

Rebecca Pritchard is an Educational Psychologist who has also undertaken a Senior Lecturer role
in Education at the University of Gloucestershire. She has worked in numerous settings encompassing early years through secondary education including specialist provision. She has been
fortunate to develop a career that has enabled a focus on her particular interests of early years,
resilience, autism and mental health through both local authority provision and private practice.
Research interests have included a European study on emotional education and she is beginning

her DEdPsy at the University College London. From supporting individuals and families with specific needs to the design and provision of training for professionals, teaching on Undergraduate and Postgraduate courses, Rebecca continues to develop her understanding and expertise across this fascinating subject.

Chapter 8
Resilience in Practitioners Working in the Field of SEND

Tristan Middleton

Abstract This chapter considers educational settings and proposes that practitioner resilience is an important part of the system and considers its impact on the resilience of children and young people. It discusses the need for practitioner resilience to be a focus and considers factors and approaches which may be key to its development. It discusses this within the context of SEND practitioners and children with social, emotional and mental health difficulties, exploring the connection between education, resilience and the educator. This will focus on the educators' capacities and readiness to work to address affective elements of student learning. The findings of a research study into the impact of working with young people in a Nurture Group setting upon practitioners will be presented. The implications of the findings of this study for practitioner resilience and learner resilience, drawing additionally on the findings of ongoing research by the author, will be considered through the use of the DIMoR (ahmed Shafi et al., 2020).

Foreword

The majority of literature related to practitioner resilience and wellbeing in the field of education refers to teachers (Day & Gu, 2020; Flores, 2018; Jennings, Frank, Snowberg, Coccia, & Greenberg, 2013; Reinders, 2018). Whilst this chapter will make use of literature related to teachers, the 'practitioners' referred to will include both teachers and paraprofessionals working pedagogically in school settings. In particular this includes Teaching or Learning Support Assistants, referred to hereafter as "LSAs", as well as mentors and pastoral support teams. Within schools in England, the LSA and other paraprofessionals play a key role in the education of children and young people and are often significantly involved in working with those who are identified as having Special Educational Needs. There is a disparity between the status and remuneration of teachers and LSAs, which often fails to reflect the

T. Middleton (✉)
School of Education and Humanities, University of Gloucestershire, Francis Close Hall, Swindon Road, Cheltenham, Gloucestershire GL50 4AZ, UK
e-mail: tmiddleton1@glos.ac.uk

© Springer Nature Switzerland AG 2020
A. ahmed Shafi et al. (eds.), *Reconsidering Resilience in Education*,
https://doi.org/10.1007/978-3-030-49236-6_8

partnership approach taken between practitioners within individual settings and the term 'practitioner' is used to intentionally balance this status and to prompt a greater emphasis in literature on the paraprofessional in schools.

The Central Role of the Practitioner in Supporting Learner Wellbeing

Fleming, Mackrain, and LeBuffe (2013) present the case that teachers are critical in supporting the wellbeing and resilience of learners and, as such, make the case for supporting teacher resilience as something of high importance and needing due consideration by national and local policy makers and leaders. Lei, Cui, and Chui (2018) identified Positive Academic Emotions on the part of the learner as being closely associated to the level of teacher support received. The wellbeing of practitioners and the impact of their personal context is something which some practitioners believe can be hidden or masked through their professional persona or approach. However, the perception and attunement of children and young people to the mood and wellbeing of the practitioner is significant (Glazzard & Rose, 2019) and the impact of the practitioners' health, wellbeing, emotional state and behaviour is of significant importance (Jennings & Greenberg, 2009; Jennings et al., 2013; Public Health England, 2016; Sanders, Munford, & Liebenberg, 2016).

The importance of teacher wellbeing is more significant when the focus is on learners with identified needs in the area of social and emotional learning. For these learners, there is a heightened importance of positive nurturing relationships (Rae, Cowell, & Field, 2017). In turn, this leads to a need for high levels of wellbeing and confidence on the part of teachers in order to be able to support the wellbeing and resilience of these particular learners (Schleicher, 2018) as these relationships demand significant 'emotional labour' (Kinman, Wray, & Strange, 2011).

The importance of wellbeing and resilience in children and young people is significant in the current context of education in England and Europe more widely. Addressing the mental health needs of children and young people is recognised by all EU member states as a priority (Caldas de Almeida et al., 2017, p. 30). The Joint Action on Mental Health & Wellbeing group (2016) identify that 10–20% of children and adolescents worldwide experience mental disorders, which impact on their educational development when untreated. The OECD/EU (2018) identifies that one in six people in 2016, approximately 84 million people across the EU, had a mental health issue in 2016, and that the cost of mental illness for EU countries is more than 4% of GDP. This report also states that half of all lifetime mental disorders begin by the mid-teens.

Impact of Negative Practitioner Wellbeing

It may seem obvious to state that negative practitioner wellbeing can impact on the individual practitioner's own work performance and family life (Hyman et al., 2011), however in the context of a profession where an attitude of keeping going until the next holiday is often evident, this perspective is important to remember. If we understand that relational safety in classrooms is supportive for students at risk of school exclusion or dropout (Sanders et al., 2016), then it is clear that negative practitioner wellbeing will also negatively impact on learners' engagement within schools. The negative impact of practitioner stress and burnout on learners' social and academic development is well documented (Fleming et al., 2013; Hoglund, Klingle, & Hosan, 2015) along with evidence of the correlation with the deterioration of teacher-learner relationships (Cano-Garcia, Padilla-Munoz, & Carrasco-Ortiz, 2005) and increased levels of conflict and difficult behaviours in learners (Bru, Stephens, & Torsheim, 2002). Furthermore, there is evidence that positive relationships between the practitioner and their learners can also support the positive wellbeing of practitioners (Milatz, Lüftenegger, & Schober, 2015).

Practitioner Wellbeing

The need to support teacher wellbeing is recognised on an international scale. In the UK, it has been recognised that teaching is a profession with a significantly higher level of work-related stress than other professions (HSE, 2017). Some reports indicate that up to 40% of teachers have left teaching within five years of joining the profession (Acton & Glasgow, 2015). There is growing concern about the rate of teachers leaving the profession, and particularly those new to the profession. Increasingly, in school systems across Europe and other developed countries, the extent of teacher attrition and turnover is cause for concern, particularly in relation to teachers who are in the early stages of their career (Avalos & Valenzuela, 2016). In England there are reports of a significant increase, of nearly 30% in one year, in teachers contacting a confidential helpline (Education Support Partnership, 2018).

The policy and guidance discourse related to adult wellbeing is firmly embedded within a workplace perspective. Notions of linking adult learning and social and emotional learning is generally discussed within the realm of skills for work and professional stress, with the focus being on the responsibility of business to provide for these areas. Whilst there is some reported development in social prescribing (Steadman, Thomas, & Donnaloja, 2017), although frequently related to vocational opportunities, there is little other support for the development of social and emotional wellbeing in adults on the part of local or national agencies beyond the management of workplace stress, through approaches such as time management, relaxation approaches and exercise (NHS, 2019).

The Case for Practitioner Resilience

In order to understand the importance of practitioner wellbeing and the centrality of the social and emotional impact of their work, it can be useful to understand the concept of 'emotional labour'. Emotional labour is described as the work undertaken to manage ones' own emotions in order to influence the production of a particular state of mind in others (Hochschild, 1983). Emotional labour is embedded in the work of the education practitioner and particularly in their support for social and emotional learning (Brown, Vesely, Mahatmya, & Visconti, 2018) and the relationships they maintain in order to do this. There are identified links between emotional labour and teacher burnout (Keller, Chang, Becker, Goetz, & Frenzel, 2014).

Working within educational settings can be viewed as existing in a wicked context, in that it is situated within a complex social organisation where there are no clear, linear, or cause and effect, solutions which can be applied from generalised principles (Middleton, 2019). Where the aim of practitioners is to develop the learners in a holistic way, with particular concern for social and emotional learning and resilience, practitioners can be seen to be at odds with the dominant ethos embodied by national policies, guidance and local and national inspection regimes, which are expressed through a normative ethos of achievement and measurement within a standards agenda (Middleton, 2019). Given the holistic, inclusive and developmental nature of the nurture group approach (discussed below), practitioners working in this field are likely to be more significantly impacted by this wicked context. Whilst it is recognised that there is an absence of focus in literature or policy on the development of practitioner capacity for resilience (Hart & Heaver, 2013), it can be argued that the need for the promotion of nurture group practitioner resilience presents an even more pressing case than for the general, mainstream practitioner.

The DIMoR presents resilience as a dynamic process which enables the individual, or wider system, to function and continue on their trajectory (ahmed Shafi et al., 2020). For the nurture practitioner, resilience factors are of heightened importance in the context of their work which is problematic in relation to the wicked context of an education system focussed on the normative, right/wrong, binary approach (Middleton, 2019, p. 3).

Summary of Research Study

This chapter uses the DIMoR (ahmed Shafi et al., 2020) to analyse the findings of a research study into the personal and professional impact of working with children with identified needs in the area of Social, Emotional and Mental Health, in a Nurture Group context (Middleton, 2018).

Nurture Groups were first established in England in 1970s and there are now over 2000 recorded Nurture Groups in the UK (NurtureUK, 2019b), with other pockets in existence in Ireland, Malta and Romania, as well as some further afield in New Zealand and Australia.

Nurture Groups are the most intensive and specialised tier of support within the taxonomy of the graduated stages of Inclusive Nurturing Practice (NurtureUK, 2019a) which are based upon the work of Bennathan and Boxall (1996). The foundational tiers of this graduated approach, applied across a whole-school, are the assessment of children and young people's social, emotional and mental health needs using the Boxall Profile (Bennathan, 1998) and a nurturing approach based upon the Six Principles of Nurture (Lucas, Insley, & Buckland, 2006). Through a focus on social and emotional learning at a developmentally appropriate level, nurture groups are an approach which provides the opportunity for children and young people to engage in learning opportunities and can help to maintain children and young people at risk of exclusions within school (March & Kearney, 2017). In practice, a nurture group is an intervention where learners who are identified as needing additional support for their social and emotional needs, attend the group on a regular basis over an extended period and are supported to develop developmentally appropriate skills to enable them to work towards learning effectively within their mainstream class context.

This research study used a narrative inquiry approach (Alleyne, 2015) to understand the professional and personal impact of working with children with Special Educational Needs (SEN) in the area of Social, Emotional and Mental Health (SEMH) difficulties. The English definition of SEMH difficulties superseded previous definitions of Social, Emotional and Behavioural difficulties (SEBD), and other combinations of those key terms, with the advent of the Special Educational Needs Code of Practice (DfE, 2015). This research study focused on the experiences of two Learning Support Assistants running a nurture group in a mainstream primary school, gathering their stories over the period of a school year.

The study identified that the nurture group practitioners' work with young people with SEMH difficulties had a significant impact on their professional identity, motivation and relationships within their place of work and also on their family and personal relationships, their leisure time and their physiological wellbeing. Further outcomes of the research provided information about factors which the practitioners identified as having the most significant impact on the areas identified above.

The research found that there were three key elements which illustrate the challenges of working with vulnerable learners linked to the practitioners' professional and personal lives. These three elements were; motivation, physiological impact and impact upon personal life and relationships.

The research also identified that the key events which impacted upon the practitioners' wellbeing, were related to two key groups; the children and young people they worked with in the nurture group setting, and the school management team.

Further findings related to factors which the practitioners identified as supporting them to continue their work with the children and young people. These were identified as three key factors; their own values and commitment to 'nurture', the friendship of their colleagues and leadership within the setting. They also identified that the year-long process of discussion and supervision, undertaken as part of the research process, gave them a sense of strength and empowerment.

Using the DIMoR to Analyse the Findings

This section will use the DIMoR (ahmed Shafi et al., 2020) as a lens through which to consider the findings of the research with educational practitioners. It will identify the risk and protective factors, the vulnerabilities and invulnerabilities, alongside the key individuals and groups with which the practitioners interacted. This will provide a picture of the relevant factors in considering the resilience of these practitioners and offer the opportunity to consider the focus of support to foster the practitioners' resilience in their work to support the wellbeing and resilience of children and young people.

The DIMoR recognises individuals as systems encountering each other within a wider system (ahmed Shafi et al., 2020). Within the systemic context and using Ungar's (2013) recognition of equifinality and differential impact, the research identified two groups which influenced the practitioners' wellbeing most significantly.

The first of these groups was the children they worked with in the nurture group setting. These children, who have been identified on the school Special Educational Needs Register as needing additional and different provision in order for them to be able to engage in learning activities in the school, often presented with physically and emotionally challenging behaviours. Their behaviours could often be emotionally distressing to the practitioners, in that they both represent the effect of trauma and very difficult life experiences for the children, which the practitioners empathise with, and that the behaviours can also present direct social and emotional challenges to the practitioners and demand significant emotional labour. Whilst some elements of the groups' identity and behaviour are perceived as being towards the 'risk' end of the DIMoR axis, their own vulnerability and need for support could be perceived as contributing as a protective factor within the DIMoR (ahmed Shafi et al., 2020), as the practitioners felt they were fulfilling a much-needed and valuable role in enacting supportive provision which the children may otherwise not be able to access. It is difficult to clearly position the impact of the children on the practitioner's vulnerability/invulnerability axis, as the empathic approach taken by nurture practitioners, whilst creating elements of vulnerability, also promotes invulnerability through the positive affective relationships and the enactment of support which are associated with the empathic approach.

The second of the groups was the school management team, a group which is identified as a key contextual influence in the recent Ainsworth and Oldfield (2019) study. This group exerted influence over the practical and organisational aspects of the practitioners' work and also influenced the practitioners' affective, or emotional, states through the nature and content of their direct interactions with the practitioners and also the influence they had in guiding, managing and mediating the opinions and interactions between the practitioners and other school staff. The management team can be regarded as a mesosystem and there is potential for the management team to impact widely across both of the axes of the DIMoR (ahmed Shafi et al., 2020) and the practitioners identified changes in the management team's attitude and discourse as having a negative impact.

Whilst these two groups were identified as the major systems impacting upon the practitioners, using the DIMoR web of connectivity (ahmed Shafi et al., 2020), it can be understood that other groups, or systems, will also be connected with, and influential upon, the practitioners and upon the two systems of the children and the management team. For example, the management team will be influenced by a range of professional and personal systems, including other practitioners, parents and carers, different learners in their setting, professional networks, family and friends. Any consideration of making changes within the two identified groups would need to consider the impact upon, and from, the other systems they are connected with or encounter more widely.

The second set of findings of the research was the factors which the practitioners identified as providing them with the strength to continue in their work to support the children in their nurture group, in spite of the significant impact of the work on their personal and professional lives.

The first of these was their commitment to their strongly held values about the importance of nurture in education. The practitioners would identify this as a protective factor on the DIMoR axes (ahmed Shafi et al., 2020), however holding strong values could be situated on the axes in a number of places, according to the context. Given the dominant policy ethos, as described above, holding strong alternative values could be identified as being located within the vulnerability section of the vertical axis. Contextual factors such as the ethos of the other practitioners within the community, or system, and the mesosystem of the management team will, as an example of equifinality (Ungar, 2013), influence the impact on the resilience of the practitioners.

The second factor was the friendship of their colleagues. This would be a protective factor on the DIMoR axis (ahmed Shafi et al., 2020) within the immediate context. This factor could move to the other axis as a vulnerability if there were a threat of the colleague leaving the setting. Once the colleague has moved, the lack of a colleague with whom a friendship was established would then be situated as a risk factor.

The third factor was identified as leadership. This concept is one which has multiple understandings and is reliant on the context of the individual and their own view and expectation of leadership. If the enactment of leadership is aligned with their own conception of the term, it is likely that the practitioners would identify leadership as a protective factor (ahmed Shafi et al., 2020). If, however, the leadership was in contrast to their own values and views, perhaps as a result of a change in personnel or external pressures forcing a change in approach, the leadership could be identified as a risk factor, creating vulnerability.

A final emergent finding from the research was that the process of the research itself was a useful empowering factor for the practitioners. As part of the research process the practitioners were provided with a form of regular supervision, in the form of a safe, confidential, supportive space in which to reflect on their practice and in frank and open discussion and explore, sometimes difficult, situations (Middleton, 2018). The availability of this resource would be situated as a protective factor. The conclusions of the research also suggested that this factor was more significant because of the particular history of the researcher, as a previous nurture group teacher, and the resultant understanding between the practitioners and researcher. This context can be identified as a further example of Ungar's (2013) notion of differential impact and cultural moderation.

Through the use of the DIMoR (ahmed Shafi et al., 2020), in the context of this research into nurture group practitioners, the initial conclusions have been re-evaluated and the dynamic and interconnected nature of the factors, which were identified through the research, has been emphasised. This has led to important conclusions relating to the potential for significant change in the influence of these factors as a result of personal and professional interactions and wider contextual relationships (Acton & Glasgow, 2015) and the dynamic nature of the emergent properties of resilience.

Resilience and the Practitioner: Conclusion

When seeking to influence the resilience of practitioners, the use of the DIMoR has clarified that any approach which aims to make changes to one isolated factor is unlikely to have a significant impact on the overall resilience. Using the axes of the DIMoR (ahmed Shafi et al., 2020) has demonstrated that where changes to resilience are desired, consideration of the interconnected systems, of the contextual influences and of the relationships within the systems, are all elements which need to be considered. The potential for factors to move along the axes of risk/protective factors and vulnerability/invulnerability has been demonstrated, thereby reinforcing the dynamic nature of emergent resilience.

This use of the DIMoR (ahmed Shafi et al., 2020) has highlighted that where attempts are made to improve the wellbeing and resilience of children and young people in educational settings, the wellbeing and resilience of the practitioner is closely connected, as is argued by Fleming et al. (2013, p. 388), and can reciprocally promote emergent resilience. Furthermore, this chapter has highlighted, in alignment with Banerjee, McLaughlin, Cotney, Roberts, and Peereboom (2016), the importance of leadership and the school organisation and ethos, within the context of the wider influences from local and national educational systems.

The role of relationships, and consequently social and emotional competencies, have also emerged as important factors within the holistic view of resilience, as identified in the argument of Masten and Garmezy (1985). The transient nature of relationships within educational settings has further emphasised the potential for change within resilience outcomes.

This emphasis on the dynamic and interactive nature of emergent resilience and the importance of relationships within the interacting systems supports the challenge that interventions aimed at teaching specific approaches or resilience skills are unlikely to have significant success. What may be more effective instead is the promotion of wellbeing and resilience for practitioners and the promotion of a holistic understanding of the complexities of interconnectedness and the understanding of the axes of risk/protective factors and vulnerability/invulnerability.

The dynamic and interactive qualities of resilience, as conceived through the lens of the DIMoR (ahmed Shafi et al., 2020), aligns with current reassessments of pedagogy and learning. Biesta's (2016, p. 27) view of learning as, "a response to what is other and different, to what challenges, irritates, or even disturbs us" is closely aligned to Masten's (2016, p. 298) view of resilience as, "the capacity of a system for successful adaptation to disturbances that threaten system function, viability or development". These perspectives support the view that by understanding of the interconnected systems and the risk/protection and vulnerability/invulnerability axes, individuals can learn to develop their capacity and potential for resilience within the connected systems in which they exist.

References

Acton, R., & Glasgow, P. (2015). Teacher wellbeing in neoliberal contexts: A review of the literature. *Australian Journal of Teacher Education, 40*(8), 99–113.

ahmed Shafi, A., Middleton, T., Millican, R., Templeton, S., Vare, P., Pritchard, R., & Hatley, J. (2020). Towards a dynamic interactive model of resilience (DIMoR) for education and learning contexts. *Emotional and Behavioural Difficulties, 25*(2), 183–198. https://doi.org/10.1080/136 32752.2020.1771923.

Ainsworth, S., & Oldfield, J. (2019). Quantifying teacher resilience: Context matters. *Teaching and Teacher Education, 82,* 117–128.

Alleyne, B. (2015). *Narrative networks: Storied approaches in a digital age.* London: SAGE.

Avalos, B., & Valenzuela, J. P. (2016). Education for all and attrition/retention of new teachers: A trajectory study in Chile. *International Journal of Educational Development, 49,* 279–290.

Banerjee, R., McLaughlin, C., Cotney, J., Roberts, L., & Peereboom, C. (2016). *Promoting Emotional Health, Well-being and Resilience in Primary Schools.* Public Policy Institute Wales.

Bennathan, M., & Boxall, M. (1996). *Effective intervention in primary schools: Nurture groups.* London: David Fulton.

Bennathan, M. (1998). *The Boxall profile: Handbook for teachers.* Maidstone, UK: AWCEBD.

Biesta, G. J. J. (2016). *Beyond learning: Democratic education for a human future.* Abingdon, Oxon: Routledge.

Brown, E. L., Vesely, C. K., Mahatmya, D., & Visconti, K. J. (2018). Emotions matter: The moderating role of emotional labour on preschool teacher and children interactions. *Early Child Development and Care, 188*(12), 1773–1787.

Bru, E., Stephens, P., & Torsheim, T. (2002). Students' perceptions of class management and reports of their own misbehavior. *Journal of School Psychology, 40,* 287–307.

Cano-Garcia, F. J., Padilla-Munoz, E. M., & Carrasco-Ortiz, M. A. (2005). Personality and contextual variables in teacher burnout. *Personality and Individual Differences, 38,* 929–940.

Caldas de Almeida, J. M., Frasquilho, D., Mateus, P., Antunes, A., Cardoso, G., Silva, M., & Parkkonen, J. (2017) *Eu-compass for action on mental health and wellbeing: Annual report 2017.* Retrieved September 19, 2019, from https://ec.europa.eu/health/sites/health/files/mental_health/docs/2017_msactivities_sum_en.pdf.

Day, C., & Gu, Q. (2020). *Resilient teachers, resilient schools: Building and sustaining quality in testing times.* Abingdon: Routledge.

DfE. (2015). *Special Educational Needs and Disability Code of Practice: 0 to 25 years. Statutory guidance for organisations which work with and support children and young people who have special educational needs or disabilities.* DFE-00205-2013. London: DfES Retrieved September 2019 from https://www.gov.uk/government/publications/send-code-of-practice-0-to-25

Education Support Partnership. (2018). *Teacher Wellbeing Index 2018*. Retrieved September 19, 2019, from https://www.educationsupportpartnership.org.uk/sites/default/files/resources/teacher_wellbeing_index_2018.pdf.

Fleming, J. L., Mackrain, M., & LeBuffe, P. A. (2013). Caring for the caregiver: Promoting the resilience of teachers. In S. Goldstein & R. B. Brooks (Eds.), *Handbook of resilience in children* (2nd ed., pp. 387–398). New York: Springer.

Flores, M. A. (2018). Teacher resilience in adverse contexts: Issue of professionalism and professional identity. In M. Wosnitza, F. Peixoto, S. Beltman, & C. F. Mansfield (Eds.), *Resilience in education: Concepts, contexts and connections* (pp. 167–184).

Glazzard, J., & Rose, A. (2019, September 10–12). The impact of teacher mental health and wellbeing on pupil progress: from the pupils' perspective In *British Education Research Association Conference*. Manchester University, UK.

Hart, A., & Heaver, B. (2013). Evaluating resilience-based programs for schools using a systematic consultative review. *Journal of Child and Youth Development, 1*(1), 27–53.

Hochschild, A. R. (1983). *The managed heart: Commercialization of human feeling* (2nd ed.). Berkeley, CA: University of California Press.

Hoglund, W. L. G., Klingle, K. E., & Hosan, N. E. (2015). Classroom risks and resources: Teacher burnout, classroom quality and children's adjustment in high needs elementary schools. *Journal of School Psychology, 53,* 337–357.

HSE (Health and Safety Executive). (2017). *Work-related stress, depression or anxiety statistics in Great Britain 2017*. https://www.hse.gov.uk/statistics/causdis/stress/stress.pdf.

Hyman, S. A., Michaels, D. R., Berry, J. M., Schildcrout, J. S., Mercaldo, N. D., & Weinger, M. D. (2011). Risk of burnout in perioperative clinicians: A survey study and literature review. *Anesthesiology, 114*(1), 194–204.

Jennings, P. A., & Greenberg, M. T. (2009). The prosocial classroom: Teacher social and emotional competence in relation to student and classroom outcomes. *Review of Educational Research, 79*(1), 491–525.

Jennings, P. A., Frank, J. L., Snowberg, K. E., Coccia, M. A., & Greenberg, M. T. (2013). Improving classroom learning environments by Cultivating Awareness and Resilience in Education (CARE): Results of a randomized controlled trial. *School Psychology Quarterly, 28*(4), 374–390.

Joint Action on Mental Health & Wellbeing. (2016). *Mental health and schools*. Retrieved September 19, 2019, from https://www.mentalhealthandwellbeing.eu/mental-health-and-schools/.

Keller, M. M., Chang, M.-L., Becker, E. S., Goetz, T., & Frenzel, A. C. (2014). Teachers' emotional experiences and exhaustion as predictors of emotional labor in the classroom: An experience sampling study. *Frontiers in Psychology, 5,* 1442.

Kinman, G., Wray, S., & Strange, C. (2011). Emotional labour, burnout and job satisfaction in UK teachers: The role of workplace social support. *Educational Psychology, 31*(7), 843–856.

Lei, H., Cui, Y., & Chiu, M. M. (2018). The relationship between teacher support and students' academic emotions: A meta-analysis. *Frontiers in Psychology, 8,* 1–12.

Lucas, S., Insley, K., & Buckland, G. (2006). *Nurture group principles and curriculum guidelines: Helping children to achieve*. London: Nurture Group Network.

March, S., & Kearney, M. (2017). A psychological service contribution to nurture: Glasgow's nurturing city. *Emotional and Behavioural Difficulties, 22*(3), 237–247.

Masten, A. (2016). Resilience in developing systems: The promise of integrated approaches. *European Journal of Developmental Psychology, 13*(3), 297–312.

Masten, A. S., & Garmezy, N. (1985). Risk, vulnerability and protective factors in developmental psychopathology. In B. B. Lahey & A. E. Kazdin (Eds.), *Advances in clinical child psychology* (Vol. 8, pp. 1–512). New York, NY: Plenum.

Middleton, T. (2018). Working with children with social, emotional and mental health needs in a nurture group setting: The professional and personal impact. *International Journal of Nurture in Education, 4*(1) 22–32. https://www.nurtureuk.org/sites/default/files/ijne_volume4_final.pdf.

Middleton, T. (2019). Thought piece—The inclusive teacher: Values and (com)passion in a wicked world. *Practice 1*(2), 169–172. https://doi.org/10.1080/25783858.2019.1659634

Milatz, A., Lüftenegger, M., & Schober, B. (2015). Teachers' relationship closeness with students as a resource for teacher wellbeing: A response surface analytical approach. *Frontiers in Psychology, 6,* 1949.

NHS. (2019). *How to deal with stress: Moodzone.* Retrieved September 19, 2019, from https://www.nhs.uk/conditions/stress-anxiety-depression/understanding-stress/.

NurtureUK. (2019a). *Nurture groups for all educational settings.* Retrieved September 19, 2019, from https://www.nurtureuk.org/sites/default/files/nurture_groups_booklet_online.pdf.

NurtureUK. (2019b). *Inclusion support solutions.* Retrieved September 19, 2019, from https://www.nurtureuk.org/sites/default/files/iss_a4_brochure_march2019_online.pdf.

OECD/EU. (2018). *Health at a glance: Europe 2018—State of health in the EU cycle.* Retrieved September 19, 2019, from https://ec.europa.eu/health/sites/health/files/state/docs/2018_healtha tglance_rep_en.pdf.

Public Health England. (2016). *Promoting children and young people's emotional health and wellbeing: A whole school and college approach.* Retrieved September 19, 2019, from https://assets.publishing.service.gov.uk/government/uploads/system/uploads/attachment_d ata/file/575632/Mental_health_of_children_in_England.pdf.

Rae, T., Cowell, N., & Field, L. (2017). Supporting teachers' well-being in the context of schools for children with social, emotional and behavioural difficulties. *Emotional and Behavioural Difficulties, 22*(3), 200–221.

Reinders, H. (2018). From dealing with teacher resistance to working on teacher resilience. *Enletawa Journal, 11*(1), 69–76.

Sanders, J., Munford, R., & Liebenberg, L. (2016). The role of teachers in building resilience of at risk youth. *International Journal of Educational Research, 80,* 111–123.

Schleicher, A. (2018). *Valuing our teachers and raising their status: How communities can help.* International Summit on the Teaching Profession, Paris: OECD Publishing. ISBN 978-92-64-29261-1

Steadman, K., Thomas, R., & Donnaloja, V. (2017). *Social prescribing. A pathway to work.* London, UK: The Work Foundation. Retrieved September 19, 2019, from https://www.theworkfoundation.com/wp-content/uploads/2017/02/412_Social_prescribing.pdf.

Ungar, M. (2013). Resilience, trauma, context, and culture. *Trauma, Violence, & Abuse, 14*(3), 255–266.

Tristan Middleton Tristan is Senior Lecturer in Education and Joint Course Leader for the MA Education suite at the University of Gloucestershire. Tristan is an experienced primary school class teacher, Senior Leader, Special Educational Needs Coordinator and Designated teacher for both Safeguarding and Looked-After Children. He also ran a Nurture Group for seven years. Tristan is Chair of Directors of Leading Learning for SEND CiC which oversees the work of the National SENCO Award Provider Partnership and also a member of NurtureUK's Research, Evidence & Ethics Trustee Sub-Group and Associate Editor of the International Journal of Nurture in Education. He is currently a member of the Erasmus+ RENYO project team focusing on the re-engagement of young offenders with education and learning, with three European partners. He has recently published "Using an Inclusive Approach to Reduce School Exclusion: A Practitioner's Handbook" with Lynda Kay, published by Routledge and the book chapter "Teaching Assistants identifying key factors to their successful work with challenging children and finding a new discourse." In: H. R. Wright & M. E. Hoyen (Eds.) Discourses We Live By: Personal and professional perspectives on education. Open Book Publishers, Cambridge.

Chapter 9
Using Assessment Feedback to Develop Resilience

Richard Millican, Adeela ahmed Shafi, Sian Templeton, and Tristan Middleton

Abstract This chapter draws on research which focuses on the everyday challenges in academic learning and argues that academic buoyancy (Martin & Marsh, 2009) is a key factor in academic success as it helps students cope with setbacks such as receiving a disappointing grade. The chapter will discuss the idea that assessment feedback offers an opportunity to contribute to student academic buoyancy. To scaffold students learning and thus to effectively support academic buoyancy, an argument will be posited that there is a need for a better understanding of (i) what students find most and least useful in their assessment feedback; (ii) how students use feedback to approach future assessments and; (iii) how students respond to feedback in terms of what they think, feel and do. 5 Key indicators of academically buoyant behaviour (which arose from the research under discussion) are suggested to increase the academic buoyancy of students and also the need for tutor/student relationships and opportunity for dialogue. Finally, using the DIMoR (ahmed Shafi et al., 2020) as a framework for analysis, the chapter will argue that individual events such as assessment feedback, need to be considered more holistically taking account of the effect they can have on other stakeholders and other interacting and surrounding systems.

R. Millican (✉) · A. ahmed Shafi · S. Templeton · T. Middleton
School of Education and Humanities, University of Gloucestershire, Francis Close Hall, Swindon Road, Cheltenham, Gloucestershire GL50 4AZ, UK
e-mail: rmillican@glos.ac.uk

A. ahmed Shafi
e-mail: ashafi@glos.ac.uk

S. Templeton
e-mail: stempleton@glos.ac.uk

T. Middleton
e-mail: tmiddleton1@glos.ac.uk

© Springer Nature Switzerland AG 2020
A. ahmed Shafi et al. (eds.), *Reconsidering Resilience in Education*,
https://doi.org/10.1007/978-3-030-49236-6_9

Introduction

This chapter draws on research conducted by the authors at a UK university that suggests there is a link between feedback given in response to assessments and resilience. The study was a piece of action research designed to improve the usefulness of feedback given. Findings demonstrated that students often experienced uncomfortable and challenging emotional reactions to feedback and grades received, which led to explorations of the notion of academic buoyancy. It revealed the opportunity that the feedback process provides to help develop buoyancy and illustrates how things are interconnected and how there is a need to view feedback within a wider context rather than as an isolated act.

The chapter will begin by discussing assessments and feedback as concepts to provide context. It will then give an overview of the research design and findings before providing a discussion that presents a conceptualization of the feedback process that situates it in a course context.

The findings will then be discussed with reference to the Dynamic Interactive Model of Resilience (DIMoR ahmed Shafi et al., 2020) showing how it can be used as a helpful lens with which to analyse the feedback process and to reflect on the resilience of the systems and actors involved.

Context

A common facet of educational programmes in formal contexts is the need for assessments. These may be initial or end point, diagnostic or placement, formative or summative, but in all cases will involve judgement of learners' work or performance against certain criteria or in comparison to others. Recent accountability initiatives and the marketisation of educational systems has meant that, in some cases, the results of these assessments are used to not only measure the learner, but also as an indicator of educator and institutional performance. This is no less true for universities that are increasingly ranked in league tables against various indices including The Teaching Excellence Framework (TEF), National Student Satisfaction Survey (NSS) results and the number of higher degree classifications.

Given this, the grading and providing of feedback on assessments is a high stakes activity. It can determine not only whether the learner succeeds or not on a programme, but can affect their feelings and emotions about themselves and the course, as well as their feelings towards the markers and teachers of the course and the institution offering it. As a consequence, it can influence evaluations given and have an impact on the status of all those involved. As a result of this, it is important that the process is carried out as effectively as possible to ensure that it is of value and use to all stakeholders involved whilst simultaneously protecting their wellbeing and reputations.

Typically, there are two elements provided in response to an assessment, the grade itself which is a statement of level or achievement, and feedback which provides a justification for the grade alongside indications of how to improve. Even within formative assessments contexts, this would render the grade as summative in nature (a summation of level at that moment) and the feedback as formative (information about performance and areas for improvement).

If feedback is providing information about performance and offering suggestions for development, then comments made need to be individualized, or personalized and targeted and arguably can be considered as part of a conversation, a dialogue between marker and learner. It has been suggested that, given this potential for feedback to provide opportunity for learning, it is more pertinent to consider it as *feedforward* (see, for example, Higgins, Hartley, & Skelton, 2002; Wheatley, McInch, Fleming, & Lord, 2015). Jonsson (2012, p. 63) goes as far as to describe feedback as 'one of the most potent influences on student learning and achievement'.

However, not all students use their feedback or do so effectively and Jonsson (2012, p. 64) argues that there is a place for explicit teaching on how to utilise feedback to optimise impact, suggesting that many students fail to read or use feedback given. Such a lack of engagement with feedback potentially leads to a significant impact on performance (Zimbardi et al., 2016) as a developmental opportunity is lost. In contrast to this, studies have shown that some students *do* use it for guidance and learning (McCann & Saunders, 2009) and it would appear useful to explore why this is the case for some and not for others.

One reason is that, for it to be effective, it is necessary for the learner to be able to interpret and understand the grade and feedback given within the context of the assessment purpose, assessment criteria and grading. Research has revealed that students can sometimes be confused by the assessment process and are not always fully cognisant of task expectations or of how grading criteria are applied. As a consequence, recent literature has suggested that to support the efficient use of feedback, students need to have what has been termed assessment literacy (see, for example, Ajjawi & Boud, 2017; Carless, 2016; Denton & McIlroy, 2017; O'Donovan, Rust, & Price, 2016; Price, Rust, O'Donovan, & Handley, 2012).

However, mindful of the fact that grading and feedback are based on a deficit model where a perceived expert makes a critique and a judgement of quality and standard (Delandshire, 2001), they have the potential to cause emotional upset. For many learners, such judgements are unexceptional events that occur during their educational journey, while for others they can be quite damaging (Poulos & Mahoney, 2008). When this is the case, it can affect the learner's motivation, self-esteem and attitude towards the course, marker and institution offering it and it can also partly account for the discrepancy highlighted above, between those learners who use feedback effectively for developmental purposes and those that do not.

Concerns about the ability to deal with such potential upsets or shocks to the system and respond in a constructive way to feedback by using it developmentally, lead to considerations of an individual's resilience (Wang & Gordon, 1994; Wang, 1997). However, given that resilience tends to refer to the ability to deal with more substantial adversity and challenges such as a family bereavement or a major health issue, Martin and Marsh (2008) suggest that a more specific form of resilience for this type of setback is academic buoyancy. This is more nuanced and targeted and is defined as a student's ability to deal with academic challenges such as poor grades, meeting deadlines, or coping with exam pressure and, in addition, coping with the unhelpful emotions associated with some of these challenges (Bouteyre, Maurel, & Bernaud 2007).

Carless (2006) observes that students who are more secure in themselves and in their academic ability and thus are less vulnerable and have more protective factors, tend to be more able to cope and to be receptive of feedback, whereas others are likely to find that it impacts on their self-concept and motivation. Consequently, he suggests that part of the function of feedback is to help students deal with their emotions and self-regulate, in other words to be academically buoyant, and notes that more successful learners tend to be those who have this buoyancy and are autonomous and able to use their feedback to develop self-regulated learning skills.

Research Phase 1

The research was conducted because the course team of a BA (Hons) Education had noted that, in a number of student evaluations, dissatisfaction was expressed around the topic of assessment and feedback. Given this, and mindful of the context as described above, the team undertook an action research project to explore student thoughts about feedback and to search for ways to improve practice.

Findings from Phase 1

Responses from the first phase (see ahmed Shafi, Hatley, Middleton, Millican, & Templeton, 2017 for more details) shed light on student activity and show that they use their feedback more than the researchers anticipated and in a variety of ways, including to develop writing skills as well as to improve content knowledge. They also demonstrated different patterns of behaviour ranging from returning to the feedback when working on a new assignment, seeking tutor advice or other support, making a plan for future assessments and taking notes for future reference. This was encouraging as it indicated that students acknowledged and were keen to exploit the learning, feedforward potential of the feedback and was thus evidence of resilient or buoyant behaviour.

The data also showed that students felt that feedback helped them manage their feelings following a disappointing grade when it provided information in terms of how they performed, by acknowledging strengths and providing reasons for the grade given, suggesting actions they might take next and giving reassurance and encouragement.

Further mining of the data led to the identification of five specific behaviours, the Key 5 (ahmed Shafi et al., 2017), which were evidence of students responding to the feedback in effective ways that helped them manage their emotions thus contributing to academic buoyancy. These were: (i) an internal locus of control - where students saw the assessment as their responsibility rather than placing blame elsewhere e.g. on the lecturer, marker, university or other external circumstance; (ii) understanding the grade - where there was a recognition as to why they received the grade and feedback that they did with relation to the task and criteria; (iii) looking forward—where the student saw the assessment as part of a longer journey and a stepping stone towards the next assessment or stage of learning; (iv) being improvement focused—where students were keen to identify how they could learn from the feedback and develop; and (v) action-orientated behavior—where they were proactive about taking steps to develop in response to feedback given.

The first phase of the research thus illustrated that our students were using the feedback more than we thought and in a variety of ways as feedforward, but also to help them manage their feelings and emotions on receipt of a disappointing grade. Zimbardi et al. (2016) had linked disappointing grades to strong emotional responses, but our research suggested that even if the initial reaction to the grade was uncomfortable and challenging and a threat to their resilience, feedback could help them deal with this response and support the development of academic buoyancy through the adoption of behaviours that were indicators of academic buoyancy.

Implications for Practice

This led to the conclusion that appropriately structured feedback that can help develop academic buoyancy (Martin & Marsh, 2008) and support the development of self-regulation (Carless, 2006) would appear to be the foundation of effective practice, as it would enable students to deal with grades that are lower than expected by encouraging and nurturing constructive strategies and behaviours.

Such constructive behaviours, as identified above, seemed to be the Key 5 (ahmed Shafi et al., 2017):

(1) Internal locus of control
(2) Understanding the grade
(3) Being forward looking
(4) Being improvement focused
(5) Being action orientated

Consequently, it would seem that effective feedback is that which:

a. Clearly recognises effort and achievement and encourages the student to take responsibility for the work and the grade given, rather than look for external reasons and excuses

b. Provides a clear indication of why the grade was given against explicit criteria and grade descriptors
c. Makes reference to the fact that the assessment does not stand alone, but is part of a longer journey
d. Provides concrete suggestions as to things that could be developed and improved in future assessments
e. Makes suggestions as to actions that could be taken to assist these developments and improvements

Given the positioning of the study as action research, the results led to three changes to practice. Firstly, to explicitly teach the concept of academic buoyancy and the five indicators of buoyant behaviour in a first year (level 4) skills module. Secondly, to adopt a redesigned course template for assessment feedback that provides: tighter shaded grade descriptors against each criterion; positive comments highlighting what was done well; an explicit section for recommendations that are encouraging and provide concrete points for development and suggestions for actions to help students improve; the grade; and a section for student-devised action points. Thirdly, to ask students to share and discuss resulting self-devised action points in personal tutor meetings.

Research Phase 2

The three changes to practice were trialled the following year on the BA Education course and then students' thoughts and opinions were collected (see ahmed Shafi et al., 2020) guided by three research questions.

(1) Do students find input on academic buoyancy and the Key 5 indicators useful?
(2) Do students find the redesigned feedback sheets useful?
(3) Do students find it helpful to discuss their action points in personal tutor meetings?

Findings from Phase 2

Findings were interesting and helpful. Responses indicated that students did find the concept of academic buoyancy useful and appreciated the input on the Key 5 indicators. They said it gave them a frame of reference as to what to do in order to respond constructively on receipt of a disappointing grade and made them more aware of the fact that it is not unusual to have an emotional response.

Reaction to the redesigned feedback sheets was also positive with students appreciating the strengths-based comments and valuing the suggestions for improvements as they helped them move away from the disappointment in what *was*, towards thinking forwards to what *might be possible.*

The majority of the respondents also found the identification and subsequent discussion of action points with their personal tutor of use. This process again helped students focus on the formative nature of the feedback and to think of an assessment as a learning opportunity.

Two new themes that emerged from the data were to do with relationships and personal attributes. Students stated that good relationships with tutors helped them deal with the emotional responses to grades and feedback and engage in discussions around their performance in the assessments and their feelings towards feedback given. They stressed the need to feel that they could trust tutors and could approach them for support and guidance and feel 'safe'. In addition, the characteristics and attributes of the students themselves were recognized as having influence as it was acknowledged that, for example, levels of determination and motivation had an impact.

Implications for Practice

Although the focus of this second phase was not directly on the emotional response, once again it emerged as having an impact on how students react to feedback. Fong et al. (2016) indicate that it is important for tutors to understand the emotional impact of feedback and how they can endeavour to ensure it is constructive (Pitt & Norton, 2017). It appears that the changes to practice implemented may help students deal with challenging emotional responses and contribute to students developing greater self-regulatory measures (Carless, 2016) and thereby increasing their academic buoyancy.

As mentioned, the findings also highlighted that part of the buoyancy to deal with disappointing grades comes from student relationships with tutors and indicated how these need to be nurtured and can be assisted through dialogue relating to feedback and a transparent assessment process. Personalised feedback and student devised action points for discussion at personal tutor meetings went some way to achieving this and suggest the need for further exploration as to ways of increasing opportunity for student/tutor dialogue and developing trust.

Findings relating to the role of individual student attributes in response to feedback adds to the work of Higgins et al. (2002) and Pitt and Norton (2017) and emphasise the interplay between self-efficacy, emotional maturity and motivation. It positions the student as a central feature in how feedback is received and interpreted and reinforces the need for personalization and dialogue throughout the feedback process.

These findings led the authors to two proposals and a new model of academic buoyancy that incorporates these factors and helps re-conceptualise feedback practice (see ahmed Shafi et al., 2020).

The first is to reinterpret indicator (ii) of the Key 5 indicators of academic buoyancy (understanding the grade) as 'assessment literacy' (Ajjawi & Boud, 2017; Carless, 2016; Denton & McIlroy, 2017; O'Donovan et al. 2016; Price et al., 2012). Reflecting further on the data from phase 1 in the light of literature and the second phase, it

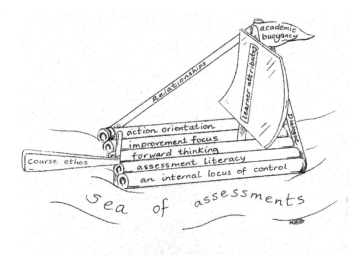

Fig. 9.1 The 'raft' of academic buoyancy

was felt that this was more apt. Assessment literacy more accurately and comprehen-
sively captures the broader aspects of understanding the grade to include interpreting
assessment and feedback within the context of its purpose, the assessment criteria
and the grading.

The second is, given the findings around student attributes and the need for relationships and dialogue that build on the work of Ajjawi, Molloy, Bearman, and Rees
(2017), Steen-Utheim and Wittek (2017) and Yang and Carless (2013), to propose
that the 5 (revised) key indicators of academic buoyancy should be underpinned by
a course ethos that values and nurtures the relationship between student and tutor,
provides opportunities for dialogue about work in general and feedback in particular
and treats the learners as individuals, recognising their attributes.

This leads to an adapted model of 'The Key 5 (revised) indicators of academic
buoyancy **plus** 2' referring to students showing: (i) an internal locus of control, (ii)
assessment literacy, (iii) forward thinking, (iv) an improvement focus, (v) action
orientation **plus** being situated within a course ethos that (1) values relationships
between student and tutor and (2) provides opportunities for dialogue about feedback
and academic progress which recognise the students' attributes and personalises
the process. This should, as Ajjawi and Boud (2018) suggest, take account of the
cognitive, socio-affective and structural dimensions and shift feedback from being
hopefully useful to something that *is* useful.

The diagram below illustrates the relationship between these factors by visual-
ising the learner remaining buoyant in the 'sea of assessments' on a 'raft' they have
constructed from the Key 5 (revised) indicators of academic buoyancy, with a mast of
their attributes supported by relationships and opportunities for dialogue and steered
by the course ethos as they sail towards academic success (Fig. 9.1).

As the second phase of an action research project, these results have led to further planned changes to practice: developing student understanding of academic buoyancy more regularly across the levels (year groups); highlighting the distinction between the *non-personal*, summative, process of grading of assessments and the *personal*, formative nature of feedback that takes account of individual attributes; explaining the rigour behind the grade; providing additional opportunities for dialogue around the feedback; and adding activities that can help build relationships and trust between tutor and student.

Further Discussion with Reference to the DIMoR (ahmed Shafi et al., 2020)

As a routine part of education processes, the act of assessing and providing grades and feedback can easily be treated as an isolated, mechanistic, stand-alone activity that just focuses on the assessment and feedback process itself. However, such an approach is in danger of disregarding the individuals and stakeholders involved and the complexities of the context and systems in which they function.

A dominant theme to emerge from the research highlighted above was the emotional impact that grades and feedback can have and how (a) the degree of this emotional response varies from individual to individual and (b) ways of dealing with the response vary between being stuck in an unhelpful mindset and externalizing the blame and taking a more positive, proactive response that views the feedback as a learning and developmental opportunity. Therefore, in order to make feedback useful, it is important to be mindful of the potential emotional impact it might have and to strive to find ways of helping recipients deal with any unhelpful emotions and turn the experience into a constructive one.

The use of resilience and in particular academic buoyancy as concepts helped explore this as they provided a lens through which to examine the ways that students were able to cope with any challenging emotional responses and aided the identification of the Key 5 behaviours that seemed to assist them deal with the response and move on from disappointment. The concept of resilience also revealed broader influences of individual characteristics and the importance of trust and relationships with tutors and the role of dialogue in facilitating this.

In no sense was there the idea that an individual's response to feedback would be the same on each occasion or that it was fixed. Rather, student responses were contextual and changed as they progressed through the course and thus moved temporally and spatially as they interacted and responded to different events and factors and developed as a person.

Traditional views of resilience were to think of it as something that an individual had, a quality or a capacity. More recent conceptualisations however, view it as something that is on a spectrum (see, for example, Daniel, Wassell, & Gilligan 1999) and built up from two axes. One considers resilience as influenced by personal qualities and traits against vulnerability caused by personal circumstances. The other weighs protective factors such as a close friend, against adversity—the threats to self.

However, whilst helpful, this view did not appear to take account of the more dynamic nature of resilience, acknowledging that individuals and their responses would change and that they were interacting with, and simultaneously affecting, others in the process of interacting. In other words that individuals, or systems, involved in an interaction have a reciprocal relationship.

Ungar's perception of resilience as a process and one that is dynamic and interactive (2013) alongside Rutter's view (2013) that we need to develop strategies in response to challenge and risk, was more useful as it provided place for the Key 5 indicators. It recognized that resilience or academic buoyancy is something that changes and seemed to accept that it could be more about process (utilizing the Key 5, engaging in dialogue, trusting others) than product (something we either have or do not have). This sense of movement, or development, was also reflected in Masten's work (2016) that suggested that the ability to cope comes in part through exposure to challenge, risk and adversity i.e. by having to respond to disappointing grades and feedback.

Further reflection on the research though suggests that, as a model of resilience, this perception of resilience is still incomplete. Personal attributes emerged as an influential theme and, alongside action orientation, link to Downes' (2017) point about agency. As individual students, they have their own attributes and their own agency and, as they interact with feedback, markers, tutors, classmates etc., they are not reverting back to the same place or bouncing back to as they were (Dent & Cameron, 2003), but changing and being changed as a result of each interaction with each aspect of the assessment and feedback process.

In addition, the research alluded to the broader context of grading and feedback processes—tutors, markers, course, university and societal structures of league tables and satisfaction surveys. Taking a systems approach allows one to explore feedback and a student's reaction to it in a more holistic way that recognizes the individual as a system within other systems. This builds on the ecological model of Bronfenbrenner (1979) and subsequent developments from Ungar (2013) that acknowledge the complex and multiple interactions that occur not just between neighbouring systems, but across and between systems.

Incorporating Morin's complexity theory (2008) attends to the fact that from these dynamic interactions between systems, things will emerge e.g. not only student academic buoyancy, resilience and learning, but new processes, systems, strategies and relationships as each system adapts in order to respond to disruption in, and to, its environment and also to protect itself. Examples of this linked to this research are: the redesigned feedback sheets that help with student self-regulation and understanding of the grade; the workload allocation models that serve to protect the marker by placing a boundary around the amount of time they have to mark and provide feedback; personal tutor guidelines and protocols that facilitate discussion of student devised action points in response to feedback; student representative systems designed to capture the student voice early and preempt and mitigate against student dissatisfaction with assessment and feedback processes; and mental health and wellbeing teams to support students when they are not coping well with grades and feedback given.

Combining these various elements, the Dynamic, Interactive Model of Resilience (DIMoR ahmed Shafi et al., 2020) helps with an analysis of the feedback process by considering the student as an individual within a complex system. It recognises that the emotional responses to feedback, and the usefulness of the feedback in helping the student deal with it, is in itself a dynamic and interactive process that will influence and impact jointly and severally the systems and stakeholders involved.

Using the DIMoR (ahmed Shafi et al., 2020) as a lens through which to examine the usefulness of feedback encourages the placement of the student at the centre of the process and recognizes the factors that might affect the student's ability to be able to deal with disappointing grades and feedback. It then accepts that student resilience is something that emerges as a result of the interactions that occur between these factors. In turn it then acknowledges that other systems could be affected by the interactions with the student through the feedback process (see Fig. 9.2).

This allows for a more complete, complex and nuanced picture of the feedback process that acknowledges that, when considering its usefulness, it needs to be considered from a broader perspective that takes account of the other systems involved.

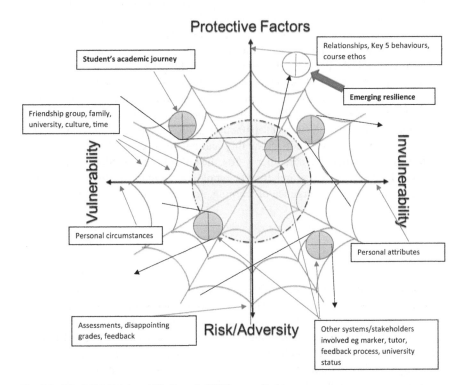

Fig. 9.2 The DIMoR (ahmed Shafi et al., 2020) as applied to assessments

Overall Implications

The Dynamic, Interactive Model of Resilience (ahmed Shafi et al., 2020) helps to serve as a framework for thinking about resilience, but also as a reminder to consider events such as feedback and the individuals involved within such an event, more holistically and from a systems perspective.

In pursuit of efficiencies, it is perhaps easy to take a reductionist approach and focus on the act itself, losing sight of the actors and other stakeholders involved. In this case, it would be possible to simply consider the efficient production and delivery of the grade and feedback without taking account of the humans involved, or their possible emotional reaction to any disappointments. A more holistic analysis allows thought for, and attention towards, individual attributes, stage of learning journey, tutor/student relationships, broader support structures and protective strategies alongside contextual structures and policies e.g. personal tutor guidelines and protocols, feedback processes, workload allocation and student voice mechanisms.

Reflecting on the research cited at the start of this chapter in the light of the DIMoR (ahmed Shafi et al., 2020) leads to thoughts about the research design. The initial design was focused on what students find most and least useful about feedback, how they use feedback and how they respond to feedback. In other words, it viewed feedback as something static and then focused on the students as recipients of the feedback and explored their reaction. As it happened, this led to thoughts about resilience and thereafter, inductively, to broader considerations. However, use of the DIMoR (ahmed Shafi et al., 2020) as a lens at the start of the research may have prompted a different research design whereby more immediately the impact of assessment feedback on the resilience of individuals was considered from a systems perspective, with thoughts for example of the interactions between markers/tutors and the students, between the design of the process and the stakeholders involved, between the emotional responses and student satisfaction and NSS responses, between workload allocation models and feedback quality and between personal tutor protocols and tutor/student relationships. In other words, the DIMoR (ahmed Shafi et al., 2020) may have helped the research search for the complexities within the feedback process and look for evidence of emergence of learning, development *and* resilience.

Conclusion

This chapter provided an overview of a research project that was undertaken with a cohort of undergraduates taking a BA Hons Education in a UK university. The project was designed to explore ways of making the assessment feedback process more effective and useful. In the process it highlighted that many students have uncomfortable emotional responses to disappointing grades that can be destructive and unhelpful. It also highlighted that students use feedback more than was anticipated by the tutors for content and writing support, but also to help them manage their emotions.

This led to thoughts about resilience and, more specifically, academic buoyancy and ways to help students develop the ability to cope with emotions during the feedback process in order to use it more constructively as feedforward. The Key 5 indicators of academic buoyancy were identified and, subsequently, the importance of trusting relationships between students and tutor and the need for dialogue. It also identified the influence of individual attributes.

A reconceptualization of the feedback process evolved that perceived the student as floating on the sea of assessments on a raft constructed of the Key 5 indicators of academic buoyancy and a mast of individual attributes supported by relationships and dialogue.

Various changes in practice followed in response to the findings designed to help the students deal with the emotional responses and to thereby use feedback constructively namely explicit teaching of the Key 5 indicators, redesigning the feedback sheets to support self-regulation, encouraging tutor/student dialogue about feedback and creating initiatives for developing relationships.

The research conducted shows the importance of widening focus from purely looking at feedback, to taking a systems approach and being mindful of the humans within the system and the system itself. The DIMoR (ahmed Shafi et al., 2020) helps with this analysis as it firmly places the student and their emerging resilience (academic buoyancy) at the centre of the process, but also acknowledges the resilience of other systems involved recognizing that resilience is a dynamic and interactive process. It thereby highlights the need to look for and at these intersections between systems and note the influence and impact the interactions can have on all stakeholders involved.

The chapter concluded by acknowledging that, whereas the research had started with a reductionist approach that focused on the use of the feedback by the learner, the data led the research towards a more systems perspective and subsequently used the DIMoR (ahmed Shafi et al., 2020) as a framework for analysis. However, it also suggested that, had the DIMoR (ahmed Shafi et al., 2020) been available at the research design stage, it may have led more quickly to a systems approach that could have helped create a more sophisticated research design that looked for evidence of the emergence of resilience and of the development of learning as a result of the feedback process in a wider range of contexts. In other words, as something that happens dynamically and interactively.

References

ahmed Shafi, A., Hatley, J., Middleton, T., Millican, R. & Templeton, S. (2017). The role of assessment feedback in developing academic buoyancy. *Assessment & Evaluation in Higher Education, 43*(3), 415–427.

ahmed Shafi, A., Templeton, S., Middleton, T., Millican, R., Vare, P., Pritchard, R. et al. (2020). Towards a dynamic interactive model of resilience (DIMoR) for education and learning contexts. *Emotional and Behavioural Difficulties, 25*(2), 183–198. https://doi.org/10.1080/136 32752.2020.1771923.

Ajjawi, R., & Boud, D. (2017). Researching feedback dialogue: An interactional analysis approach. *Assessment & Evaluation in Higher Education, 42*(2), 252–265.

Ajjawi, R., Boud, D. (2018). Examining the nature and effects of feedback dialogue. *Assessment & Evaluation in Higher Education 43*(7):1106–1119.

Ajjawi, R., Molloy, E., Bearman, M., & Rees, C. E. (2017). Contextual influences on feedback practices: An ecological perspective. In *Scaling up Assessment for Learning in Higher Education* (pp. 129–143). Springer.

Bouteyre, E., Maurel, M., & Bernaud, J. (2007). Daily hassles and depressive symptoms among first year psychology students in France: The role of coping and social support. *Stress and Health, 23,* 93–99.

Bronfenbrenner, U. (1979). The ecology of human development: experiments by nature and design. Cambridge: Harvard University Press.

Carless, D. (2006). Differing perceptions in the feedback process. *Studies in Higher Education, 31,* 219–223.

Carless, D. (2016). Feedback as dialogue. In *Encyclopedia of educational philosophy and theory* (pp. 1–6).

Daniel, B., Wassell, S., & Gilligan, R. (1999). *Child development for child care and protection workers.* London: Jessica Kingsley Publishers.

Delandshire, G. (2001). Implicit theories, unexamined assumptions and the status quo of educational assessment. *Assessment in Education, 8*(2), 113–133.

Dent, R., & Cameron, R. (2003). Developing resilience in children who are in public care: The educational psychology perspective. *Educational Psychology in Practice, 19*(1), 3–19.

Denton, P., & McIlroy, D. (2017). Response of students to statement bank feedback: The impact of assessment literacy on performances in summative tasks. *Assessment & Evaluation in Higher Education,* 1–10.

Downes, P. (2017). Extended paper: Reconceptualising foundational assumptions of resilience: A cross-cultural, spatial systems domain of relevance for agency and phenomenology in resilience. *International Journal of Emotional Education, 9*(1), 99–120.

Fong, C. J., Warner, J.R., Williams, K.M., Schallert, D.L., Chen, L.H., Williamson, Z.H. & Lin, S. (2016). Deconstructing constructive criticism: The nature of academic emotions associated with constructive, positive, and negative feedback. *Learning and Individual Differences, 49,* 393–399.

Higgins, R., Hartley, P., & Skelton, A. (2002). The conscientious consumer: Reconsidering the role of assessment feedback in student learning. *Studies in Higher Education, 27*(1), 53–64.

Jonsson, A. (2012). Facilitating productive use of feedback in higher education. *Active Learning in Higher Education, 14*(1), 63–76.

Martin, A. J., & Marsh, H. W. (2008). Academic buoyancy: Towards an understanding of students' everyday academic resilience. *Journal of School Psychology, 46*(1), 53–83.

Martin, A. J., & Marsh, H. W. (2009). Academic resilience and academic buoyancy: Multidimensional and hierarchical conceptual framing of causes, correlates and cognate constructs. *Oxford Review of Education, 35*(3), 353–370.

Masten, A. (2016). Resilience in developing systems: The promise of integrated approaches. *European Journal of Developmental Psychology, 13*(3), 297–312.

McCann, L., & Saunders, G. (2009). *Exploring student perceptions of assessment feedback.* SWAP report. York: HE.

Morin, E. (2008). *On complexity.* Cresskill: Hampton Press.

Middleton, T., Ahmed Shafi, A., Millican, R., Templeton, S. Developing effective assessment feedback: academic buoyancy and the relational dimensions of feedback. Teaching in Higher Education:1–18.

O'Donovan, B., Rust, C., & Price, M. (2016). A scholarly approach to solving the feedback dilemma in practice. *Assessment & Evaluation in Higher Education, 41*(6), 938–949.

Pitt, E., & Norton, L. (2017). 'Now that's the feedback I want!' Students' reactions to feedback on graded work and what they do with it. *Assessment & Evaluation in Higher Education, 42*(4), 499–516.

Poulos, A., & Mahony, M. J. (2008). Effectiveness of feedback: the students' perspective. *Assessment and Evaluation in Higher Education, 33*(2), 143–154.

Price, M., Rust, C., O'Donovan, B., & Handley, K. (2012). *Assessment literacy: The foundation for improving student learning.* Oxford: The Oxford Centre for Staff and Learning Development.

Rutter, M. (2013). Annual research review: Resilience—Clinical implications. *Journal of Child Psychology and Psychiatry, 54*(4), 474–487.

Steen-Utheim, A., & Wittek, A. (2017). Dialogic feedback and potentialities for student learning. *Learning, Culture and Social Interaction, 15,* 18–30.

Ungar, M. (2013). Resilience, trauma, context, and culture. *Trauma, Violence, & Abuse, 14*(3), 255–266.

Wang, M. C., & Gordon, E. W. (1994). *Educational resilience in inner-city America: Challenges and prospects.* Oxon: Routledge.

Wang, M. C. (1997). Next steps in inner-city education: Focusing on resilience development and learning success. *Education and Urban Society, 29*(3), 255–276.

Wheatley, L., McInch, A., Fleming, S., & Lord, R. (2015). Feeding back to feed forward: Formative assessment as a platform for effective learning. *Kentucky Journal of Higher Education Policy and Practice, 3*(2), 2.

Yang, M., & Carless, D. R. (2013). The feedback triangle and the enhancement of dialogic feedback processes. *Teaching in Higher Education, 18*(3), 285–297.

Zimbardi, K., Colthorpe, K., Dekker, A., Engstrom, C., Bugarcic, P., Victor, R., … Long, P. (2016). Are they using my feedback? The extent of students' feedback use has a large impact on subsequent academic performance. *Assessment and Evaluation in Higher Education.* https://doi.org/10.1080/02602938.2016.1174187.

Richard Millican is a Senior Lecturer in Education and the Course Leader for the BA (Hons) Education at the University of Gloucestershire where he has worked for the past 10 years. Prior to that he has a long history of working within education, but in different contexts and phases. These include as a Drama and Music teacher across age ranges, a teacher of learners with social and emotional difficulties 5–18, a teacher of English as a Foreign Language to children and adults and a teacher trainer. He has worked in various countries including Spain, Oman and Egypt and in schools, further education colleges and universities including Leeds and Birmingham.

His current interests are in social justice and sustainability and in the role of education in helping to create a fairer and sustainable world. He is currently working on an international research project, A Rounder Sense of Purpose, which is developing a framework of competences for educators of sustainable development linked to the Sustainable Development Goals. This has led to various recent publications alongside work into developing academic resilience and buoyancy with higher education students.

Dr. Adeela ahmed Shafi has a background in psychology and education and has been teaching in higher education for over 17 years. Her research draws on psychological theories to explore how to re-engage young offenders with formal education and learning in a secure custodial setting. Adeela's other research includes how to develop academic resilience and buoyancy in higher education students. She has also worked on international projects in Rwanda and Pakistan as well as an EU project on emotional education. Adeela has recently won two EU bids of 3 years duration, each running parallel. The first is on re-engaging young offenders with education and learning with three European partners. The second is a project designed to develop social and emotional competencies through active games in young people in conflict with the law. This is with ten partner across seven European partners. Adeela has an established publishing profile and leads the REF submission for Education at the University of Gloucestershire. Adeela is an active community worker and also stood for MP in 2010.

Sian Templeton is a Senior Lecturer in Education at the University of Gloucestershire and a practicing Educational Psychologist working with teaching staff, children, young people and their families. She has worked in a variety of educational settings with a focus on supporting the social, emotional and cognitive needs of vulnerable learners to enable them to engage with education. She achieved this through working directly with the young people, with the families, teaching staff and a range of professionals from health and social care. In addition to direct work, she also believes in exploring more systemic opportunities for promoting and supporting access to education for all. She teaches on both Undergraduate and Postgraduate courses within her University role across a range of areas within education and leads on a number of psychology-based education modules. She is involved in ERASMUS + projects related to her areas of interest. Sian's research includes resilience, emotional education and supporting young offenders in re-engaging with education and she is just commencing her DEdPsy at University College London.

Tristan Middleton is Senior Lecturer in Education and Joint Course Leader for the MA Education suite at the University of Gloucestershire. Tristan is an experienced primary school class teacher, Senior Leader, Special Educational Needs Coordinator and Designated teacher for both Safe-guarding and Looked-After Children. He also ran a Nurture Group for seven years. Tristan is Chair of Directors of Leading Learning for SEND CiC which oversees the work of the National SENCO Award Provider Partnership and also a member of NurtureUK's Research, Evidence & Ethics Trustee Sub-Group and Associate Editor of the International Journal of Nurture in Education. He is currently a member of the Erasmus+ RENYO project team focusing on the re-engagement of young offenders with education and learning, with three European partners. He has recently published "Using an Inclusive Approach to Reduce School Exclusion: A Practitioner's Handbook" with Lynda Kay, published by Routledge and the book chapter "Teaching Assistants identifying key factors to their successful work with challenging children and finding a new discourse." In: H. R. Wright & M. E. Hoyen (Eds.) Discourses We Live By: Personal and professional perspectives on education. Open Book Publishers, Cambridge.

Chapter 10
Educator Conceptualisations of Emotional Education and the Development of Resilience

Sian Templeton, Adeela ahmed Shafi, and Rebecca Pritchard

Abstract This chapter draws on data from an Erasmus + project on emotional education and its potential for developing competencies to prevent early school leaving in partner organisations spread across six countries in Europe. Emotional competencies are a part of the protective factors that can help the development of resilience, which is known to be relevant to success in school, including staying on at school. Particularly, this chapter is focused on educators—at the forefront of interactions with learner—and their conceptualisations of emotional education and how these can affect engagement and delivery of emotional education. The Chapter uses the dynamic interactive model of resilience (DIMoR) to understand the broader contextual and systemic factors that can shape educator conceptualisations and uses the opportunity to discuss and recommend that transnational interventions need to consider the wider context of settings in their design of programmes, if they are to be effective.

Introduction

This chapter presents how emotional education can contribute to the development of resilience. This is based on the recognition that emotional competencies can form part of the protective factors (see Chap. 2), which can aid an individual's resilience and support them to succeed in school (Brooks & Goldstein, 2012; Heckman & Kautz, 2012) and life in general (Sklad, Ritter, Ben, & Gravesteijn, 2012; Klapp et al., 2017), such as employment, well-being and developing to one's full potential (Heckman & Kautz, 2012). Positive psychology underpins the view that it is possible to promote resilience through teachable elements of emotional education (Seligman, Ernst, Gillham, Reivich, & Linkins, 2009). Emotional education incorporates behavioural, cognitive and emotional components (Taylor, Oberle, Durlak, & Weissberg, 2017). These enable learners to apply knowledge, attitudes and skills

S. Templeton (✉) · A. Shafi · R. Pritchard
School of Education and Humanities, University of Gloucestershire, Cheltenham, UK
e-mail: stempleton@glos.ac.uk

© Springer Nature Switzerland AG 2020
A. ahmed Shafi et al. (eds.), *Reconsidering Resilience in Education*,
https://doi.org/10.1007/978-3-030-49236-6_10

necessary to set and achieve positive goals, demonstrate empathy, engage in healthy relationships, responsible decision making and emotionally regulate (Axelrod, 2010).

As key deliverers of interventions, educator conceptualisations of emotional education are the focus of this chapter because of the important role they play in the relational context. This chapter reflects on findings from an Erasmus funded[1] emotional education project entitled EUMOSCHOOL[2] with educators in six partner based in Austria, Romania, Italy, Turkey, Hungary and the UK. Emerging themes that arose from this project in relation to the delivery of intervention programmes was the need to first appraise education professionals' conceptualisations of emotional education, the extent to which they valued emotional education and where they attributed responsibility for emotional education. This theme reinforced the importance of an adaptable and dynamic approach to emotional education, which in turn can influence resilience within learners.

Using the Dynamic Interactive Model of Resilience (DIMoR), ahmed Shafi et al. (2020), this chapter considers the wider dynamic and complex systems, which surround not only the children for whom the intervention/programmes is aimed, but also the educators tasked with delivering them. The project highlighted how the teaching of emotional education should not be viewed as an isolated mechanism through which to build resilience but part of a wider positive sustained school climate (Cohen & Geier, 2010). As Doll Brehm and Zucker (2014) remind us 'resilience is a characteristic that emerges out of the systemic interdependence of children with their families, communities and schools' (p. 400, 2014). Whilst emotional education can provide a mechanism through which to support the development of resilience, it is important to consider the wider implications and influences upon the delivery of such interventions, including the educators themselves.

This chapter will begin by presenting the EUMOSCHOOL Project, followed by how the DIMoR, (ahmed shafi et al., 2020), can illuminate the range of actors within the system when delivering the emotional education intervention. The chapter then discusses the findings from an exploration of educator conceptualisations from the partners in the different countries.

The EUMOSCHOOL Project

The EUMOSCHOOL project was funded by Erasmus + to research how emotional education can help prevent early school leaving (ESL)[3] as a potential risk factor for the development of resilience. The European Commission (EU), (2010) considers

---

[1] European Union funded research.

[2] Eumoschool https://eumoschool.eu/.

[3] As a statistical measure, ESL is the percentage of 18–24 year olds with only lower secondary education or less and no longer in education and training (European Commission, 2013). This stimulated the funding allocation for projects such as Eumoschool that aimed to contribute towards reducing ESL.

reducing ESL a means to resolve labour market issues in Europe in its EU2020 strategy and the use of transnational policy to address shared problems collectively (Moutsios, 2010). The EUMOSCHOOL project was based upon these principles and the use of a competence based emotional education intervention programme from Italy entitled 'Didactics of Emotions' (DoE) which focused on educator professional development. Six project teams from the partner countries in Italy, Austria, Romania, Hungary, Turkey and the UK collected qualitative and quantitative data from over 600 educators as part of the needs analysis stage of the project. A broad sample of educators conceptualisations of emotional education were gathered from; teachers, school leaders, teaching assistants and educational psychologists.

Educators from the partner countries were trained on the delivery of the 'Didactics of Emotion' intervention programme in order to deliver it in their respective educational settings. The project involved the development of online educational resources to support the training of educators and their delivery. The project highlighted that an understanding of educators' contexts was important in developing appropriate interventions and associated resources. The DIMoR, (ahmed Shafi et al., 2020), presents a visual representation of the way in which the contextual factors in each system interact and influence potential pathways. Within the project, educators were uniquely placed to comment on their specific contexts.

Using the DIMoR to Understand a Context and System

The DIMoR, (ahmed Shafi et al., 2020), was developed (see Chap. 2) as a way to bring together many of the established models of resilience to better understand the dynamic, interactive, complex and emergent nature of resilience. In order for emotional education interventions to be effective, a recognition of this complexity is important and particularly so when the same intervention is to be applied to a range of very different contexts. This is apparent both in terms of the different countries and the very specific and local context of the partners and participants in the project. The figure below illustrates the way in which local country contexts can differentially influence the conceptualisation of emotional education and impact on how the interventions are delivered (Fig. 10.1).

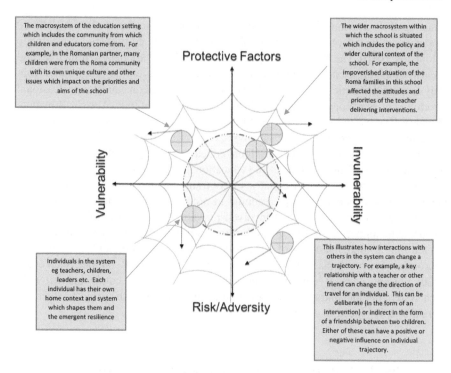

The macrosystem of the education setting which includes the community from which children and educators come from. For example, in the Romanian partner, many children were from the Roma community with its own unique culture and other issues which impact on the priorities and aims of the school

The wider macrosystem within which the school is situated which includes the policy and wider cultural context of the school. For example, the impoverished situation of the Roma families in this school affected the attitudes and priorities of the teacher delivering interventions.

Protective Factors

Vulnerability

Invulnerability

Individuals in the system eg teachers, children, leaders etc. Each individual has their own home context and system which shapes them and the emergent resilience

Risk/Adversity

This illustrates how interactions with others in the system can change a trajectory. For example, a key relationship with a teacher or other friend can change the direction of travel for an individual. This can be deliberate (in the form of an intervention) or indirect in the form of a friendship between two children. Either of these can have a positive or negative influence on individual trajectory.

Fig. 10.1 Using the DIMoR to understand a context and system

The figure above illustrates how the context of educators' settings can influence their conceptualisations of emotional education, which is also likely to be shaped by the local context within which they are situated, as well as the wider macro level context. For example, for the Turkish partners, gender role expectations were identified as important as well as families' financial situations, which shaped their engagement with education. The Hungarian partners were situated in a location with a very high number of Roma families who also experienced high deprivation and poverty which again was different to the Italian partner context. This highlights the differences between contextual expectations and therefore can potentially lead to a challenge to the notion that one particular intervention can work in multiple contexts.

The DIMoR, (ahmed Shafi et al., 2020), also enables us to see how the trajectory of individuals in the systems can be changed by interacting both with the system and other individuals in the system. These may be deliberate interactions such as an intervention, or more indirect such as a friendship between children that could foster resilience. The DIMoR, (ahmed Shafi et al., 2020), thus enables us to examine the range of actors with a given systems so that we can explore how they play a part in the system for the emergence of resilience. An often forgotten element are the actual educators as key deliverers in intervention programs. We return to them as a focus later in the chapter when we examine the data, but the following section first examines emotional education itself and its relationship to resilience.

Emotional Education, Emotional Competence and Resilience

As discussed earlier in this chapter, one of the aims of the EUMOSCHOOL project was to 'teach' skills relating to emotional competence using emotional education through the highly structured programme; Didactics of Emotion. Part of the rationale for this explicit teaching of emotional competence through emotional education is that it is widely recognised that possessing the sub-skills of emotional competence (such as self-regulation, empathy, self-awareness etc.) has been shown to be important for success not only in school, but life in general (Sklad et al., 2012; Klapp et al., 2017), including employment, well-being and developing to one's full potential (Heckman and Kautz, 2012). Emotional competence is also recognised as a protective factor which contributes to individual resilience (Werner & Smith, 1979).

Emotional education can be explored as an *approach* to working with learners or a discreet *curriculum*. Specific social emotional curriculum interventions provide an evidence base on which to determine the impact on skills/emotional competencies (Jones & Kahn, 2017; Durlak, Weissberg, Dymnicki, Taylor, & Schellinger 2011; Humphreys, 2013). Within the field of emotional education, 'emotional intelligence' and 'emotional literacy' are key conceptual terms that are often highlighted. An issue with focusing on these broader terms such 'emotional intelligence' and 'emotional literacy' is the potential to concentrate on 'within child' factors (Weare & Gray, 2003) and, consequently, there is a danger of ignoring the more complex interactive nature of other contributory systems around the child such as schools, families and communities (Haddon, Goodman, Park, & Deakin-Crick, 2005).

Emotional education as part of a pedagogical repertoire has the potential to contribute towards developing resilience for our young people and thus prepare them for challenge, change and flux. However, often interventions which focus on emotional education take place once learners have been identified as being 'at risk' and therefore needing support in this area. This model of 'identify' and 'intervene' is driven by a deficit model in which skills are seen to be lacking and requiring further support. Many researchers therefore argue for recognition of a broader contextual understanding through earlier interventions focusing on increasing students overall social and emotional competencies through a wider systemic approach rather than individualised programmes (Gutman & Schoon, 2013; Klapp et al., 2017) with Weare and Gray (2003) emphasising the importance of creating appropriate environments in order to optimise the success of these programmes. These 'emotional education' or 'social and emotional learning' approaches which take into account the learning environment in addition to the specific content of the programmes have been found to demonstrate positive effects on intra and inter-personal affective competencies, Klapp et al. (2017).

The conceptual grounding of emotional education being a key contributor to academic engagement is based on the argument that if a learner can self-regulate their emotions during learning, they are more resilient to setback and challenge and thereby more likely to remain engaged with their learning (ahmed Shafi et al., 2017; Hatzichristou & Lianos, 2016) support the connection between resilience and components of social emotional learning/education within a multi-level conceptual framework, the importance of schools and communities, including the impact of wider social and economic factors that can impact on engagement are empahasised; this is further considered through the DIMoR, (ahmed Shafi et al., 2020), model in Chap. 2.

There are many programs designed to support children's emotional education implemented in schools around the world (Humphrey, 2013). This movement seeks to transform educational practice into a 'humanizing experience' (Elias et al., 2015) where emotional education is not merely a 'subject' that is added to the curriculum, but embedded within a whole school context and, as a result, recognises the positive impact on behavioural and academic outcomes. This elevates the status of emotional education as an essential underpinning across the whole school curriculum, influencing resilience of learners and facilitated by teachers as key deliverers of the curriculum. This 'humanising experience' is upheld by Banerjee, Weare, and Farr (2014), in their analysis of the UK government led 'Social and Emotional Aspects of Learning' programme (SEAL, DfES, 2005). They emphasised that a socially and emotionally literate school ethos is more influential than a programme per se.

The links between children's emotional health and wellbeing, cognitive development and future wellbeing and in turn resilience has been widely reflected in the literature (see Banerjee et al., 2014; Panayiotou & Humphrey, 2018). Klapp et al. (2017) suggest that the development of emotional competencies reduces the likelihood of engaging in risk taking activities such as violence and drug misuse, which are highlighted as risk factors for the development of resilience. For example, the analysis by Dietrich (2012) found that lack of emotional resources was a common characteristic of unemployed youths (who are generally recognised as being less resilient than their employed counterparts). Young people's emotional competence also links with their short-term achievement and longer-term outcomes into adulthood (Weare, 2015). All of these indicate the potential of emotional education as a protective factor that optimises support to members of a school community for these longer-term (Reynolds et al., 2011) and short-term outcomes (Durlak et al., 2011) and thus positively impact on their emerging resilience. This is highlighted by the work of Banerjee, Weare and Farr (2014) where they establish a clear link between a socially and emotionally literate school ethos and learner achievement results and attendance. Gutman and Schoon (2013) emphasise the necessity of taking a holistic approach to promoting skills and addressing risks rather than isolated skill development as key in the development and delivery of emotional education programmes. The need to therefore focus on a more holistic approach that takes account of, and is responsive to, the context to support the development of resilience. This is also reinforced by the observation from Downes (2017, p. 16) that '…resilience [is] an interactive directional process more than a static trait'. In this, Downes has recognised that resilience is on-going rather than something that you can 'remedy' with an intervention.

Emotional competencies can be seen to serve as protective factors in dealing with change and as predictors of academic success (Heckman and Kautz, 2012) and can be developed through emotional education. This ability to manage change is well linked to the resilience literature (Masten, 2015; Rutter, 2013; Werner, 1993) and is explored more fully within Chap. 2.

These ideas around the competencies developed through emotional education complement the key factors of the dynamic processes of behavioural, cognitive, emotional and psychological factors within individual levels of resilience. The cognitive-emotional skill of emotional regulation developed as part of a wider, holistic emotional education programme can also protect against risks, such as offending behaviour (Taylor et al., 2017) or early school leaving and dropout (Christenson & Thurlow, 2004), factors clearly linked to 'risks' identified within the resilience literature.

The Role of the Educator

The DIMoR, (ahmed Shafi et al., 2020), illustrates that we cannot solely focus on individuals and 'within-learner' factors of what may/ may not be recognised as resilience; the role of the educator within this process may be argued as being at least equally important. There is growing evidence that teachers' beliefs, feelings, and behaviours have an impact on student engagement and outcomes (e.g. Arens & Morin, 2016; Klassen & Tze, 2014; Leventhal et al., 2018). The importance of the individual qualities of the educator and their pedagogy as a means to facilitate engagement, develop academic resilience (Martin, 2002) and emotional competencies (Klapp et al., 2017) should not be underestimated (Goldspink & Foster, 2013). Developing these ideas around the importance of individual qualities of the educator, Goldspink & Foster (2013) also emphasised the significance of the proximal and distal learning context, echoing the work of Skinner, Furrer, Marchand and Kindermann (2008). Within this work, the essential role of the educator and their pedagogical approach was emphasised in delivering impact on the developing resilience of learners through a focus on emotional competency development.

However, educators' role perception within emotional education intervention literature has not been fully explored. Even in the socialisation literature, teacher beliefs or conceptualisation of socialisation practices in the school environment, have been ignored in many studies, despite the prolonged contact and impact they have on learners as illustrated by Zinsser, Shewark, Denham and Curby, (2014). Their study explored educators' beliefs about the value of social and emotional learning; their perceptions of socialisation practices and strategies; and their beliefs about their role in children's emotional development. They concluded that differences in teacher beliefs could affect both outcomes and delivery of intervention programs. This points to how the educator plays a significant role in developing emotional education and how individual qualities can influence the success or not of a programme and re-emphasises the importance of considering wider factors than the programme per-se when trying to develop factors which may contribute to emerging resilience.

Educator Conceptualisations of Emotional Education

Educator conceptualisation of emotional education is therefore central to understanding and implementation of interventions; how educators define, value and understand emotional education is potentially key to the efficacy of implementing an intervention (Jennings and Frank, 2015) alongside where they attribute responsibility for
the development of emotional competencies in learners in order to develop resilience.
For example, it is possible to have a shared understanding of emotional education
and value it (Reeves & Le Mare, 2017), but this does not automatically mean that
educators believe it to be their responsibility to support this in practice especially
if an 'interventions' approach is taken. Educator self-efficacy about their ability to
implement emotional education in their settings is likely to be influenced by their
perceptions around barriers and opportunities within their learning environments
(Alridge & Fraser, 2016). Like learners, educators are a dynamic product of their
culture, context, experience and personality all of which are likely to shape their own
resilience and conceptualisation of emotional education within their context (Ungar
& Liebenberg, 2013). These in turn impact on their motivation and skills in imparting
the programme (Leventhal et al., 2018).

The challenges of emotional education are copious and reflect the dynamic nature
of reciprocal interactions between and within systems which include both the learner
and educator as illustrated within the DIMoR, (ahmed Shafi et al., 2020). Factors
such as the family, community, culture, context and the setting all affect emotional
education and how it is 'delivered' and received. Within the EUMOSCHOOL project,
it emerged that the crux of a number of these issues centred on educators and their
conceptualisations of emotional education as key deliverers of interventions and in
particular, whom they believed should provide it and the value that individual schools
placed on it.

Four Components of Emotional Education

The issues around educator conceptualisation was reinforced further from the findings from educator survey responses as part of the EUMOSCHOOL project. Within
the survey, educators were asked to ascribe perceived importance of a list of relevant emotional education competences and these were subjected to an exploratory
factor analysis which revealed four main components of emotional education (see
Table 10.1). These components connect with the protective factors which enable
resilience (see Catalono et al., 2004; Luther et al., 2000; Werner 1993 in Chap. 2) and
were labelled as *Relatedness, Mindful Awareness, Emotional Agency* and *Empathic
Understanding* (see ahmed Shafi, Templeton, Huang & Pritchard, under review).
Relatedness refers to co-operation, managing conflict, working in groups or helping
others. *Mindful Awareness* refers to the awareness of own and others' emotions
and developing positive relationships. *Emotional Agency* refers to acting on areas of

Table 10.1 Four components of emotional education and their related competencies

	Interpretation of the component	Items of related competences
1	Relatedness	Cooperating
		Managing conflict non-violently
		Working effectively in groups
		Help-seeking and help-giving
2	Mindful awareness	Recognising emotions in self and others
		Approaching others and building positive relationships
		Recognising own strengths and areas of need
		Regulating and managing strong emotions (unpleasant and pleasant)
3	Emotional agency	Recognising own strengths and areas of need
		Listening actively
		Communicating accurately and clearly
		Setting positive and realistic goals
4	Empathic understanding	Taking others' perspectives and sensing their emotions
		Showing ethical and social responsibility
		Respecting others and self and appreciating differences

Adapted from: Ahmed Shafi, Templeton, Huang & Pritchard, under review

strength and need in relationships. *Empathic Understanding* is about empathy, social responsibility and respect of self, others and difference, implying the competence of taking others' perspectives and sensing emotions. There was broad consensus on the components of emotional education across the six countries. The strength of emphases on each of these components varied across the partners and appeared related to the extent to which educators felt equipped to provide emotional education.

A Context and Systems Level Approach

The differences between partners on the attribution of responsibility for emotional education referred to the local context, culture, policy and pupil intake of the local networks of the participant samples in each of the countries. It pointed towards the importance of culture and context, illustrating how the educator is an individual embedded within a cultural and societal system, just as the individual learner is. This nuanced perspective underlies how the educator themselves can sometimes be a 'forgotten' element within the system. The DIMoR, (ahmed Shafi et al., 2020), recognises and acknowledges the educator as one of the actors situated within the (school) system. It somewhat challenges the finding from Gershon and Pelliterri (2018) that some emotional education programmes have potential in terms of cross-cultural usage. Instead, it connects more to the ideas put forward by Hatzichristou & Lianos (2016) who advocate the importance of recognising the wider social and economic context within which schools are situated in order for social and emotional learning interventions to be effective in achieving their aims. This also reinforces the argument put forward by Weare & Gray (2003) about the significance of the school environment in determining levels of social and emotional competence and the importance of the quality of daily interactions and subsequent impact on people's feelings and the development of resilience (Haddon et al. 2005).

This was echoed in the finding within the EUMOSCHOOL project on the value for emotional education where there was greater variability between partners. This variability appeared to be due to the sociocultural context which determined the extent to which emotional education was seen to contribute to improved longer term outcomes. The priority of these outcomes was again, connected to the local context. For example in Romania, the importance of self-awareness and empathy was linked to diversity, the tolerance of others and reduced prejudice (further supporting the *Relatedness* component from the questionnaire data). This positioned these findings within the *relational approach* put forward by Reeves and Le Mare (2017). In the UK, the longer-term outcomes related to academic attainment, encased within a school and policy culture that is attainment driven. In this way, educators assessed the value of emotional education according to their social, cultural (and policy) contexts. Utilising the DIMoR, (ahmed Shafi et al., 2020), it is possible to map the relative influencing factors within any given system including the external drivers, such as policy and culture.

The range of system based factors that have contributed to how educators conceptualise emotional education illuminate the importance and complexity of educator engagement. For example, if educators do not attribute themselves to be responsible for emotional education, then they are less likely to engage in interventions. Further, if the educator does not feel an intervention has value, then they are less likely to engage with it beyond the level of compliance. This has implications for learner engagement and the development of resilience especially if the intervention is part of an overall approach taken by the setting to develop resilience. There is plenty of literature (e.g. Goldspink and Foster, 2013; Zinsser et al., 2014) which points towards the importance of the educator in delivering interventions, as well as how educator engagement impacts on learner engagement (Perera, Vosicka, Granziera, & McIlveen, 2018; Arens & Morin, 2016; Goddard, Hoy, & Hoy, 2000; Klassen & Tze, 2014). Klapp et al., (2017) emphasise that through engaging in good quality pedagogy and the qualities of the educator, emotional competences can be developed. This suggests that the development of emotional skills is important and valuable for learners, but that this in isolation is not sufficient, further pointing to how the development of, for example how resilience can only be fostered or facilitated through a system level approach. Thus, the educator and their ecology of the learning context merits attention. This is further reinforced by the work of Zinsser et al. (2014) and Leventhal et al. (2018) who emphasised the individual value and belief systems of educators and how these might impact on the success of emotional education whether part of a specific programme or something wider in the ecology of the learners. Research more generally has demonstrated the potential of emotional education can be increasingly realised when embedded within a whole school approach to developing resilience (Banerjee, Weare, & Farr, 2014; Gilbert, Rose & McGuire-Snieckus, 2014). These findings illustrate how the educator is an individual embedded within a professional, cultural and societal system and that in order for emotional education interventions to have traction, it is important to engage educators through a recognition of the system/s within which they are situated and their key drivers. This has implications for the effectiveness of interventions which require the 'buy-in' and engagement of the educator.

The DIMoR, (ahmed Shafi et al., 2020), offers a way in which a context or setting can assess the range of factors at play within any given system by enabling leaders of interventions to develop emotional education and thereby resilience to visually map their system and its interacting factors. This would provide an opportunity to design interventions that could identify some of the potential challenges within that system to better work across contexts. At the same time it can enable enough flex for each context to not only recognise the various factors that might impact the success of the intervention, but also then respond to those so that the intervention/s are responsive to such factors rather than oblivious. Indeed, the DIMoR, (ahmed Shafi et al., 2020), can also illuminate opportunities which may otherwise be missed when considering interventions in a narrow way.

Conclusions

The findings from the EUMOSCHOOL project focused on educators' conceptualisations of emotional education and the extent to which they perceive their role to be a part of that. Whilst emotions have been cited as significant for resilience and for promoting effective learning, there has been little research which has explored educator conceptualisations of emotional education and how his may affect engagement and delivery. Given that educators are at the forefront of interactions with learners, this seems an important endeavour. Whilst there is a general consensus of defining what is meant by emotional education, the value educators placed on it and attribution of responsibility in terms of who provides it, varied between partners.

This chapter provides some unique insights into how educators in several different contexts conceptualise emotional education which helps build resilience. As a transnational piece of work, this project highlights how whilst a number of nations can make a collective pledge to resolve a particular education issue, how interventions are implemented locally, has to take account of the local socioeconomic, policy and cultural context of which the educator is an important part. It highlights how the educator is an active and agentic social being who is situated within a political and social context. Cross-national programmes that adopt a context specific system level approach that recognise differing interpretations and attributions of emotional education are likely to be more effective in developing resilience. This has implications for transnational intervention programmes designed to be implemented in a range of contexts. Ironically, for too long educator conceptualisations of interventions have been ignored. Our research shows how educators conceptualise emotional education, who they believe is responsible for providing and how they value it, can play an important role in how effective emotional education interventions are. The implications of this are that before interventions are delivered, consideration be given to educators' beliefs and values as these are likely to determine the extent to which they engage with the intervention and its subsequent success. Using the DIMoR, (ahmed Shafi et al., 2020), is one way to capture the importance of educator conceptualisation alongside the other factors, acknowledging their pivotal role in the system and enable greater success of interventions designed to develop resilience through emotional education.

References

Ahmed Shafi, A., Hatley, J., Middleton, T., Millican, R., & Templeton, S. (2017). The role of assessment feedback in developing academic buoyancy. *Assessment and Evaluation in Higher Education*.

ahmed Shafi, A., Templeton, S., Middleton, T., Millican, R., Vare, P., Pritchard, R. et al. (2020). Towards a dynamic interactive model of resilience (DIMoR) for education and learning contexts. *Emotional and Behavioural Difficulties, 25*(2), 183–198. https://doi.org/10.1080/136 32752.2020.1771923.

Alridge, J. M., & Fraser, B. J. (2016). Teacher's views of their school climate and its relationship with teacher self-efficacy and job satisfaction. *Learning Environment Res, 19,* 291–307.

Arens, A. K., & Morin, A. J. (2016). Relations between teachers' emotional exhaustion and students' educational outcomes. *Journal of Educational Psychology, 108*(6), 800.

Banerjee, R., Weare, K., & Farr, W. (2014). Working with 'Social and Emotional Aspects of Learning' (SEAL): Associations with school ethos, pupil social experiences, attendance, and attainment. *British Educational Research Journal, 40*(4), 718–742.

Brooks, R., Brooks, S., & Goldstein, S. (2012). The power of mindsets: Nurturing engagement, motivation, and resilience in students. In *Handbook of research on student engagement* (pp. 541–562). Boston, MA: Springer.

Catalano, R., Haggerty, K., Oesterles, S., Fleming, C., & Hawkins, D. (2004). The importance of bonding to school for healthy development: Findings from the social development research group. *Journal of School Health, 74*(7), 252–326.

Christenson, S. L., & Thurlow, M. L. (2004). School dropouts: Prevention considerations, interventions, and challenges. *Current Directions in Psychological Science, 13*(1), 36–39.

Cohen, J., & Geier, V. K. (2010). School climate research summary: January 2010. *School Climate Brief, 1*(1), 1–6.

Dietrich, H. (2012). Youth unemployment in Europe. *Theoretical considerations and empirical findings., 16*(7), 2012.

Doll, B., Brehm, K., & Zucker, S. (2014). *Resilient classrooms: Creating healthy environments for learning.* Guilford Publications.

Durlak, J. A., Weissberg, R. P., Dymnicki, A. B., Taylor, R. D., & Schellinger, K. B. (2011). The impact of enhancing students' social and emotional learning: A meta-analysis of school-based universal interventions. *Child Development, 82*(1), 405–432.

Elias, M. J., Leverett, L., Duffell, J. C., Humphrey, N., Stepney, C., & Ferrito, J. (2015). Integrating SEL with related prevention and youth development approaches. In J. A. Durlak, C. E. Domitrovich, R. P. Weissberg, & T. P. Gullotta (eds.), (2017), *Handbook of social and emotional learning: Research and practice* (Paperback edn, pp. 33–49). New York: Guilford Press.

European Commission. (2010). *Europe 2020: A strategy for smart, sustainable and inclusive growth: Communication from the commission.* Publications Office of the European Union.

Goldspink, C., & Foster, M. (2013). A conceptual model and set of instruments for measuring student engagement in learning. *Cambridge Journal of Education, 43*(3), 291–311.

Goddard, R. D., Hoy, W. K., & Hoy, A. W. (2000). Collective teacher efficacy: Its meaning, measure, and impact on student achievement. *American Educational Research Journal, 37*(2), 479–507.

Gutman, L., & Schoon, I. (2013). The impact of non-cognitive skills on outcomes for young people: Literature review. *Education Endowment Foundation.*

Haddon, A., Goodman, H., Park, J., & Deakin-Crick, R. (2005). Evaluating EL in schools: The development of the school emotional environment for learning survey. *Pastoral Care, December, 2005.*

Hatzichristou, C., & Lianos, P. G. (2016). Social and emotional learning in the Greek educational system: An Ithaca journey. *The International Journal of Emotional Education, 8*(2), 105–127.

Heckman, J. J., & Kautz, T. (2012). Hard evidence on soft skills. *Labour economics, 19*(4), 451–464.

Humphrey, N. (2013). *Social and emotional learning: A critical appraisal.* Washington, DC: Sage.

Jennings, P. A., & Frank, J.L. (2015). Inservice preparation for educators. In J. A. Durlak, C. E. Domitrovich, R. P. Weissberg, & T. P. Gullotta (eds.) (2017), *Handbook of social and emotional learning: Research and practice* (Paperback edn., pp. 422–437). New York: Guilford Press.

Gershon, P., & Pellitteri, J. (2018). Promoting Emotional Intelligence in preschool education: A review of progams. *International Journal of Emotional Education, 10*(2), 26–41.

Gilbert, L., Rose, J., & McGuire-Snieckus, R. (2014). Promoting children's well-being and sustainable citizenship through emotion coaching. *A child's world: Working together for a better future. Aberystwyth, UK: Aberystwyth Press. Google Scholar.*

Jones, S. M., & Kahn, J. (2017). The evidence base for how we learn: Supporting students' social, emotional, and academic development. *The WERA Educational Journal, 10*(1), 5–20.

Klapp, A., Belfield, C., Bowden, B., Levin, H., Shand, R., & Zander, S. (2017). A Benefit-Cost Analysis of a Long-Term Intervention on Social and Emotional Learning in Compulsory School. *International Journal of Emotional Education, 9*(1), 3–19.

Klassen, R. M., & Tze, V. M. (2014). Teachers' self-efficacy, personality, and teaching effectiveness: A meta-analysis. *Educational Research Review, 12,* 59–76.

Leventhal, K., Andrew, G., Collins, C., DeMaria, L., Singh, H., & Leventhal, S. (2018). Training School Teachers to promote metnal and social well-being in low and middle income countries: Lessons to facilitate scale-up from a participatory action research trial of *Youth First* in India. *International Journal of Emotional Education, 10*(2), 42–58.

Martin, A. (2002). Motivation and academic resilience: Developing a model for student enhancement. *Australian journal of education, 46*(1), 34–49.

Moutsios, S. (2010). Power, politics and transnational policy-making in education. *Globalisation, Societies and Education, 8*(1), 121–141.

Panayiotou, M., & Humphrey, N. (2018). Mental health difficulties and academic attainment: Evidence for gender-specific developmental cascades in middle childhood. *Development and psychopathology, 30*(2), 523–538.

Perera, H. N., Vosicka, L., Granziera, H., & McIlveen, P. (2018). Towards an integrative perspective on the structure of teacher work engagement. *Journal of Vocational Behavior, 108,* 28–41.

Reeves, J., & Le Mare, L. (2017). Supporting Teachers in Relational Pedagogy and Social Emotional Education: A Qualitative Exploration. *International Journal of Emotional Education, 9*(1), 85–98.

Reynolds, A., Temple, J. A., Ou, S., Arteaga, I. A., & White, B. A. B. (2011). School-based early childhood education and age-28 well-being: Effects by timing, dosage, and subgroups. *Science, 333*(6040), 360-364.

Seligman, M. E., Ernst, R. M., Gillham, J., Reivich, K., & Linkins, M. (2009). Positive education: Positive psychology and classroom interventions. *Oxford review of education, 35*(3), 293–311.

Skinner, E., Furrer, C., Marchand, G., & Kindermann, T. (2008). Engagement and disaffection in the classroom: Part of a larger motivational dynamic? *Journal of educational psychology, 100*(4), 765.

Sklad, M., Diekstra, R., Ritter, M. D., Ben, J., & Gravesteijn, C. (2012). Effectiveness of school-based universal social, emotional, and behavioral programs: Do they enhance students' development in the area of skill, behavior, and adjustment? *Psychology in the Schools, 49*(9), 892–909.

Taylor, R., Oberle, E., Durlak, J., & Weissberg, R. (2017). Promoting Positive Youth Development through school-based social and emotional learning interventions: A meta-analysis of follow-up effects. *Child Development, 88*(4), 1156–1171.

Ungar, M., & Liebenberg, L. (2013). Ethnocultural factors, resilience, and school engagement. *School Psychology International, 34*(5), 514–526.

Weare, K. (2015). *What works in promoting social and emotional well-being and responding to mental health problems in schools.* London: National Children's Bureau.

Weare, K. & Gray, G. (2003) *What works in developing children's emotional and social competence and wellbeing?* DfES Research Report No 456.

Werner, E., & Smith, R. (1979). A report from the Kauai Longitudinal Study. *Child and Adolescent Psychiatry, 18*(2), 292–306.

Zinsser, K. M., Shewark, E. A., Denham, S. A., & Curby, T. W. (2014). A mixed-method examination of preschool teacher beliefs about social–emotional learning and relations to observed emotional support. *Infant and Child Development, 23*(5), 471–493.

Sian Templeton is a Senior Lecturer in Education at the University of Gloucestershire and a practicing Educational Psychologist working with teaching staff, children, young people and their families. She has worked in a variety of educational settings with a focus on supporting the social, emotional and cognitive needs of vulnerable learners to enable them to engage with education. She achieved this through working directly with the young people, with the families, teaching staff and a range of professionals from health and social care. In addition to direct work, she also believes in exploring more systemic opportunities for promoting and supporting access to education for all. She teaches on both Undergraduate and Postgraduate courses within her University role across a range of areas within education and leads on a number of psychology-based education modules. She is involved in ERASMUS + projects related to her areas of interest. Sian's research includes resilience, emotional education and supporting young offenders in re-engaging with education and she is just commencing her DEdPsy at University College London.

Adeela ahmed Shafi has a background in psychology and education and has been teaching in higher education for over 17 years. Her research draws on psychological theories to explore how to re-engage young offenders with formal education and learning in a secure custodial setting. Adeela's other research includes how to develop academic resilience and buoyancy in higher education students. She has also worked on international projects in Rwanda and Pakistan as well as an EU project on emotional education. Adeela has recently won two EU bids of 3 years duration, each running parallel. The first is on re-engaging young offenders with education and learning with three European partners. The second is a project designed to develop social and emotional competencies through active games in young people in conflict with the law. This is with ten partner across seven European partners. Adeela has an established publishing profile and leads the REF submission for Education at the University of Gloucestershire. Adeela is an active community worker and also stood for MP in 2010.

Rebecca Pritchard is an Educational Psychologist who has also undertaken a Senior Lecturer role in Education at the University of Gloucestershire. She has worked in numerous settings encompassing early years through secondary education including specialist provision. She has been fortunate to develop a career that has enabled a focus on her particular interests of early years, resilience, autism and mental health through both local authority provision and private practice. Research interests have included a European study on emotional education and she is beginning her DEdPsy at the University College London. From supporting individuals and families with specific needs to the design and provision of training for professionals, teaching on Undergraduate and Postgraduate courses, Rebecca continues to develop her understanding and expertise across this fascinating subject.

Chapter 11
Young Offenders and the Complexity of Re-Engaging Them with Education and Learning Whilst Incarcerated: A Case Study

Adeela ahmed Shafi

Abstract This chapter draws on research on re-engaging young offenders with education and learning in a secure custodial setting in England as a case study to examine the range of complex and interacting factors that shape the educational experiences of young offenders. It uses the Dynamic Interactive Model of Resilience (DIMoR) (ahmed Shafi., 2020) as an analytical framework to consider the risk-protective/vulnerability-invulnerability matrix against the backdrop of the micro, meso, exo and macrosystems, which structure the experiences of the young people. In so, doing this chapter illustrates how the DIMoR can provide an opportunity to consider a system wide approach to interventions which can support their success.

Introduction

As discussed throughout this book resilience is a multi-dimensional, domain and context specific construct (Masten, 2018). Resilience has been the focus of research across many disciplines ranging from engineering to psychological resilience; community and organisational resilience to educational resilience, each with their own sub-disciplines. This demonstrates the versatility and importance of the concept but also runs the risk of meaning everything and therefore nothing (Brown, 2015). As a concept that is currently 'in vogue', it also runs the risk of having 'buzzword' status, viewed as a silver bullet for a multitude of problems. We have thus argued elsewhere in this book how resilience is a complex construct and put forward the case for a particular approach to resilience (see Chap. 2) which addresses some of these issues to a certain extent. In this Chapter, resilience is explored in a very specific context and with a very specific group of learners: young offenders in a secure custodial context. This is because in addition to complex and challenging backgrounds, there is considerable evidence that experiences of education and formal learning for young

A. ahmed Shafi (✉)
School of Education and Humanities, University of Gloucestershire, Cheltenham, UK
e-mail: ashafi@glos.ac.uk

© Springer Nature Switzerland AG 2020
A. ahmed Shafi et al. (eds.), *Reconsidering Resilience in Education*,
https://doi.org/10.1007/978-3-030-49236-6_11

people who come into conflict with the law tend to have been disruptive and unful-filling (Cripps & Summerfield, 2012; Little, 2015). Many of them become disengaged and disaffected early in their educational careers (Hirschfield & Gasper, 2011; Kirk & Sampson, 2013; Graham, Van Bergen, & Sweller, 2015). Many also have other education related adversities, which place them at even greater risk of education failure. The educational 'failure' is indicated through the 9 out of 10 young people in custody who have dropped out of school before being incarcerated (Little, 2015) with dropout being an indicator of disengagement (Rumberger & Rotermund, 2012; Kirk & Sampson, 2013). Thus, young people in custody have a number of risk factors for which a dynamic, complex systems approach is required to re-engage them with education and learning.

This chapter considers the significance of the secure educational context and its interaction with wider contexts to understand how best to foster resilience in incar-cerated young people. Wang (2012) first discussed resilience with a focus on educa-tional contexts in the 1990s, as interest in disadvantaged children and young people with adverse life experiences and circumstances such as poverty, poor housing, poor employment opportunities, poor health care or exposure to crime and addictions, indicated that they were at an increased risk of educational failure. She defined educational resilience as 'the heightened likelihood of educational success despite personal vulnerabilities and adversities brought about by environmental conditions and experiences (Wang, Haertel, & Walberg, 1994, p. 4). Wang et al. were inter-ested in how children and young people at risk succeeded in education, despite their adverse circumstances. Young people who come into conflict with the law have a series of these disadvantages and adverse life circumstances and the evidence suggests that they have not been able to overcome them to succeed in education. The Dynamic Interactive Model of Resilience (DIMoR) introduced in Chap. 2 is used as an analytical framework to examine the wide range of interactive (and competing) factors which can affect the educational resilience of young people serving custodial sentences.

Understanding the Circumstances of Young People in Conflict with the Law

Family breakdown, lower socioeconomic status, education attainment, learning diffi-culties and mental health are all circumstances that can impact learning. As many as 34% of boys and 61% girls in conflict with the law reported being in the care of the local authority at some point (Murray, 2012; Kennedy, 2013). Other research by Jacobson, Bhardwa, Gyateng, Hunter and Hough (2010) found that 76% of young people who offended had an absent father and 33% had an absent mother. The same study also found that over 51% had come from deprived or unsuitable accommoda-tion. Young people who offend are also more likely to have parents who have been incarcerated (Farrington, Ttofi, Crago, & Coid, 2015) and more likely to have been exposed to drugs and alcohol abuse (Manly, Oshri, Lynch, Herzog & Wortel, 2013).

Further, half of the 15–17 year olds entering custody have levels of literacy equivalent to that expected of primary age children of 7–11 years (Education Funding Agency, 2012). This may be because 86%-90% of 15–17-year-old boys and 74% girls coming into custody have been excluded from school at some point and many (36% boys and 41% girls) had not been to school since they were 14 years old (Murray, 2012; Little, 2015). As well as the lack of attendance or being excluded, young people who find themselves in custody are also likely to have higher levels of learning disabilities (Williams et al., 2015) with a prevalence of 23–32%, the figure is 2–4% in the general population (Hughes 2012). Such circumstances would reflect a number of the risk factors for educational resilience. The imbalance of risk and protective factors around children in these circumstances contribute to them coming into conflict with the law and subsequent incarceration (Farrington, Ttofi, & Piquero, 2016).

Factors that Promote Educational Resilience

As discussed in Chap. 2, it is possible to mitigate against risk factors for resilience by developing and promoting protective factors. These protective factors come in a range of guises and these are based on individuals as well as environmental conditions. The resilience research in the psychological literature has given much credence to the importance of these protective factors as a way to develop resilience in at-risk children. Consequently, there has been a plethora of research in this area (e.g. Luthar, 2006; Masten 2001, 2007; Wright et al., 2013) and remarkably the range of these protective factors have remained fairly stable over the last two decades of research (Masten, 2015). Protective factors include within-child factors and the interaction of a range of environmental factors. This 'short list' (Masten, 2015) of protective factors include effective caregiving/parenting and close relationships with other capable adults, intelligence and problem-solving skills, self—regulation, direction and agency, optimism and hope. These protective factors may be organised at several levels depending on their proximity to the child and often arranged within the ecological model (Bronfenbrenner, 1979) in terms of the micro and macro systems that support resilience i.e. family, school/community and culture/society.

For the purposes of this book, we are largely interested in the importance of the educational context. Schools, as educational settings, have been shown to be a protective factor from some of the earliest resilience research even before the educational resilience literature came into the fore (e.g. Werner, 1993). For example, the school environment nurtures many of the adaptive systems in the individual that foster the development of resilience. This includes an environment that helps the development of caring and nurturing relationships—in some cases replacing that which is not provided within the family context. This has been even more important for children from disadvantaged backgrounds who are at high risk of school dropout (Doll et al.,

2013). Teachers can also promote engagement in the classroom which can prevent children from dropping out of school (Goldspink & Foster, 2013). Schools and educational settings represent a sense of stability and continuity for some children who may come from chaotic family backgrounds (Barnert et al., 2015). Indeed Henderson (2012) highlight how teachers that provide a caring and supportive environment, have high expectations and create opportunities for participation which foster resilience in children at risk.

In creating nurturing and supportive environments, (turnaround) teachers (and schools) can create the conditions to develop motivation, efficacy and agency, all of which are also protective factors. The body of research on the importance of school and its protective factors has been conducted using a range of methodologies and generally, come to similar conclusions regards the role of the school. A more recent paper from Downey (2014) decided to take the perspective of children in understanding the factors that promote educational resilience. She found that the 50 children in her study described eight factors that fostered educational resilience. These were intelligence, feelings, behaviours, home environment, family assistance, school support, community connections and organized programs that improved their academic performance. These do not differ so much from the extant literature in this area.

However, the children in Downey's study, whilst described as facing serious life difficulties were still attending school and presented as fairly engaged. As mentioned earlier, young people in conflict with the law have already disengaged from education and often dropped out, therefore this aspect has already failed them. We would also be mindful that school can also become a risk factor when it does not engender the qualities of an effective school (see Chap. 4). Hence, the need to foster the protective elements of schools within a custodial setting where they are still entitled to 30 h of education provision per week. However, this comes with its own challenges as the secure custodial setting is not a replica of a mainstream school or even that of alternative provision (ahmed Shafi, 2018a). These include the fact that the secure setting is primarily punitive in nature rather than educational which shapes the culture and environment of the setting (see Case (2018) for a discussion on the welfare vs justice debate). Nevertheless, despite its challenges, it also has opportunities. For example, the students are there full-time and the risks of innovation or trying something new are less because the pressure of achieving exams and qualifications is more relaxed (ahmed Shafi, 2019). Further, the young people are also cared for under the same roof, so effectively you have the 'family' and 'educators' in the same place meaning greater opportunity for continuity of approach, or indeed greater tension as educators and carers focus on different priorities (Andow, 2016; ahmed Shafi, 2018b). However, it is important to get a better understanding of how this may happen in reality by understanding the secure and locked environment of a custodial setting for young people.

The Educational Context in Custodial Settings

Secure Youth Provision in England and Wales

The type and form of custody and secure accommodation for young people in conflict with the law has changed shape and form ever since the first structure for youthful offenders, Parkhurst Prison on the Isle of Wight in 1838 was built. Most of the structures and forms of custody reflect the dominant political and ideological debates of the time (McAra, 2010). Currently, in the UK, there three main types of custody for children and young people and are typically dependent on age. Young people aged 10–15 years are placed in Secure Children's Homes (SCH), those over 15 are usually placed in Young Offender Institutions (YOI) or Secure Training Centres (STC) for a Detention and Training Order (DTO). In a DTO, offenders spend half their sentence in a secure setting and the remainder in the community, supervised by a Youth Offending Team[1] (YOT). There are currently circa 900 young people under 18 in custodial settings (Youth Justice Board, 2018a, 2018b) with approximately 605 young people in YOIs, 171 in STCs and 100 in SCHs.

Education Provision in Custodial Settings

The Ministry of Justice (2013) states that a period in custody represents the structure and boundaries which many young people in conflict with the law, have not experienced in their lives. A good quality educational experience can form the basis of this structure (Ministry of Justice, 2013). However, research on education within the secure context is not plentiful (Hart, 2015) and much of it is focused on specific education interventions rather than the overall approach to education provision.

Challenges in the education of young people whilst in a secure setting are copious. They include: navigating a youth justice system with both welfare and punitive elements; individual challenges, such as emotional, behavioural or learning difficulties; previous (negative) educational experiences; complex social backgrounds; a lack of educational records; constrained resources and; a workforce who may not be qualified as teachers or trained to the needs of young people in custody (Jeanes et al., 2009). Research by Smeet (2014) from the Netherlands and Ball and Connolly (2000) in England illustrated the challenges centred around patchy previous educational records as young people entered the secure estate. The UK Office for Standards in Education (OFSTED) also identified that many establishments described considerable difficulty in accessing documentation from schools, local authorities or other professionals and in some instances the information did not exist at all

---

[1] A youth offending team is a multi-agency team and are co-ordinated by local authorities in England and Wales. The YOT works with young people in conflict with the law as they go through the youth justice system with a view to supporting the young person and preventing reoffending.

(King, 2015). This results in education within youth justice that cannot be seamlessly picked up from the previous institution/s, nor respond to any additional needs without conducting full assessments on arrival of the young person at the secure unit.

There were a number of reasons for the difficulty in accessing information, including that many young people who offend have not been in school for some time (Smeet, 2014; Little, 2015) and the most recent schools were not especially proactive in forwarding educational records nor were they up to date (Ball & Connolly, 2000; Smeet, 2014). Again, there are a range of reasons for this, such as schools removing a perpetually absent child's name from the register to avoid skewing their data—recently termed 'off-rolling' (Danechi, 2019). Whatever the reason, considerable time is consequently spent on ascertaining educational levels before devising an education plan and if the sentence is short, the time is potentially wasted. Such challenges risk educational interventions whilst in custody being applied as a 'blunt instrument' without consideration of the specific needs, education level or background prior to incarceration. These circumstances create yet another adverse set of circumstances that may be considered as risk factors for developing resilience.

Furthermore, previous research has suggested that education and training in custody is fragmented and of a lower quality than mainstream schooling (Frolander-Ulf & Yates, 2001) holding a marginal status in custodial settings (Jones & d'Errico, 1994). 'Instructors' rather than qualified teachers are more likely to be employed as prison educators, contributing to the marginal status and high staff turnover (Jeanes, McDonald, & Simonot, 2009). Staff do not always see the fruits of their efforts as students move on and the education or training may not continue, thus teacher expectations can also be low (Houchins, et al., 2010). This means that the literature which supports education settings as protective factors for resilience, due to the relationships that may be developed, is thwarted. This is further compounded by the transient nature of setting and the desire or focus to achieve is somewhat diminished from both the teacher and pupil perspective (Sander, Sharkey, Olivarri, Tanigawa, & Mauseth, 2010). Consequently, educational aspirations are limited (Stephen & Squires, 2003; Oser, 2006). These are all conditions that do not facilitate protective factors for resilience that are associated with educational settings.

The complexity of these circumstances do not lend themselves to educational resilience or success despite adversity. Thus, whilst it was mentioned earlier that the secure custodial setting offers opportunities, these come with considerable obstacles. A first step in facilitating the opportunities afforded is an understanding of the multifariousness of the context, the dynamic and interactive nature of it in order to suggest ways of fostering educational resilience within it. We can, however, draw on ahmed Shafi et al. (2020) DIMoR (presented in Chap. 2) as a starting point in understanding the context. Combined with some recent research on re-engaging young people in secure educational settings, we can create a rich picture of the setting and the areas which can be focused on to develop the conditions for educational resilience within the setting. This may seem an ambitious task given the discussions in the chapter so far. However, if we are to work towards mitigating negative early experiences of these young children, then we need to be serious about understanding where they are, where they came from and where they are likely to go. Resilience is important not only for life in general, but particularly in helping the young people transition from custody to the community. Developing educational resilience is important, especially as those who engage in education whilst in custody are also likely to continue when back in the community (Lanskey, 2015). However, as young people in custody are generally disengaged with education and learning, this creates its own particular issues and require specific strategies for re-engagement. This can contribute to resilience in order to persist and succeed, despite the adversities both whilst incarcerated and in transitioning back to the community.

Adopting the DIMoR in Custodial Settings to Foster Resilience

The DIMoR

The DIMoR, which is the focus of Chap. 2 in this book, was developed by ahmed Shafi et al. (2020) by building upon existing and well-established models of resilience. In this newly built DIMoR, resilience is an emergent property of risk-protective/vulnerability-invulnerability and for this reason, we present resilience as emerging from the reciprocal interactions of these factors. Resilience is thus context and domain specific, based on Ungar's (2013) principles of equifinality, differential impact and cultural moderation as well as Downes' (2017) notion of agency, all encased within Bronfenbrenner's (1979) ecological model of human development. The result is presented as the image in the figure below, which aims to encompass the key ideas from these models in all their complexity. It demonstrates the complex, multidimensional, dynamic, interactive, context and domain specific nature of resilience that emerges from the interaction of all these properties.

The DIMoR Applied to Secure Custodial Settings

The DIMoR can be applied to secure custodial settings as it can to any other setting in order to understand the complexity of resilience as an emergent property, both at an individual and organisational level. The model can help to conceptualise the various actors and structures within the secure setting that can affect individual resilience. The case study in the next section shows how peers, staff and the context play a key role in their behaviour (social and emotional) in custody (and probably beyond). Understanding this complexity is useful in planning and developing a resilience-fostering environment (see below a visual version of the DIMoR).

The ecological system represented by the 'spider web-like' structure in the DIMoR demonstrates the interconnectedness of the various ecosystems. The microsystem in the case of the secure custodial setting consists of the staff (care, education and

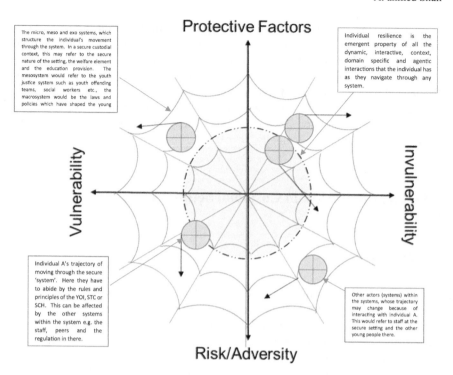

Protective Factors

The micro, meso and exo systems, which structure the individual's movement through the system. In a secure custodial context, this may refer to the secure nature of the setting, the welfare element and the education provision. The mesosystem would refer to the youth justice system such as youth offending teams, social workers etc., the macrosystem would be the laws and policies which have shaped the young

Individual resilience is the emergent property of all the dynamic, interactive, context, domain specific and agentic interactions that the individual has as they navigate through any system.

Vulnerability

Invulnerability

Individual A's trajectory of moving through the secure 'system'. Here they have to abide by the rules and principles of the YOI, STC or SCH. This can be affected by the other systems within the system e.g. the staff, peers and the regulation in there.

Other actors (systems) within the systems, whose trajectory may change because of interacting with individual A. This would refer to staff at the secure setting and the other young people there.

Risk/Adversity

Fig. 11.1 The Dynamic Interactive Model of Resilience (DIMoR) as applied to a secure custodial setting

specialist staff), the peers at the secure setting, the secure, the locked physical environment of the setting *and* the interactions of these with the young person. The mesosystem refers to the interactions between those in the microsystem, particular the staff at the setting but also other external agencies which may not directly interact with the young person. This could include YOTs, onward or previous educational establishments, doctors, lawyers and so on. Their interactions affect the young person, for example, if a YOT is unable to place the young person for when released in a timely and appropriate place, the uncertainty affects the young person's behaviour (Lanskey, 2015). The macrosystem features include wider laws, policies or the media that shape the experiences of all within the secure context. For example, a high profile case that is covered in the media means the secure setting needs to take measures to protect the young person's identity at the secure unit. The macrosystem is affected by the wider cultural approach to young people who offend and has shaped the tensions surrounding what is known as the welfare-justice debate on youth offending (see Haines and Case, 2015 for a discussion on this). This has shaped how the youth justice system is primarily characterised by a punitive approach, manifested in the secure locked nature of custodial settings and the welfare approach due to the age of the young people (Fig. 11.1).

If one is to view the secure custodial setting as a system, it is possible to begin to identify the risk-protective factors and the vulnerability-invulnerability aspects within the system. An example of a risk factor is the transient nature of the young people and indeed the staff turnover at the setting that prevents the development of relationships. Relationship have consistently shown to be an important protective factor for resilience (e.g. Luthar, 2015) and the challenge of developing ans sustaining them can be challenging. A vulnerability of the secure setting is the changing policy landscape to which the setting has to continually respond. For example, a change in policy with regards to first-time entrants (FTEs) into the youth justice system through diversionary measures or the use of restorative justice has resulted in a significant drop in young people in custody (Bateman, 2014). This meant that the youth estate shrunk significantly, meaning children were being sent to secure settings far from their home. This again acts a risk factor to maintaining relationships with family and home networks, which have been shown to be effective in rehabilitation (O'Neill et al., 2018). Nevertheless, a protective factor could emerge from the secure and '24 hr' presence of the young people at the setting where there is an opportunity for relationships between young people and the staff as well as peers to be fostered and nurtured. Education provision at the setting is another opportunity to develop a protective factor because it can foster a sense of purpose and future. However, at the same time, an invulnerability is the rigid rules and secure regime, which restrict and structure both physical movement and autonomy—risk factors in resilience.

Ungar's (2013) notion of equifinality helps us to understand how in some circumstances one system or another can become more influential to the outcome, for example the environmental context can have a considerable impact on the young person in custody. However, within the education space at the secure setting it is possible to enable individual factors and relationships to become more important. This is illustrated through ahmed Shafi et al. (2020) DIMoR model by the shaded circles (orbs) which represent individuals within a system. Each orb (A) is an individual, navigating the secure custodial setting as the broader system. Each orb as a system in itself also has its own DIMoR with risk-protective factors/vulnerability-invulnerability, all embedded within the individual's own ecosystem. In the figure above, individual A's trajectory is shown as it moves through the secure setting 'system'. Here the individual has to abide by the rules and principles as they do their time, but is shaped and influenced by the other systems within the system e.g. the staff, peers and the regulation in there (the spider web-like structure). If A has a challenge with one of the staff/peers (other systems), this can have an impact on them in that they may be withdrawn from activities and possibly even affect their sentence, which can then affect their own trajectory. This can be illustrated in the DIMoR where the interaction with the system or other individuals in the system can alter trajectories of one or all in the interaction and therefore their emergent resilience. Thus, an individual does not unproblematically move through systems but the interactions can change trajectories. As Downes (2017) suggested, interaction with others and agency can shape that movement for the individual and even other individuals. In some instances an individual can even change the broader system by campaigning for change or even through the occurrence of tragedy (such as a death in custody). The following section describes an ethnographic case study of young people in custody that aimed to re-engage them with education and learning. It serves to illustrate some of these interactions in a real context.

An Ethnographic Case Study

An ethnographic case study conducted over two main phases in one secure children's home in England aimed to re-engage young people with education and learning whilst in custody (ahmed Shafi, 2018a, b, 2019). Phase I explored how young people in secure custodial settings perceived education, school and learning in relation to their own lives. Phase II was concerned with exploring the nature of engagement in young people with education and learning within the secure context, consisting of case studies of 5 participants, involving the use of Authentic Inquiry (AI) (Crick 2009, 2012) as a means to re-engage them. AI was developed as a pedagogical model, placing the learner at the centre, typically starting with a concrete place, object or experience that is of importance to the learner. Through the process, this can develop into, for example, a product such as a poster, presentation, artwork, essay, poem which can be assessed for English, Maths or Art. AI offers a way to connect the participant's own interest and knowledge creation with formal education and has been shown to appeal to disengaged learners (Jaros & Crick, 2007). The process provided a framework for data collection at various points offering insight into the nature of engagement in this particular group. The findings of this research and associated methodological and ethical challenges are discussed elsewhere (see ahmed Shafi, 2018a, b, 2019) and for this chapter, the study is used to illustrate how the DIMoR could be used to support the setting to enable resilience to emerge—despite its challenges.

Using authentic inquiry, it was possible to re-engage all the young people involved in the case studies, representing varying levels of resilience i.e. success despite the adversities of the context. However, this was to different degrees and much of the challenges were down to the secure context and the difficulties it presented for each of the young people. It demonstrated how the secure context was a defining feature in the education and learning of young people in custody (ahmed Shafi, 2019). The figure below summarises the conditions that in resilience terms acted as risk and protective factors in order to facilitate or hinder engagement (Fig. 11.2).

A context of autonomy enabled the young people to feel they could express themselves in terms of their own interests and choices and featured as important for re-engagement. A supportive mentor emerged as an essential protective factor in creating the context of autonomy despite the secure setting. They were also vital in enabling the access to resources, such as the internet, books or stationary and time to engage in their authentic inquiry. However, the absence of or a poor mentor also acted as a risk factor. Task value is a term associated with the expectancy-value theory ((Eccles & Wigfield, 2002) and is based on the degree to which one expects to succeed (expectancy) and the value one places on the task itself (value). In the case

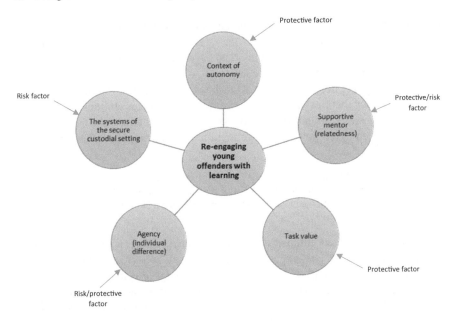

Fig. 11.2 The conditions which can act as protective and risk factors for resilience in engaging with education in a secure custodial setting

studies task value was an important protective factor for the individual to engage, however, task value alone was insufficient. For example, the lack of a supportive mentor meant that the resources and support needed for continued engagement were absent and so the task had no value.

All participants demonstrated agency by agreeing to participate. However, agency was demonstrated to varying degrees and, depended on the other conditions being favourable. The organisational features compounded by the locked and secure nature of this environment presented as a major risk factor to re-engaging young offenders with education and learning and these represented challenges that were difficult for some of the young people to overcome. The DIMoR model presented by ahmed Shafi et al. (2020) provides a useful framework to be able to visualise some of these structures and interaction. This is embodied in the case of Jeremy, which illustrates some of these conditions.

The Case of Jeremy

The case of Jeremy who was one of the five case studies and illustrates these conditions in the context of the DIMoR model. Jeremy was 16 years old born in Britain and of mixed European heritage. He was serving a long-term sentence (18 + months) for manslaughter with no previous known offence. Staff described Jeremy as polite and generally non-disruptive but arrogant and un-cooperative, though never aggressive; intelligent, but not engaged with the education provision, often refusing to answer questions, participate in activities and daydreaming. Jeremy had dropped out of school well before he was convicted.

Once Jeremy had decided that the AI task was of value, relevant to him (his AI was on conspiracy theories) and he was already confident in his abilities, Jeremy was engaged and he was resilient to the setbacks that occurred due to the constraints of the setting. When asked how he was getting on after starting his authentic inquiry, his response was:

> It's going very well! I'm almost finished [...] and I'm researching on the internet about conspiracy theories and trying to find some way to put it into something like a workbook or some sort of documentation so I can explain to people, I guess, but I'm just trying to get it organised. (Jeremy, aged 16)

Jeremy demonstrated enthusiasm, passion, agency, effort, action and planning with an awareness of challenges—all indicators of behavioural and emotional engagement as per Skinner et al. (2008) model of engagement. Reeve and Tseng (2011) point out, learners do not just react to learning, but pro-act too. Jeremy demonstrated that he was pro-active which was the driving force in shaping his learning, resulting in his actions being intentional, proactive and constructive—indicators of engagement and acted as the agentic element needed for him to be resilient and shape his trajectory and in some ways change the system as he demanded time with his mentor. Jeremy's engagement with his authentic inquiry demonstrated that even a disengaged, disillusioned and disaffected learner can be re-engaged with education and learning within a relatively short space of time. That Jeremy could navigate a range of setbacks in order to achieve his aims was evident and reflects Downes' (2017) view of individual agency and appraisal of a situation which depended on the relational space.

However, whilst Jeremy engaged for a relatively long while, he was still a fragile learner and experienced barriers (risks) which challenged his resilience. Initially, driven by excitement, he was able to overcome these, however persistent setbacks impacted him emotionally. For example, he felt embarrassed when he could not fulfil what he believed to be his obligation and therefore he disengaged in the process and was not able to navigate (be resilient) the structural constraints for much longer. This reflects Ungar's (2013) notion of equifinality whereby in certain circumstances one system or another can be more influential to the outcome. At one point, it was the opportunity to engage and then it was the limitations of the secure system. Jeremy's frustrations were directed at the Head Teacher as the authority figure, demonstrating his awareness of the structure of the context that had prevented him from persevering. Teachers and Head Teachers also pointed to the context, its systems and structures as a key challenge in offering the opportunities needed to engage or maintain engagement of their pupils. The invulnerability and rigidity of the secure system had made it challenging for Jeremy. Combined with his own individual vulnerability in terms of his desire to appear successful, this became a risk factor. Whilst the opportunity to engage with a genuine learning opportunity was a protective factor, combined with the relationship with his mentor, the risk factors became too great and hence Jeremy's emergent resilience was not sufficient for him to feel that he had succeeded. Jeremy thus abandoned the authentic inquiry and disengaged. This illustrates the notion of the differential impact in Ungar's work where different factors can have different impacts in different contexts. Jeremy's case also illustrated how he had attempted to be autonomous and agentic and show resilience in his learning, however he was overcome by the invulnerability of the setting and his own vulnerability. This case demonstrated how an individual can be resilient but that they can also be worn down by cumulative and perpetual risk factors. Using the DIMoR model could have enabled the setting to map out the risk and protective factors and consider what can be fostered/overcome within the structures of those aspects that cannot be changed. This could have enabled a holistic and system view of the situation that Jeremy was in so that his emerging resilience may have been further developed. Instead, it was quashed.

The DIMoR in Practice

The DIMoR offers a way to map the risk-protective/vulnerability-invulnerability factors within any particular context. This enables an organisation to assess which areas they may be able to focus upon in order to foster educational resilience even within a secure custodial setting. It enables an organisation to consider both its own organisational features as well as other external systems that it also interacts with. In doing so, it provides an opportunity for leaders to consider how and where interventions may be best targeted. For example, one of the biggest risks in the case of Jeremy was the lack of being timetabled to work with his mentor and access resources. This was due to the line management issues between education and care staff. Creating a more coherent and unified approach could eradicate this problem and facilitate the relationships, the absence of which are a risk factor in resilience. This enables the protective relationship to detect and respond to individual vulnerabilities so they do not obstruct the learner. At the same time, this would address the invulnerabilities of the overall organisation and what can be done to manage this, whilst complying with their external obligations as a custodial youth justice setting.

In using the approach suggested by ahmed Shafi et al. (2020) DIMoR approach a setting is enabled in examining some of the complexities of their organisation, its structures and how all these interact with the people in the system and other systems. In doing so, it is possible to create a rich picture of the range of dynamic interactive systems in any given setting and how these may be maximised (or minimised) through the use of 'intelligent' interventions. At present many interventions are employed without due regard to the complexity of the systems within which they are to be used and then all too quickly discarded or credited with having made a difference without fully understanding how it has worked/not worked. Using the DIMoR model can enable a secure custodial setting to maximise the time that young people have in custody and the opportunities that it can afford in terms of re-engaging them with education and learning.

Conclusion

This chapter has considered how the dynamic interactive model of resilience proposed by ahmed Shafi et al. (2020) built on the established ideas and theories of Gilligan (2004), Ungar (2013), Bronfenbrenner (1979) and Downes (2017) can help identify the dynamic interactions of organisational and individual risk-protective factors. This provides the opportunity to position them as they are, situated within the secure custodial system, wider systems of youth justice, policy and wider still, cultural contexts. This enables one to build a much more complete and complex picture of any given system and the range of dynamic interactions. In doing so, there is a greater scope for identifying the best form of interventions and at which levels in order to enable young people to develop a resilient approach to life and its challenges.

References

ahmed Shafi, A., Templeton, S., Middleton, T., Millican, R., Vare, P., Pritchard, R. et al. (2020). Towards a dynamic interactive model of resilience (DIMoR) for education and learning contexts. *Emotional and Behavioural Difficulties, 25*(2), 183–198. https://doi.org/10.1080/136 32752.2020.1771923.

ahmed Shafi, A. (2018a). Re-engaging young offenders with education in the secure custodial setting. *Children and Their Education in Secure Accommodation: Interdisciplinary Perspectives of Education, Health and Youth Justice.*

ahmed Shafi, A. (2018b). Researching young offenders: Navigating methodological challenges and reframing ethical responsibilities. *International Journal of Research & Method in Education*, 1–15.

ahmed Shafi, A. (2019). The complexity of disengagement with education and learning: A case study of young offenders in a secure custodial setting in England. *Journal of Education for Students Placed at Risk (JESPAR)*, 1–23.

Andow, C. (2018). Roles and relationships of care and education staff inside a secure children's home. *Children and Their Education in Secure Accommodation: Interdisciplinary Perspectives of Education, Health and Youth Justice. Oxon: Routledge.*

Ball, C., & Connolly, J. (2000). Educationally disaffected young offenders. *British Journal of Criminology, 40*(4), 594–616.

Barnert, E. S., Perry, R., Azzi, V. F., Shetgiri, R., Ryan, G., Dudovitz, R., & Chung, P. J. (2015). Incarcerated youths' perspectives on protective factors and risk factors for juvenile offending: A qualitative analysis. *American Journal of Public Health, 105*(7), 1365–1371.

Bateman, T. (2014). Where has all the youth crime gone? Youth justice in an age of austerity. *Children & Society, 28*(5), 416–424.

Board, Y. J. (2018). Youth justice statistics 2016/17 England and Wales. *Youth Justice Board/Ministry of Justice Statistics Bulletin.*

Bronfenbrenner, U. (1979). *The ecology of human development.* Harvard university press.

Brown, K. (2015). *Resilience.* Development and Global Change: Routledge.

Crick, R. D. (2012). Deep engagement as a complex system: Identity, learning power and authentic enquiry. In *Handbook of research on student engagement* (pp. 675–694). Springer.

Cripps, H., & Summerfield, A. (2012). Resettlement provision for children and young people' and 'The care of looked after children in custody': Findings from two HMIP thematic reviews. *Prison Service Journal, 201*, 31–38.

Danechi, R. L. S (2019) Off-rolling in English schools. House of Commons Library Briefing Paper Number 08444, 10 May 2019. file:///C:/Users/s2112630/Downloads/CBP-8444.pdf. https://dera.ioe.ac.uk/34217/1/CBP-7388%20%28redacted%29.pdf.

Deakin Crick, R. (2009). Pedagogical challenges for personalisation: Integrating the personal with the public through context-driven enquiry. *The Curriculum Journal, 20*(3), 185–189.

Doll, B. (2013). Enhancing resilience in classrooms. In *Handbook of resilience in children* (pp. 399–409). Springer.

Downes, P. (2017). Extended paper: Reconceptualising foundational assumptions of resilience: A cross-cultural, spatial systems domain of relevance for agency and phenomenology in resilience. *International Journal of Emotional Education, 9*(1), 99–120.

Downey, J. A. (2014). Indispensable insight: Children's perspectives on factors and mechanisms that promote educational resilience. *Canadian Journal of Education, 37*(1), 46–71.

Eccles, J. S., & Wigfield, A. (2002). Motivational beliefs, values, and goals. *Annual Review of Psychology, 53*(1), 109–132.

Education Funding Agency. (2012). Internal analysis of admin data, unpublished analysis.

Farrington, D. P., Ttofi, M. M., Crago, R. V., & Coid, J. W. (2015). Intergenerational similarities in risk factors for offending. *Journal of Developmental and Life-Course Criminology, 1*(1), 48–62.

Frolander-Ulf, M., & Yates, M. D. (2001). Teaching in prison. *Monthly Review-New York, 53*(3), 114–127.

Gilligan, R. (2004). Promoting resilience in child and family social work: Issues for social work practice, education and policy. *Social Work Education, 23*(1), 93–104.

Goldspink, C., & Foster, M. (2013). A conceptual model and set of instruments for measuring student engagement in learning. *Cambridge Journal of Education, 43*(3), 291–311.

Graham, L. J., Van Bergen, P., & Sweller, N. (2015). To educate you to be smart': Disaffected students and the purpose of school in the (not so clever)' lucky country. *Journal of Education Policy, 30*(2), 237–257.

Haines, K., & Case, S. (2015). *Positive youth justice: Children first, offenders second*. Policy Press.

Hart, D. (2015). *Correction or care? The use of custody for children in trouble*. London: Churchill Memorial Trust.

Henderson, N. (2012). Resilience in schools and curriculum design. In *The social ecology of resilience* (pp. 297–306). Springer.

Hirschfield, P. J., & Gasper, J. (2011). The relationship between school engagement and delinquency in late childhood and early adolescence. *Journal of Youth and Adolescence, 40*(1), 3–22.

Houchins, D. E., Shippen, M. E., McKeand, K., Viel-Ruma, K., Jolivette, K., & Guarino, A. J. (2010). Juvenile justice teachers' job satisfaction: A comparison of teachers in three states. *Education and Treatment of Children, 33*(4), 623–646.

Hughes, N. (2012). *Nobody made the connection: The prevalence of neurodisability in young people who offend*.

Jacobson, J., Bhardwa, B., Gyateng, T., Hunter, G., & Hough, M. (2010). *Punishing disadvantage-a profile of children in custody*.

Jaros, M., & Deakin-Crick, R. (2007). Personalized learning for the post-mechanical age. *Journal of Curriculum Studies, 39*(4), 423–440.

Jeanes, J., McDonald, J., & Simonot, M. (2009). Conflicting demands in prison education and the need for context-specific, specialist training for prison educators: An account of the work of the initial teacher training project for teachers and instructors in London prisons and offender learning. *Teaching in Lifelong Learning: A Journal to Inform and Improve Practice, 1*(1), 28–35.

Jones, R. L., & d'Errico, P. (1994). The paradox of higher education in prisons. *Higher Education in Prison: A Contradiction in Terms*, 1–16.

Kennedy, A. (2013). Education in custody: Young males' perspectives. *Contemporary Social Science, 8*(2), 104–119.

King, A. (2015). Fostering in England, 2014–15. Retrieved from https://dera.ioe.ac.uk/24918/1/Fostering_in_England_2014-15.pdf.

Kirk, D. S., & Sampson, R. J. (2013). Juvenile arrest and collateral educational damage in the transition to adulthood. *Sociology of Education, 86*(1), 36–62.

Lanskey, C. (2015). Up or down and out? A systemic analysis of young people's educational pathways in the youth justice system in England and Wales. *International Journal of Inclusive Education, 19*(6), 568–582.

Little, R. (2015). Putting education at the heart of custody? The views of children on education in a young offender institution. *British Journal of Community Justice, 13*(2).

Luthar, S. S. (2015). Resilience in development: A synthesis of research across five decades. *Developmental Psychopathology: Volume Three: Risk, Disorder, and Adaptation,* 739–795.

Luthar, S. S., Sawyer, J. A., & Brown, P. J. (2006). Conceptual issues in studies of resilience: Past, present, and future research. *Annals of the New York Academy of Sciences, 1094,* 105.

Manly, J. T., Oshri, A., Lynch, M., Herzog, M., & Wortel, S. (2013). Child neglect and the development of externalizing behavior problems: Associations with maternal drug dependence and neighborhood crime. *Child Maltreatment, 18*(1), 17–29.

Masten, A. S. (2001). Ordinary magic: Resilience processes in development. *American Psychologist, 56*(3), 227.

Masten, A. S. (2007). Resilience in developing systems: Progress and promise as the fourth wave rises. *Development and Psychopathology, 19*(3), 921–930.

Masten, A. S. (2015). Pathways to integrated resilience science. *Psychological Inquiry, 26*(2), 187–196.

Masten, A. S. (2018). Resilience theory and research on children and families: Past, present, and promise. *Journal of Family Theory & Review, 10*(1), 12–31.

McAra, L., & McVie, S. (2010). Youth crime and justice: Key messages from the Edinburgh study of youth transitions and crime. *Criminology & Criminal Justice, 10*(2), 179–209.

Murray, R. (2012). *Children and young people in custody 2011–12: An analysis of the experiences of 15–18 year olds in prison.* Stationery Office.

O'Neill, S. C., Cumming, T. M., Strnadová, I., & Grima-Farrell, C. (2018). Transitions from behind the fence to the community: The Australian experience. In *Incarcerated Youth Transitioning Back to the Community* (pp. 97–113). Springer.

Oser, C. B. (2006). The criminal offending–self-esteem nexus: Which version of the self-esteem theory is supported? *The Prison Journal, 86*(3), 344–363.

Reeve, J., & Tseng, C.-M. (2011). Agency as a fourth aspect of students' engagement during learning activities. *Contemporary Educational Psychology, 36*(4), 257–267.

Rumberger, R. W., & Rotermund, S. (2012). The relationship between engagement and high school dropout. In *Handbook of research on student engagement* (pp. 491–513). Springer.

Sander, J. B., Sharkey, J. D., Olivarri, R., Tanigawa, D. A., & Mauseth, T. (2010). A qualitative study of juvenile offenders, student engagement, and interpersonal relationships: Implications for research directions and preventionist approaches. *Journal of Educational and Psychological Consultation, 20*(4), 288–315.

Skinner, E., Furrer, C., Marchand, G., & Kindermann, T. (2008). Engagement and disaffection in the classroom: Part of a larger motivational dynamic? *Journal of Educational Psychology, 100*(4), 765.

Ungar, M., Ghazinour, M., & Richter, J. (2013). Annual research review: What is resilience within the social ecology of human development? *Journal of Child Psychology and Psychiatry, 54*(4), 348–366.

Wang, M. C., & Gordon, E. W. (2012). *Educational resilience in inner-city America: Challenges and prospects.* Routledge.

Werner, E. E. (1993). Risk, resilience, and recovery: Perspectives from the Kauai Longitudinal Study. *Development and Psychopathology, 5*(4), 503–515.

Werner, E. E. (2000). Protective factors and individual resilience. *Handbook of Early Childhood Intervention, 2,* 115–132.

Williams, H., Hughes, N., Williams, W. H., Chitsabesan, P., Walesby, R. C., Mounce, L. T., & Clasby, B. (2015). The prevalence of traumatic brain injury among young offenders in custody: A systematic review. *Journal of Head Trauma Rehabilitation, 30*(2), 94–105.

Wright, M. O., Masten, A. S., & Narayan, A. J. (2013). Resilience processes in development: Four waves of research on positive adaptation in the context of adversity. In *Handbook of resilience in children* (pp. 15–37). Springer.

Youth Justice Board. (2018). Youth justice statistics 2016/17 England and Wales. *Youth Justice Board/Ministry of Justice Statistics Bulletin.*

Adeela ahmed Shafi MBE is an Associate Professor in Education. She has a background in psychology and education and has been teaching in higher education for over 17 years. Her research draws on psychological theories to explore how to re-engage young offenders with formal education and learning in a secure custodial setting. Adeela's other research includes how to develop academic resilience and buoyancy in higher education students. She has also worked on international projects in Rwanda and Pakistan as well as an EU project on emotional education. Adeela has recently won two EU bids of 3 years duration, each running parallel. The first is on re-engaging young offenders with education and learning with three European partners. The second is a project designed to develop social and emotional competencies through active games in young people in conflict with the law. This is with ten partner across seven European partners. Adeela has an established publishing profile and leads the REF submission for Education at the University of Gloucestershire. Adeela is an active community worker and also stood for MP in 2010

Chapter 12
Developing an Emergent Resilience Through Self-Organised Learning Environments

Jenny Hatley

Abstract Resilience can be seen as an emergent property resulting from reciprocal interactions in complex systems. Self-Organised Learning Environments (SOLE) are a complex system which foster an emergent learning. This chapter considers whether SOLE can be used to also foster an emergent resilience. The internet is a central component of this system but its potential increase in use carries concerns about the additional online risk young people may be exposed to. This chapter discusses the nature of risk aversion and that exposure to some measure of risk is necessary for the development of resilience. Three further factors which are important for the development of resilience are explored which are social capital, a sense of agency and autonomy. These three factors and the exposure to some risk have implications for pedagogy. The use of SOLE to foster these factors, potentially developing both an emergent resilience and an emergent learning, can assist educators when helping young people to develop individual resilience.

Case Study—Using SOLE in Higher Education with 2nd Year Undergraduate Students

During a module on the Education Studies degree course which examined a range of contemporary issues within education, a session was delivered using a Self-Organised Learning Environment (SOLE). Prior to the SOLE, the module itself had taught several skills encouraging the students to take a critical approach to information in the context of issues they had chosen, such as whether there is a gender bias in education, whether school choice is socially just and whether higher education should be free for all. It was hoped that with the freedom and independence afforded by the SOLE pedagogy, that students would utilise their critical skills to look deeply into their topic, achieving lasting learning. However, it was also clear that in general, students of this age found it difficult to take risks in their learning and wanted reassurance and structure to guide them towards the 'right' answer; so it was uncertain whether they would be able to take advantage of, and subsequently experience, all that SOLE promised. Would they be able to work independently, work well together, be critical in their approach and manage their learning without the direct instruction and guidance from the lecturer?

J. Hatley (✉)
Dept. Education & Inclusion, University of Worcester, Henwick Grove, Worcester WR2 6AJ, UK
e-mail: j.hatley@worc.ac.uk

© Springer Nature Switzerland AG 2020
A. ahmed Shafi et al. (eds.), *Reconsidering Resilience in Education*,
https://doi.org/10.1007/978-3-030-49236-6_12

This chapter picks up the concept of resilience discussed in Chap. 2 and focuses on resilience as emerging from reciprocal interactions between and within systems, where the reciprocity can influence the trajectory of individual resilience. In this chapter, the internet is located within the DIMoR's web of ecological systems (ahmed Shafi, et al., 2020) and as such permeates all layers of Bronfenbrenner's micro-meso-exo and macro systems and is mindful of person, place, context and time (PPCT) (Bronfenbrenner & Morris, 2007). The internet is also considered a central component of the complex system of a Self-Organised learning Environment (Mitra, 2014). This chapter discusses the role of self-organised learning environments (SOLE) (Mitra, 2014) in facilitating an emergent resilience.

This chapter presents a discussion on the potential contribution of SOLE to the fostering of resilience in the context of formal education environments which include schools and universities. This discussion was stimulated by the above case study and the feedback sought from the students after the SOLE had ended. After their use of SOLE, they reported that they needed to 'choose information, judge sources, be involved, analyse, synthesise and use critical skills' and asserted that they 'use so many more skills than a traditional lecture [meaning an interactive yet predominantly didactic teaching approach], SOLE helps it stick'. They also discussed their sense of autonomy in choosing their sources rather than having the lecturer provide them. This feedback is reminiscent of some of the factors that promote resilience (including self-efficacy, autonomy, taking responsibility and personal agency, discussed in Chap. 2). This provided the springboard for an exploration of whether and how SOLE may foster resilience, which this chapter presents.

Firstly, the concept of SOLE is explored with the emergent nature of learning being compared to the emergent nature of resilience. Secondly, the internet is discussed in relation to risk and resilience. Following this a discussion of 'negative affects' and 'promotive factors' (Wisniewski, 2015), situates the internet and SOLE within current debates, including about the nature of risk aversion, and picks up the assertion from Chap. 2 that a certain amount of risk exposure is necessary to develop resilience. Finally, implications for pedagogy are highlighted such that the SOLE environment can be used not only for emergent learning, but for emergent resilience as well.

SOLE, Complexity and Resilience

Suggested as a 'new approach to primary education' Self-organised learning environments are challenging traditional notions of pedagogy (Mitra, 2014, p. 547). Using the internet as a provider of content, the teacher's role is no longer to be the provider of knowledge but the facilitator and encourager of learning that emerges when groups use the internet to answer 'Big Questions'. Big Questions 'are the ones that don't have an easy answer. They are often open and difficult; they may even be unanswerable. The aim is to encourage deep and long conversations, rather than finding easy answers' (School in the Cloud, 2019). Examples of Big Questions include 'Is life on Earth sustainable?' and 'How do my eyes know to cry when I'm sad?' (Mitra, 2015,

p. 18). As Mitra states 'groups of children can learn almost anything by themselves using the internet' (Mitra, 2014, p. 549). Further, the teacher is not to intervene in the learning but act as observer, allowing learning to happen. That learning just 'happens' is reminiscent of the science of emergence which is part of complexity. 'Emergence, a common phenomenon in nature, is the appearance of properties that are not evident in the parts of a system' (Mitra, 2014, p. 556). SOLE as a system of individual components consists of the learners, the internet and—to maximise the learning—an encouraging but non-interventionist 'other', all of which form part of the DIMoR's web of interrelating systems (ahmed Shafi et al., 2020). The amount of computers is restricted to about a quarter of the number of learners so that they have to form groups. The groups are fluid. Learners can interact within and across groups, so the group's structure and size changes. This creates what Mitra (2014) terms an 'edge of chaos' effect which is a state that is 'neither strictly ordered nor completely chaotic' (Mitra, 2014, p. 556). This is very important for emergent behaviour to occur which, as Mitra further states, 'it indeed does, frequently' (Mitra, 2014, p. 556). Being on the edge of chaos means that the environment has become self-organising. This has an effect of 'downward causation' (CALResCo, 2007)—what has emerged from the dynamics of the system exerts an effect on the individual components. In the case of a SOLE, the emergent learning has an educative effect on the individual learner and different groups of learners within the overall system of the learning environment. This has been described as a 'SOLE contagion' which creates a positive norm for educational growth (Weisblat & McClellan, 2017, p. 311).

SOLE can be described as a dynamic reciprocal system where each part interacts with the other which exemplifies the DIMoR (ahmed Shafi et al., 2020). Because emergence occurs within a self-organised complex system and SOLE is such a system, and if resilience is also an emergent property which Rutter further situates as a dynamic process (Rutter, 2013) and Ungar (2013, p. 349) states develops from 'children's interactions with multiple reciprocating systems', how can an emergent resilience be fostered such that it has a downward causal effect on the individuals and groups within the learning environment? In other words, how can SOLE foster resilience?

Research highlights a number of factors which are important in the fostering of resilience. This chapter will focus on three: social capital (Southwick et al., 2014), a sense of agency (Downes, 2017) and autonomy (Rutter, 2013), each of which will also be explored in relation to pedagogy later in the chapter. If SOLE is going to allow resilience to emerge and achieve the downward causation necessary to affect an individual's and group's resilience, these factors are ones which need to have a high chance of being present within a SOLE so that they can feed into the reciprocal interactions of the system. From the aforementioned feedback from undergraduate students resulting from the case study above, this seems likely. Social capital is important for building resilience (Southwick et al., 2014; Rutter, 2013). This is exemplified by Bonanno who, in his discussion of Super Storm Sandy, describes the way in which texting between individuals became vital for keeping lines of communication open, receiving updates and gaining knowledge of where resources were located (Bonanno in Southwick et al., 2014, p. 8). He states that this social capital was of 'crucial importance' in helping people cope with adversity. This would have contributed to their resilience. Rutter (2013) also highlights the importance of social capital for the building of resilience. He states that 'interventions need to serve the provision of good social relationships...they are best acquired through relevant experiences that are guided but not instructed' (Rutter, 2013, p. 483). SOLE can be considered one such experience. It is a 'shared social experience' which 'provides new opportunities for social connectivity' (Weisblatt & McCellan, 2017, p. 310). The teacher guides the experience of the SOLE, they do not instruct it. SOLE can develop social capital which in turn may foster resilience.

Another factor important to the fostering of resilience is a sense of personal agency in which one is able to act to improve one's situation (Werner, 1993; Rutter, 2013; Downes, 2017). Werner (1993) suggests that this is most effective in the context of social relationships and cooperation with others, reinforcing the importance of developing social capital. Further, Rutter (2013) describes factors including 'being able to take responsibility, exercise a degree of autonomy, and have the opportunity of learning from their own mistakes' as factors important to developing resilience (Rutter, 2013, p. 482). Weisblatt and McClellan (2017, p. 311) describe how SOLE facilitates these factors. They highlight increasing personal agency through the change in a student's self-identity occurring as a result of seeing themselves as 'architects of their own [learning] journeys'; they state that community is changed and sustained as students increasingly become citizens of their environment, increasing social capital; they highlight that students take responsibility for their learning; that SOLE allows learning from failure; and that the teacher is enabled to emphasise student relationships and growth, further building social capital and community citizenship, rather than focusing solely on delivering content. An example of how SOLE builds community citizenship, social capital and self-efficacy can be seen through the work of Sanjay Fernandes who is using SOLE with ex-combatants and child soldiers in Colombia, most of whom have never turned on a computer, to 'foster trust and curiosity in communities' and combat isolation so that they may build a future of peace (Healy, 2018, p. 27). The benefits of SOLE reported by Weisblatt and McClellan (2017) across a range of educational contexts and those reported by Fernandez in his peacebuilding initiative (Healy, 2018) align with research on resilience and echo the feedback from my own undergraduate students. It would seem possible that inputting these factors into the complex system of SOLE and its reciprocal interactions may increase the likelihood that resilience will be an emergent property of a SOLE with subsequent downward causation to the individual and groups.

The Internet, Risk and Resilience

The use of SOLE requires the use of the internet as a central tool. The use of the internet in the lives of young people has caused concern in some areas which highlight the risks that it, and the subsequent increase in screen time, may carry. The prevalence of these risks in media coverage (Hern, 2019; Davis, 2019; Walton, 2018; Dunckley,

2015) may present a limiting factor to practitioner's use of SOLE and subsequently the potential fostering of resilience, and therefore warrants discussion.

In the case of screen time, one of the health complaints that is often mooted is a rise in obesity. The use of screens is often demonised as the cause of obesity. However, it is not the screen itself but the increased sedentary lifestyles many 'screenagers' adopt due to the increased amount of time they spend interacting online that is suggested as the problem (Griffiths, 2010). Indeed, some concerns about the rise in screen use may be seen as a moral panic. Campos et al. (2005) inform that 'moral panics are typical during times of rapid social change and involve an exaggeration or fabrication of risks...'. The moral panic is both assisted and exemplified by media headlines where the dangers of screen time range from causing a 'global epidemic of blindness' (Kekatos, 2017) to causing depression in children (Burrell, 2013). Stiglic and Viner (2018) carried out a systematic review of evidence on the effects of screen time on children and young people's health and well-being and found inconsistent results. They state that 'a prominent group of scientists recently argued that messages that screens are inherently harmful is simply not supported by solid research and evidence' (Stiglic & Viner, 2018, p. 14). Further, the evidence they looked at also focused mainly on TV screens and as they acknowledge, the research on the use of mobile technology or computer screens and also the influence of the types of content they are used to access, such as educational content, is currently lacking. To date, the best advice seems centred around the need to balance screen time with other 'positive activities (socialising, exercise, sleep)' which may be displaced by screen time (Viner et al., 2019, p. 6). Applied to SOLE in formal educational environments, this suggests that there is no evidence that increased use of screens to access the internet will have any adverse effects; especially when balanced against other positive activities which can promote social capital and exercise, such as university sports clubs, school playtimes and lessons in Physical Education.

In the case of increased internet use, concerns centre around increased exposure to online risks. These include sexual images, online bullying, sexting and meeting new online contacts offline (Livingstone, 2013), with many fearing that simply being exposed to the risk and seeing such content will cause harm. However, it should be noted that there is not a single response to online risk and exposure to online risk does not automatically equate to harm (Livingstone, 2013). There are various dependent factors including social context and stage of development plus existing levels of resilience pre-risk exposure which will moderate the potential harm done by online risks. Concerns about online risk encompass 'negative affect' (Wisniewski, 2015). Negative affect is a reaction of displeasure when experiencing online risk that might include 'anger, contempt, disgust, guilt, fear, and nervousness...and is associated with anxiety, stress, poor coping, and health complaints' (Wisniewski 2015, p. 4031). In contrast to Wisneiwski's (2015) negative affect and associated negative outcomes, resilience is considered a 'promotive factor' that 'can moderate the relationship between risk exposure and a negative outcome, either by neutralising the relationship between the two, or weakening it' (Wisniewski, 2015, p. 4031). In other words, resilience can significantly reduce negative affect or reduce any harm done when risks are experienced. Resilience has a key role to play in enabling young people to not only cope with the online risks they may experience but also to enable them to thrive in spite of the risks they experience. Everyone is different and each person will experience online risk differently. That said, whilst each person may experience negative affects to a greater or lesser degree, all young people will benefit from developing the promotive factor of resilience.

A potential hindrance to the development of resilience is the way in which adults may attempt to eliminate risk altogether, believing that this will keep young people safe. The advice often given to young people when they have experienced negative affect, is to just stop using the website or device. Further, schools often have strict filters in place designed to eliminate young people's exposure to risk, also believing that this is keeping them safe. Solutions are often targeted towards restriction and risk prevention (Wisniewski, 2015). But there is a danger that overly restrictive behaviours may trigger 'deeper psychological problems' if underlying needs for 'social interaction, acceptance and support' are not addressed (Wisniewski, 2015, p. 4034). After all, these may be the needs which led to using the internet in the first place. Yet it is unrealistic to expect that adults can eliminate young people's exposure to online risk entirely or indeed whether they should. If young people are never exposed to risks online, how are they to learn ways to deal with it constructively? Indeed, some children become resilient 'precisely because of their exposure to a degree of risk' (Livingstone et al., 2011, p. 144). Further, how are they to develop the skills needed to self-regulate the emotions that may occur through negative affect, a key factor in developing resilience? (Ungar, 2013). A way forward through the potential moral panic, fear and uncertainty may lie in a balance between risk and protection (Rutter, 2013). Solutions could be offered that enable risk management, not risk avoidance. Otherwise, there is a danger that young people are denied the opportunity to develop the promotive factor of resilience that can help them moderate negative affect, because the adult desire to keep them safe drives their experience of exposure to online risks.

This is not to suggest that there should be no filtering of online content in schools allowing young people to experience whatever content is delivered, but neither should filter systems or other risk prevention measures be so strict that 'there is no scope for participants to try out their own ideas and to learn from their own mistakes', in other words to foster their resilience (Rutter, 2013, p. 483). What can likely foster their resilience, is 'controlled exposure to manageable challenge' [in this case online risk] rather than its avoidance (Rutter, 2013, p. 484). The fostering of resilience in order to mediate the possible negative affect of online risk exposure is important. As discussed above, resilience can moderate negative affect if it is present before risk exposure. Resilience can be proactive and have a somewhat feed-forward effect on future risk experience. Wisneiwski (2015, p. 4031) describes this proactive resilience as having an 'inoculation effect, where past negative experiences may facilitate the development of coping strategies, which can directly influence adolescents' future online activities and behaviours, including avoidance of or protection against online risk'. This thinking illustrates the dynamic nature of the interaction between resilience and online risk exposure.

The factors that foster resilience can form part of the dynamics of SOLE. Due to its complex systemic nature, SOLE may potentially enable resilience to become an emergent property with a downward causal effect on individuals, which can help to inoculate them against online risk and mitigate negative affect. This will be influenced by how a SOLE is run which brings us to a discussion of elements of pedagogy which may be beneficial to the success of SOLE in fostering resilience.

Implications for Pedagogy

As discussed, with the internet as a provider of content the teacher's role is no longer to be the provider of knowledge but the encourager of learning that emerges when groups use the internet to answer 'Big Questions' (School in the Cloud, 2019). The groups of learners are fluid—learners can interact within and across groups, so the group's structure and size changes. This creates the 'edge of chaos effect' and is the state of maximum information (Mitra, 2014, p. 556). The edge of chaos effect should be maintained for emergence of learning to occur. This effect, mediated by the way a SOLE is delivered, can also potentially increase the likelihood of an emergent resilience (ahmed Shafi et al., 2020). Teachers, through their pedagogy, can facilitate the factors that are known to foster resilience, enabling them to become part of the complex reciprocal interactions within the system of SOLE. Therefore teachers, as part of their guidance and encouragement of the SOLE experience, need to promote social capital, autonomy and a sense of personal agency. These factors are also shown to deepen learning, suggestive of an already complex and possibly reciprocal interaction between learning and resilience. The factors which foster resilience are now considered in turn.

Social Capital

As stated by Salloum et al. (2018, p. 282) 'Social capital resides in the quality of social relations'. The characteristics of social capital include trust, respect, affection (Ergün et al., 2018, p. 106) and supportive relational networks (Salloum et al., 2018) all of which are said to enhance student learning and as we have seen, social capital is also important in fostering resilience. Salloum et al. (2018) also confirm the importance of trust, calling it 'social trust' (Salloum et al., 2018, p. 283) which, expanded by Li and Choi (2013, p. 3), is important for 'reciprocal action, mutual support…and collective endeavour'. These are ingredients of a successful SOLE as learners act together and engage in reciprocal interactions to answer Big Questions as part of a group collective action. As Li and Choi (2013, p. 3) further state, 'social trust creates a context of predictability and stability for genuine, open dialogues, as well as for critical reflection and risk taking when individuals are confronted with the need for change'. The exploration of Big Questions will often include the need to take risks and critically reflect on previously held understanding in order to learn and, when working together, genuine open dialogue is understandably important between learners and between learners and teacher. Ergün et al. (2018) also name respect as part of social capital. Whilst what it means to show respect will vary from person to person, Goldson (2018, p..587) states that part of respect is recognition, aligning this with teacher behaviour by stating that 'a teacher must recognise a student's needs, even if the teacher cannot actually meet them' (Goldson, 2018, p. 587). In terms of pedagogy, the teacher may facilitate the building of social trust by explicitly recognising a student's needs in order to show respect, encourage and ensure respectful relationships between learners, encourage risk taking in learning perhaps by asking questions which take learners into Vygotsky's zone of proximal development and encourage open dialogue between learners. Vygotsky's theory forms the basis of much current pedagogical practice, as does the encouragement of respectful relationships, but the importance of these skills for SOLE is to use them explicitly in this context so that they become part of the complex reciprocal system which can foster not just an emergent learning but an emergent resilience (ahmed Shafi et al., 2020), with associated downward causation to the individual.

Autonomy

In addition to social capital, as stated, autonomy is also important to foster resilience. Autonomy is 'freedom from external control', linked to learners having a say in their education (Goldson, 2018, p. 592). Notwithstanding the teacher's need to maintain some control over the learning environment in order to ensure student safety and so forth, SOLE does provide a measure of autonomy in the learner's choice of which Big Question to pursue, which sources to use on the internet and which group(s) to work with. The feedback given by the undergraduate students in the case study supports this. They reported the sense of autonomy that they experienced through SOLE, plus their sense of involvement with the group and use of critical skills; also supporting the existence of social trust. The teacher can encourage this autonomy throughout a SOLE session by reminding learners that the groups are fluid and they can make a choice to pursue learning that is of interest to them. Inherent in autonomy, is the teacher's trust that learners know how to learn (Sennett, 2003 in Goldson, 2018), reminiscent of Mitra's assertion that teachers should 'get out of their way' during a SOLE and allow learning to emerge, rather than directly intervening in the learning (Mitra, 2014, p. 552). This is challenging to traditional notions of pedagogy that imbue the teacher as the one in charge, in control and as the knower. Perhaps this requires the teacher to embrace the challenge of teaching differently.

Agency

So far we have seen how social capital and autonomy, two factors that foster resilience, can be present within a SOLE with implications for pedagogy. The third factor under consideration is agency. Goddard (2000, p. 688) defines agency as 'the intentional pursuit of a course of action'; the behaviour in SOLE can be considered agentic when learners purposefully pursue answers to Big Questions. Davis and Singh (2015, p. 73) further state that a sense of agency develops when learners feel a personal connection to what they are learning and are recognised as 'competent, valued contributors within the community of practice'. Related to autonomy, this reinforces the need for teachers to trust that their learners know how to learn. In terms of pedagogy, teachers can foster agency by encouraging learners to reflect on how their learning may relate to their real-life contexts such that learners derive personal meaning from their experience.

The factors that foster resilience may be encouraged within SOLE through a teacher's pedagogy. Whilst many of these pedagogical recommendations may currently be considered simply part of effective teaching, explicitly doing so in SOLE sessions will input these factors into the complex dynamic system of SOLE such that resilience may emerge and create downward causation to the individual learner, influencing their resilience trajectory. After all, 'resilient children and youth are often those who have teachers who accept, respect and trust them, as well as those who are provided opportunities to express themselves inside institutional settings' (Ungar, 2013, p. 353). However, as discussed, it is also important to be mindful of the need to balance risk and protection (Rutter, 2013) when using the internet and teachers need to adopt an approach of risk management, not risk avoidance. This is accompanied with an understanding that a certain amount of risk exposure is necessary to the building of resilience. Teachers can be reassured that exposure to risk online does not necessarily equate to harm, and as long as they are confident in helping learners navigate any initial 'negative affects' they may experience (Wisniewski, 2015), then learners may become inoculated against experiencing negative effects when exposed to future risk.

This chapter has presented an exploration of the contribution SOLE may make to the fostering of resilience in formal educational environments and considered the DIMoR (ahmed Shafi et al., 2020) as a lens through which to think of its interrelating systems. It is acknowledged that classrooms and the formal institutions they exist within are themselves complex environments with many intersecting factors influencing success, but the focus here has been on the environment of SOLE as a complex reciprocal system and the factors which may facilitate an emergent resilience within it. However, alongside viewing SOLE in the context of the DIMoR (ahmed Shafi et al., 2020), the model can also provide a lens through which to consider these wider factors. Further research is needed to consider that in more detail, and to provide the evidence base for an emergent resilience within SOLE, however this chapter has provided a discussion regarding the use of SOLE to potentially enable an emergent resilience and is positioned as a contribution to current debates on these issues.

References

ahmed Shafi, A., Templeton, S., Middleton, T., Millican, R.,   Vare, P., Pritchard, R. et al. (2020). Towards a dynamic interactive model of resilience (DIMoR) for education and learning contexts. *Emotional and Behavioural Difficulties, 25*(2), 183–198. https://doi.org/10.1080/136 32752.2020.1771923.

Bronfenbrenner, U., & Morris, P. A. (2007). The bioecological model of human development. In W. Damon, R. M. Lerner, & R. M. Lerner (Eds.), *Handbook of child psychology* (Chapter 14). http://doi.org/10.1002/9780470147658.chpsy0114.

Burrell. (2013). Overload of screen time causes depression in children. The Independent. Retrieved May 16, 2019, from https://www.independent.co.uk/life-style/health-and-families/health-news/overload-of-screen-time-causes-depression-in-children-8786826.html.

CALResCo [Complexity & Artificial Life Research Concept]. (2007). *Complex systems glossary.* New Mills: CALResCo. Retrieved May 16, 2019, from https://www.calresco.org/glossary.htm.

Campos, P., Saguy, A., Ernsberger, E., & Glenn , O. (2005). The epidemiology of overweight and obesity: Public health crisis or moral panic? *International Journal of Epidemiology, 35*(1), 55–60.

Davis. (2019). Study links high levels of screen time to slower child development, The Guardian. Retrieved May 16, 2019, from https://www.theguardian.com/society/2019/jan/28/study-links-high-levels-of-screen-time-to-slower-child-development.

Davis, K., & Singh, S. (2015). Digital badges in afterschool learning: Documenting the perspectives and experiences of students and educators. *Computers & Education, 88,* 72–83.

Downes, P. (2017). Reconceptualising foundational assumptions of resilience: A cross-cultural, spatial systems domain of relevance for agency and phenomenology in resilience. . *The International Journal of Emotional Education , 9*(1), 99–120.

Dunckley. (2015). Screentime is making kids moody, crazy and lazy 6 ways electronic screen time makes kids angry, depressed and unmotivated, psychology today. Retrieved May 16, 2019, from https://www.psychologytoday.com/us/blog/mental-wealth/201508/screentime-is-making-kids-moody-crazy-and-lazy.

Ergün, B., Uzunboylu, H., & Altinay, Z. (2018). An investigation of high school students' social capital development within organizational climate. *Quality and Quantity, 52*(S1), 105–113.

Goddard, R., Sweetland, S., & Hoy, W. (2000). Academic emphasis of urban elementary schools and student achievement in reading and mathematics: A multilevel analysis. *Educational Administration Quarterly, 36*(5), 683–702.

Goldson, D. (2018). Showing respect in school: What does it mean? *Reflective Practice, 19*(5), 586–598. https://doi.org/10.1080/14623943.2018.1538948

Griffiths, M. (2010). Trends in technological advance: Implications for sedentary behaviour and obesity in screenagers. *Education and Health, 28*(2), 35–38.

Healy, H. (2018). Meet the peacemakers, new internationalist. Retrieved July 11, 2019, from https://newint.org/features/2018/09/21/meet-peacemakers-heroes-paintbrushes-rec onciliation-not-revenge-talking-down.

Hern, A. (2019). Screen time has little effect on teenagers' wellbeing, says study. The Guardian. Retrieved May 16, 2019, from https://www.theguardian.com/society/2019/apr/05/screen-time-has-little-effect-on-teenagers-wellbeing-says-study.

Kekatos, M. (2017). 'Global epidemic of blindness' on the horizon, experts warn: Hours spent staring at screens 'will rob millions of their sight decades early', Daily Mail Online. Retrieved May 16, 2019, from https://www.dailymail.co.uk/health/article-4149734/Global-epidemic-blindness-scr een-time-blinding-kids-adults.html.

Li, S. C., & Choi, T. H. (2013). Does social capital matter? A quantitative approach to examining technology infusion in schools. . *Journal of Computer Assisted Learning, 30,* 1–16.

Livingstone, S., Haddon, L., Görzig, A., & Ólafsson, K. (2011). *Risks and safety on the internet: The perspective of European children. Full Findings.* LSE, London: EU Kids Online.

Livingstone, S., Kirwil, L., Ponte, C., Staksrud, E. (2013). In their own words: What bothers children online? With the EU Kids Online Network. EU Kids Online. London, UK: London School of Economics & Political Science.

Mitra, S. (2014). The future of schooling: Children and learning at the edge of chaos. *Prospects, 44,* 547–558.

Mitra, S. (2015). SOLE toolkit—How to bring self-organised learning environments to your community. School in the Cloud. Retrieved July 11, 2019, from https://www.theschoolinthecloud.org/how-to/sole-toolkit/.

Rutter, M. (2013). Annual research review: Resilience—clinical implications. *Journal of Child Psychology and Psychiatry, 54*(4), 474–487.

Salloum, S., Goddard, R., & Berebitsky, D. (2018). Resources, learning, and policy: The relative effects of social and financial capital on student learning in schools. *Journal of Education for Students Placed at Risk (JESPAR), 23*(4), 281–303. https://doi.org/10.1080/10824669.2018.149 6023.

School in the Cloud. (2019). *Choose a big question.* Retrieved May 16, 2019, from https://www.theschoolinthecloud.org/how-to/how-to-choose-a-big-question/.

Southwick, S. M., Bonanno, G. A., Masten, A. S., Brick, C., & Yehuda, R. (2014). Resilience definitions, theory, and challenges: Interdisciplinary perspectives. *European Journal of Psychotraumatology, 5*(1), 25338. https://doi.org/10.3402/ejpt.v5.25338.

Stiglic, N., & Viner, R. M. (2018). Effects of screentime on the health and well-being of children and adolescents: A systematic review of reviews. *BMJ Open, 2019*(**9**), e023191. https://doi.org/10.1136/bmjopen-2018-023191

Ungar, M. (2013). Annual research review: What is resilience within the social ecology of human development? *Journal of Child Psychology and Psychiatry, 54*(4), 348–366.

Viner, R., Davie, M., & Firth, A. (2019). The health impacts of screen time: A guide for clinicians and parents. *Royal College of Paediatrics and Child Health.*

Walton, A. (2018). How too much screen time affects kids' bodies and brains, forbes. Retrieved May 16, 2019, from https://www.forbes.com/sites/alicegwalton/2018/04/16/how-too-much-screen-time-affects-kids-bodies-and-brains/.

Weisblat, G., & McClellan, J. (2017). The disruptive innovation of self-organized learning environments. *Childhood Education, 93*(4), 309–315. https://doi.org/10.1080/00094056.2017.134 3584.

Werner, E. (1993). Risk, resilience, and recovery: Perspectives from the Kauai longitudinal study. *Development and Psychopathology, 5*(1993), 503–551.

Wisniewski, P., Jia, H., Wang, N., Zheng, S., Xu, H., Rosson, M., & Carroll, J. (2015). Resilience mitigates the negative effects of adolescent internet addiction and online risk exposure. In *Proceedings of the 33rd Annual ACM Conference on Human Factors in Computing Systems, Seoul, Republic of Korea* (pp. 4029–4038).

Jenny Hatley Jenny's main concern within education is social justice. This is a focus in all her areas of interest which have evolved from her development of educational provision across settings in both the UK and overseas. She began in museum education at the Science Museum in London, working as a Science Educator and as Assistant Curator for Space Technology. Following this, Jenny was programme manager for an aid agency working in conflict zones and areas of natural disaster to lead and deliver trauma and conflict resolution programmes in schools and villages, health counselling and disease prevention education. Following this, Jenny taught in primary schools in both the state and independent sectors developing relationships education and global citizenship. She has been lead teacher for PSHE and Citizenship and has also worked in Sweden as Associate School Leader, focusing on the whole school development of IT and associated pedagogy. Jenny currently teaches in Higher Education and enjoys bringing a critical eye and research base to studies in Education.

Part III
Looking Forwards

Chapter 13
A Rounder Sense of Purpose: Educator Competences for Sustainability *and* Resilience

Richard Millican and Paul Vare

Abstract This chapter takes the premise that, in order to create a sustainable world, we need to repurpose and refocus the education system to better equip individuals with the ability to recognise what changes need to be made to move towards sustainability and then how to participate in the implementation of these changes. It argues that there is a close link between sustainability and resilience and that by equipping individuals in this way not only helps to create a sustainable and resilient world, but one in which resilient societies and individuals will emerge. It reports on an Erasmus project, A Rounder Sense of Purpose, that developed a set of educator competences for sustainability designed to help facilitate this process through appropriately trained educators. It then uses the Dynamic Interactive Model of Resilience (DIMoR) (ahmed Shafi et al., 2020) to analyse the role of the competences and to illustrate how they can help develop individual, societal and biodiversity protection and thus in the emergence of resilience.

Introduction

This chapter builds on themes introduced elsewhere in the book. It takes as a premise that resilience is needed—by individuals to cope with and act within a stressful and changing education system and with and within rapidly changing societies, and by individuals *and* societies to deal with environmental change and the climate emergency (Chap. 1). However, as previously discussed, (see Chaps. 4 and 5) one perspective is that resilience can be considered as something that is needed to cope with what is, and thus needs to be taught or added eg strategies given to an individual to help them deal with stress, or something done to a society to help it deal with the impact of climate change eg construct a higher sea defence wall, or find a fall back

R. Millican (✉) · P. Vare
School of Education and Humanities, University of Gloucestershire, Francis Close Hall, Swindon Road, Cheltenham GL50 4AZ, Glos, UK
e-mail: rmillican@glos.ac.uk

P. Vare
e-mail: pvare@glos.ac.uk

© Springer Nature Switzerland AG 2020
A. ahmed Shafi et al. (eds.), *Reconsidering Resilience in Education*,
https://doi.org/10.1007/978-3-030-49236-6_13

supply of energy in case one fails. This can be considered as resilience *for* education, or resilience *for* life. This, however, suggests a fatalistic approach to the status quo and a passive acceptance. An alternative perspective is to think of education and societies as being structured in such a way that they do not demand resilience to be able to cope with them, but that they generate resilience in stakeholders at various levels through the process of education and the interactions that occur as part of this, and through the way that society is structured and acts (see Chaps. 3, 4 and 5). In other words, resilience emerges *through, or because of,* education and *through, or because of,* societal processes. It encourages actors to take a proactive, agentic, role in turn in creating education and societies that are conducive to the development of resilience.

The challenge is however, how to arrive at that point. In much of the world there is a long-standing tradition of education, democratic processes and economic theory and yet we have arrived at a situation where individual and societal health and wellbeing are threatened and the planetary systems that support and provide for human life forms are also at risk (see Chap. 1). If we take these threats seriously, then this suggests that something needs to change, that perhaps education needs to be refocused and repurposed and that our individual and collective actions and behaviours need to be scrutinised and evaluated through a lens that considers whether they are damaging other individuals, societies and/or the environment, or are constructive and helpful—therefore judging as to whether they are sustainable actions which are helping to build individual, societal and ecological resilience.

The chapter reports on a European Erasmus plus project 'A Rounder Sense of Purpose' (RSP) that was designed to consider this by focusing on educators and the competences they would need in order to be educators for sustainable development. In other words, if education were to be considered as an engine or catalyst for change towards creating a sustainable and resilient world of resilient societies and individuals, what abilities would the educators need to be able to facilitate this. The chapter will present the framework of competences that was the outcome of this work and present its heritage and rationale. It will then analyse the result using the Dynamic Interactive Model of Resilience (DIMoR) (ahmed Shafi et al., 2020) to show how such an approach to education can help create resilient individuals, structures and societies and thereby contribute towards creating a sustainable world.

The Project

Some Context

Over the last century and particularly since the 1950s (see for example Carson, 1962), there has been growing unease and concern about the impact of human activity on the environment. The epoch in which humans have been roaming the planet and exploiting nature for benefit has been dubbed the Anthropocene (see for example

Lewis & Maslin, 2018). Human nature and ingenuity is such that as a species we are constantly looking to explore and discover and to develop, progress and improve (Harari, 2015). This has clearly led to myriad exciting inventions and innovations that have enabled us to live longer and more healthily and in a way that is less labour intensive.

However, during this process, we have also been growing in number and as the human population increases, so have our expectations for food, housing, health-care, comfort, travel and entertainment and this intensifies pressures on land use and production as we look to produce greater amounts to satisfy demand and endeavour to do so ever more efficiently and cheaply. This accelerating demand means the date at which we consume the Earth's annual supply of replenishable resources each year is getting steadily earlier and, at the time of writing, was 29th July for 2019 (https://www.overshootday.org/about/).

The planet has been able to absorb and cope with much of this and has allowed us to continue to capitalise on its resources and exploit the potential provided. However, the signs that this is placing strain on planetary systems is increasingly evident and much research draws our attention towards melting ice caps, rising sea levels, increasing global temperature, species extinction, desertification and extreme weather conditions. In short, a climate and environmental crisis caused by human activity (see for example International Panel on Climate Change (IPCC) reports at https://www.ipcc.ch/about/).

It thus seems evident that things are going to change. This change could be forced upon us as ecological systems that we rely on break down or material resources run out, or we face up to the challenges ahead of us and work to avoid and mitigate where possible and prepare to deal with them where not.

However, this would take a radical shift in individual and societal attitude and approach whereby we accept the stresses we are creating, embrace the need to look for new ways of being and search for mechanisms that allow us to live in such a manner that does not rely on constant economic growth but has individual, collective and planetary health and wellbeing as a focus. In other words, it seeks to build sustainable and resilient individuals and societies.

The Role of Education

The world is constantly changing and at an ever-increasing rate (see Chap. 1), but any change is predominantly based on the same fundamental principles that are mostly emanating from Western civilisations. These principles are underpinned by capitalist ideology and assumes that planetary resources are there for our use and for us to exploit in pursuit of wealth creation and accumulation (Moore, 2016). However, whilst this system has worked effectively in many ways, the profit motive has a tendency, if not unchecked, to lead to short termism and a belief that the planet can keep providing allowing us to continue to take, make, use and dump and to continue to grow and find new markets without factoring in and giving due consideration to environmental and social costs.

To change economic and social principles that have evolved over centuries will not be easy to achieve and if that change is to be a managed process rather than forced, it will be harder still. If it *is* to be managed and led by us in a conscious and deliberate way, then that means a change in our thinking and understanding—what Freire might call conscientisation (1972). A large influence on the way we think and understand the world comes from our education.

Much has been written about the purpose of education, but a crude distinction comes between (a) the idea that it is there to protect and perpetuate current societal values and practices and to preserve the status quo and (b) that it is there to encourage free and critical thought and thereby act as an instigator and engine of change. Arguably, much of Western education has been based on the former as it has focused on producing engineers, business leaders and workers able to fit into existing systems and to continue to produce efficiently and effectively to maximise profit using similar business and economic models (see for example Bates & Lewis, 2009; Curtis & Pettigrew, 2009; Marples, 2010).

So, if we accept that we are damaging the planet's support systems and threatening their, and consequently our, ability to be resilient and that we thus need to find sustainable ways of living, then there is a compelling argument to change the focus of education—to repurpose it so that people develop a different consciousness that encourages them to adopt a critical eye that is looking at our actions, structures and behaviours through a sustainability lens to see if they need to change in order to move towards a sustainable world, or at least to mitigate against the worst of climate disaster.

The Purpose of the Project

There have been a number of initiatives that have attempted to address this issue and to encourage thought and care for the environment through, for example, Environmental Education (EE), Education for Sustainable Development (ESD), Learning for Sustainability (LfS) and the Eco-Schools movement (https://www. eco-schools.org.uk/). More recent examples have focused on teacher education and there have been various attempts to produce frameworks that can guide and inform initial and in-service training. Perhaps the most notable of these was the United Nations Economic Commission for Europe (UNECE) Competences in Education for Sustainable Development (2011).

Whilst these efforts have all had some impact, recent government policy in the UK has been to side-line sustainability education and much headway that was made is now starting to lose traction (see Vare, 2014). Aside from the influence of governmental policy, another barrier to the widespread adoption of the UNECE competences was the fact that there are 39 of them which is, perhaps, over-complicated and unwieldy.

With this in mind, the Rounder Sense of Purpose Erasmus plus project was established with the aim of creating a simplified, distilled, user-friendly set of educator competences that built on the work that had gone before. Competences that could be used with and for different contexts and that developed educator ability to educate for sustainable development and, therefore, resilience.

The project was led by the University of Gloucestershire who worked in partnership with Tallinn University, Estonia; Duurzame PABO, The Netherlands; Italian Association of Sustainability Science, Italy; Frederick University, Cyprus; and the Hungarian Research Teachers' Association, Hungary. It was a 3 year project that, as well as creating a set of educator competences, aimed to design a pan-European qualification in Education for Sustainable Development.

Project Outcomes

The process for creating the educator competences was a rigorous one. It began with a careful reading of the UNECE competences and a distillation process in which statements with similar learning outcomes were matched together. New labels were given to the matched statements that encapsulated the essence of each competence and then the result was compared to other frameworks to search for any concepts that were missing. This was an iterative process that involved not only the six project partners, but consultation with experts from each of the partner countries.

A new set of 12 competences emerged that continued to fit into the UNECE framework of three columns and four rows. These were tested through a Delphi research procedure and trialled in different contexts. Results were shared and gradually a consensus formed around the content and wording of the competences. The final 12 were: Systems, Futures, Participation, Attentiveness, Empathy, Engagement, Transdisciplinarity, Innovation, Action, Criticality, Responsibility and Decisiveness. The three columns were entitled 'Holistic Approach', 'Envisioning Change' and 'Achieving Transformation' and the rows 'Integration', 'Involvement', 'Practice' and 'Reflection'.

Whilst the table form conveyed its UNECE heritage and had a neatness to it, there was concern that such a presentation suggested that the competences were separate and distinct and would be used in isolation. This was not the intention as clearly there was overlap between them and it was evident that in practice they would, and should, be employed flexibly and in different combinations. Different designs for representation were experimented with until agreement settled on the image of an artist's palette with the competences represented as different coloured paint that could be combined and used differently for different purposes.

The project team were pleased with the outcome of the work around the competence framework, but to achieve a pan-European qualification for Educators of Sustainable Development proved more problematic as (a) it was difficult to find an awarding body that was recognised in all participating countries and (b) each partner had different ambitions in terms of level and size of the award and as to which sector eg primary, or secondary it would focus towards. It was thus agreed that rather than attempt to create a single, one size fits all qualification, a more valuable approach was to use the framework as something to inform, guide and underpin qualifications and training programmes that were bespoke and which could be devised and implemented at a local level.

This revised approach to the qualification and the fact that, during the project cycle The United Nations' Sustainable Development Goals (SDGs) (2015) were launched, led to a further 3 year Erasmus plus project that aims to integrate the RSP framework with the SDGs and to provide example qualifications in each context.

The addition of new partners from Universitaet Vechta, Germany; Universitat Oberta de Catalunya, Spain and HEP Vaud, Switzerland have provided additional opportunities for testing the framework which is now presented in table form below (Table 13.1).

Or, as a palette as in Fig. 13.1.

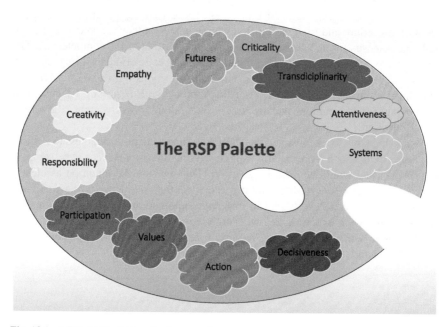

Fig. 13.1 A Palette illustrating the framework

Table 13.1 The RSP framework in table form

Thinking holistically	Envisioning change	Achieving transformation
Integration		
Systems The educator helps learners to develop an understanding of the world as an interconnected whole and to look for connections across our social and natural environment and consider the consequences of actions	**Futures** The educator helps learners to explore alternative possibilities for the future and to use these to consider how behaviours might need to change	**Participation** The educator helps learners to contribute to changes that will support sustainable development
Involvement		
Attentiveness The educator helps learners to understand fundamentally unsustainable aspects of our society and the way it is developing and increases their awareness of the urgent need for change	**Empathy** The educator helps learners to respond to their feelings and emotions and those of others as well as developing an emotional connection to the natural world	**Values** The educator develops an awareness among learners of how beliefs and values underpin actions and how values need to be negotiated and reconciled
Practice		
Transdisciplinarity The educator helps learners to act collaboratively both within and outside of their own discipline, role, perspectives and values	**Creativity** The educator encourages creative thinking and flexibility within their learners	**Action** The educator helps the learners to take action in a proactive and considered manner
Reflection		
Criticality The educator helps learners to evaluate critically the relevance and reliability of assertions, sources, models and theories	**Responsibility** The educator helps learners to reflect on their own actions, act transparently and to accept personal responsibility for their work	**Decisiveness** The educator helps the learners to act in a cautious and timely manner even in situations of uncertainty

Each competence has been listed with a set of Learning Outcomes that the educator should help the learner to achieve and a set of underpinning components that the educator should be able to do. For example:

Systems

The educator helps learners to develop an understanding of the world as an interconnected whole and to look for connections across our social and natural environment and consider the consequences of actions.

Table 13.2 Learning Outcomes: The educator helps learners to…

Learning Outcomes: The educator helps learners to…
1.1 Understand the root causes of unsustainable development and that sustainable development is an evolving concept
1.2 Understand key characteristics of complex systems such as living environments, human communities and economic systems, including concepts such as interdependencies, non-linearity, self-organisation and emergence
1.3 Apply different viewpoints and frames when looking at systems, e.g. different scales, boundaries perspectives and connections
Underpinning Components for the educator   In order to achieve the above Learning Outcomes the educator should be able to:
UC1 Identify the level of complexity and abstraction to be tackled with students and use techniques such as concept mapping, systems analysis, games, or structured research-based activities to make complexity accessible to them
UC1.1a Identify and discuss causes of unsustainability, be they environmental, social, cultural, political or economic
UC1.1b Understand and critique different models of sustainability
UC1.2a Explain the difference between systematic and systemic thinking
UC1.2b Understand and apply boundaries and frames to systems, look for interconnections and emergence and recognise feedback and unpredictability
UC1.2c Understand the difference between linear and circular economies
UC1.3a Analyse issues and contexts from different perspectives and from different levels of detail
UC1.3b Use different forms of thinking and logic to aid analysis, e.g. linear vs systemic approaches, scientific method and artistic interpretation

The project has produced a series of activities, materials and theoretical papers to support delivery of the framework which can be found at www.aroundersenseofpur pose.eu/, including materials to show how it could also help the educator to address the SDGs simultaneously. For a more detailed overview of the project process and outcomes, please visit the website, or see Vare et al. (2019).

A Rounder Sense of Purpose and Sustainability

The title of the project 'A Rounder Sense of Purpose' (RSP) hopefully encapsulates the essence of the framework. As mentioned earlier, arguably the existing focus of much of our education is on preparing learners to fit into society and to be ready to serve the needs of business. Indeed, on occasions we hear business leaders remark that young people are not equipped with the skills they need for work and politicians argue that education needs to be tweaked to better serve the economy. However, if we are to address climate and environmental concerns then it is not just more education we need but, as Schumacher states, 'education of a different kind' (in

Sterling, 2001). A Rounder Sense of Purpose aims to equip educators to provide education of 'a different kind'.

Rather than train educators to be technicians who are carrying out the wishes of others by delivery of prescribed syllabi, the framework encourages educator, and learner, agency and criticality.

Competences in the first column are about the need to think holistically—to recognise that we are all interconnected and that things that are happening in one context, ie to and within one system, have implications and impact on others. This is a fundamental need in order to achieve a sustainable world. There has to be widespread realisation that actions elsewhere eg forest clearance, dumping of waste, polluting of air cannot be ignored as the planet is a closed system and such events will not remain within the boundary of the place it is happening, but will have knock on effects that will continue to spread across boundaries with long lasting impact.

This column encourages individuals to be attentive and aware of what is happening in the world and to not just accept actions and behaviours, but to evaluate them and critique them and to judge whether they are damaging to planetary systems, or are supportive. It recognises that there are different sources of knowledge and that there is a need to draw on these and operate in transdisciplinary ways in order to make judgements about actions and to consider alternatives.

Given that we are currently experiencing a climate emergency, there clearly is a need to change the way we behave individually and collectively. The first column is about identifying where those changes might need to take place and so the second column refers to competences needed to envision a different way of acting and being, in other words to envision the changes we need to make to ensure that we are living in a sustainable way.

Futures thinking is part of that, alongside the ability to be creative and innovative and to be able to imagine other ways of doing things. It is also about accepting the need to be responsible for one's actions and to be willing to be held to account for what we do. There are times when, particularly with hindsight, it becomes clear that actions taken were not the most appropriate and may have had a negative impact on the environment and we need to be willing to acknowledge and accept when this happens and learn from such occasions.

This middle column also contains the important competence of empathy as it recognises that change is difficult and that identifying evidence of, and causes of, climate and environmental disaster and consequent changes of behaviours needed can cause distress and upset. As a result, change needs to be managed carefully and sensitively with awareness of the needs and feelings of others. It is important to maintain hope for the future, but this needs to be realistic and based on what is achievable and therefore should not deceive or misrepresent reality.

Having acknowledged that changes are needed and alternatives identified, the final column is about developing the ability to achieve transformation, to make a difference. It encourages learners to appreciate that there are different ways to participate in change and to be aware of values that underpin beliefs and actions. It draws attention to the fact that sometimes it is difficult to make decisions as necessary information is not always available, but it helps learners to develop the confidence and ability to weigh up information available and to make decisions and take action where and when necessary.

The framework is intended to be used flexibly and could be used to inform a dedicated training course for educators and/or a dedicated education for sustainability course for learners. However, perhaps more importantly, it is intended to equip educators in general with the skills and attitude to approach any educating they do with an ESD mindset so that whatever the focus of the lesson or course they are encouraging learners to think holistically, to envision change and to act to help achieve transformation towards a sustainable world.

Sustainability and Resilience

Analysing the RSP framework and sustainability using the DIMoR (ahmed Shafi et al., 2020), links between sustainability and resilience soon become apparent. Using Bronfenbrenner's (2007) notion of surrounding systems of Micro to Macro, it can be seen that these are housed within the local Ecosytem which is itself within the global planetary support system. In terms of the Chronosystem, the current time is the Anthropocene and of climate crisis. These in turn influence the development of systems within, which will then reciprocally influence the development or sustainability of the Ecosystems and Planetary support systems.

Taking a systems perspective, individual and societal trajectories will mean encounters with and within other systems. Individuals and societies can be considered vulnerable because of their circumstances e.g. the surrounding planetary support systems (environment, ecosystem, water, air) are threatened or damaged, or invulnerable because the environment and ecosystems are healthy, diverse and strong. They can also be deemed to be protected because people are aware and have a positive mindset towards sustainable development (in other words have developed RSP competences), or at risk because of climate change denial, short termism, ignorance and a focus on continued growth.

Individuals and societies then, continue to change and develop throughout their life course. As they do so they will encounter and react to other systems, which will in turn react to them. Resilience emerges when there is a healthy balance between risk & protection and vulnerability & invulnerability and when individuals and societies recognise and accept that they are not just responding to climate crises, but also causing them and that there is a symbiotic relationship between us, individually and collectively, with the ecological systems surrounding us.

So, individuals and societies have agency and consequently have a responsibility to acknowledge and accept responsibility for their actions and decisions and to consider their impact on the systems around them. RSP competences help protect individuals and societies and thus can play a role in developing resilience and creating a sustainable world. By helping individuals to develop the confidence to critique, envision difference and participate in creating change, it empowers and gives a sense of individual agency and thus resilience. In so doing it creates societies of individuals who

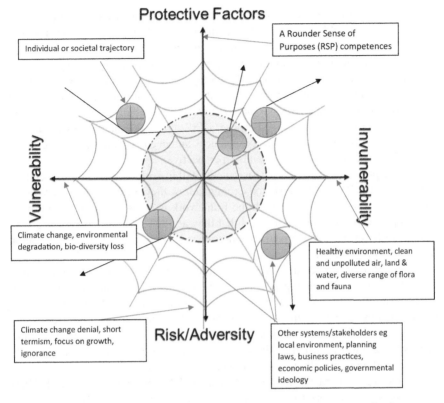

Fig. 13.2 The DIMoR (ahmed Shafi et al., 2020) and RSP competences as protective factors

have a sense of whole, of interdependence, who have awareness of, and empathy for, humans and other life forms. This 'ubuntu' further empowers by giving a sense of shared agency and the belief that together it is possible to make a difference and to create a fairer, sustainable world. A virtuous circle of individuals working together for sustainability, and the societies developed offering more safety and protection for its individuals can then be imagined, whereby sustainability and the resilience of societies, the individuals within and the surrounding ecosystems go hand in hand.

Figure 13.2 uses the DIMoR (ahmed Shafi et al., 2020) to show how the RSP competences can be perceived as protective factors and can help to develop a sustainable world in which, in turn, resilient individuals and societies emerge.

Conclusion

This chapter has argued that the planet is in an environmental and climate crisis and that this will enforce change upon the human race unless there is the collective will to tackle the root causes in order to avoid, or at least mitigate against, damaging possible outcomes. This would involve adopting a different mindset—one that views actions and behaviours with a critical lens, that recognises and acknowledges connections between and within systems and that has a sense of responsibility and agency.

It suggested that education has a role to play in developing this mindset, but that it needs to be refocused and repurposed if it is to do so. It thus makes the case for Education for Sustainable Development (ESD). It reported on a European Erasmus Plus project 'A Rounder Sense of Purpose' (RSP) that was established with various partner countries, to consider the competences an educator would need in order to approach education with a sustainability perspective.

The chapter then provided an overview of the twelve educator competences produced in the RSP framework and explained how they were developed providing a rationale for its design. Although the framework is a convenient way to present the competences, the chapter stressed that they are better viewed as on an 'artist's palette' to be utilised and mixed together as and when appropriate rather than as separate and individual.

It showed how these competences are important in moving towards a sustainable world by collectively helping people to take a holistic, systemic view, to be able to envision alternative futures, and to have the confidence and ability to be able to participate in working towards change towards a fair and sustainable world.

The chapter then made a link between sustainability and resilience, arguing that working towards sustainability in fact increases resilience in both individuals, societies and more broadly in planetary support systems.

The Dynamic, Interactive Model of Resilience (DIMoR) (ahmed Shafi et al., 2020) was used as a framework for analysis to help illustrate these links. By representing individuals and societies within webs of support structures and interacting with and within other systems, it showed how, for example, the health of the planet can cause vulnerability or invulnerability. It then showed how RSP competences can act as protective factors as they develop individual and collective awareness, empathy and agency.

The chapter then posited that in such a way a virtuous circle could be created whereby individual and collective systems are seeking to create the conditions for sustainability in which resilient individuals, societies and ecosystems can emerge.

References

ahmed Shafi, A., Templeton, S., Middleton, T., Millican, R., Vare, P. & Pritchard, R. et al. (2020). Towards a dynamic interactive model of resilience (DIMoR) for education and learning contexts. *Emotional and Behavioural Difficulties, 25*(2), 183–198. https://doi.org/10.1080/136 32752.2020.1771923 https://www.aroundersenseofpurpose.eu/.

Bates, J., & Lewis, S. (2009). *The study of education*. London: Continuum.

Bronfenbrenner, U., & Morris, P. A. (2007). The bioecological model of human development. In W. Damon, R. M. Lerner, & R. M. Lerner (Eds.), *Handbook of child psychology* (Chapter 14). doi.org/10.1002/9780470147658.chpsy0114.

Carson, R. (1962). *Silent spring*. New York: Houghton Mifflin.

Curtis, W., & Pettigrew, A. (2009). *Learning in contemporary culture*. Exeter: Learning Matters.

Eco-Schools. Retrieved April 10, 2019, from https://www.eco-schools.org.uk/.

Freire, P. (1972). *Cultural action for freedom*. Harmondsworth: Penguin.

Harari, Y. (2015). *Sapiens: A brief history of humankind*. London: Harvill Secker.

International Panel on Climate Change (IPCC). Retrieved April 10, 2019, from https://www.ipcc. ch/about/.

Lewis, S., & Maslin, M. (2018). *The human planet: How we created the anthropocene*. London: Penguin Books Ltd.

Marples, R. (2010). What is Education for? In R. Bailey (ed.), *The philosophy of education*. London: Continuum.

Moore, J. (ed). (2016). *Anthropocene or capitalocene? Nature, History, and the Crisis of Capitalism*.

Sterling, S. (2001). *Sustainable education, re-visioning learning and change*. Dartington: Green Books. Retrieved June 10, 2019, from https://www.overshootday.org/about/.

United Nations. (2015). Retrieved June 10, 2019, from https://www.un.org/sustainabledevelopment/ development-agenda/.

United Nations Economic Commission for Europe (UNCECE). (2011) *Learning for the future: Competences in education for sustainable development*. Retrieved April 10, 2019, from https:// www.unece.org/fileadmin/DAM/env/esd/ESD_Publications/Competences_Publication.pdf.

Vare, P. (2014). *Are there inherent contradictions in attempting to implement education for sustainable development in schools?* EdD thesis, University of Bath.

Vare, P., Arro, G., de Hamer, A., Del Gobbo, G., de Vries, G., Farioli, F., Kadji-Beltran, C., Kangur, M., Mayer, M., Millican, R., Nijdam, C., Réti, M., & Zachariou, A. (2019). Devising a competence-based training program for educators of sustainable development: Lessons learned. *Sustainability, 11*, 1890.

Richard Millican is a Senior Lecturer in Education and the Course Leader for the BA (Hons) Education at the University of Gloucestershire where he has worked for the past 10 years. Prior to that he has a long history of working within education, but in different contexts and phases. These include as a Drama and Music teacher across age ranges, a teacher of learners with social and emotional difficulties 5-18, a teacher of English as a Foreign Language to children and adults and a teacher trainer. He has worked in various countries including Spain, Oman and Egypt and in schools, further education colleges and universities including Leeds and Birmingham.

His current interests are in social justice and sustainability and in the role of education in helping to create a fairer and sustainable world. He is currently working on an international research project, A Rounder Sense of Purpose, which is developing a framework of competences for educators of sustainable development linked to the Sustainable Development Goals. This has led to various recent publications alongside work into developing academic resilience and buoyancy with higher education students.

Paul Vare is Postgraduate Research Lead and Course Leader for the Doctor of Education at the University of Gloucestershire's School of Education. Before joining the University in 2013, Paul worked for over 35 years in environmental education and education for sustainable development in the UK and on international development projects, chiefly in sub-Saharan Africa. For over a decade Paul represented European ECO Forum, a coalition of citizens' organisations, on various expert groups of the United Nations Economic Commission for Europe (UNECE) where he assisted in drafting the UNECE Strategy for Education for Sustainable Development. He is currently leading an international research project, A Rounder Sense of Purpose, which is developing a framework of competences for educators of sustainable development. Paul has a Masters of Philosophy Degree from Bristol University and a Doctor of Education from the University of Bath. Recently he co-authored a book with Prof. Bill Scott (University of Bath) called The World We'll Leave Behind: grasping the sustainability challenge that introduces a wide range of issues, concepts and strategies related to sustainable development. Paul's lifelong passion for the environment has been expressed through research, habitat management, drawing, painting, or simply walking in all weathers.

Chapter 14
Conclusion

Richard Millican

Abstract This chapter summarises issues raised in Chap. 1 surrounding the need for resilience and discusses how the Dynamic Interactive Model of Resilience (DIMoR) (ahmed Shafi, Middleton,Millican, Templeton, Vare, Pritchard, & Hatley, 2020) helps consider ways of developing resilience by positioning it as something that is dynamic and interactive and operating at and across different levels. It reflects on key themes that have emerged in each chapter and shows how the DIMoR (ibid.) provides a lens through which to look at educational systems and illustrates how they can contribute to helping resilience emerge in individuals, structures and societies.

The opening premise of the book was that there is a growing need for resilience. Chapter 1 argued that, although change is a given, if the pace of change is too quick it can cause stress to individuals, societies and, arguably, the very structures that support and nurture them. These structures, or systems, might be, for example, societal ones of family, neighbourhood and community networks, governmental ones such as health, care and youth services, or environmental ones like biosphere, climate and food supply. History and science have shown that where systems are robust they will evolve, adapt and survive change and possibly thrive within new contexts. However, they also show that change can be too extreme and too fast and cause too much of a shock in which case it can threaten the very well-being of, and ultimate survival of, the system.

By looking at various metrics, the first chapter made the case that the increasing pace of change experienced since the industrial revolution has brought immense benefits to the health and well-being of humans and increased opportunities for travel, leisure and work, but that alongside the benefits are rising indicators of stress to individuals and society as illustrated by the numbers suffering from poor mental health and other social ills such as suicide, murder, poverty and abuse. It also suggested that this pace of change has wider implications by placing increasing demands on

R. Millican (✉)
School of Education and Humanities, University of Gloucestershire, Francis Close Hall, Swindon Road, Cheltenham GL50 4AZ, Glos, UK
e-mail: rmillican@glos.ac.uk

© Springer Nature Switzerland AG 2020
A. ahmed Shafi et al. (eds.), *Reconsidering Resilience in Education*,
https://doi.org/10.1007/978-3-030-49236-6_14

our planetary support mechanisms through consumption rates of both finite global supplies of natural products like coal, oil and precious metals and renewables like wood, fish and fresh water. It posited that there are indicators of stress that this demand is causing to the planet manifested through, for example, climate change, rising sea levels and species extinction rates.

The argument presented was that to adapt and survive will take resilience, the resilience of individuals, societies, structures and planetary systems. However, it also suggested that systems are not only passive and responsive, but have agency and can push back and resist and can be proactive in trying to shape the direction of travel of their own system, or others, and purposefully redirect trajectories and cause change. This too takes resilience: the resilience to withstand stress and risks caused by change and shocks to the system, to deal with tensions caused by conflicts of values, beliefs, ideology and the resilience to, where desired, resist and fight back to create new behaviours, new ways of thinking and new ways of being.

Viewing resilience in this way leads to a new way of conceptualising it. Earlier models portrayed it as something within the individual, or within the structure or system. There was consideration of whether the individual/system were vulnerable or not and acknowledgement that there were ways of providing protection against risks that could occur to build resilience. There was a sense that to be resilient was to be able to withstand shocks and change and to be able to revert back to original state afterwards.

However, Chap. 2 argued for a more systemic approach that recognised that systems were interconnected and affected by other systems, but in turn affected other systems. In other words were interactive and had reciprocal relations with other systems. It also recognised that nothing ever stayed the same and that systems are in a constant state of flux and change as they interact with other systems and move through time and space and are thus dynamic. Considering resilience in this way led to the Dynamic Interactive Model of Resilience (DIMoR) (ahmed Shafi et al., 2020). The chapter suggested that resilience emerges through the intersection of vulnerabilities-invulnerabilities/risks-protection, surrounding structures and interactions with other systems.

This approach moves away from reductionist approaches that might atomise individuals (systems) and look at them in isolation and suggests that any analysis must look more holistically and take account of wider context and other interacting systems. The model thereby serves as a lens, or a tool that helps with considerations of, and with the development of, resilience.

As a further illustration of this interactive and multi-layered nature of resilience, Chap. 3 considers resilient societies and shows how they can only become so if they recognise and seek to build resilient individuals, structures and networks and also acknowledge and protect the systems within and around them. It discusses the diverse nature of systems and the complexity of resilience and the challenge of achieving it. It highlights the role of education and learning and the need for transparency, openness and the proactive sharing of ideas and power alongside cross-disciplinary connections.

The rest of the book then focuses on education, itself a system, and explores various ways it can contribute towards the development of resilience in learners and also in other stakeholders and educational structures and, thereon, how it might help build resilient societies and, perhaps, a more resilient world.

Chapter 4 picks this up by questioning the very purpose of education. It suggests that the recent pace of change of education policy and moves towards more target and data driven agendas are in danger of placing increasing stress on learners, educators and institutions as public facing measures of performance are used to compare and contrast performance in a competitive way. It also suggests that this process, arguably implemented in a quest for equality of opportunity, has tended to move towards a more standardised and uniform approach to education with the instrumentalist agenda of preparation for work. The chapter suggests that the DIMoR (ahmed Shafi et al., 2020) helps analyse such an approach and show how it is not conducive for resilience and that, rather, more freedoms and autonomy should be available for the actors within to respond to individual need and to develop their own and each other's autonomy and agency. This would better prepare them for uncertain futures and help equip them with the confidence, ability and skills necessary to navigate their own future in which they might feel fulfilled and at ease. In so doing this would develop their own resilience, those of others and in turn help contribute to resilient societies.

Probing further into the role of education, Chap. 5 uses the systems approach of the DIMoR (ahmed Shafi et al., 2020) to consider the development of resilience through education from different perspectives: (1) from a systems perspective, (2) from a pedagogical point of view and (3) from a programme-based approach. It argues that the latter has the potential to become a checklist of strategies and implies that there are easy 'solutions' and ways of becoming resilient. It also suggests that a programme-based approach does not take sufficient account of individual context and agency. Instead, the chapter advocates that educational institutions should be organised in such a way that encourages agency and does not over-protect from risk, but instead provides a safe, nurturing environment in which individuals can explore, experiment and take risks at their own pace. This has implications not only for institutional ethos and underpinning values, but also for pedagogy which, the chapter contends, needs to put the individual at the centre of learning and encourage them to take responsibility for their actions and behaviours and, as also suggested in Chap. 4, develop autonomy and agency and thereby resilience.

The theme of a learner centred pedagogy is picked up in Chap. 6 which focuses on the early years' foundation stage. It applauds the key person approach advocated in this phase to nurture and support children and the role of challenge and risk to aid development. The DIMoR (ahmed Shafi et al., 2020) is used to illustrate how this can help create a positive early trajectory towards the development of resilient individuals. It emphasises the importance of this period in laying resilient foundations in children, whilst acknowledging that resilience is contextual, contingent and time bound.

Chapter 7 draws attention to rising incidences of, and concerns about, poor mental health in education. It explores links between mental health, well-being and resilience and the challenge of responding to and meeting needs. The DIMoR (ahmed Shafi et al., 2020) is used to help analyse and search for causes of poor mental health and to look for interventions that might help improve it and develop well-being and resilience. It argues that a more systemic, holistic approach is needed in order to address these issues and that the DIMoR (ahmed Shafi et al., 2020) can assist with this. It also illustrates that, due to the interconnections between systems and the dynamic and interactive nature of resilience, making positive developments to try to improve well-being for learners is likely to have a reciprocal positive effect on the educators too.

An action research project into feedback practices is summarised in Chap. 8 and relays how the research revealed that many students had an emotional response to disappointing grades and feedback which could be uncomfortable and challenging. Students responded in various ways to this: in some cases they seemed to get stuck in this space which could be detrimental to motivation and wellbeing, while in others they took actions to move on in a developmental way. This led to links with resilience and, specifically, academic buoyancy and highlighted again the need to consider things holistically and not to view events, in this case feedback, in an isolated and unconnected way. Having identified indicators of academic buoyancy (the Key 5), the research proceeded to highlight the importance of relationships and dialogue and the impact of learner attributes. In so doing, the chapter showed how the resilience of learners could be supported and developed by creating a supportive, nurturing environment built on relationships and dialogue and by encouraging the adoption of certain behaviours i.e. internal locus of control, assessment literacy, forward thinking, improvement focus and action orientation. However, alongside this it illustrated how the DIMoR (ahmed Shafi et al., 2020) approach helps reflect on the feedback process and notice how systems are interacting and having an effect on each other. This drew attention to the symbiotic relationship between student, tutor/marker, feedback systems, student motivation, workload allocation models, league tables and, ultimately, student and institution wellbeing.

Chapter 9 builds on themes raised in earlier chapters. It centres on research conducted with practitioners working on a nurture group for young children with Special Educational Needs and Disabilities (SEND). Findings revealed that the stresses and emotional demands of running such a group had impact on the mental health and well-being of the practitioners. This highlighted again the interconnected nature of systems and how changes to one can affect others. It showed the importance of taking a systems approach and looking holistically at contexts, recognising the role of relationships and individual attributes in helping to provide protection alongside factors such as leadership, institutional ethos and policy context.

The influence and dynamic interconnection and interaction of context, culture and actors was further explored in Chap. 10 which reported on an Erasmus plus research project that investigated the impact of an intervention programme designed to develop emotional intelligence in learners in the hope of reducing the number who left school early. This focus on emotional intelligence and the notion of self-awareness and self-regulation is relevant as they are recognised as protective factors and can thus potentially help build resilience in individuals with the belief that this would make them more likely to remain in education. The project adopted a highly structured scheme called the Didactics of Emotion and, as such, used the programme-based approach as discussed in Chap. 5. The programme was implemented in the six partner countries with varying degrees of success and indicated that the attitudes, values and beliefs of the people implementing the programme impacted on the effectiveness of the programme as did cultural context. The use of the DIMoR (ahmed Shafi et al., 2020) as a lens through which to analyse the project threw light on the importance of giving due consideration to these other human and systemic factors that are involved in the implementation of, and provide a context for, the intervention and thus affect the trajectory of the individuals involved and their developing resilience.

Chapter 11 develops this theme further. It discusses how education may be viewed by many as a protective factor and indeed for some as something that might compensate for the protective factors that might be perhaps lacking within the family. However, using research with young offenders, it illustrates that, again, this cannot be assumed due to myriad influences on systems and individuals within them. It reveals that, indeed, education in custody may even be detrimental to the development, resilience and well-being of the individual and add to risk factors due to the poor training of educators, the fragmentation of provision, high turnover of staff and the transient nature of individuals concerned. The author suggests that the DIMoR (ahmed Shafi et al., 2020) helps the custodial setting take a holistic, systems view and map risk-protective and vulnerability-invulnerability factors within a context and consider the complexities of the organisation, the organisational structures and the interactions with internal and external systems and individuals together. The chapter argues that this would enable a more complete picture to be developed that would help with the targeting of interventions which would then be better positioned to help the individuals involved develop a resilient approach to life's challenges.

In Chap. 12, the author makes reference to research conducted with 2nd year (level 5) BA Education Studies undergraduates and draws a number of themes together. The chapter contends that the internet, itself a system, plays a pivotal role in the education of young people and permeates the systems that surround us, as suggested by Bronfenbrenner. As a consequence, it can act as both a risk and a protective factor depending on use. Drawing on ideas discussed in Chap. 5, it proposes use of Self Organising Learning Environments (SOLE) as a pedagogical approach. This approach has its foundations in complexity theory and the idea that, from complexity, things emerge. The notion discussed is that, presented with a 'Big Question' by the educator acting as a facilitator, the learners self-organise into groups as they use the internet to explore the question posed. From the activity a fluid and organic situation is created in which learners can change groups and direction during exploration. This, coupled with both the interplay between the learners as they move around and interact and the interplay with the internet and the facilitator creates a sense of chaos from which learning occurs. The author proposes that from such an approach not only learning, but resilience can emerge. Using the DIMoR (ahmed Shafi et al., 2020) approach the chapter shows that such a pedagogical approach as espoused by SOLE can present learners with risk from both the fluidity of the activity itself and also from the use of and exposure to the internet, but in a supportive environment that encourages the development of social capital, agency and autonomy—all components and essential aspects of resilience.

The final chapter, Chap. 13, revisits the central theme of Chap. 4 and, reporting on an Erasmus plus project involved in developing competencies for Educators of Sustainable Development, questions the purpose of education. The chapter makes reference to environmental, ecological and climate change and shows how actions and behaviours of humans threaten the very structures and systems that sustain us. It argues that education has been based on economic models that assume constant growth that is predicated on unlimited supplies of food sources, water and the materials used in production of consumables and on the notion that the Earth can continue to absorb the waste that we produce without damage or long-term effect. In so doing, it shows how the DIMoR (ahmed Shafi et al., 2020) helps us to view sustainability from a systems perspective and recognise how all systems are interconnected. It can thus be seen that our individual and collective actions are damaging other systems e.g. water, climate, ecological and the consequences are that the climate is showing signs of becoming more unpredictable, species are becoming endangered or even extinct and supplies of items that we rely on to produce 'necessities' for our lives in the twenty-first century are rapidly diminishing. This illustrates again the reciprocal relationship of systems within our planetary system and how individual and collective behaviours are affecting the resilience of other systems, which in turn will affect our own resilience, and how it is thus vital to view the interactions and effects holistically. The chapter posits that education is not fit for purpose as existing education systems have created this situation. The project was entitled 'A Rounder Sense of Purpose' as it started from the premise that education should be about more than preparation for employment and economic growth and that it should equip learners with the critical thinking skills, awareness and ability to effect change i.e. the resilience to deal with the changes taking place, to cope with tensions that might be felt between what is happening and with what they feel should be happening and with the resilience to resist and to redirect the current direction of travel, as discussed in Chap. 1.

The premise of the book has been that a reconceptualization of resilience is needed. Whilst examples drawn upon have been European and largely UK based, the ideas presented are applicable more widely to other contexts. The book suggests that there has been a tendency to view resilience as something that is within—whether that be within an individual, an institution, a society or an organisation—and something that needs to be developed. It argues that this can lead to risk aversion and over-protection as stakeholders look to develop that resilience within the given system. Building on models and ideas from Bronfenbrenner; Daniel, Wassell & Gilligan; Ungar; Masten; Rutter; and Downes, introduced in Chap. 2, the book argues that whilst it is useful to consider the risks that the system is exposed to against protective factors; its vulnerability against its invulnerability; and that it is also useful to consider the layers or webs of support surrounding the system and the agency and trajectory of the system itself; it is also important to recognise that the system is not static. It contends that all systems move in time and space and interact with other systems and are in a constant state of flux. From these interactions and this state of change, or chaos, as long as the shocks caused by the interactions are not too great, resilience emerges and the systems continue to adapt and develop.

The book therefore suggests that a systems approach to resilience needs to be taken whereby it is acknowledged that it is not something that is a fixed state, but something that is dynamic and constantly changing in response to interactions with other systems. It thus argues that resilience is not something that is simply within, but that emerges temporally as a result of past and current interactions between and within other systems. The Dynamic Interactive Model of Resilience attempts to capture this by representing systems within systems, each with their own trajectory, each with a mix of protective and risk factors and vulnerabilities and invulnerabilities, interacting with each other. As they do, new trajectories emerge.

The book also highlights agency as a key feature of resilience and notes how this can enable systems to accept change and adapt to it, but also at times to resist change and even to predict it and to influence the direction of travel so to avoid a particular interaction or disruption. The implications of this approach are that, as argued, individuals and systems in general need resilience—the resilience to cope with change, the resilience to deal with tensions and inconsistencies within and across systems and the resilience to be able to deal with the pressure and stress of resisting and redirecting pathways when desired.

The DIMoR (ahmed Shafi et al., 2020) helps with an analysis of the resilience of systems and with the realisation that it is not possible to view any system in isolation, but as part of a bigger system. To accept that we are all interconnected suggests the need to nurture and care for others/other systems given that the wellbeing and trajectory of others will ultimately impact on that of our own, symbiotically. This is as apposite within an educational institution when considering the learners within, as within society when we are thinking about the members within, as within the planet when considering our place as humans living within and alongside life planetary support systems.

The authors present the DIMoR (ahmed Shafi et al., 2020) as a model to encourage a shift in the way that resilience is conceptualised and approached. It will enable practitioners to analyse systems more broadly and think more holistically and contextually as to how to create the conditions for resilience to emerge and be nurtured. To facilitate this process, research plans are in place to develop a practical guide in the form of a framework which can be used by practitioners to help understand the emerging resilience of systems, including the individual as a system in their own right. This framework will provide a strong perspective from which to try to create conditions that would further help emergence of resilience within the system/s under consideration.

The DIMoR (ahmed Shafi et al., 2020), therefore, contains broad messages. Messages about how, as educationists, we might consider and support the emergence of resilience in our learners, but also how, collectively, we might need to consider how we live and work together and how our actions might affect the resilience of other systems around us, including those that we need for our very survival. We are, after all, all interconnected.

Reference

ahmed Shafi, A., Templeton, S., Middleton, T., Millican, R., Vare, P., Pritchard, R. et al. (2020). Towards a dynamic interactive model of resilience (DIMoR) for education and learning contexts. *Emotional and Behavioural Difficulties, 25*(2), 183–198. https://doi.org/10.1080/136 32752.2020.1771923.

Richard Millican is a Senior Lecturer in Education and the Course Leader for the BA (Hons) Education at the University of Gloucestershire where he has worked for the past 10 years. Prior to that he has a long history of working within education, but in different contexts and phases. These include as a Drama and Music teacher across age ranges, a teacher of learners with social and emotional difficulties 5-18, a teacher of English as a Foreign Language to children and adults and a teacher trainer. He has worked in various countries including Spain, Oman and Egypt and in schools, further education colleges and universities including Leeds and Birmingham.

His current interests are in social justice and sustainability and in the role of education in helping to create a fairer and sustainable world. He is currently working on an international research project, A Rounder Sense of Purpose, which is developing a framework of competences for educators of sustainable development linked to the Sustainable Development Goals. This has led to various recent publications alongside work into developing academic resilience and buoyancy with higher education students.

CPI Antony Rowe
Eastbourne, UK
September 07, 2020

SO THIS IS ECSTASY?

To Anne
My Mother and friend

SO THIS IS ECSTASY ?

Bernard O'Mahoney

MAINSTREAM
PUBLISHING

EDINBURGH AND LONDON

Author's Note

Some names have been changed in the text and therefore should not be confused with any real people of that name.

Photo Credits

All the photographs are from the author's collection

First published in Great Britain in 1997 by
MAINSTREAM PUBLISHING COMPANY (EDINBURGH) LTD
7 Albany Street
Edinburgh EH1 3UG

ISBN 1 85158 896 5

A catalogue record for this book is available from the British Library

Typeset in Plantin
Printed and bound in Great Britain by J.W. Arrowsmith, Bristol

CHAPTER 1

Leah Betts was not the only one who was placed on the danger list with little hope of survival after she collapsed at her 18th birthday party. As the media descended on her family for news of her condition, the final curtain was descending on the gang who ultimately supplied the pill that killed her.

Murder may sound dramatic, but as the police closed the net on those who might have supplied Leah's ecstasy tablet, the gangland leaders were preparing to take out anyone they thought might blow their cover, and that included me. But even I couldn't have known how many of my associates were to be affected by the events that followed, or how many of us were going to follow Leah down.

The tragedy was a nightmare for everyone it touched. Her death was to result in the end of a way of life for many; betrayal, misery and death for others. The investigation that followed Leah's collapse tore apart the gang, or 'firm', I was part of. It had controlled the drugs trade in several clubs across Essex and London, including Raquels where Leah's pill had been obtained. The truth about the brutality and ruthlessness of our regime was about to be exposed. It ripped apart the inner sanctums of the Essex gang who were involved in the drugs trade which led to Leah being supplied her pill.

It was Monday morning, 13 November 1995. I was filling my car up with petrol at the garage, thinking about Christmas, of all things. It had been a bad year. I'd suffered enough grief to last me a lifetime: police raids, internal feuds within the firm – and I was on bail for possessing firearms. It couldn't get any worse. As I walked to the garage kiosk, I glanced at the news-stand. Every newspaper had a picture of a girl on the front page. Her eyes were closed, her mouth slack, agape, and there were tubes everywhere. I picked up a tabloid out of curiosity, and paid for the petrol. I looked at the picture and thought to myself, what a waste. I turned the page. There was a picture of Raquels, the Basildon nightclub where I was the head doorman. My heart sank. I knew this was going to cause us serious grief.

When I got in I sat on the stairs and put my head in my hands. I wasn't sure what to do. In the end I decided to ring Dave Simms, the general manager of Raquels. The night before we'd had a furious row about staffing levels. Since his arrival he'd cut the door staff down from the original ten and the previous night we only had four door staff on. Three were male, and the fourth was my wife, Debra, who used to work searching females who entered the club. Of those three males, two were in a bar next door called the Buzz Bar which held up to 250 people, which left me to police the whole of Raquels – the front door, the main dance hall and the dining area above. Three levels, really, which was impossible.

At about 10.30 that night I closed the doors at the club because 400 people had entered. I told the promoters and Simms that no one else was getting in because we simply couldn't police the club. I was very abusive to him. He had cut the door to save money – and because he felt threatened by our firm. With a promise to review the situation, he left at about 11 p.m. Rod Chapman, the assistant manager, whom I had a lot of respect for, agreed with most of what I'd said. He was basically under the same strain as me. He asked me to open the doors because if I didn't he'd get into a lot of trouble with head office. Out of sympathy for him, I agreed.

Basildon is a very violent town. Around midnight a fight broke out behind the DJ stand, involving about 15 male customers. Knives came out, ammonia was squirted and, because of the numbers of doormen, it was very difficult to break up. I was furious that we'd been put in a position which was obviously dangerous. When you're outnumbered, you have to play for keeps. When somebody goes down they have to remain so. Inevitably, people get hurt. It's distasteful, but that's the nature of the business we're in.

At about a quarter to one, as we were dusting ourselves down after the fight, Janet Betts picked up the phone in the nearby village of Latchingdon, and dialled 999. Her stepdaughter Leah had just collapsed.

The first thing I said to Dave Simms when he answered the phone on that Monday was: 'Have you seen the papers today?'

'What do you mean?' he replied. I repeated the question.

'What's the problem, Bernie?' Simms asked.

'Some girl's collapsed after being in our club and she's in a coma.'

I read him the text on the front page. 'There goes our four o'clock licence,' Simms muttered, which was a reference to Raquels being in the process of applying for an extension to their current two o'clock licence. That was all he seemed to be concerned about.

The next person I rang was Rod Chapman, the assistant manager. He had already heard about it on the radio. Rod really couldn't do anything, because he was answerable to Simms. Then I called Martin who was I suppose my right-hand man in Raquels, and also my best friend and the person I relied on most. I told him what Dave Simms had said and we discussed what might or might not happen in the next few weeks. He suggested, and I agreed, that I contact Mark Murray, who was the firm's main drug dealer in Raquels, and sit down and discuss our position.

When I say Mark Murray was the firm's main dealer in Raquels, I don't mean that he was the sole dealer in the club but he ran the drug dealing operation. I have never dealt drugs, but because I was head doorman, Mark dealt with me. I was my firm's representative if you like.

Mark would usually have around six dealers under him working in and around the club. One of his gofers would bring in the drugs for him, which had already been divided into bags of 20 to 50 pills. He very rarely sold drugs himself, but he would hold gear for the dealers and give them new bags as and when they sold out.

Recently, though, there had been a lot of falling out among his dealers, and because he was down to one or two on this particular weekend he had been selling himself.

7

Mark would farm out the work of selling the goods to his dealers in Raquels and profits were divided accordingly. For every pill they sold, they would get a pound. Which does or doesn't seem a lot of money. They would usually sell roughly 100 pills each. In four hours they would earn more than they could working forty hours a week in a straight job. It's easy to understand why people turn to crime. The hours are good, and the pay substantial. But there is a downside. Getting the bullet isn't a phrase used when your services are terminated. It is usually the method used to bring about that termination.

The firm would also take a pound for every pill Murray's dealers sold, and they would also have a free supply of ecstasy, cocaine or speed for themselves. Mark would then have the remainder of the profits. I would estimate that Mark made three pounds on every pill sold. He probably sold 400 plus per night.

In the event of an incident, Mark and I had devised a plan of action. Each Friday night when I saw him at the club we would name a different meeting place for the following week. If something happened beforehand that might endanger his operation, I could just ring him – or he could ring me – and say, for example, 'See you at five o'clock.' If the police were monitoring our calls they would have no idea of what we were talking about or where we were going to meet. This particular week we'd arranged to meet at a pub called the Darby Digger in Wickford, approximately three miles from Mark's house and the same from mine. I rang Mark but his phone was unobtainable.

The first person to call me was a drugs squad officer, whom I'll call John Hughes, from Essex Police HQ in Chelmsford and who'd been taking an interest in me and the firm's activities for some time. He had had me under surveillance and searched my house on a number of occasions. He asked me what was going down my end, and I said I'd only just heard what had happened. I enquired about the girl's condition and he said that Leah was going to die. She was only on the life support machine for the benefit of her family, but all avenues of hope were being explored. I offered to see if I could – and I'm sure that I could have done – get a similar pill to the one she had taken for doctors to analyse in the hope that, knowing the breakdown of the chemicals used, they could somehow help her. He told me that the police were already in possession of several of the pills from the same batch.

At this time everyone believed that the pills were contaminated, which I found hard to believe. The pill Leah had taken was called an Apple, which was a relatively new kind of ecstasy on the scene. The most common type at the time was a pill called Dove, which had a dove motif. Leah's pill, with its apple motif, was considered to be very strong.

Policemen are remarkably like villains: they don't like talking on the telephone. Hughes suggested that we meet. He told me in the meantime to expect a 'spin' (search), because my name had come up continuously on the hotline set up by the police hunting the pushers who had supplied Leah. Because of the interest he took in me, he knew I wasn't a drug dealer.

The reasons were firstly that I was head of security at Raquels, and secondly I was involved with the firm which controlled the drugs in the club.

Nobody else was in touch with me on that Monday. I tried ringing a few people, but they were either all out or unavailable. I tried ringing Tony Tucker: he ran several doors across Essex, south London and Suffolk. In each of the premises Tony appointed a head doorman who was in charge of that particular club, but overall he gave the orders. Our arrangement was slightly different, as I had control of Raquels initially and I later asked him to come in with me. Tony was a huge man – very handy. We had known each other for a few years, but in the past 12 or 18 months, Tony had changed. Things had started to go wrong.

The following day I was out of town. I had a court case in Birmingham to attend – various driving offences. I was banned for 12 months and fined £330. (I was not bothered by such a trivial matter. I had far more important things to attend to.) Driving back down from the court case I heard nothing but the Leah Betts case on the radio. Four addresses were raided that morning in Basildon. One of the addresses raided was a firm member's flat – Pat Tate's. He was one of Tucker's main henchmen and had a flat in Swanstead, Vange.

9

This flat was occupied by Tony Tucker's mistress, a girl called Donna Garwood, 17 years old. Tucker had installed her there.

A quantity of amphetamine was found; not a lot, just a bit of personal. But the fact that they'd raided Pat's flat spoke volumes. Donna was a regular in the club; Pat was a member of the firm and had only been out of prison for two weeks. It was quite obvious that it was only a matter of time before the rest of us got spun. My big concern was all the main players were running a mile, leaving me to face the music. So much for loyalty.

While those on the inside were trying to get out, there were people on the outside trying to get in. A man called 'Vic Peters' appeared in the *Daily Mirror*, his face hidden, obviously. His claim was that he had dealt kids pure poison. He also claimed he had sold ecstasy at Raquels, although I'd never heard of him. He claimed that the pills could be laced with rat poison, guitar wax or toilet cleaner and coated with hairspray. 'Peters' said that whoever sold Leah that pill knew they were selling her poison. 'The pushers don't give a damn,' he added.

The man was a publicity-seeking idiot. He may have been in Raquels, but he'd certainly never sold ecstasy there. It's quite obvious drug dealers wouldn't sell guitar wax or strychnine, because they wouldn't sell many pills. They'd get rid of one or two, cause one or two deaths, and they'd be out of business.

He claimed that they deliberately laced tablets or capsules with deadly rubbish to maximise their profits and that none of the dealers cared if people died or suffered brain damage, because they had made a sale and they wouldn't see that person again anyway. He said he used to sell 100 pills a night in Raquels. This is near enough impossible because what our firm used to do was recruit people who weren't actually willing to sell drugs. They would be told: 'Here's £20, you go into the club and see if you can buy ecstasy or any other drug off anyone. As soon as you find someone selling, buy it off them, come back to us and point them out; we'll take them to the fire exit, spin them, take all their money and take all their drugs.'

Our firm took half and half went to our recruit for his

SO THIS IS ECSTASY?

personal use. Either that or we paid him the money. Those
drugs would more than likely be sold back to the firm's
dealers who would benefit because a rival would have been
taken 'out of the game'. That was the way we'd keep rogue
drug dealers out of Raquels. It was very difficult to see how
this man was selling 100 every Friday and not come to our
attention.

On Wednesday, 15 November, I still hadn't located Mark
Murray, despite going to his house and leaving messages with
everyone. I finally managed to speak to Tony Tucker, and he
didn't want to talk to me. He said he'd got the hump over
Donna Garwood, because she had claimed she had been
grassed up by a doorman, even though at that time no
doorman had been spoken to by the police. Already, though,
a menace fuelled by paranoia was growing. Everyone was
putting their back against the wall and somebody else's name
in the frame.

John Hughes and another detective called round on the
same morning. They telephoned first and told me to meet
them in a street at the back of my house where the garages
were. I went round and sat in the back of the car. They told
me my name had constantly been brought up for supplying
Leah Betts, and they were surprised that I hadn't been spun.
They explained this away by saying the police investigating
Leah's death were probably busy making a case against me.
They were quite sure that the police would descend on me
when they had all the evidence they needed. I wasn't
surprised. Our reign at Raquels had won few friends.
Everyone who had a grudge was now on the phone to *Crime
Stoppers*. True or false information – it did not matter. People
knew it would cause me or the firm grief whatever.

That Wednesday night was the first night that the Buzz Bar,
an annex to Raquels, had been open since Leah had
collapsed. As usual Martin and I were working that night. We
went into work at about eight-thirty, nine o'clock. There was
an eerie atmosphere in there. It was as if everyone had their
eyes on me – half looking for a reaction, I think. I felt like a
condemned man. What made it even more strange was the
fact that in the Buzz Bar there were four television screens.
Every time there was a news item, images of Leah lying in bed

11

with tubes coming out of her were coming up on these four screens. We had this dark room full of kids Leah's age, some on drugs, some not, loud music and pictures of Leah lying in hospital as a result of what went on in this very building. Strange, very strange. And unnerving really.

There were the usual fools, coming up asking for my opinions on Leah. A couple of reporters were in there trying to buy drugs. So obvious: long raincoats, short, tidy hair, middle-class accents, and going up to people asking if they could 'score'. I was just glad to get out of work that night.

I got home early, around 11 o'clock, and there was a telephone call from a local man who asked me if I had a problem with a person called Steve Packman. I'd never heard of Steve Packman in my life.

'Assure him I haven't,' I said.

'Is it all right if I give him your number?' the man asked. I said, 'By all means,' and went to bed thinking that was the end of it.

About ten minutes later, there was another telephone call. I got out of bed, rather reluctantly, picked up the telephone and sat on the stairs. 'This is Steve Packman,' said the voice.

'I'm sorry, I don't know you,' I replied.

'I'm on police bail for the Leah thing. I've got to go back to the police station for allegedly supplying the pills which Leah took.'

'What has that got to do with me?' I asked.

'I've been told that you and the doormen have got a problem with me because of all the trouble at Raquel's,' said Packman. 'I was told that you were after me because of all the trouble at the club.'

'No such thing,' I replied. He was very nervous and didn't seem to believe me, despite the fact that I'd never heard of him. He wanted us to meet so he could explain it all.

I'm always very wary of these sorts of telephone calls but they went with the game I was in and I thought I should meet him in case it was important.

'Can you come out now and meet?' he asked.

'Look mate, it's fucking half 11 at night, I've just come in from work. I don't particularly want to get out of bed and go and meet you and listen to something which doesn't concern me,' I said. 'Ring me tomorrow, and if you wish I'll see you.'

I didn't have a very good night's sleep that night. The call played on my mind. The more I thought about it, the more I was convinced that someone was trying to set me up.

The following day, Debra and I were due to move. We'd bought a house in Saffron Walden. She'd gone over there to wait for the removal van and I took my children to school. I was driving there when I heard on the car radio that Leah had died in the early hours of the morning. Even though I knew two or three days prior to the event that Leah was going to die, I still felt saddened, particularly when I heard her family on the radio.

When I arrived Debra was at the front door, standing outside. 'Have you heard what's happened?' she asked. She had been very upset by what had happened to Leah. Debra had no idea of the firm's involvement. She had never been privy to the business side of things.

Around lunch-time Tony Tucker rang me. He was going mental. He was saying he wanted it sorted out and he wanted it sorted out today. There was too much police attention both on him and on the firm in general, he said. Now Leah had died, the shit was going to hit the fan. He was involved in a bit of serious business at the time, and he didn't want this to interfere with it. I explained to him about the phone call from this Steve Packman, and I explained that I didn't really want to meet the guy because I didn't trust him.

'Look, if he's on fucking bail for it, he's the one who's going to be nicked, not us,' he said. 'If he's already in the frame, there's nothing we can do about it. It's not grassing. But I want the Old Bill off our backs. I don't need this now.'

I wasn't sure how we were going to do that. It wasn't going to be easy. The world and his mother thought that we were responsible. People I had known for years had stopped speaking to me. Reporters were ringing Raquels and my house. They were saying to me, 'Is that Bernie?' Then asking, 'Look Bernie, can you get hold of anything for us tonight?' It was just incredible. Everyone was convinced that either I or one of the other doormen had actually supplied Leah. I agreed with Tony Tucker, the spotlight should be taken off us. But how we were going to do that, I just didn't know.

Not long after Tony rang me, Steve Packman phoned again. He said he couldn't meet me that day because he had to work on his father's market stall in London. He assured me, however, that he'd meet me the following day. I still didn't trust him, but I said okay. I rang round a few people and asked about Packman, who he was and what he was up to. It seemed that a story was circulating in Basildon that on the Wednesday prior to Leah's collapse Martin and I had confiscated approximately 30 ecstasy tablets (Apples, the same type Leah had taken) from a drug dealer named Danny Smith in the Buzz Bar. After confiscating the drugs from Smith, it was alleged that somehow the drugs had found their way to Leah Betts.

The story was partially true. We had confiscated the Apples from Smith because we had found him selling them in there 'unauthorised'. He'd gone away and spoken to his main dealer, a man called Gary Murray. Gary did deal drugs in Raquels, but only on Saturdays. He had come into the Buzz Bar on that Wednesday night and said it was a misunderstanding. Smith was meant to meet someone outside, but it was cold so he came in to wait for them and we caught him selling the pills. I told him I couldn't care less about misunderstandings. 'If you don't like it do something about it,' I said. At no time did any of those pills get given to Steve Packman.

The Thursday night after Leah's death, the Buzz Bar was empty. It's not usually busy anyway, but that night it was deserted. A couple of people – ghouls, I call them – came in to look, then left. I spent most of the evening sitting down trying to decide what to do about Steve Packman. People needed to know he was on bail for allegedly supplying Leah. He couldn't be named on the news at that time because he was under-age – he was only 17. I thought the only way to stop the witch-hunt against me would be if Packman was identified in a newspaper. That way everyone would know that a person had been arrested and he was not a member of our firm or in any way connected to us.

I rang Tony Tucker and started to explain. He didn't want to discuss it. 'Do what you think best, but get it sorted,' he snapped.

I spoke to a reporter I'd known for several years. He and everybody else was aware that people had been arrested and bailed, but nobody was quite sure who they were. Obviously they were keen to find out. He had told me that my name had been offered up to newspapers as the supplier, which I was obviously aware of because of the reporters coming in to the club and ringing my house. I said: 'Look, I'm not involved in this shit.'

I told him about Packman and, although I didn't know at that stage where the meeting would be, that I would ring to give him the details.

The following day was Friday 17 November. There were more raids by Basildon police. During the previous four days there had been a total of 13 arrests. Everyone was becoming paranoid. The members of the firm were all too frightened to speak to each other on the telephone. No one was going out. It was a strange time. I'd have thought that rather than hide from each other, people would get together and confront the problem. But they were running everywhere.

Packman rang me and told me he was again in London and he had an appointment with his solicitor. However, he did say as soon as he was finished we'd meet. I agreed, and arranged to meet him on a garage forecourt. I chose the location for two reasons. Firstly, I feared he may be trying to set me up. This garage forecourt was always busy, so he couldn't say he was being threatened. Secondly, we would be on the garage video so he couldn't later say he was being intimidated or anything else. I insisted we met there rather than in a pub or somewhere else where he could allege something that wasn't true.

I rang the reporter and told him where we were going to meet. I also had reservations about the newspaper's involvement, because I was an obvious suspect. The newspaper man said that the conversation would have to be recorded. This was for two reasons: one to alleviate my fears; but mainly because if Packman tried to sue them they could prove the meeting had taken place. They arranged to photograph him, and the tape would prove that the man I talked to was the man on bail.

I felt I was probably being set up. I armed myself with a

15

tape recorder to record anything that was said to me by the news people. Packman turned up about six o'clock. We shook hands, and the first thing he asked was had I got a problem with him? 'I've got no problem at all with you,' I said. We went into the shop. He had long hair and he was very, very nervous. I remember he kept touching his mouth and pushing his hair back. I think he was expecting me to assault him, because he had heard these rumours. I tried to reassure him.

'Look, we didn't mean to cause you this trouble,' he said.

I asked him what went on.

He said that he knew Leah and her friend Sarah Cargill. They were planning Leah's forthcoming 18th birthday party which was going to be held at her father's house in Latchingdon. Leah and her friends wanted gear for the party, and had approached a friend, Louise Yexley, who was unable to get anything, but said she would ask her boyfriend Stephen Smith (the second person who was on bail). Smith and his friend, Steve Packman, were going up to Raquels that Friday, and Smith said he would try to get some ecstasy at the club.

Smith had made some amateurish efforts to obtain drugs for Leah's party. He had approached several people who told him they didn't know what he was on about. He said to Packman that if he was approached by a dealer, to come and tell him. While Packman was standing at the top bar, he was approached by a man who asked him if he was sorted (had drugs). He described the man as wearing a blue Schott bomber jacket and had long, curly shoulder-length hair. He was describing Mark Murray to me.

He said he returned to Stephen Smith, who gave him the money. He told me he then bought the pills which were later passed down the chain to friends. But he only told me this, he said in court, because he was so frightened of me and Tucker. Our reputation had even reached an innocent teenager.

I said he hadn't caused us any problem, it was just one of those things. My parting words to him were: 'If I were you, take a bit of advice; keep your mouth shut.' We shook hands and he walked off into the night.

I went over to the reporters who were in a van and had been photographing Packman. Nothing untoward had been said. I hadn't implicated the firm. The reporters had a photograph of the man who was on bail and who ultimately was going to be photographed when he appeared in court. It's just that they were getting there first. Tony Tucker would be happy because the spotlight on the firm would be switched off as soon as Packman's picture appeared. Raquels would be happy because Leah hadn't been in the club. I was happy because it was all over, or so it appeared.

I gave my copy of the tape to the reporters. I said I didn't want to see them again and walked off. I wasn't offered money for the story or the picture, and I wasn't paid any.

Two hours later I was at work at Raquels. It was the first night that the main club had been opened since Leah had collapsed. It was very unnerving. There were teams of camera crews everywhere: Sky TV, London Weekend Television, the BBC. There were even a couple of foreign TV crews there. It was just full of media. I felt as if they were all looking at me because my name had been bandied about so much in the past week. They were asking: 'How do these people get these drugs past security?' 'How do these people sell them unnoticed?' I felt like I was the centre of attention, as if I was on trial.

The police had gathered there to hand out leaflets. They said that on Saturday 11 November 1995 Leah Betts collapsed during her 18th birthday party at home, having taken an ecstasy tablet which was obtained from a supplier in Raquels nightclub. Below this was the now famous picture of Leah lying stricken in a hospital bed. Below that were the words: 'She has since died. Do you know the identity of the supplier? Can you provide *Crime Stoppers* with the name of this supplier? Your call is free, you do not have to give your name. You may receive a reward.'

People from everywhere were flocking to get these leaflets from the police. It seemed the queue for the leaflets was bigger than the queue for the club. Dave Simms, the general manager, had made himself scarce, like everyone else that week. He'd left Rod Chapman, the assistant manager, to man the telephones and answer the stream of questions from reporters and journalists. Rod had done a marvellous job, really. I felt quite sorry for him. He was inundated with reporters, cameramen, people trying to catch him out.

Simms was due back in that night, and I was quite keen to see him. We were told that all staff had to attend a meeting in the office prior to opening the doors of the club. The area manager, Colin Agar, was there. Basically we were told that we weren't to talk to the press. All questions were to be directed to the management. And we were to keep a low profile. There was to be strict searching. They had told us the day before that there would be extra door staff. We were even given brand new jackets (previously we hadn't worn a uniform), I suppose so we'd look a bit efficient. It was too little, too late. Getting made up for the TV cameras wasn't going to change anything, particularly as the back of the jackets said Gold, from another club they ran. None of them fitted. In their haste to make us look efficient they also provided us with black T-shirts with 'Security' emblazoned across the front. The only problem was security was misspelt on some, and they read: 'Securtiy'. Gold was going to be the new name for Raquels if it got its four o'clock licence. Quite ironic, really. There was to be no new club and no four o'clock licence. Not for some time anyway.

When the management had finished telling us what we must and must not do, they were quite emphatic that there must be no violence. Incidents must be played down and handled discreetly. They asked if anyone had any questions.

'Has David Simms got anything to say?' I asked.

'What do you mean?'

'Well have you got anything to say about last Saturday?' Simms obviously hadn't told the area manager about the fight. I was still very annoyed. 'Come on then, tell us what happened last Saturday,' I said. 'Four people working 400 people in the club, people pulling knives out, ammonia and everything else. Now the door has nearly trebled to what it was last week. Why couldn't you have given me these people last week?'

'All I can say is that I apologise,' he said.

I really was furious. But of course, no one person was to blame. I was asked to curb my language by the area manager. When I'd finished my bit, they said: 'One more thing, we'd like you to go in twos to Basildon police station because they want to interview you. Bernard, you go last.'

I started laughing. I said: 'Why have I got to go last? Does that mean that they're going to keep me the longest?' He said that when you're called over, if you don't know anything, you can't say anything.

I was expecting something like this from the police, but the more I thought about it, the more concerned I got. So I called my own meeting with the doormen downstairs. I said: 'Look lads, no one's going over to the police station. This is a very very serious matter and if the police want to question you they'll either arrest you or ask you to be questioned, in which case you'll need a solicitor with you, or some sort of legal advice. I don't suggest we go over to the police station willy nilly and hope for the best.'

So I called down the area manager. 'Look, basically we're not going to the police. So ring them up and tell them.'

He rang them, and I believe the police said it was nothing formal, it wasn't to be a statement, or made under caution. I said if people wished to go, they could, but I wasn't going. I believe four went over. They were asked if they knew certain people, if they saw anything suspicious. Just general questions, basically.

Later on in the evening, we were warned to expect Mr and Mrs Betts, who, we were told, were going to come down to the club and possibly walk around. I really, really didn't want this to happen. One, I think it would have created a terrible atmosphere in the club; and two, I didn't really want to face these people. Not that I had any personal guilt, it just didn't seem right. We were told that if they did arrive we should be courteous and give them full access to the club. The doormen should not stay with them, but keep a discreet distance in case an idiot – and there always is one, especially in Raquels – should do anything silly or controversial.

Fortunately they never did arrive. But it was that night that I first set eyes on Superintendent, or I think he was then Chief Inspector, Brian Storey, who was leading the Leah Betts investigation. He came through the main doors of Raquels after giving numerous interviews outside, and he had a cup of coffee in his hand. The first thing I said to him was, 'Where's mine?'

'You can have this one, if you want,' he said.

'No, you're all right,' I said, and he walked off. I was quite surprised that he didn't want to question me. But later on, as future events unfolded, I got to know him more and more.

I would have thought the Leah Betts tragedy would have deterred our regular idiots from performing that night. But as I said, Basildon is a very violent town. In full view of the television cameras and the police, a group of youths came to the doors and wanted to fight the doormen. They didn't give a particular reason – they never do. They were just abusive, using threatening words and behaviour, trying to make the news, I guess. I tried to calm them down and all the doormen were going, 'Watch it Bernie, the Old Bill's here, the Old Bill's here, they're watching you.'

I'd never been one to be really too concerned about the police and so I hit a particularly mouthy one who seemed to be in some sort of authority. There was a scuffle and a doorman pulled me away. The person I'd hit stood in the street shouting. Fortunately for him, the police intervened. We didn't usually stand for that type of behaviour.

Several police officers approached him, and he ran. They chased him through the town and I believe he was arrested. From there on in the mood grew uglier.

Later that night there was a second fight outside. This time a man was nearly murdered. Charlie Ayers, a 20-year-old, was attacked outside Raquels. He staggered to the nearby taxi rank where he collapsed in a pool of blood. He pleaded with the two taxi drivers to take him to hospital but they refused. Charlie lost almost four pints of blood and nearly lost his life. He suffered a punctured lung and more than six stab wounds. He was rushed to Basildon's intensive care unit after police arrived at the taxi rank and called an ambulance. It was alleged in the local paper that taxi drivers had refused to take him because of the amount of blood he was losing and the mess it would have caused in their cars. A man was arrested later that night and charged with grievous bodily harm with intent.

It was business as usual. Leah's tragedy may have touched the nation, but it certainly wasn't touching the nutters in Raquels.

I waited all night at the club, expecting word from Mark Murray. I didn't expect him to turn up in person, but I did expect somebody to come with a message, so we could meet. I also expected Tony Tucker to show his face, or for him to send some sort of message. Surely they were curious as to what was going on. But nobody came.

On Saturday 18 November, the police were still making themselves busy. I heard on the radio that there had been a raid in Brentwood. Nine hundred ecstasy tablets had been seized at a café. Two men had been arrested. I was losing count now of the number of people the police had arrested or pulled in for enquiries. I was just so concerned that they hadn't come to me. Not officially, anyway. But as John Hughes told me, the only reason they hadn't was that they were probably building a case against me.

I didn't know what to do. I'd had it up to here with Raquels, and so had my family. If the firm had pulled together during the crisis, it would have made it so much easier, but I just couldn't reach anyone or see anyone or get to talk to anyone. Once you are in that situation, it's only a prison van, hearse or monumental tragedy that's going to get you out of it.

One of the doormen said jokingly to me, this would be a good time to make some money. He said: 'You're the head doorman, imagine how much money you'd get if you told the whole story about this place to a newspaper.'

'The way I feel now, I'd fucking do it,' I answered. 'I tell you what, I'll give it a lot of thought.'

I rang a reporter I'd known for some time, named Ian Cobain, on the *Daily Express*, and he expressed an interest. We agreed on £8,000, but I told him I'd only give him the ins and outs on the club. This didn't involve naming people, naturally. It related to the short staffing and the dispute I'd had with the management. It was such a difficult decision to make, I called a meeting with the door staff and explained to them my predicament.

Whatever happened regarding the Leah Betts enquiry, common sense told me that the management would want to show that there had been changes, i.e. changes in security. If I was put out of work, nobody was going to pay me any money, and nobody was going to look after my wife and children. So I said to them, 'I've made my decision and I'm going to do this story.' No one objected. Everyone understood my position. I did my story with the paper and went into work that night.

It was very quiet, as I recall it. All night long I just wanted to get out of there. I'd had enough of the place. I hated it, I loathed it. I was meant to stay until two o'clock. There was me, Martin, Debra and a couple of other doormen. I didn't do anything at all that night, work-wise. I just sat at the bar and had a drink. About 11 o'clock, I said to Martin, 'Fuck this, let's go.'

I went to Maurice, a doorman from Bristol, whom I had a lot of faith in. I had first known about him from a previous manager of Raquels. He'd told me that his friend Maurice was in prison for breaking a man's arm during a road rage incident and was looking for work when he got out. I told him to bring him up on his release, and we'd sort him out. The evening he arrived in Basildon, he was given a bit of money and a job. He had worked for me ever since.

He was a very sensible guy. I said to him: 'Look, Maurice, I want you to be head doorman.' We agreed, shook hands. I went up to the office. I knew the manager would never agree to Martin, my best friend, getting the door, because he was too much like me. Maurice was the sort of person the management would get on with. He was very professional. He wasn't a villain doorman.

I went to the office with Martin. 'I'm leaving,' I told Simms.

'What's the problem?' he asked. 'There ain't no problem. I don't like you, you don't like me, I'm leaving. See you later,' I said, and walked out.

I went downstairs to the main dance area. I said goodbye to the barmaids, I said goodbye to Rod. I felt quite saddened leaving him. I felt too much responsibility had been put upon him. When things went wrong he was the fall-guy, so saying goodbye was particularly difficult. I didn't really care about anyone else. The doormen had got their jobs, I'd remained loyal to them. I said to Martin and my wife, 'Let's get out of here.'

We walked out of the door together and the last five or so years were just forgotten, goodbye Raquels. The firm, the violence, the police, the grief, it all meant nothing now. It was a thing of the past. Or so I thought.

CHAPTER 2

8 July 1986. The prison warder unlocked the door, and I stepped onto the street. 'See you soon, O'Mahoney. Next time bring a friend,' he said. I turned to answer but the main gate of Stafford Prison slammed behind me.

I'd just finished six months of a 12-month sentence for wounding with intent. It was no big deal. I'd cut a man with a bottle following an argument in a pub in Staffordshire. I was in my mother's home town and arguing with a friend about village gossip, where people were bad-mouthing me and my friends. Another man, named Mark Green, kept getting involved, which made it doubly annoying. I kept telling him to go away, but he persisted in interfering. Eventually I was so angry I hit him across the forehead with a bottle.

Prison didn't agree with me at all. It wasn't so much the Victorian environment, it was the company one was forced to keep. I was sick of petty rules, petty screws and wannabe movie-star gangsters.

It was good to be out. It was two years since I had been free in England. I'd gone to South Africa following the bottling incident, as I'd previously been convicted of the same offence and I knew I would go to prison. I was arrested when I tried to make my way back into the country. But now that was history, and I was thinking all the philosophical shit you have to believe in: a fresh start; new beginnings; no more trouble. Futile, but essential to raise one's hopes.

My first port of call was the mandatory appointment with one of my probation officers in Basildon, Essex. When I was convicted, she had been appointed to give me supervision and guidance. She certainly had her work cut out. She had spent

23 years of a sheltered life in school and college earning qualifications. But she had skipped the practical side of her subject. The first time we met I explained politely that she couldn't begin to assist me, or understand the world I inhabited. Without much argument, she agreed.

Instead of paying regular visits to me in prison, as per regulations, she used to have a day out of the office shopping, and I used to write to her saying what a good and fruitful visit we had enjoyed together. That way she would not have to bother me and she could enjoy an all-expenses-paid day out on the town with her mum.

On the train journey south, I was considering my prospects. I had never been to Basildon before. I had met Debra in Johannesburg. She lived in Basildon and had helped me secure parole by allowing me to use her address. Debra was in South Africa working as a rep for a British hairdressing company and I was out there distancing myself from the constabulary.

There was no romance between us in South Africa. Debra and I were just very good friends. Our first embrace had been in the police cells in Dover where she'd come to meet me as I re-entered the UK. Sadly, two detectives had also decided to welcome me home. They took me back to Staffordshire that day and the following morning I was in Crown Court having pleaded guilty to bottling Mark Green.

Debra had been very loyal to me, visiting me in every dustbin the Home Office had sent me to. We were not Richard and Judy but we were happy.

Because of my reluctance to conform, I had been in five prisons in six months. First was Shrewsbury, then Birmingham, which was an allocation place. After that I went to Ranby in Nottinghamshire. It was full of low-intelligence criminals: shoplifters and petty crooks. I was accused of trying to escape from there, which wasn't true. I had only been there six or seven hours and I was put into an isolation unit. Then I was moved to Lincoln, which was full of northern prison officers who thought they were on this earth to persecute the prisoners. I asked to be moved near to my home town, and they said they'd never move me under any circumstances.

But I thought of a way round that. They have a box for mail, but a lot of cons put notes in there about other prisoners. Another guy and I devised a plan where we would put notes in this box about myself, saying O'Mahoney's got a works (a syringe), so a prison officer would search my cell for heroin every morning. We stepped the notes up to say O'Mahoney's selling bad gear and we're going to kill him. The plan worked. After that note, the governor decided he didn't want drugs in his prison, and we were moved to Stafford via Birmingham.

My first sight of Basildon new town was Laindon Station and the Alcatraz Estate, so called because of the warren of alleyways and Legoland-type flats it was made up of. The plan was I was to ring Debra from the station, but as she said she only lived five minutes away, I thought I would surprise her. Armed with her address I set off. The only person I did surprise was myself.

I spent an hour walking round identical streets hopelessly lost before I finally found her home. I was very pleased to see Debra. Unfortunately, the Home Office do not allow for such feelings. I had to report to my probation officer within one hour of reaching the town. I've had several probation officers in my life, so I know the ritual. Sit down, smile, 'How are you? How are you feeling? Do you regret the crime? Do you think you'll be in trouble again? Congratulations, Mr O'Mahoney, you've just won your freedom. See you again next month. Goodbye.'

Coming out of prison is a shock to the system. Employers tend to shun you and socially you have an unacceptable stigma. But eventually Debra and I did settle down to what most would consider to be a normal life.

Debra had her own hairdressing business, and I used to commute to London every day for my job as a heavy goods vehicle driver. The hours were very, very long, leaving my house at quarter to five in the morning and returning at seven in the evening. But it kept our heads above water. I didn't really mix with anyone from Basildon. My friends were in south London where I'd lived before going to Africa.

In June 1987, Debra and I had our first child, Vinney. We both wanted children, and Vinney brought us a lot of happiness. We lived a pretty uneventful life, really. Vinney took up most of our time, but he was a labour of love rather than a chore.

Debra and I had never got married officially, but because of the rather outdated views on children born out of wedlock, I had adopted her surname. In 1988 this simple exercise of changing my name brought rather surprising results. I had heard of young children and deceased persons being summoned for jury service due to clerical errors. But an ex-prisoner with at least five different reasons for being disqualified did seem rather bizarre. Nevertheless, the thought of me, an habitual criminal, sitting in judgement on others was intriguing. The desire to see for myself what went on on the other side was the major factor in my deciding to go.

I was asked if I had any convictions, and my denial was accepted without any checks being made. Once inside the jury's waiting room, I sat for the entire morning with approximately 50 other potential jurors, the vast majority of them obviously middle-class. The main topics of conversation seemed to revolve around bringing back the birch and the need to reinstate national service. A group of middle-aged ladies at an adjoining table talked as if they were already on the point of passing sentence on the as-yet unseen defendant. They agreed on suitable punishments for burglars, rapists (quite unprintable), car thieves and vandals. They were not quite so ready to discuss the question of innocence or guilt.

It struck me that by extracting jurors from a group of people of 'good character', we were in fact denying the accused person the chance of a fair trial. Judging by the blinkered views of the people I was mixing with at Chelmsford Crown Court, anyone charged with a crime must carry a degree of guilt.

The second thing I learned in a short time was that judges' directions are ignored. Jurors do discuss their cases with other people, and they are influenced by other people's views. In this room of 50 or more people the majority were discussing the cases they were on with jurors from other cases. It was during these conversations that I learned just how easily I could influence these people. Because we were not known to each other, nobody wanted to say the wrong thing to upset the other person. For the vast majority of them, it was the first time they had been part of such a sinister and exciting world.

SO THIS IS ECSTASY?

They kept their mouths shut and their ears open. They wanted to absorb knowledge from the learned and not expose their innocence.

I sat on two rather minor cases. One was a fraud case where a man had relieved a company of some money. And the second was a family dispute which had escalated into minor family warfare.

After hearing all the evidence, the jurors are ushered into a room and locked in. They select a foreman and then they are supposed to discuss the case and come to an agreed verdict. On both occasions, none of us had met before, other than to exchange pleasantries. We all sat round a big table, and there was nervous sniggering and an uneasy silence. No one wanted to begin talking. I took the initiative and suggested that they elect a foreman.

I knew straightaway who they were going to elect. It was an elderly gentleman wearing a regimental badge on his blazer. Something signalled doom for the accused man who was sitting in the cells below waiting for us to decide his fate. They started off going down the track of guilt. I learned in the waiting room outside that to be outspoken is to be heard. I attacked the evidence with vigour and before too long I had everyone in the room in agreement.

I've always believed that law and justice are two separate things. Law is man-made, and justice is natural. In the family dispute case a teenager had assaulted an elderly gentleman who lived next door. The gentleman's sons had gathered and gone round to the teenager's house and assaulted the teenager and his brothers. They were guilty in law, but it was justice to me. The gentleman in the fraud case had fallen on hard times, and had acquired a bit of money, not a lot, from a very large national company for his family, which to me was fair enough. In the end both cases were found not guilty.

People may say that my actions are the very reason that persons with convictions shouldn't sit on a jury, but I'd argue that most of these cases should not have come to court in the first place, and if there were more people with knowledge of life involved in the judicial system many of them wouldn't come up. Criminals do not set crime figures, the law does. Fifteen years ago, if a boy stole apples from a farmer's field and he was chased by the farmer with a stick, there would be no action. It's an everyday occurrence of no relevance. Today the youth would be charged with theft and probably trespass, the farmer would be charged with carrying an offensive weapon, using threatening words and behaviour and possibly assault. This is why crime figures are spiralling out of control, not because young people are any worse. I know from personal experience that if you treat an impressionable young juvenile like a criminal, you will create a criminal.

In October 1988, I read a newspaper article about a 10-year-old boy named James Fallon. He'd been the victim of an horrific accident in Johannesburg, South Africa. James was riding his bicycle when he was struck by a car being driven by a 17-year-old schoolboy who had no licence. The vehicle dragged him 30 metres along the road. There was virtually no hope that he would live. He was unconscious with serious internal injuries and a crushed leg. James also suffered severe spinal injuries and 'died' twice. Top surgeons from all over South Africa managed to save his life with a seven-hour operation which received worldwide publicity.

It was the first time such an operation had been carried out in South Africa, and only the fourth time anywhere in the world. James could not talk, breathe or swallow without the aid of a life support system. His mother, Elaine, had been brought up in the same street as me in the Midlands. I read that James needed a computer similar to those needed by jet fighter pilots which would allow him to communicate by eye movement.

As Elaine was from my home town, I decided I would try to help them raise this money and that the best way to do this would be to stage a charity auction. I set about writing to more than 150 celebrities requesting that they send me something which they had signed or was somehow connected to them. Phil Collins, U2, Tina Turner, the Rolling Stones, the Who, Liverpool FC, Manchester United, Arsenal and countless other people responded. Probably the most surprising response I got was from Ronald and Reggie Kray. Reggie rang my house and said he had heard about James and my efforts through the Dire Straits PR person, and he and his family were touched by James's plight and wished to help me.

It seemed pointless trying to raise money for a boy from the Midlands in the South of England, particularly as he was in a South African hospital – this was the height of the anti-apartheid period and feelings were running high against South Africa – so I decided to stage the event at a hotel on the outskirts of Birmingham.

I booked the hotel and travelled to Birmingham with my brothers, Michael and Paul, and we began to try and sell tickets for it. However, my reputation went before me and the locals didn't show much enthusiasm, not because they didn't have feelings for James, but because they deemed a criminal assisting another human somehow unethical.

I thought their actions were far worse then any act I had committed. While travelling from pub to pub in our efforts to sell tickets, we encountered a group of young men hanging about in the street acting loutishly. One of these boys, a Stuart Darley, shouted an obscenity. I stopped, turned round and asked him what he had said. He denied saying anything. I turned and began to walk again with my brothers. Again he shouted an obscenity and I turned round. He had had his chance. I walked up to him and hit him in the face. He started saying: 'Don't hit me, please don't hit me, I haven't done anything.'

His friend ran to a nearby telephone box and tried to ring the police. I ran over to the telephone box and prevented him from doing so. Meanwhile, Stuart Darley began to get brave again. He started shouting further obscenities. I walked over and again I hit him.

Vulnerable people walking the streets may have to endure this behaviour, but I certainly wasn't going to. The following day, Paul and I returned to the south (Paul lived in south London) and Michael remained in Birmingham. At about midday I received a phone call and I was told that the police were searching for us. Throughout my youth I had experienced quite a volatile relationship with the local police, and I wasn't too concerned. I certainly wasn't going to jump into my car and go and hand myself in.

I rang James Fallon's grandmother and explained that I would not be able to attend the event because of personal problems. However, it had been advertised in the local papers and pubs, it was all organised, and there was no real reason for me to go.

I wasn't surprised to later learn that only 20 people attended. I had half-expected it. The local people had let James down badly. They had snubbed James Fallon's needs in an attempt to get at me.

Debra was still running her hairdressing business, and I was still commuting to London driving heavy goods vehicles. Meanwhile we moved out of the flat on the Alcatraz estate to a three-bedroomed house nearer to Basildon town centre. In November 1989, our second child was born: Karis, a girl. I had no sisters and I'd never imagined myself having a daughter. Debra and I were overjoyed.

The snub by local people in my efforts to raise money for James had become a personal matter. Although my efforts on behalf of James began to take a strain on my family life – I'd been doing this for over a year – I travelled to Broadmoor Hospital in Berkshire on 16 November 1989 for my first meeting with Ronnie Kray, who wished to discuss with me ways of raising money for James Fallon.

I was quite surprised when I first met Ronnie. He was a small man, and good manners personified. He and I got on very well. We sat in a visiting room, which was very much like a hospital day room, and drank can after can of Kaliber alcohol-free lager. Ronnie was genuinely concerned about James Fallon. He told me that he considered himself to be lucky. He had his health, he had his strength. He had his new wife, Kate. He said he could smoke and drink and wasn't complaining about his lot. 'Anybody with feelings would be concerned about what happened to James,' he said. 'It's one of the most terrible cases I've heard of in my life.' After that, I started to visit Ronnie on a regular basis, sometimes twice a day.

Ronnie was on the same ward as the Yorkshire Ripper, and on occasions he would be in the same visiting room at an adjacent table. Ronnie despised him. He considered it an insult that Peter Sutcliffe had been given a 25-year recommendation after butchering 13 women and attempting to murder a further seven, while he had been given a 30-year recommendation after shooting a fellow criminal. 'It is as if,' he would say, 'the law considers me a worse man than him.'

After toying with various ideas, Ronnie, his brother Reggie and I decided to stage a charity boxing show for James Fallon in the south of England. The twins said that I shouldn't concern myself with the events in Birmingham as they would ask their friends and the numerous people who supported them to rally round and support it. Again I threw myself wholeheartedly into preparing for a fund-raising event for James Fallon.

The police in Birmingham, meanwhile, were still trying to track down me and my older brother. They had arrested my brother Michael and he was on police bail.

In January 1990, I was in Peckham, south London, having a drink with my friends Colin Allabyrne and Ray Cartland. Colin was on the run from the Army over a compassionate leave application. During the winter of 1987, a very good friend of ours, Adrian Boreham, from Battersea, south London, was killed in a road accident while serving with the British Army in West Germany. He was 19 years old. Colin had gone on the run from the Army because they refused him permission to attend his friend's funeral as he was not immediate family. Colin had attended the funeral anyway.

It was a Sunday and we were in the Heaton Arms, Peckham Rye, near where Ray lived. At about 10.30 he said he was going home and asked Colin, who lived in Stratford, East London, how he was getting back. Colin replied, 'I'm going to get the tube to Stratford.'

Unknown to us, a group of very large men, probably in their 40s, were standing nearby listening to our conversation. Apparently Millwall FC, the local team, and their arch Docklands rivals, West Ham United, had been playing at the Den in New Cross that day and I can only assume that when Colin said he was returning to Stratford, these people thought we were West Ham supporters. Ray went home first and afterwards at closing time Colin and I left the pub. I was walking in front of Colin when I heard a loud thud. I turned around and saw four or five men, the 40-year-olds, with baseball bats and Colin lying flat out on the floor. He had been hit in the face with the baseball bat between his chin and nose. His jaw was broken, his cheekbone was broken and his teeth hadn't been knocked out: they had been pushed flat underneath and above his tongue.

I ran to assist Colin and they knocked me unconscious. The police were told by a witness that I was laid on my back and my knees were smashed by the bats, and that my assailants were shouting: 'Cripple the bastard, cripple him!'

When I awoke I was in King's College Hospital, East Dulwich. I had stitches in my head and both my knees were swollen to twice their normal size. I had no money on me. Whether this had been stolen or whether it had been lost *en route* to hospital or in hospital, I really didn't know. My first reaction when I woke up was to tell the nurses I was going home. They thought this rather amusing: I could barely sit up or move because of my injuries. But I still got out of bed and managed to reach the street.

All my clothing was covered in blood. It was about eight o'clock in the morning and I scrambled onto a bus full of commuters. I said to the driver, 'I've just come out of hospital. I've got no money on me. I've got to get to a Tube,' and I just sat down. He didn't say anything to me.

I managed to get onto the tube network and eventually on a train to Basildon. This was at about a quarter to nine. I must have looked like a lunatic sitting there, smothered in blood, disorientated because of the injuries to my head. I reached Upminster, two stops from Basildon, thinking I was home and dry, when suddenly a ticket inspector appeared. He demanded a ticket. I said to him: 'Look mate, I've had a bad fucking day. Leave me alone. I'm not in the mood. Go away.' To my surprise, he did.

Since the assault I've had an operation on my knees and I underwent physiotherapy every week for almost two years. I still suffer from arthritis and other related injuries. I have returned to the pub on a number of occasions with my friends to seek revenge, but I've never found who was responsible.

During the preparations for the boxing show for James Fallon, I was contacted by a man called James Campbell, who had been appointed by the Kray twins to assist me in promoting the show. He in turn had appointed a partner, a man called David Brazier, whom Campbell worked for in a taxi office in Chigwell, Essex. I didn't particularly see the need for persons to be named as promoters etc and was not happy with the situation. But I was grateful for the twins' assistance and let matters be.

Reggie Kray sent me a list of phone numbers and addresses of all his friends and persons he thought could assist me or attend. These were people from the criminal world: Charlie Richardson, Frankie Fraser, Tony Lambrianou, whom I had met on various visits with Ronnie Kray, John Masterson and the Scotsman Jimmy Boyle. Celebrities included Barbara Windsor, Bob Hoskins, Roger Daltrey, Jon Bon Jovi, who had been in contact with Ronnie, and the Kemp twins who were at that time making the film *The Krays*. Another person on the list was a man named Keith Bonsor. He, the letter said, was the manager of a local nightclub in Basildon called Raquels, and Reggie suggested I go and see if he might attend and also sell tickets via the nightclub.

I went to see Keith Bonsor one Wednesday afternoon, 21 March 1990, two days before the event, which was to be held at the Prince Regent Hotel in Woodford, Essex. Keith said he was unable to attend, and would pass on my phone number to people he thought would be interested.

Debra and I were still encountering financial problems because of our new house. We also wanted to give our children everything, so I was looking for further employment.

Reg suggested I ask Keith Bonsor if he had any door work available, which I could do on Friday evenings and the weekends for additional income. Bonsor told me that they employed a security company and the head of that security company was responsible for the hiring and firing of all the doormen. This person was Dave Vine and he would be in on Friday and Saturday evenings. If I was to attend an adjacent bar, which was called Strings – the Piano Bar – any Friday or Saturday evening, I would be able to speak to him personally, and he would be able to assist.

That same Wednesday evening, I had a meeting with James Campbell and David Brazier at a pub in Epping. When we'd finalised discussing Friday's event, I rang Debra to tell her I was on my way home. She told me that James Fallon had lost his fight for life that day. I really felt sorry for the boy and his family. He had put up a terrific fight, and so had they.

I went back to Campbell and Brazier and told them that James had died. Their reaction was, well what should we do with the money? I felt sick. I told them that James's family had incurred huge debts in their fight for James, as there was no national health service in South Africa, and all monies from the event would go to the family.

Reg and Ronnie I know were deeply moved and upset by the news of James's death. It was reported at the time that Reg wept. It certainly wouldn't surprise me, because when he talked to me on the phone, he was really choked up. On the night of the event, a telephone was connected to the public address system and the 200 diners, who had each paid £40 to attend, fell silent as Reggie Kray paid a moving tribute to James – he'd been granted special permission to telephone the hotel from Lewes Prison.

It was a sight to see so many criminal heavyweights standing sombre, paying tribute to ten-year-old James Fallon. Charlie Kray attended, so did Ronnie's new wife Kate, Joey Pyle, former Page 3 model Flannagan, Chris Lambrianou and his brother Tony, who had both been convicted with the Krays for the murder of Jack the Hat, and various other people who did not want to publicise their presence as they were normally residents in exile in Spain, but had risked attending at the express wishes of Reg.

TV stars including Glenn Murphy and Ray Winston also attended. It was at this event that I met Geoff Allen, who is said in various books and newspaper articles to be the man they call the Godfather of the Krays. Geoff was 70 but had the mind and heart of a young man. He was jailed at Norwich for seven years in 1976 for masterminding a £300,000 insurance swindle after an historic building named Briggatt Mill was burned down. It was also believed in police circles that Geoff was the man behind the Great Train Robbery. Geoff told me it was to his house in Suffolk that Ronnie and Reggie went to lie low after murdering Jack the Hat.

The event raised a reported £15,000. However, at the end of the evening when I went to collect this money, I could not find Campbell or Brazier. The hotel and other expenses had been paid, but there didn't seem to be any balance forthcoming. Despite my efforts I was unable to contact either of the men that evening.

During the following days calls from Ronnie and Reggie were fast and furious. They demanded that the money be handed over to the family. I was in total agreement, but I could not find the men. Promise after promise followed meeting after meeting, but the money never did materialise. To this day it remains a mystery as to where it went. The promoters insisted that it was swallowed up by expenses. I find that hard to believe. I thought it rather ironic when I read one year later, on 22 December 1991 in the *Sunday People*, that David Brazier had taken the dying for a ride when he pocketed the proceeds of a charity football match.

I told the twins after James Fallon's event that I wanted to seek some sort of retribution, but Reg was adamant that it be forgotten, because the Krays had always been associated with charitable funds, and understandably, they didn't want to be associated with a charity rip-off. I rang the Fallon family and told them I would be unable to attend the service being held in this country for James as I still had problems with the local police force who were looking for me for the earlier assault. The truth of the matter was, I was too embarrassed to show my face.

The following weekend Debra and I asked her mother if she would babysit for us. We were going to the cinema in Basildon to see the film *Ghost*. At the end of the film Debra and I had to wait until everyone else had left the cinema because she was in tears over the film. She was still quite tearful when we had walked the 500 yards or so to the entrance of Raquels where I was due to go and see Dave Vine. It's ironic, looking back now, that my arrival at Raquels was shrouded in sadness and my departure would be in much the same vein.

CHAPTER 3

The bar was fairly quiet when I went in. On a small stage there was a white grand piano, a memorial to the man who tried to bring culture to Basildon. He'd called his bar Strings – The Piano Bar.

Although it was done out like a fancy cocktail bar, the clientele were mainly middle-aged heavy drinkers and peroxide blonde Essex girls. The pianist had been replaced by a DJ who had put his record decks on the piano lid and wrapped flashing rope lights around the legs. I asked the barmaid where I could find Dave Vine. After undergoing the 'Who wants to know?' formalities, I was finally introduced to him.

Dave was about six foot tall, balding, and very powerfully built. He told me he had a partner, Micky Pierce, and they ran a couple of clubs and most pubs in the Basildon area. He offered me £40 a night and told me I could start on Friday. We shook hands. I wasn't surprised to be offered the job straightaway because of Reggie's recommendation and the fact that doormen know doormen, by the way they look and act. I'd done the job before. You speak the same language, you're all on the same level.

Wearing a dinner suit and a bow-tie and being surrounded by drunks is quite an unpleasant experience, so I was pleased to learn on my first night that I would be working at the top bar rather than at the front door. But it wasn't long before I discovered that this was where most of the heavy drinkers gathered and where most of the trouble took place.

Vine introduced me to my fellow doormen. There was no unity among them. Most of them were like me, there just for a bit of extra money. There wasn't a gang or a firm as such. I wasn't impressed. I said hello, and went straight to work.

About two hours into the night a pot-man, the guy who collects the empty glasses, came over to me and said somebody was causing trouble on the dance floor. He pointed to probably the largest man in the club. He had another man by his neck and was threatening him. I went over and said: 'Leave it out mate, or you'll have to go.'

'It's all right, I know the score, I'm a doorman,' he replied.

I said: 'It's not all right, and if you are a doorman and you do know the score, then you will leave it out. If you wish to sort it out you'll have to sort it out outside.'

He let go of the man, and started walking down the stairs with me following him. We went down one flight of stairs and he stopped at the cloakroom and began to talk to a female, I assume it was his wife or girlfriend. I was insistent: 'I'm sorry, you've got to leave.'

'Who the fuck are you, anyway?' the man shouted. 'No fucking northerner tells me what to do.'

I grabbed him in a headlock and tried to force him down the stairs. He struggled and I began to punch him in the face. We both rolled down the stairs and at the bottom, as I was fighting with him, his girlfriend hit me across the nose with a champagne glass, took off her high-heeled shoe and started to hit me across the head with it. It was laughable, really, but we continued fighting down the stairs.

He was quite a large man, so it was difficult to fight him and defend myself from the blows from his girlfriend. I somehow managed to keep going until eventually we were fighting in the foyer where five or six of the other doormen were. I remember fighting and thinking: 'Why aren't they helping me?'

I saw Micky Pierce, Dave Vine's partner, laughing. I couldn't work it out at all. Eventually the doormen split us up and the man went out of the door of his own free will. I was livid: 'What the fuck do you think you're doing? Do you work on your own here or what?' Pierce calmly explained to me that the man I'd thrown out of the door was a doorman who worked with us, but it was his night off.

It wasn't the best impression I've made on my first day at a new job, but it was to secure my reputation. It was an impression people retained about me throughout my time at Raquels.

Raquels was a very violent club. I would expect to be involved in at least two fights each night I worked. However, it wasn't all gloom. One evening, Keith Bonsor had booked a fire-eater to do a stage show. The fire-eater turned up drunk and was quite unsteady on his feet. During the show he tipped flammable fluid in his mouth and blew out a large cloud of fire over a naked flame. But because he was drunk, when he swigged back the fluid, he'd poured it down his chest and his arm, and set himself alight. He fell off the stage backwards, into the curtains behind the stage, and the curtains caught fire. The doormen were despatched to put him and the curtains out. It was a funny moment.

Things were going okay for me and Debra now I had extra income, so I decided to get the matter with Stuart Darley sorted out at my convenience rather than waiting for the police to catch up with me and arrest me when it may not have been convenient.

My brother and I travelled to the Midlands and gave ourselves up. Over a period of time we went through the rigmarole of attending numerous magistrates courts waiting to be committed to crown court. Eventually we were told we had to appear at Stafford Crown Court for trial. However, no date was fixed. When you're sent to a Crown Court, you are not given a date; you are told usually two or three weeks prior to the trial that you're being put on a waiting list. Judges and the police don't know how long a trial's going to last, because a defendant could change his plea or a witness might fail to attend or whatever. It could be over in a day, for example, so you are told to ring your legal representatives each evening to find out if you're in court the next morning.

One evening I was in Newcastle driving a heavy goods vehicle and I rang my legal representative. I was told I had to attend Stafford Crown Court the following morning at 10.00 a.m. I told him that I would be unable to reach Stafford by then because of legal restrictions on the hours you can drive heavy goods vehicles, but that I would be there not long afterwards. My brother Michael was with me at the time.

We set off as soon as we could and made our way to Stafford. On the way there we rang the Court to tell them where we were and our expected time of arrival. However, when we did arrive at 11.30 we were told that a warrant had been issued for our arrest and the case put off to a later date.

Two weeks later the trial started. We were all charged for not answering our bail. This matter related to the one and a half hours that we were late on the first day. For this heinous offence we were each fined £50. We all pleaded not guilty to the charge of assaulting Stuart Darley. The police suggested we had tried to intimidate witnesses prior to the trial and intimidate Darley himself. The prosecution were throwing plenty of mud at us, but it was hard for them to make it stick because we all decided to exercise our right not to enter the witness box. However, our trump defence card was Stuart Darley himself. We knew the type he was, and we knew when he entered the witness box, he would do all our work for us.

True to form, Darley was rude, sarcastic and brazen. He insulted our Counsel and we could see the straight people on the jury were not impressed. After they retired they returned very quickly with a not guilty verdict. The law failed and justice prevailed.

I was still visiting Ronnie Kray on a regular basis. On one occasion Ronnie told me that he was quite upset by a new house rule brought in at Broadmoor. He said they were now banned from smoking in the day room and were forced to go to a room set aside especially for smoking. Ronnie was a chain smoker, and this caused him a lot of distress. What made me laugh was that he was ranting and raving at me, saying it was a fucking liberty that he had to sit in a smoke-filled room with a load of nutters and he couldn't sit where he wanted to and smoke in peace.

Ronnie asked me to write to Broadmoor and say that I had met prison officers in a nearby pub. I was to say that they were outraged at the unhappiness that this was causing inmates and they were concerned it was going to cause incidents. I wrote the letter from a friend's address and used a false name in the hope that this matter could be resolved for Ronnie.

On my next visit to Broadmoor the manager called me into an office on my way out. I had made a silly mistake. He

39

showed me the letter I had written to Ronnie and the letter I had written into the hospital. Both were in my handwriting. From that time onwards, because I would not reveal the names of the prison officers who allegedly told me about this matter, I was banned from visiting him. I thought it was quite amusing that I had been banned from Broadmoor Hospital.

Once I had settled in at Raquels it became quite clear to me that things were not running the way they should be. It was as if a handful of local hardmen were running the club, and not the doormen. Local men with reputations would fight in the club and the following evening they would be allowed in. Because, as the other doormen said, 'It's not worth the trouble.' The doormen thought that if they barred one of these local hardmen who kept causing trouble, they may meet him in the street, or the man may call round at their house and they would end up the victims of an assault. I was of the opinion that if someone wanted trouble, they could fucking have trouble. And if they came into the club they either behaved themselves, or they weren't allowed in. Simple as that.

Dave Vine and I became quite good friends. I was moved from the top bar down to work on the front door with him. We were able to fiddle a bit of door money by letting customers in and pocketing the cash ourselves. Some Saturday nights we would make an extra £200 each. Christmas Eve and New Year's Eve were always sold out and they were ticket-only events. We decided to buy a ticket for each night at Raquels and another local disco and have our own printed. We asked Debra's brother, Keith, to sell these tickets outside the venues on Christmas Eve and New Year's Eve.

We sold approximately 200, but unfortunately the other club had already sold out its quota of tickets. When the extra 200 people tried to enter, the people inside were crammed shoulder-to-shoulder and there were disturbances when it was discovered they'd bought forged tickets. Those people who were turned away were so irate at having their Christmas Eve night out ruined, they came in search of Keith. Eventually we had to hide him in the toilet upstairs in the club.

I could never understand why Dave allowed local people to

take liberties with him. He certainly was no fool. But it was as if he couldn't be bothered with the trouble – hardly the attitude for a doorman.

In January 1992 things started to come to a head. Dave did security with Micky Pierce at a local pub called the Bullseye. An 18-year-old local man named Shaun Dunbar had been asked to leave by the manageress, and he had refused. The manageress rang Dave Vine and asked him to come down to eject the person. Dave rang round all the doormen and we went down there. There was a scuffle. A man named Tim Whidlake hit Dunbar and his jaw was broken. The following evening Tim and another doorman, Ronnie Downes, were working in the Bullseye. Some local men who had taken exception to what had happened to Dunbar went into the pub and attacked them with machetes. Tim escaped unhurt but Ronnie suffered severe injuries to his hands trying to protect himself. Once more we were all called out to attend to the incident. I was of the opinion that we should have gone after those responsible and sorted it out there and then. But Dave Vine said that we should leave it till later. I really felt it was the wrong way to handle things.

The next evening a man named Les Murphy came into Raquels. Vine said that he was one of those responsible when the attack took place on the doorman in the Bullseye. I said it should be sorted out, but he told me to leave it. A doorman friend of Ronnie Downes was in Raquels and told Tim that because he was the intended victim and Ronnie had ended up injured, it was Tim who should confront Les Murphy.

Tim went over to Les and said: 'You've got to leave.'

'The only cunt who's leaving here is you,' said Murphy, and with that he picked up an ashtray.

Somebody whom I couldn't see squirted cleaning fluid, industrial ammonia, at Les Murphy which hit him in the eye, and he fell against the bar. He was then hit over the head with a water jug and kicked and beaten. He had head injuries and we later learned he was blind in one eye. If Les had any idea that he was going to be subjected to this kind of attack, I don't think he would have come into the club in the first place. It seemed that Dave Vine's way of solving things wasn't working.

He was being too soft and no one had any respect for him. It was becoming clear to me that combating violence with violence was the only way to gain control of the club.

Vine's partner quit near enough directly after the Les Murphy incident. He had had enough of working the doors, and went to work on his father's farm. Vine had been relying too much on him and as a result lost more and more control.

Further unrelated incidents followed. A man who refused to be searched returned to Raquels and petrol bombed the front doors. Jason Riley, a local man and friend of ours, put a gun to someone's head on the dance floor. He was barred by the management when the customer complained. The manager, Ralph Paris, came in. Because Riley was a friend, I actually told the manager that he had been to a fancy dress party and come to the club as a German and the firearm was an imitation. But he was not fooled. He said the customer was going to go to the police and it was in everyone's interest that Jason be barred – for the time being, anyway.

The following week Jason came to the club and asked if he could come in. As I said, we were Jason's friends and the gun he had pulled on this person was in fact still owned by the Raquels door staff. Jason had ordered it but, although it remained in his possession, he still had not paid for it. We explained the situation to him regarding the management and suggested he go over to Time, another local disco, for a couple of weeks until things had died down. Jason agreed and went over with his friend, Simon Wally.

Jason and Simon were in Time when a girl accused Jason of pinching her backside. He said it wasn't him, and she said she was going to tell a man who was with her. The man came over and hit Jason on the nose, Jason began fighting with his attacker and the doormen became involved. He was ejected from the club and was furious because he had done nothing. He told the doorman and the man involved that he would be back. It's a phrase people who work on the door hear at least once a week. Few take notice of it, everybody should.

Jason jumped into a taxi and told the driver to take him home. Simon got into the taxi with Jason and was trying to calm him down, but Jason was furious. He told the taxi to wait outside and he went into his house.

When Jason got back into the cab, he had a gun in his pocket, and he kept saying that he was going to 'shoot the bastards'. All the time Simon was telling him to calm down. Jason shouldn't have said what he did in front of the cab driver, and he should have listened to Simon.

But he went back to Time, got out of the cab, walked up to the front doors and fired into the reception area at the people who had assaulted him. They were still talking to the bouncers there. He was incensed that they hadn't been kicked out. One man was hit in the ankle and the other man put his hand up to protect himself. The bullet entered his wrist and came out through his elbow.

I got a phone call at Raquels and was told what had happened. I had a flat in London and, because the door staff owned the gun with which he had committed the crime and Jason was a friend, I thought we should help. Dave Vine and I went over to Time to see what we could learn over there. Everybody was saying that it was Jason Riley who had shot the two people.

I rang Jason's girlfriend and told her to tell him to stay wherever he was and we would be in touch. When Raquels closed that night, Dave Vine and I met Simon Wally and Jason's girlfriend outside a pub not far from Jason's house. I told Simon that he should go to Jason and meet me round the corner at an agreed time. I would take him to my brother's flat in south London. On the way we could dispose of the gun and wait to see what happened when the dust settled. He would then be in a far better position to give himself up and get the matter resolved.

We were the only people who knew where he was. Dave said he had to go home and he left us. I went to the agreed meeting place to pick Jason up, but he never arrived. Nobody knows how the police knew where to find him. But armed police stormed the house where he was hiding and he was arrested.

Jason's friends believed it was Dave Vine who had told the police where he was. It may have been chance. Nobody will ever know. In this world where there's always doubt, rumours never decrease, they always increase. People will always try and discredit you when it's in their interests to do so. At his trial Jason was sentenced to 12 years' imprisonment for two attempted murders.

Dave Vine had been working at Epping Forest Country Club, which is frequented by various celebrities. He asked me if I would do his Wednesday nights up there as he had other commitments, and I agreed.

It was while working at Epping I first met David Dunne from Romford. Dave was a fanatical body builder. We got on very well and not long after starting at Epping, Dave had come to work with me and Dave Vine at Raquels.

On Sundays at Epping, they started playing rave and house music, and I was asked to work there. They were very busy. All club people who had worked Friday and Saturday used to go to Epping socially, as it was their night off, so I soon got to know many people in clubland throughout London.

One of the people I met, and became quite friendly with, was Tony Tucker. Tony was in his mid-30s and a mountain of a man. He ran a very big and well-respected door firm. He was strange in many ways. He spoke to few people and was quite abrupt. He had a very dry sense of humour. He was quite aggressive to those who tried to enter his circle without invitation.

I learned some years later that it was in August 1992, while I was working at Epping, that the police had begun watching me. My way of dealing with problems, compared with the way Dave Vine handled them at Raquels and elsewhere, had begun to earn me something of a reputation in Basildon, and this had brought interest from the police.

Geoff Allen, the old gentleman I had met at the James Fallon boxing show, had become a good friend to me. I would meet Geoff occasionally in the village of Lavenham in Suffolk. Dave Vine had told me about a scam which was going down in the City: people working in a bank would put dodgy cheques or amounts of dirty money into your account, and for this service they would get 25 per cent, the manager of the bank would also get 25 per cent, and you would get the other 50 per cent.

It sounded too good to be true to me. The catch apparently was the bank manager insisted on the money being paid into a healthy bank account as they were talking about amounts in excess of £100,000, and an average account of course wouldn't be able to contain such amounts without it arousing suspicion.

Vine suggested I ask my friend Geoff. I didn't want to involve him in something which may have resulted in him spending his last years in prison, but I did mention it to him, and he did express interest. He suggested that I and those involved meet at his home.

Myself, Dave Vine, a man named Tony Bones, and two other men who allegedly worked in the bank, travelled to Geoff's house and we had a meeting. Geoff was a very wise man, though. He said he would not commit himself to anything unless he spoke to the bank manager involved. Bones, Vine and the other two people approached were not so wise. It transpired that these two people were not bank employees, but cleaners. Their rather sad attempt at defrauding the bank from within failed miserably, and the person they *had* talked into putting the cheques into his account was promptly arrested and charged.

I was furious that Vine and Bones had tried to get my friend Geoff into such a stupid thing. They insisted that they had been told in good faith that it was a good earner and it was the other two and not they who were responsible. I saw this as the turning point in my friendship with Vine.

On 9 September 1992, Vine left Raquels and was driving home. He was stopped by the police and it was found that the car was ringed (a stolen car with false number plates). Further searches at his home revealed 25 ecstasy tablets and a knife. He was never convicted of possessing an offensive weapon, driving a stolen car or being in possession of the ecstasy tablets. I suspect he told the police that he had confiscated the ecstasy tablets from somebody at the club; he had bought the car in good faith and the knife was not kept for any sinister purpose. However, this event certainly caused Dave a lot of problems among those in clubland.

Many people suggested that he had not faced prosecution because he was a police informant, particularly in view of the fact of what had happened to our friend Jason Riley four months previously. That's the way things are when you fall out of favour.

Raquels continued to be a hotbed of trouble. Not only from

the customers, but seemingly from everybody loosely associated with it. Opposite the main doors of the club there was a small round market shop, brick built and a permanent fixture, and a man sold fancy goods there. He complained to the club that when revellers were leaving Raquels, they were breaking his windows and he wanted the club to put up shutters on his windows at the club's expense, otherwise he would object to their licence. The area manager agreed with the man that he or the club would pay for these shutters. I thought it was a right liberty that this man could just come along and demand money from the club on a whim and the club agree to pay it. However, it was their choice.

The following Sunday night, Dave Vine, Tim Whidlake and I were driving home from working at Epping. We stopped near the shop at a burger van to buy a cup of tea, and then we went home. I lived not far from the nightclub at the time, and I heard sirens heading towards the town. I learned the next day that the shop had been burned to the ground. The man never did get his shutters.

On Christmas Eve 1992, my friend Geoff Allen died. Geoff's wife Annie rang and told me. I was very upset. Geoff was a real gentleman. I attended Geoff's funeral with Dave Vine. Charlie Kray attended, as did Bill Wyman of the Rolling Stones, a good friend of Geoff and his family.

When a person who makes such an impression dies, I find it hard to believe that they have gone. Annie, Geoff's wife, and I were having a drink at his house after the funeral, and I said to her, 'Geoff's probably upstairs now. It's probably another insurance fiddle.' We had a good laugh, but it was a very sad occasion.

Dave Vine seemed to be losing confidence all the time at Raquels. Paul Trehern, a local doorman in Basildon who used to work with us, was getting married and he was kind enough to ring and tell us that he was having a stag night and he and perhaps 30 other doormen from various clubs would be coming into Raquels for a drink. It was to be expected that they'd be rowdy, but they were doormen like us. Paul had worked with us on a number of occasions and he had had the courtesy to ring us days before the event to inform us that he would like to come into the club for a drink with his friends.

I told Vine that he should go and see Paul and explain to him that there would only be four or five of us working and it would be inconceivable for us to control 30 door staff: we would expect Paul to supervise his own friends and then they would be most welcome to come into the club. However, Dave discussed it with the management, and together they decided that Paul Trehern and his friends would not be allowed in. I thought it was ridiculous.

When the night came around, Paul and his friends turned up and were quite rightly disgusted to learn that they were not allowed in the club. Paul ended up grappling on the floor with Dave Vine and, despite objections, they still all entered the club and drank at the bar. Apart from the trouble with Dave Vine getting in, they weren't a bit of bother at all. I was quite embarrassed to be working with doormen who turned other doormen away for no reason whatsoever, particularly doormen who had worked with us.

The following night Dave Vine didn't come into work. He knew I had the serious hump with him. Dave Godding, a good friend of his, and a man named Joe had trouble in the Piano bar. Joe had hit a man and dislocated his arm. Godding insisted that an ambulance be called. I refused, because if you rang an ambulance, the police would attend also. He went behind my back and rang them. He also said he was going to ring Dave. I went berserk. I shouted at him and I told him what I thought of Dave, and he left the premises at about 1.00 a.m.

The following day I received a phone call from the manager, Ralph Paris. Ralph asked me to come in and see him during the day. Ralph told me that that morning Dave Vine had resigned. He thought he could no longer work with me. I was in total agreement. Prior to my arrival at the club people had taken liberties all the time. By using excessive violence to combat violence, I had reduced the amount of trouble, and people were thinking twice about starting anything in the club.

It's easy to say with hindsight now, but I should have realised that excess would eventually be met with excess.

CHAPTER 4

Now I had control of Raquels. I wasn't sure that I really wanted it. The door was still made up of Basildon men, and they still feared local men with reputations. They had earned them in the playground, and they were going to take them to their graves. The only way to regain control of the club was to bring in outsiders. But for now, the local doormen were all I had and I would have to make do. To be honest, I was nervous about my position, but the game's all about front. I couldn't walk away.

My first problem was going to be obtaining invoices as Raquels would only pay cheques to a limited company. I approached Dave Vine's old partner Micky Pierce to see if he knew anybody who could front the door for me. He suggested a man I had met several times, Peter Clarke, a local Mr Fixit, who agreed to supply the invoices in return for one or two of his doormen being given work.

I was rather concerned that he was involved with a rival door firm, run by a man called Charlie Jones. Jones was very interested in taking over the Raquels door. While Vine was in charge he had approached the manager on several occasions. But for the time being it was all that was available to me.

Word soon got round Basildon that Vine had given up the door and I had taken over. I was preparing myself to be tested. I knew trouble was going to come, but I wasn't sure from whom, or in what form. Somebody was bound to try and make a name for themselves, that was certain.

To this day, I have been unable to find out who was behind one particular incident. A man named Israeli Frank, a well-known villain, came to see me one evening and asked me if I knew anybody who could get hold of some bullets. I asked him what calibre. He said he needed some nine millimetres, and I agreed to give him some. It's not uncommon to do something like this, it's almost like giving someone a sample. I hadn't paid for the ones I had myself – there were only six, and people wouldn't charge for that quantity.

The following Friday, Israeli Frank came to see me and we went into the back fire exit out of view from people and the noise of the disco. We spoke about things in general, and the conversation got round to why he needed the bullets, which I'd handed over to him. He told me that he'd been approached by a doorman in Basildon; someone had come on the scene recently and taken over a club and he was being paid to shoot him. He had been given the gun and was waiting for the bullets. Since there are only three or four nightclubs in Basildon, it seemed quite obvious that I was the intended victim. Frank, of course, would at that stage be unaware it was me.

When I said this to Frank, he gave the bullets back to me but would not disclose who his employer was. I've never been able to get to the bottom of this, but I have my suspicions as to who was behind it: Dave Vine.

Micky Pierce visited me at the club on several occasions and told me that Vine had been badmouthing me to other people. Vine was now working at Time and had brought in a new partner. On a couple of occasions, when Pierce had told me that Vine had been badmouthing me, I'd gone over to Time looking for him and threatened his doormen.

The new partner, whom I had met while I was at Epping and always got on with, would ring me the following day, and we would meet and resolve the matter. He used to tell me that what Pierce was saying was untrue. Pierce, he said, was trying to cause trouble between me and Vine so I would be arrested and lose the door at Raquels so he and his sleeping partner, Jones, could take over the club from me. I was completely taken in by Micky Pierce, and with hindsight, that was probably foolish. (It's worth mentioning here that a door registration scheme operates in Basildon and it's a condition of nightclubs and all licensed premises that they employ registered doormen. The police can object to your registration or your licence if you're convicted of an offence. If you lose your door registration licence the club obviously has to get rid of you.)

It was around this time that the farm Pierce lived in near Basildon was raided by the police following a surveillance operation and a tip-off. Police uncovered a firearm and various pieces of equipment they said had been used in the manufacture of amphetamine sulphate. They said it was a speed factory. Pierce automatically blamed Vine.

David Done was at this time my closest friend. He was a fanatical body builder and had a serious problem with steroids. I used to warn him about the excessive doses he was taking. His problems with steroids led to problems with money. He was even resorting to being a pizza delivery boy to help finance his drug-taking. He wouldn't listen to reason and his addiction began to affect his judgement.

One Monday morning, Dave rang me up and told me he had been sacked from Epping Country Club for allegedly selling drugs. I knew this was false. Dave did not sell drugs. I told him that if he was out then all the doormen should be out, myself included. I said I'd go with him and see the head doorman, Joe.

I asked Joe who had said that Dave was dealing. He said that the club had received a telephone call. I got quite annoyed and said that if the person who alleged Dave was a dealer didn't do it openly, then he shouldn't be believed. Eventually Joe said that Dave could have his job back, and we both went home. However, that evening I received a phone call from Vine – it was a split door up there: the club employed Joe, but he farmed out half of his work to Vine, who employed me and supplied invoices for Joe – and I was told that I had been sacked in his place. No reason was given. I was later told that Dave Vine was behind these phone calls to the club. What particularly annoyed me was that now I had been sacked, Dave Done refused to stand by me. He said that he needed the money, and the fact that I'd lost my job was unfortunate, but there was nothing he could do. I was furious.

Within a couple of days Dave Done left Raquels and went to work at the Ministry of Sound in south-east London. He suggested that I should work with him there on the odd nights when extra work arose. I agreed. Unknown to me at that time there was a lot of doorman's politics connected to the Ministry of Sound. A notorious East End villain and doorman, Rod, had just been asked to give up the door by the management because he was under police surveillance. Two very well-known south London brothers had taken over. Everybody was expecting an all-out war. I was acquainted with Rod, but Dave was a friend of his, so I was surprised when he asked me to go and work with him for the two south London brothers, Paul and Tim. I told him that it would be insulting to his friend and we should stay out of it. However, he told me he had discussed it with his friend and that it was okay, and so I agreed to work with him.

On my first night there, we were standing on the door and there was a discussion about the problem between Rod, Paul and Tim. Dave Done started siding with those loyal to Paul and Tim. 'You shouldn't get involved, Dave, Rod's your friend,' I said. Dave ignored me – he obviously needed the work.

A couple of days later I learned that Dave had lied to me. When he'd approached Rod about working at the Ministry of Sound Rod had told him he'd rather Dave didn't work for Paul and Tim. When Dave explained that he needed the money, Rod said he'd pay him his wages – £100 a night – not to work there. Dave was taking the money from both of them. I wanted nothing more to do with it, and we fell out.

I was still seeing a fair bit of Tony Tucker, the man I had met socially at Epping Country Club. He was also a friend of Rod's. Tucker asked me what had gone on between me and Dave Done and subsequently told Rod about the incidents when Done was in the company of people badmouthing him. Dave denied it and slagged me off, so when he rang me, I taped the conversation to prove he had been badmouthing Rod and the things he'd said about me in return were untrue.

Around the same time an article appeared in the *News Of The World* about two of the Ministry of Sound doormen, Mark Rothermel and a South African, Chris Raal. Rothermel had left before I joined and Raal was working during my time there. He was in this country on the run from the South African police after it was alleged that he had shot dead a nightclub manager. I had never met Rothermel, and up until reading this article hadn't heard of him. The Ministry of Sound had at that time won one of its many awards and the article was referring to men with violent pasts working there.

In November 1989 Mark Rothermel was sentenced to six years imprisonment for assisting in the disposal of a body. Mark had been working at Hollywoods in Romford, one of Tony Tucker's doors, with another man, Pierre St Ange. Pierre had been having an affair with Pamela, the ex-wife of a DJ named Bernie Burns. Eventually Pierre, another body-builder who was six-foot-four, moved in with Pamela in Ilford. But Burns kept calling round, pestering and sexually harassing Pamela.

Pierre thought he was a 'little runt', and decided to teach him a lesson by slapping him around. Bernie Burns was cornered in the Ilford flat, where he was beaten up and throttled by a mystery assailant, helped by Pierre. Initially Pierre had told police that it was Mark Rothermel who had strangled Bernie Burns. He later retracted this in court.

The body was wrapped in a red blanket, put in the boot of a car and taken to a quiet copse in Longspring Wood near Chelmsford, Essex. It was there that Mark, who was nicknamed the Colonel because of the way he planned things with military precision, took an axe to the body. He hacked off Bernard Burns's head and both of his hands to avoid identification. Mark is reported to have told a friend: 'The hands came off easily, but the head was more of a problem because of the veins in the neck.' Burns was then buried in a shallow woodland grave. His head and hands have never been recovered. Police found Burns's body after a tip-off and collared Rothermel at the same time. He was hiding neck-deep in a pond near the grave. A police helicopter pilot spotted his head as the chopper skimmed across the tops of trees, and armed detectives moved in. Rothermel was ordered out of the pond at gun-point.

Mark was found not guilty of murder and not guilty of manslaughter, but he received six years for disposing of the body. Pierre was found not guilty of murder and sentenced to ten years for manslaughter.

It wasn't the only time a member of Burns's family had

been a victim of violent death. In July 1984 his father Peter was killed when former soldier James Melloy thrust a four-foot metal stake through his eye. The 60-year-old railway guard died ten days later in hospital.

Dave Done was still working at the Ministry of Sound. At first people blamed Rod for the newspaper article. In order to win favour, Done told people that it was me. It must have been easy to believe. I made no secret of the fact that I had many newspaper contacts which I had picked up during my days working on the James Fallon fund-raising events. It was Ronnie and Reggie Kray who had shown me the importance and usefulness of a relationship with members of the press.

It was a childish and dangerous thing for Dave to say; Mark and Chris were certainly no fools. But if Dave Done was trying to cause me trouble, he couldn't have picked two better people to cause it for me.

I was unaware of what he said. And the next time I worked at the Ministry of Sound you could have cut the atmosphere with a knife. It soon became clear that it wasn't the atmosphere that people wanted to cut. I went out to the front door and said: 'What the fuck's going on, Dunny?' He said nothing, although I could tell by his manner that whatever was going on he was behind it. I went inside and spoke to South African Chris. He seemed okay, but I could tell that something was brewing. There was an air of menace, but I wasn't going to run anywhere. I hadn't done anything. I stayed until the end and left.

On Sunday evenings there was a house and garage night on a boat permanently moored at the Embankment. The following Sunday I went to the boat and had a drink with David Courtney, whom I'd met on the club circuit. Again I noticed the atmosphere was odd. So much so that when I sat with Courtney everyone around us began to move away, a sure sign that something was going to happen. I asked Courtney what was going down, and he said nothing was the matter.

As I was leaving the boat, I saw David Courtney arguing with a tall man with a pony tail who had a knife with a green handle in his hand. Courtney was telling him: 'Not here, not here.' It was quite obvious what they were talking about. I went over to Courtney and said: 'What the fuck's he doing with a knife?' He denied the man was carrying one. I knew it was bollocks. As we left the boat, Courtney asked me if I would give a friend of his a lift to a party in north London. I thought that if something was going to happen, it was going to happen here at the boat, so I agreed.

The person who got into my car was in his 20s. He said he was from Coventry. He didn't look up to much. He said the party was in a house in north London. It sounds corny, but you can actually sense fear, or the coming of violence. The atmosphere in the car was very, very tense. He was asking me if I knew South African Chris and also about Dave Done. He asked too many questions, because the penny had dropped straightaway with me. I kept a First World War bayonet down the side of my seat in the car. The first wrong move this person made, he was going to get it.

The so-called party was in a house on a main road heading towards the A1. He kept saying to me: 'This looks like it, this looks like it.' By pure coincidence, every place that looked like it happened to be a dark, unlit, uninhabited area. He told me the number of the house the party was meant to be at and we were unable to find it. He kept saying pull over here and I'll knock a door. Each time I ignored him and pulled into a brightly lit garage forecourt or similar spot. As we were driving up the dual carriageway I noticed going down the other side to the roundabout in order to get behind us were two cars. Dave Courtney was driving one of them, and the tall man with the pony tail was driving the other one.

I wasn't thick. It was an amateurish attempt to corner me. My confidence grew when I realised the type of people I was dealing with. I stopped the car, grabbed my passenger and shoved him onto the street and slammed the door. As I drove away, I noticed he had left a lock-knife on the seat.

The following day, I rang Tony Tucker, because he knew all these people and Rothermel and Raal had worked for him. I told him what had gone on. I said there was only one way to sort it out: ring Rod, ring Rothermel, ring South African Chris and arrange a meeting.

A meeting is not a democratic discussion. Each person says their piece, and whoever is not believed does not usually get to leave the room under his own steam. Despite being disadvantaged, as I was from the Midlands and these people already knew each other, I was still keen to let the meeting go ahead. Later that day Tucker rang me and said the meeting was on for the following morning at a Portacabin in Essex. The following morning, I got a call and was told it was called off because they had been unable to get hold of David Done. Another meeting was arranged. On this occasion they had been able to reach him, but he said he did not want to go to any meeting. The matter, I was told, was then closed. Dave had an excuse for his actions: his drug problem. The rules could be changed when it suited them. I doubt if I would have enjoyed the same privilege.

I was furious. People had been plotting to stab me for no reason, and now I was told to forget it. I reluctantly agreed. I didn't want any more enemies. I had had enough in Basildon. The standard of doormen being provided by Peter Clarke was deteriorating rapidly. It was as if he was supplying me with people not up to the job on purpose in the hope that we would come unstuck against the locals who were testing us.

The only effect it did have was that every time there was an incident, the violence to counteract what had occurred became more and more excessive. The legacy of the last door firm was over, and I wasn't going to make the same mistakes as Vine. More and more people were getting seriously hurt. Knives and other weapons were being used. On the surface revellers were beginning to see a decrease in violence, but behind the scenes those who wished to cause trouble were paying dearly.

In one incident a local man came to the front door and became abusive because I insisted that he be searched before he entered the club. He went away and returned with a rounders bat. Maurice Golding, a doorman from Bristol who worked for me, was hit across the head and the man ran away. We all chased him and the new manager, Ian Blackwell, followed, trying to reason with me to calm down. We caught the man approximately 500 yards away from Raquels outside the local bingo hall.

The doorman who caught him began to hit him, but I told him to stop. The man was cut twice with a sheath knife, once

SO THIS IS ECSTASY?

in the face, and once in his upper thigh. The manager was outraged. I told him that if he had chased Maurice with the bat and Maurice had fallen over, what would he have done with the rounders bat? It was only right that he got a bit of his own medicine.

In another incident a man from Leeds was refused entry because he was drunk. He produced a knife and began waving it and shouting obscenities. I told him to put the knife down. But he kept shouting: 'Do you want some? Do you want some?'

'It's up to you which way this goes,' I said. 'Put the knife down.'

He refused. He was slashed and received a serious injury to the left-hand side of his face

Again I justified this by asking what would have happened if I had walked towards him without a knife and he was still brandishing his? I've always said they dictate the way things go. If they put their hands up, I'll put my hands up. If they pull out a weapon, I'll pull out a weapon. It's entirely their choice. Violence is a messy business.

It wasn't all one-way traffic. On Friday 4 April 1993, I'd been to the Ministry of Sound on a social visit. When I left in the early hours of the morning, four or five black youths were following me up the Borough High Street, and I sensed that there was trouble. I turned around and stopped, and one of them asked if I had a problem. I said no, and he hit me on the side of the face. We began fighting and ended up bundled into a shop doorway. I had one of them by the head, and was hitting him. With the force of us fighting and me being shoved backwards, the window of the shop broke and an alarm went off. I felt what seemed like a hard punch in my stomach and the youths ran away. When I looked down blood was pouring from my stomach. I had been stabbed. I found it hard to stop the flow, but I applied pressure to the wound with a cloth, and drove home.

I lost a lot of blood and tried to dress the wound myself. However, four days later I was admitted to Basildon Hospital. I had an infection, and the wound was an inch-and-a-half to two-inches deep and was causing me quite a lot of problems. I later discovered that these youths had been in the Ministry

SO THIS IS ECSTASY?

of Sound selling drugs which had been confiscated. They were
waiting for a doorman to leave. They assumed that I worked
there as I dressed as a doorman – black trousers, white shirt
and a black bomber jacket – so they attacked me. I never
found out who they were. It's one of those things.

One afternoon I received a phone call from Rod Chapman,
the assistant manager at Raquels. He told me that my
partners had been in to have a meeting with the manager of
the club about security and there were a few points he wished
to discuss with me. I was furious. I went down to the club and
asked who my partners were. I was told that Peter Clarke and
Jones had been having a meeting with the manager.

I asked Clarke what was going on, and he told me that the
management asked them to go in for a meeting about the
levels of violence being used in the club, because he wasn't
happy with it and there were a couple of doormen who
worked for me whom they wished to get rid of. I went mad. I
told them that it was my door, nothing to do with him, and
Jones should stay out of the club. I would choose the doormen
I wanted to work with me, I insisted, and I wouldn't be told
what to do by anybody, particularly Jones. If he wanted to
take the door from me, he should come and try man-to-man
and not do things behind my back.

That night Clarke sent three of the saddest doormen I have
ever seen in my life. I told them all to go home. I rang Peter
Clarke and I told him I didn't want any doormen from him or
his partner (whom I wasn't meant to know about) Charlie
Jones, ever again. In fact any agreement we had was then
terminated. That Friday night, I and another doorman
worked at Raquels on our own.

I had arranged to go to Epping Country Club that week
with Steven Richards, Noel Palmer and David Thomkins.
They were from the Bristol area. I had met them in the
Ministry of Sound. On Sundays they used to come to Epping.
This particular Sunday I was to introduce them to Tony
Tucker as he was looking for dealers for his clubs. At the same
time I thought I would use the opportunity to discuss a deal
concerning Raquels with Tony.

I'll always remember introducing Steve and Noel to Tony.
He asked me if they had any drugs with them. I asked them if

57

they could sort Tony out. They asked Tony for £40. Tony started to laugh and said to me: 'Tell them to hand over what I asked for, or I'll take the fucking lot.' It was typical of Tony. He wasn't in the habit of paying for things.

That same evening I told Tucker about the problems I was having, and said I needed the back-up of a strong firm. I told him I would run the door and he could reap whatever benefits there were from providing invoices and any other 'commodities' – drugs, protection, debts and so on. I would not bother him with the day-to-day running of the club. The only time I would call on him was if I had a severe problem and I needed back-up. In return he would make money each week from the club. We shook hands and on 4 September 1993, Tony Tucker and I began our partnership at Raquels.

CHAPTER 5

Less than two weeks after our partnership began, I made the front page of the local papers for all the wrong reasons. On 15 September I was outside the club near a burger van when a man made a few silly remarks about the Raquels door staff. I told him to shut up, but he wouldn't. So I hit him. He was knocked out when his head hit the pavement. His friends had difficulty bringing him round. They called an ambulance and, as a result, the police attended.

At the hospital, Dave Case, the injured man, told police he wished to press charges, and the police appealed for witnesses on the front of the local paper, saying it was an unprovoked attack by a man approximately 40 years old, heavily built, with a Birmingham accent. I was outraged. I was only 33 at the time.

Within a day or so I was arrested. The police found the number of calls they had received giving my name quite amusing; it seemed I was the only heavily built man in Basildon with a Birmingham accent. I told the police it was self-defence and I had been attacked first, and provided numerous witnesses from the club. Case was seen in a public house in Basildon by a mutual friend, and he suddenly remembered that it was entirely his fault and the case against me was dropped.

The agreement with Tucker brought new faces onto the scene in Basildon. Men who worked for him and were looking for a change would come and work for me at Raquels. Troublemakers began to go to other clubs and the violence in Raquels began to die a death. Local hardmen who did remain as customers became more friendly and wanted to get on with our firm.

A man called Jason Vella was at that time up-and-coming in Basildon. He had a firm of men who were causing chaos across the South East. He used to come to Raquels, and we got on quite well. Vella was quite short, but stocky. He was in his early 20s, but had a fearsome reputation. He was considered more of a nutter than a hardman. People who crossed him wouldn't get an opportunity to fight him: they would be cut, shot or stabbed. I always thought Vella was all right. He certainly wasn't loud. He was quiet and he never put himself about. His victims entered the business through their own choice. If he had let them go unpunished, he would have become a victim himself. That's the way things were in the world we inhabited.

Another man was Jason Draper. Jason was also in his 20s. Few messed with him in the Basildon area. He too became quite friendly with me and the other doormen.

Tony Tucker told me he was having his birthday party at the Prince of Wales in South Ockendon, and he invited me and all the other doormen from Raquels. He also asked me to bring along Steve and Noel from Epping so that there would be a supply of drugs for him and his guests. The party was a real success. Doormen from everywhere were there. Most were out of their face on cocaine, Special K or ecstasy or a cocktail of all three and more. Tucker was in a really good mood.

In the early hours of the morning I was sitting on the floor of a room with Steve and Noel and my wife Debra. A man in his early 20s pushed open the door, which hit me. I looked at him, waiting for him to apologise, and he asked me what the matter was. I said to him: 'You've just knocked the fucking door into me.' He said: 'Well you're a doorman, aren't you?' It was a stupid thing to say, because it was obviously intended to cause trouble. I got up and walked towards the man. He walked out to the kitchen and I followed him. Friends of Tucker's also followed us but, before the fight could start, we were separated.

I later learned he was Tony's closest friend, Craig Rolfe. He was possessive of his friendship with Tony. I told him that out of respect for Tony he shouldn't cause trouble at his birthday party. He seemed all right afterwards, but he still had an attitude. It was Tony who told me a few days later, when I was explaining what had gone on, why Craig had this chip on his shoulder.

On Christmas Eve 1968, a man was found murdered in a van in a lay-by at the side of the A13 between Stanford-Le-Hope and Vange in Basildon. The dead man had been found slumped in the seat of a grey Austin van. He was Brian Rolfe, a market trader from Basildon. At the post mortem later that day the cause of death was determined as a fractured skull. In less than 24 hours the case had been solved. On Boxing Day a 19-year-old motor fitter, John Kennedy from Basildon, was charged with the murder together with 23-year-old Lorraine Rolfe, the wife of the murdered man.

When she was charged, it is reported that Lorraine said: 'I never touched him, honest, on my baby's life.' Lorraine was at that time the mother of three children and was expecting a fourth – Craig. Kennedy and Rolfe were lovers. When the case came to trial at Maidstone in March 1969 the prosecution alleged that Lorraine and Kennedy murdered Brian Rolfe and tried to fake a roadside robbery. Both pleaded not guilty to the murder charges and Lorraine not guilty to making false statements. The prosecution alleged the murder was committed so the accused could simultaneously get rid of Rolfe and acquire his money. It was said that Rolfe was hit over the head in the early hours of Christmas Eve in the bedroom of his Linford Drive home with a ten-pin bowling skittle which weighed nearly four pounds. His skull was crushed like an eggshell. Kennedy was found guilty of murder and jailed for life. He was also given a concurrent sentence of seven years for breaking and entering Rolfe's home and stealing £597.10/-. Lorraine Rolfe was found not guilty of murder, but sent to prison for 18 months for making false statements to impede Kennedy's arrest. It was while serving this sentence that Lorraine gave birth to Craig in Holloway Prison. Little wonder he had a chip on his shoulder and he'd chosen a life of crime.

Craig and I never really did see eye to eye after that first meeting. Our views clashed on most things. However, my association with Tony Tucker was business, Rolfe's was personal, so like and dislike didn't really come into it. Craig had a fairly serious cocaine problem, and hanging around with Tony helped, because there was a constant supply at a discount price, if not free.

Merging with anyone in business is always potentially hazardous, but particularly so if you're involved in our line of work. When I had taken over Raquels from Dave Vine I had, in the eyes of those concerned, become top of that particular heap. However, when I merged with Tucker, who ran a much larger door firm, my position was automatically questioned. Long-standing members of his firm resented me. It's sad but true, men are like children. They feel threatened in some way by a newcomer. The fact that I was also introducing people like the drug dealers, Steve and Noel, into the situation caused further resentment. Tucker's doormen had their own people they were earning out of. I didn't know they had dealers, and thought I was being helpful.

Shortly after Tucker's birthday party, Steve and Noel and their runners, who included Dave Thomkins, began work at Club UK in Wandsworth, where Tony Tucker ran the security. (Their position had been discussed at Tucker's birthday party.) For the exclusive rights to sell drugs in there, they paid Tony £1,000 per weekend. On average their return for Friday and Saturday night was £12,000.

Christmas 1993 and the firm celebrated in style. My brother, Michael, and his wife, Carol, came to a party we were attending at the Café de Paris in the West End. It was one of the most exclusive clubs at the time. There were queues of people outside, which we ignored as a matter of course. These events where the firm got together were extraordinary. Nobody connected to us paid to get in anywhere. Nobody paid for drugs. Huge bags of cocaine, Special K and ecstasy were made available to the firm and their associates. You look around the dark room, you're surrounded by 40 or more friends, all faces (well-known figures). Everyone else in the place knows it, too. The music's so loud it lifts you; you're all one – you have total control. Those on the firm created an atmosphere which demanded respect from other villains. Straight people hardly noticed. On the surface, everyone was friendly, but there was this feeling of power and evil. Tucker felt it, too. Often he would look across the club, and smile knowingly. Looking back, we revelled in the atmosphere we created wherever we went.

It was a memorable Christmas. After the party we went back to Steve and Noel's flat at Denmark Court in Surrey Quays, an exclusive development in the south London Docklands. Strewn across the floor, spilling out of a carrier bag, lay over £20,000, the proceeds of that weekend. The dealers had so much money about them, they didn't know how to spend it or where to put it.

Around that time in London, there was a little firm going around the clubs who used to look out for the dealers, follow them home and rob them of their proceeds. It was quite a lucrative operation because the victims couldn't go to the police. Steve and Noel had been victims of this firm in south London while dealing in the Ministry of Sound. A man had knocked on the door while Steve was in the house alone. When Steve had answered, the man pushed his way in with another man, tied Steve up and threatened him with a knife, but Steve had not divulged where the money was. The man cut Steve several times in the mouth, demanding to know where it was hidden. Eventually, fearing for his life, Steve handed over £4,000 and the robbers left.

Steve feared another attack, and on occasion he would pay me to protect them. During their career in the drug world, he was to call on me many times for assistance.

On Sunday 23 January myself, Debra and some other friends were at the Gass club in central London when we heard that a friend of mine and well-known villain, Michael McCarthy, had been shot in Basildon. Mick was sitting at a table having breakfast with his wife at his father-in-law's café, Rebels. They heard a woman screaming and a door bang open. The gunman entered and it was reported that he said, 'I'm going to kill you, McCarthy.' As Mick stood up, he shot him in the back. The gunman then stood over Mick, put the gun to his head and fired it again. Beverley, Mick's wife, wrestled with the gunman, and pleaded with him not to shoot any more. She caught her finger in the buttonhole of his coat, and couldn't get away. It is reported he swung around and pointed the gun at her forehead at close range. She said: 'I don't know whether the gun went off or not. He went to pull the trigger. I saw that.' Other customers grabbed the gunman and bundled him out of the door.

Mick McCarthy is lucky to be alive in some respects. However, he's paralysed for life from the waist down. To this day nobody has been convicted of the attack.

I had known McCarthy for some time. He often came to Raquels, and his children attended the same school as mine. A lot of people were not surprised by what happened, but I thought it was a tragedy none the less. It was a sign of the times, and a prophecy of things to come.

Guns had always been set aside for special occasions. But more and more often they were being used to sort out trivial arguments. Drugs, too, were becoming more prevalent, bringing in huge rewards for villains. The more money there was, the more violence there was. The more violence there was, the more guns were being used. The stakes were being upped all the time. Every Tom, Dick and Harry was strolling round Essex with a gun, although McCarthy's shooting wasn't drugs related, but due to another feud.

Business at Raquels was not booming, and so the powers that be decided a change was needed. Out went the grand piano from the Piano Bar – Strings, and in came framed gold discs, electric guitars, trumpets, American football jerseys, American football helmets and baseball bats (purely for décor, nothing else). They turned it into an American-style bar, and called it the Buzz Bar. It had the desired effect and attracted more people.

Along with the good came the bad. Raquels is situated in Basildon town centre, next door to a butcher's in the middle of a market. In that market square there was a pub called the Bullseye. It was the place where Vine's doormen had been attacked by machetes. The regulars were known as the 'Bullseye'. They had a reputation for violence. When the Buzz Bar opened they began drinking in there. The most well-known member of their 'gang' was Jason Draper.

Draper could be quite friendly when he was just with one or two of his friends. However, when the Bullseye firm was together his minions seemed to play up for him. I thought everybody deserved a chance, so I thought we would allow

SO THIS IS ECSTASY?

them to drink in there up until the time that they outstayed their welcome.

In January 1994 there was a bomb scare on the Southend to Fenchurch Street British Rail line. All trains were prevented from leaving Basildon station. Passengers were not allowed to go into the station and so in a short period of time there was a large group of people hanging around the town centre. Rather than wait in the street on a cold winter's night, they came into the Buzz Bar for a drink. As soon as I went into work, I told the manager, 'You should get some more doormen down here, there is going to be trouble.'

There was a group of between eight and ten men from Romford and between six and eight men from the Bullseye. By half past eight the Buzz Bar was completely packed. One of the men from the Bullseye came up to me and said: 'Look Bernie, we don't want to cause trouble in here, but one of those geezers from Romford is giving it to us.' I said: 'What do you mean, "giving it"?' He said: 'Every time he walks past, he knocks into us, and it's going to go off in here in a minute.'

I said: 'I don't want no grief in here, so if you want, I'll ask them to leave, and do what you want outside. I don't want it to happen in here.' I went downstairs to get some tea from the burger van and I was followed outside by one of the Bullseye firm. He said it was definitely going to go off and a man named Joe Wright had some CS gas. He didn't want to fall out with me and was advising me that Joe was going to use it. As I was walking upstairs I could hear the sound of smashing glass and people screaming. I ran up the stairs and there was a huge fight in progress. The Bullseye firm were hammering the men from Romford. Someone had dispensed CS gas and people were running and screaming everywhere. I was trying to pull people apart, and the fight went out onto the stairs. Several men were bleeding heavily. I managed to get the men from the Bullseye out of the doors and lock the men from Romford in the Buzz Bar. One of the men from Romford hit me and I began fighting with him.

Eventually the doors burst open. The Bullseye lot came back in and the fight continued. Some of the men from Romford had escaped into the street but they were being attacked there also. Eventually I managed to get both parties outside as the police were pulling up. I looked up to the bus station and one man was lying on the floor. Blood was gushing from a wound in his head. I ran over to him and saw that it was a very, very serious injury. There was a gaping gash around his eye. I couldn't see whether he'd been stabbed above his eye or glassed. I took my coat off, put him on his side and wrapped my coat around his head to try to stop the flow.

The police pulled up and jumped out and grabbed me. I said: 'I'm a doorman, I'm trying to help him.' An ambulance then arrived and took the man to hospital. Through police enquiries I later learned the man had lost his eye and suffered severe injury to his face. He had been repeatedly glassed. I wasn't very happy with the people from the Bullseye, as they should have sorted their problem with these people outside. They had brought police attention to me.

In the following few days I learned that the man who'd been blinded was a friend of a friend of Mark Rothermel's. Tony Tucker, whom Mark used to work for, rang me and told me this. He asked me who Jason Draper was and where he could be found. I had a photograph of Draper and me which had been taken at a social night out at Epping Country Club. But the firm's business came before friendship and Tucker asked me to take it over to his house in Chafford Hundred, which I did.

When I got there Tucker was suggesting ways of mounting a revenge attack on Draper and his friends from the Bullseye. All the plans were pretty gruesome. While we were talking, Craig Rolfe arrived and saw the photograph. He asked Tucker why he had a photograph of Jason Draper, whom Rolfe knew, as he had been brought up in Basildon. When Tucker told him, Rolfe was furious. He was arguing that Draper was all right and nothing should be done about the attack on the man from Romford.

Again I was in confrontation with Rolfe. I said to Tucker: 'If this man is a friend of Mark's, then it's down to Mark what is to be done. And if Mark wants to do something about it, I'm going to help him.' Tucker said he'd ring me later, and I left.

Tucker rang me that night and told me to ignore Rolfe. He said if Mark was going to do something about it, then we would back him. To my surprise it was the man who had lost the sight of one eye who came to Draper's rescue. He said that he didn't want any repercussions. I think he had had enough of violence. The firm from the Bullseye stayed away for a few weeks. I think they were expecting a comeback, but because the injured party had declined, none was forthcoming.

On 11 February they turned up at Raquels. I told them to fuck off. A fight started on the door and they backed off. They smashed pallets up and produced weapons from their cars which were parked nearby. They threw bottles, bricks and bars at the doors, so I closed them. They then charged the doors trying to smash them with an axe and iron bars. They doused the doors in petrol and tried to burn them. I opened the doors and we ran at them.

Draper, the man they looked up to, wasn't with them, so they didn't have that much heart. They dropped the bars, which were ineffective anyway – they were the rods used to construct the nearby market stalls – and ran. We gave chase. We caught two or three of them. One of the men who was beaten stopped breathing. The police arrived and went to his assistance, and an ambulance was called. I was arrested and kept in the police station until 5.40 a.m. the following morning.

It was self-defence, and I had the usual coach-load of witnesses from the club to verify the fact. No charges were ever brought. The man lived and both sides were happy.

Violence I can deal with. Intrigue has never been my forte. Micky Pierce, Dave Vine's old partner, was still on the scene, lurking in the background. He came to me and asked me to assist him with the charges he was facing in relation to the gun and the equipment used to manufacture amphetamine. He explained the situation and I said I would assist.

On 21 February I went to his solicitor in London and made a statement. I told the solicitor I worked occasionally for Micky Pierce on a casual basis repossessing cars, vans and commercial vehicles. I said at the end of January 1993 I was asked to repossess an Iveco box van from a yard at the Amstrad factory in Shoeburyness. I said Micky had phoned me the previous evening to ask if I was available for a day's work because he would be busy on the farm all day and unable to do it. I was to go to the yard at Amstrad's and pick up the van for one of the finance companies Mr Pierce had a contract with. I was then to take the van to Mr Pierce's house, remove all the items from the vehicle except the spare wheel, the jack and the wheel brace and place any excess items in a shed at the rear of Mr Pierce's property. I said I did this.

The excess items were two boxes which I described as resembling tea chests. These contained glassware, a radio, a multi-coloured folding deck chair. I said there was nobody at Mr Pierce's property. I then completed my instructions by taking the empty vehicle to Mr Pierce's father's farm a little further up the road. I said this was standard procedure regarding all the vehicles I was involved in repossessing for or with Mr Pierce.

When Micky Pierce's case came to court the charges relating to the drugs were dropped and he was fined £1,000 for possessing the firearm. I thought I had done him a good turn. He, unknown to me at the time, was not grateful at all and together with others was plotting my downfall.

Tony Tucker and I took over security at the Towngate Theatre in Basildon, where they held pop concerts. It was hardly a lucrative contract, but it was work, nevertheless, and additional money. One evening I was told that there were doormen already there. To my surprise a security company from Kent had taken over our contract, albeit a verbal one, without me or Tony being notified. I asked the Towngate Theatre manager what was going on, and he said that these people had gone in there cheaper than us and he had therefore hired them. I explained to him that things didn't work like that, and they would not remain there.

A few days later on 25 February, I and another doorman from Raquels went over to the Towngate Theatre to have a drink. There was a disturbance, and the Towngate Theatre security ran off and telephoned the police. The police attended in large numbers and insisted that the other doormen and I, who were in there having a quiet drink, should leave at once.

As a result of that disagreement, I was visited at Raquels by the licensing police in Basildon, who weren't keen on me anyway. They told me that they would revoke my licence if this behaviour persisted. They suggested that if I had a grievance with the way things were being run with regard to doormen on premises, I should approach the council who ran the door registration scheme, and not take matters into my own hands.

They were also concerned about doormen working for me who were not registered. They said anyone with a conviction in recent years should be excluded from working. They told me I had to register all my doormen. If they were concerned about people having convictions for fisticuffs who were working with me, I thought I better not mention that Mark Rothermel had also begun working on an occasional basis at Raquels.

They weren't all dark days. We had good times too. Tony Tucker used to lead Nigel Benn, the boxer, into the ring at all his fights and on occasion we would be invited to parties in honour of Nigel and his friends. After one of his fights a party was held at the Park nightclub in Kensington High Street. Everyone was there. We really had a good time. Tucker was in his element. Out of his head, shitfaced on coke and Special K, one of his favourite cocktails.

All sorts of people attended these parties. I became very friendly with Dave Lea, who came from England, but now lives in Hollywood. He started out working as Sam Fox's bodyguard. He was the British kickboxing champion and used his skills to further his career as a stuntman. He worked on the Batman films, *Hook* and *Tango & Cash*. He had trained Sylvester Stallone, and many other Hollywood names. When he was in England, Dave lived in Basildon, and we often went out together. As a favour, he had gone with me to collect my boy from school with his Batman outfit on. The other six- or seven-year-old boys could not believe it. They thought my son really knew Batman. The people we knew were like that, they would do anything for you.

In March 1994 a 20-year-old, Kevin Jones, died in Club UK. Shortly after his death the police, who had Steve and Noel under surveillance, found 1,500 ecstasy pills in a stolen car from Bristol in an underground car park at the back of their flat. At the same time Dave Thomkins was arrested at his home in Bath. Steve and Noel were arrested, as was Noel's girlfriend, an Asian princess, Yasmin. This was on 6 May 1994.

Dave Thomkins was bailed. He rang me and told me what had happened. I organised a 'proper' solicitor for Steve and Noel to have and we attended their Court hearing at Tower Bridge Magistrates Court in London. Yasmin turned up for the hearing, as did Steve's girlfriend, a stunning Swedish girl. Yasmin and the Swede had initially been arrested, but were put on police bail and had to return to the police station at a later date.

Our first problem was going to be getting Steve and Noel out on bail. Bail was set at £10,000 each. Thomkins and I met Yasmin the following day and she gave us £20,000 in cash. We took this to Leman Street Police Station in the City, plonked it on the counter and asked for our friends to be released. The officer at the desk was unsure what to do. Dave and I were kept waiting for several hours while enquiries were made as to what the procedure should be. We were taken into a room and asked about our identities and where the money had come from etc. We said a family friend had loaned the money, but the police officer said they were going to refuse it. Bail would be granted only if it could be shown that the money was in an account prior to their arrest. After making several frantic phone calls, we found someone who was able to do the necessary and the following morning they were released on bail.

No charges were ever brought against Yasmin, Steve's girlfriend or Dave Thomkins.

At the first trial, the jury could not reach a verdict. At the final trial Steve and Noel were acquitted and returned to their native Bath. Tucker was furious about their arrests. He claimed they'd been grassed up because of the person dying in the nightclub. It seemed obvious to me that people involved in this trade only have a limited time. To be successful you have to tell as many people as possible what you are doing. It's no good standing in a nightclub with 500 ecstasy pills in your pocket and keeping the fact to yourself. The more people you tell, the more pills you sell, but the chance of your being arrested rises dramatically. Tucker was concerned that they were going to grass on him for taking rent, but there was no fear of that, and I reassured him of the fact.

Back in Basildon I was asked to attend a meeting with

David Britt and Dawn French, two environmental health officers who ran the door registration scheme for Basildon Council. The manager of Raquels, Ian Blackwell, was also asked to attend. At the meeting the subject of the Towngate Theatre incident arose. I told the council they were getting involved in something they knew little about. People couldn't just turn up from another town and undercut you and take over your door and expect nothing to happen. They argued that competition was good. They obviously didn't understand. I got rather angry and David Britt mentioned that they had received reports that I had been taking protection money from a pub in Basildon called the Castlemayne. I told him this was nonsense. I had taken money from the pub, but it was for a favour I'd done the manager. Some hooligans had been causing problems in there. I had spoken to them and told them to stay out. Britt told me that Basildon was not Chicago. His inference was clear. 'Maybe it's not Chicago,' I thought, 'but there are people in the town who wish it was. Events were becoming far more violent.'

CHAPTER 6

As the notoriety of the firm grew, so too did the number of people who wanted to be known as our associates. The presence of the firm in pubs or clubs in the area prompted respect, and I have to admit it was a good feeling.

Because of the firm's reputation for sorting out problems – and people – we were now doing a lot more than running the door at weekends. Additional work was forthcoming. Protection, punishment beatings and debt recovery were all added to the firm's CV. It wasn't just local work, either. Cries for help came from as far afield as Sunderland, Manchester, Bristol and the Midlands. The work was diverse. Some of it was legal, some of it gratuitous, some of it downright illegal. It seemed that everybody who had a grievance wanted to use our violent firm to get their revenge on whoever had slighted them.

Peter Singh, an Asian from Basildon, paid me and another doorman to protect his brother who had been threatened in a family feud. His brother had entered an arranged marriage, and after a couple of years he decided to divorce. The girl's family took it as a great insult and they had threatened his life. At the divorce proceedings in Southend Crown Court, there was pushing, shoving, shouting, and threats were issued. The judge removed me and my friend from the Court after the girl's family said they'd been threatened. Eventually Peter's brother got his divorce.

A man from Leicester named Martin Davies contacted us and asked us to recover a series of debts in Leicestershire which had accumulated following the collapse of his video hire shop chain. I and two other men travelled to

Leicestershire and soon discovered most of the debts were useless. The people involved had lost heavily in the business also, and they had no money to repay the outstanding debt. One of the men who owed money was a taxi driver named Danny Marlow. I went to his house, knocked on the door and a lady, whom I assumed was his wife, answered. She told me he wasn't in and she had no way of contacting him. Through a neighbour I learned which cab office he worked at and went to visit him there. The controller was persuaded to contact Danny on his radio. He told him to come back to the cab office, but Danny refused. I gave the controller my number, and Danny rang me. We had a row and I threatened him. He said he was going to contact the police.

Sometime later, at about 11 p.m. one evening, Danny was outside his home and was struck by a speeding car. He was killed. He had received a phone call at his local pub, the Bell, at 10.30 p.m. He left about ten minutes later. A witness heard two men talking. The voices got louder, then he heard a high-revving car and Danny's pool cue case clatter to the ground. Danny died on his way to hospital. Forty minutes later, a stolen Ford Granada was found burnt out nine miles away.

The police interviewed me, Martin Davies, and the other two men. They were convinced that Marlow had died for the £800 debt he owed. That may have been the case. It was certainly nothing to do with our firm. We would hardly kill anyone for a third of £800. We were furious that Davies had revealed our identities during questioning to the police, and decided that we should be compensated. We fined Davies £3,000, £1,000 for each member of the firm whose name he had given. He paid, and we have not heard or seen him since.

We hardly ever did the work as agreed, but tended to have these people over. They were not from our world, and were considered easy pickings. We were contacted about a man named Jackson in Southend. He had borrowed £60,000 to invest. The business venture had gone horribly wrong and the man who was holding their money had disappeared to Geneva. We descended on Jackson. He was very middle-class: nice house, nice wife, nice job. He didn't like our kind of people around so after a bit of intimidation he agreed to pay us £3,000 expenses to fly to Geneva to try and apprehend and hold talks with the man who was holding their money. We took Jackson's money, and never went as far as the end of Southend Pier.

A week later we returned to his house and told him we had been without success and needed to go on further trips. I think he smelled a rat, because eventually he had an injunction put on us preventing us from approaching him.

We devised a set of rules for straight people requiring our services for debt recovery. When someone came to us with a debt we used to tell them that there was no fee for our services until money had been recovered. Then we would require a third of everything we had collected. Most of these people had been through solicitors or the Courts and paid huge fees for little or no result and so the deal we offered seemed quite good. After all, they had nothing to lose – or so they thought. The other clause in the agreement was that once we were on the debt it remained ours and they couldn't employ other people to chase it. Also, once we'd agreed to take it on, we would remain with it until the money was recovered; the person who employed us couldn't change his mind, or if he did, he had to pay us a third of the debt as our fee. It all seemed fair, and everyone agreed.

However, what we used to do was intimidate the person owing the money, or cause a scene at his home so he would call the police. As they would not know our identities, the police would go to the person the money was owed to and tell them that if there were any more problems, they would be prosecuted. So the person who was owed money would get in touch with us and ask us to pull out because the police had threatened to prosecute. We would remind them of the clause that if they called it off, they would have to pay us a third. Fearing prosecution from the police on one side, and violence from us on the other, they had no choice but to pay.

The illegal side of our operation was far less complex. We did a job for one man who'd been hounded by a motorist in a flashy car. He used to do wheel spins in his road, play loud music from his car stereo, and the man who hired us was at his wits' end. He said the driver was using his road as a race track. He feared for his children. He couldn't get any peace and quiet because of the music. The man's car, which was causing the problem, was his pride and joy. We were told he was putting it in for a re-spray and contacted the people at the garage to find out when he was picking his car up. For a fee of £500 paid by the aggrieved, the man was followed on the day he collected his newly re-sprayed car, and when he parked it outside his home and went inside, it was petrol bombed, burned out, absolutely gutted.

The firm was also employed as minders on drug deals. The fee would depend on the size of the parcel. When the two parties met to do the deal, a member, or two members, of the firm were present just to make sure one side didn't have the other over. They weren't required to say or do anything unless something didn't go according to plan.

When things didn't go to plan, we were often called in to make matters right. A man named Kevin Gray came to see us. He was a drug courier who worked for a firm from West Ham in the East End of London. Kevin had been sent to Sunderland with a parcel of £16,000-worth of ecstasy he would trade with a firm of Geordies run by two brothers named Billy and John Carruthers. When Kevin got to Sunderland he was taken to a house and the brothers told him that they didn't have the money in the house because they feared the police were watching them. They told Kevin to give them the parcel and said they would go and fetch the money.

Rather foolishly Kevin handed it over. Once a person becomes a courier and is given a parcel it is his responsibility. If it goes missing, he has to pay. Billy Carruthers stayed with Kevin and his brother went off with the parcel. Half an hour later his brother came running back into the house appearing flustered. He told everyone to get out of the house, and everybody ran. Kevin couldn't find anyone. When he went back to the house some hours later, a girl was there. She told him that John Carruthers had been going to another house with the parcel and the police stopped him. He had jumped out of his car, run down the railway embankment and thrown the parcel away. She told Kevin that John assumed that the police had picked up the parcel.

Kevin couldn't do anything because he was alone, and came back down to London. I was surprised that he swallowed the story. Normally you would ask people to produce paperwork to prove that the police have been involved. I was even more surprised he'd handed over the parcel. It was quite obvious the Geordies had had him over. The firm from West Ham was now onto Kevin. He owed them £16,000 and they wanted to know what he was going to do about it.

I felt the only way to get his money back would be if we kidnapped one of the Carruthers brothers and brought him down to London. We could then contact the other brother, and tell him that when we got the parcel back he would get his brother back.

During the interim period the brother whom we had would not be having a very good time. A place was prepared for one of them. We armed ourselves and headed up north to have it out with the Geordies. Billy and John weren't new to this game. They had upped and left long before we arrived. We did manage to get hold of an associate of theirs known as Alan. He was either very brave, or didn't know the whereabouts of his friends. From the beating he received, I believe he didn't know their whereabouts. He was pushed to the floor and stamped and kicked repeatedly. If he did know, then he would have told us.

Already £16,000 in debt, the courier could not afford the cost of us remaining in Sunderland searching for people who had obviously left, so he cut his losses and we returned south. To recover the money he was forced to sell his car and run drugs around the country for no payment. The Geordies had a result that time. But blagging (robbing) shipments of drugs is not an occupation one tends to live up till retirement age doing.

Our new manager, named Mark Coombes, took over Raquels and there was soon an agreement that the way forward was to have house and garage nights rather than three hours of chart music and five slow dances at the end of the night, which had been the format up until his arrival.

To the revellers, Raquels was now trouble free. Most of the violence was behind the scenes, away from the premises. The noticeable change brought offers from promoters who wanted to hire out the club. The rave scene had no place for violence; all the kids now were into this peace and happiness thing.

Mark Coombes was approached by a promotions team from Southend who were very professional and very successful. They were currently hiring out a club in the Southend area which didn't hold enough people to fulfil the demand. They were looking for larger premises and had heard about the changes at Raquels.

An agreement was made and a date was set for them to begin. The following day, Mark Murray, and his partner, Bob Smith, whom I had not previously met, came into the Buzz Bar and asked to speak to me. They told me that they sold most of the gear in the clubs around the Basildon and Southend area and they had heard that the promotions team from Southend were coming into Raquels. They asked me if we could strike up a deal whereby they were allowed to sell their drugs exclusively in our club.

I called Tony Tucker and he told me to let them start. The fee depended on the amount of drugs they sold per night. If it became busy, then it would become more lucrative. Both parties agreed to see how it went. It was going to be the door's job to ensure there was no trouble from other dealers and also that an early warning was given about any police presence

I wasn't concerned about men like Jason Vella. He often used to come in to the club and I'd become friendly with him. Murray, not being a violent man, had heard, like everyone else, what Vella was up to in the Essex area. He was concerned that Vella was going to muscle in and put his operation out of business. Although only 23 at the time, Vella was a big man on the Essex drugs scene. Vella specialised in kidnapping, torturing and humiliating his opponents. One man had a broomstick inserted into his backside and Vella took pictures of him. These were then circulated to show what happens to people who cross Vella.

Another man named Mark Skeets sent Vella's girlfriend a Christmas card. Vella decided that he was taking a liberty. He invited Skeets out for a drink to lure him into a trap. Skeets was tied up and beaten. Vella then chopped off Skeets' hair and shaved his eyebrows off. Again photographs were taken to humiliate him. He was jabbed with knives, and burned with cigarettes. The soles of his feet were also burned. He was forced to take the hallucinogenic drug, acid, and snort 12 lines of cocaine. Skeets was completely drugged out of his brains. Coupled with the assault, the effects must have been terrifying.

Another man named Dean Power was trapped in a similar way. He was whipped with a metal coat hanger and flogged with a bamboo stick. In a second attack some time later, Power was jabbed with a roasting fork and beaten with lumps of wood. His crime: he had tried to restrain Vella in a pub argument over money. His head was also kicked, his feet and arms were stamped on. He was totally disfigured. Power told people Vella was like the devil, he was possessed. Although the police were well aware of Vella's activities, nobody would give evidence against him.

The police attended many incidents. One man was admitted to hospital with burns to the back of his hands from a hot iron. He wouldn't talk. Another had been shot at close range with a handgun. He wouldn't talk. One house had the door kicked in. The people inside were sprayed with CS gas and the TV was blown out by a sawn-off shotgun. They refused to complain.

A man named Reggie Nunn owed Vella £7,000. He had been sent to Scotland as a courier and he had spent some of the profits on what he called expenses. Vella lured him to his home in Basildon to discuss the debt. When Nunn couldn't explain to Vella's satisfaction what had happened, he was beaten and kicked. Then a sword was produced and Vella stabbed him. Afterwards Vella walked about shouting at Nunn. He said: 'There's blood on my settee, stop whimpering like a little boy. You know it's not going to end here, Reg.' Vella gave him a few more slaps and swipes and went out of the room. Reggie overheard Vella saying he would be kept overnight and finished off in the morning. In panic he jumped through the upstairs window, falling nearly 20 feet to the ground. He staggered to a neighbour's door begging for help, and they called the police. There was no need. At that time, 40 officers from Essex had been assigned to an investigation against Vella, known as operation Max, and his flat was under surveillance. Police video cameras had caught Nunn jumping from the window and staggering to the neighbour's house. It was the end of the road for Vella and his firm. Shortly afterwards they were all arrested and remanded in custody to await trial for various offences ranging from drug dealing to serious assault. But to secure that conviction, three men had to be given new identities after giving evidence – an expensive business.

In the same month that Vella's world collapsed, a new outlet for drug users in Basildon opened up, and the firm started its ascendancy. Its activities would make Vella's seem user-friendly.

On Friday, 25 July 1994, Raquels opened its doors for the first house and garage night promoted by the team from Southend. It was absolutely packed, because this type of event was rare in a violent town like Basildon where peroxide blondes, cheap drinks and drunken nights were commonplace. We kept all those types out, and for those not involved in the politics it really was an enjoyable night. There was no trouble among the customers and the atmosphere in there was fantastic. It's hard to describe. You could feel the music, it was so loud. You could see little because of the darkness and smoke, but already there was a feeling of unity among the revellers.

I had begun to experience a new feeling myself which at first I dismissed. In the firm you had a sense of security. On your home ground, you felt safe. Everyone in that particular jungle knew who to avoid. It was when we moved to seemingly greener pastures working in northern England, the Midlands or Bristol that the problems for me started. Danger was everywhere, yet you couldn't see it – there was just a feeling that something was going to happen. It is then that paranoia creeps and for me it struck deep. I started to become suspicious of everybody.

If a car pulled up outside the club, I was expecting somebody to get out and launch some sort of attack upon us. Groups of men in the club talking probably about everyday business aroused suspicion in me. The pressures of my environment were beginning to affect me. I wouldn't leave the house unless I was armed. Even during the day if I went to fetch a newspaper or post a letter in the town I took a sheath knife with me. My car had weapons hidden in the boot and under the dashboard on the driver's side. There could be anything from a knife to a gun, depending on where I was going and what I was up to. I even kept a gun in my bedroom and there was a rounders bat and squirt (ammonia) in the cupboard by the front door. I considered every possibility. If they kicked the door in and I was upstairs in bed the weapons by the door were useless. I therefore had to have a weapon in my bedroom. If I was getting something out of the boot of my car and they came, the weapon in the dashboard was useless, therefore I had to have one in the boot. I tried to convince myself of the stupidity of it all, but paranoia had taken a grip of me.

With the crowds and the house music came a demand for ecstasy. Raquels was hit by an avalanche of drugs. Local men were quickly recruited by Murray. Dealers were everywhere in the club. The demand was being met.

I had now recruited what I considered to be an ideal door. I had doormen who were not bullies. They were friendly and could mix with the people who were entering the club and were not seen as intimidating. Yet if someone wanted trouble, they would fucking get it, and they would regret it. None of the men were from the Basildon area: they came from south and east London. They weren't impressed by local men's reputations. They took people how they found them. They dealt with them accordingly.

Without exception everybody accepted it. On the face of it the police now had a peaceful club, they could divert their attentions elsewhere. The occasional victim was of our own kind and so of little concern to them. Previously we had endured twice weekly visits from the constabulary, but we rarely saw them now, and on the odd occasion we did, it was only as they drove past to buy tea from the burger van. We now had a club full to capacity with peaceful people. The customers were getting what they wanted, and the firm had got what it wanted. The lunatics had taken over the asylum.

In that same July of 1994 another explosive ingredient was added to what was to become an increasingly volatile situation. Pat Tate was released from prison after serving four years of a six-year sentence. In December 1988 Pat had robbed a restaurant in Basildon. He had been in a Happy Eater with his girlfriend and had got into a dispute with the staff about his bill. To compensate himself he decided to help himself to the takings.

When he was arrested he was found to be in possession of a small amount of cocaine, which was for his personal use. On 29 December 1988, Billericay magistrates decided that Pat would see the New Year in within the confines of Chelmsford Prison.

Pat, however, had made other plans. He jumped over the side of the dock and made for the door. Six police officers joined the jailer and jumped onto his back, but he broke free and ran off. One WPC received a black eye and another police officer was kicked in the face as they tried to block Pat's escape. He ploughed his way out of the Court to a waiting motorcycle. Roadblocks which were immediately set up failed to trap him. His escape was so speedy, the police couldn't say what type of motorcycle it was, or whether he was alone or travelled as a passenger.

Several days later, Pat surfaced in Spain. He remained there for a year, but he made the mistake of crossing over into Gibraltar where he was arrested by the British authorities.

Everybody in Basildon had a good word for Pat. But he had become a drug user in prison and this caused a marked change in his character. I call prisons hate factories, because all they produce is people full of hatred. Pat came out of prison much that way. He wanted the world to know he was out and he was not happy about the way he had been treated.

Tucker warmed to men like him. He was six-foot-two, very broad, 18 stone and no fool. He also had a glamorous bit of history. His fight with the police in Court and his escape on a motorbike were talking points in criminal circles. He was soon recruited by the firm.

Pat's arrival was met with resentment by some members. Chris Wheatley had returned from America some time before Pat's release. Tucker had latched on to him, giving him control of one of his clubs in Southend, and he became a close friend. However, when Pat came out, he dropped Chris as if he didn't exist. Chris is one of a few of my former associates that I have any time for. I do not think he deserved the treatment he received from Tucker; he turned on him for no reason, and the firm followed suit. Pat Tate took his place.

Others who had no reason to dislike Pat felt their position was threatened. Few felt comfortable about his appointment because he had an explosive temper. Tony, on the other hand, was loving every minute of it. He loved to pitch people against one another.

On one occasion a doorman from Chelmsford mentioned in conversation that he thought another doorman was a police informant. Tucker rang this alleged informant and asked him to meet him outside McDonald's in Chelmsford. Then he told the other man that if he thought someone was a grass, he should confront him and not talk about him behind his back. He was allowed to arm himself with a machete and was then taken to the meeting at McDonald's. Fearing he was going to lose face, he accused the man of being a grass in front of Tucker. The man denied it, of course.

'He's just called you a fucking grass,' said Tucker. 'What are you going to do about it? I'd fucking hit him if he said that to me.'

The so-called grass threw a half-hearted punch and the other man slashed his arm with the machete before he fled. You didn't get a P45 in our firm.

Pat Tate brought with him ideas of grandeur. He had met lots of useful contacts in prison whom he thought we could work with or exploit. Prison is the university of crime, and such meetings are inevitable. However, dealing with the unknown is a dangerous business.

I was all for looking after what was already there rather than expanding into unknown territory. Tucker and Tate felt everyone was there for the taking. They began to talk about lorries bringing in drugs from the continent and small aircraft dropping shipments in the fields around Essex. However many times I told them it was risky, they wouldn't listen. Being king on your home ground is one thing, but going on an international crusade with the attitude and regard for other people they had was a recipe for disaster.

Since Steve and Noel's arrest and the death of 20-year-old Kevin Jones, Tucker had employed various dealers in Club UK. None was up to the job, really. In August 1994 a 19-year-old man from Essex came close to death at Club UK after a mixture of cocaine, speed and ecstasy brought on a fit. It attracted more publicity for the club, so Tucker decided to withdraw all dealers from the premises for six to eight weeks. He rang me and asked how Mark Murray and his dealers were performing in Raquels. I told him they were discreet and no problem.

Tucker asked me to take Murray over to his house in Chafford Hundred for a meeting. Tucker told him that he wanted him to take over the sale of drugs in Club UK. Murray would have to buy all his drugs from Tucker and pay £1,200 rent each weekend. But in return, Tucker told him, he could earn in excess of £12,000.

Murray stuck out his hand without hesitation. The deal was struck. He was to start in six to eight weeks' time when the publicity over the kid who collapsed and nearly died had abated. For introducing Murray to Tucker, Murray said he would pay me £500 a week once he started. I would have no further involvement. It was, he said, a drink as a favour. It had been quite a lucrative ten-minute meeting.

CHAPTER 7

It's sad but true, that there are those in all walks of life who take a favour as a sign of weakness. Jason Draper was regarded as a fearless hardman in Basildon. He had temporarily paralysed a man, Tony Aldridge, by attacking him with a machete which caused brain damage. He had used a girl to drink with Aldridge and lure him out by asking him to take her to a taxi rank. I had welcomed him and his cronies into Raquels, but there had been trouble on occasion. It had now reached the stage where I would let Jason Draper in with his girlfriend, but not with his firm because they all acted out their parts for each other's benefit when they were together.

One Friday night, there was a large disturbance at the top bar and the DJ called for security to attend. When I got there, Draper was beating a man. I tried to separate them and Draper got upset, saying the man had assaulted his girlfriend. I knew this was nonsense and I told him to calm down. The manager came and I told Jason he would have to leave. He was getting more irate, saying he had done nothing. I told him just to go, and if he had a problem to see me the following day. He was still stroppy, but eventually he left.

I had a feeling that this would not be the end of this particular story. People with reputations don't like being put out, because they lose face. The following evening Draper came back to Raquels' front door and asked if he could come in. I told him he was not allowed. He said he wanted to speak to me. We went outside and again he began getting angry, saying he had done nothing wrong, but I insisted that he would have to stay away for a few weeks.

Maurice, from Bristol, came outside and asked me if

84

everything was all right. Draper took exception to this, and said: 'If it wasn't, what would you do about it?' Maurice laughed at Draper and said if he had a problem with him, they should sort it out. Draper started shouting. Maurice said: 'If you want to have a go, come on then,' and he started to walk towards Draper. He backed off, getting more and more angry, shouting obscenities, offering violence, and saying he would be back. I said to Draper: 'What's the point of going away if you're going to come back? If you're going to do something, let's do it now.' He walked away shouting.

Ten minutes later, he returned. He said he was sorry. He had just got upset. I said to him again: 'Come back in a week or so and we'll sort it out. The manager won't let you into the club under any circumstances, so all this is pointless. When the dust settles, things may be different.'

The following weekend, Draper came into the Buzz Bar. He was quite a nice bloke, really, when he didn't have his cronies around him. We had a drink together and I explained that he couldn't come into Raquels. He agreed that I was right. He said he was going for a drink the following day in the Bull public house in Pitsea, and invited me out for a drink to show that there were no hard feelings. When the pub closed Jason, his girlfriend, Debra, and I went up to a nightclub called Gass in the West End. We had a very good evening. Jason was apologetic about the trouble in the club and he agreed that he wouldn't come back for a few weeks until the dust had settled.

It was all left on friendly terms. I was making the same mistakes Vine had made. I should have fucked him up when he put his first foot wrong. I considered him a friend. I now know you don't have friends when it comes to business.

During the week I got a telephone call from the Bath dealers Steve and Noel, who were with Dave Thomkins, one of their friends who dealt in the clubs in London for them. They told me they were having trouble with some doormen from Bristol who, seeing them driving round in BMWs and knowing they had a flat in London, wanted to get in on the act. I told them I would make some phone calls and sort it out. I rang the doormen and told them to leave it out with Steve, Noel and Dave, otherwise they would have trouble. I gave the doormen the impression that they were working for a much more powerful operation. I knew them and they didn't know us, which always puts you in a powerful position in our circles. The doormen argued that Steve, Noel and Dave were the cause of the trouble, but they said it wasn't worth falling out over, and the matter would come to an end.

The next morning, I got a frantic phone call from Noel. He said that he had been driving through Bath in his BMW when two men had flagged him down. He was dragged from the car and told that they were taking it and keeping it. He said he wanted his car back, but he was scared of the men who had taken it. I told him and Steve that if we were going down to Bath to recover a car, we would have to go firm-handed as we did not know what we were up against until we got there. I asked them how many men we'd need, and they said if I could get ten down there, they would pay us £300 each.

I asked for a contact number for the man who had taken the car and I said I'd be down that evening with ten people. I told them to stay out of the way until the matter was resolved.

The man holding the car was called Billy Gillings. He had a reputation in the area as a hardman. He had just come out of jail for robbing a security van. I rang Billy and asked him if he had Steve and Noel's car. He got all shirty at first, and I told him to calm down and listen. I pointed out to him that I knew where he lived, and he didn't even know my name. I was coming to Bath to recover the car whatever. I had no particular loyalty to Steve and Noel, and therefore we could come to an agreement. 'Falling out over a BMW was hardly worth it,' I said. Billy agreed. I told him for recovering the car I was going to be paid £1,000, and he should meet me at Bath railway station and give me the car. I would give him half the money. He would be able to return to his friends and tell them that we had chased him, assaulted him, and taken the car back. We'd both be £500 better off and everyone would be happy.

I rang Steve and Noel and told them there were ten of us going down to Bath in two cars. They were to stay out of the way until we called them. I drove to Bath on my own and met Billy as arranged. I told him the plot and that I would meet him there again in an hour's time, but first he would have to give me the car. He agreed. I phoned Steve and Noel and drove to meet them. I said there had been a bit of trouble with Billy and the other people with me had driven out of Bath. I added that I was to meet them afterwards because they feared the police may be looking for them. I gave Steve and Noel their car, and they gave me the £3,000.

Dave Thomkins, who had arrived with them, was going mad. He said another man, named Steve Woods, had burgled his house and stolen quite a lot of electrical equipment – televisions, videos, etc – and covered his children's bedroom floor and walls with excrement. He was under the impression that we were to do Steve Woods as well for this money. He claimed that Woods and Gillings were in on it together. Gillings had the car. Woods, he alleged, had done the burglary, and gave the goods to Gillings to fence. I told them it was the first I had heard of it. I said if he wanted, we would resolve that matter for him also. But he was adamant he wanted it sorted that night. 'Suit yourself,' I said. I shook hands with Steve and Noel, jumped into a cab, and went to meet Billy.

I gave Billy his £500 and kept the £2,500 for myself. Late that night I got a call from Dave Thomkins. He told me he couldn't stand the thought of knowing Steve Woods had robbed his house and covered his children's bedroom in excrement and got away with it. I told him that Woods hadn't got away with it. He said: 'Too right he hasn't, I've just fucking shot him.'

He explained what he had done. After leaving me, he was in a rage. He had gone home and picked up a shotgun. He had gone to Woods' house and put on a balaclava before knocking on the door. Woods' girlfriend answered the door. Dave pushed her aside. Woods was in the hallway. It must have been a terrifying sight for him to see a man in a balaclava with a shotgun. Dave fired and hit Woods in the upper thigh. He then ran over to Woods, who had collapsed on the floor, put the gun to his head and shouted: 'I want my fucking television back.' Woods' girlfriend was screaming. Dave levelled the gun at her head and told her to shut up. Then he made his escape. I remarked to Dave that this kind of behaviour was a bit over the top over a 14-inch Nicam television. He obviously did not think so. This was becoming the norm for more and more people in these firms. It was all front. Dave obviously wanted people to know you couldn't take liberties with him.

Now Dave had calmed down, he didn't have a clue as to what he was going to do. It wasn't really my problem, but he was associated with us, and you have to help your own. I suggested he conceal the weapon, jump in a car and meet me in Basildon as soon as possible. I didn't know if Woods still had Dave's television or not. It didn't really matter. I thought Dave Thomkins was in luck. According to the tabloids everyone who is sent to prison these days gets given their own television anyway.

I could have done without Dave's problem at that particular time. The police in Basildon, although maintaining their distance, were keeping a very watchful eye on my activities. Whatever, Dave was in trouble, and I felt obliged to help. I wouldn't be able to keep him at my house because the police often watched those who came and went. I rang Pat, the landlady at a pub called the Owl And Pussycat in Basildon. I had sorted out a bit of trouble for her when she ran a pub in Southend. I asked her if she would put my friend up for the night. Pat asked me what the problem was. It was no good lying. I told her Dave had shot somebody. At first she was reluctant to help me, which is understandable; she had never even met the man, and he had just attempted a murder. The thought of spending the night alone with him must have been quite unnerving. However, in the end, she relented.

I met Dave in Basildon in the early hours of the morning. I took him to Pat's pub, where he spent the night. We would decide what we were going to do in the morning, when he had a clearer picture.

The following day we contacted people in Bath to try and find out about Steve Woods' condition. We learned that Dave had blasted a large hole in Woods' upper thigh. It was unlikely that he would ever be able to walk properly again. His life was not in danger, but we learned the police were treating it as attempted murder. We arranged for people to pick up the gun and dispose of it and then for Dave to go and stay with some people in Liverpool for a few days while the dust settled.

Around the same time Jason Vella and his firm went on trial for numerous offences. All were drug- or violence-related. One of the defendants, Wally Birch, was released halfway through the proceedings by the judge, because there was no evidence against him. Wally turned up at Raquels with all his supporters to celebrate. Unfortunately, his party included Jason Draper who had agreed only five days earlier that he would stay out of Raquels for a few weeks. He came to the door saying that this was an exception. He was only out celebrating Wally's release: would I let him in? I said no.

He got all stroppy and offered to fight me. I walked out into the street and the doormen were calling me back, telling me to leave it, he was not worth it. He continued to call me out, so I pulled out my sheath knife. He backed away, rather wisely. I turned around and walked back into the club. If somebody wanted to fight, they wanted to fight. At my age I wasn't going to chase him around the town. I went upstairs and told a doorman named Liam to stand by the fire exit and ensure that nobody went in or out, because on previous weeks people had opened the fire exits to let people in without paying. Liam wasn't what I consider to be a proper doorman. He was one of a minority one has to employ when running a door. They are not up to much, these people, when it comes to handling trouble. You just use them for guarding fire exits, collecting tickets and other menial jobs such as searching, which the proper doormen don't really do. He was one of those people who thought it a glamorous world, and he was useful to me. He was under-age, so I fixed him up with a false birth certificate and he applied to the police and the council with it to get his registration.

I was standing at the bar talking to Wally Birch. Wally was upset about the way he had been dragged into the Vella trial. He said he had popped around to Vella's home in Basildon to buy a car. When he arrived a man named Reggie Nunn was in dispute with Vella, so he left. Unknown to Wally, the police had the house under surveillance and he was captured on their video. As a consequence he had been roped in. He was adamant he was innocent.

Vella's was not a firm anyone wished to be associated with at that particular time. The police had the serious hump with them because of their activities and anyone found guilty at his trial was going to be severely dealt with. When the trial was concluded, Vella and five other gang members were found guilty. Vella's second-in-command, Simon Renaldi, who was 23, was sentenced to six years and eight months' imprisonment after he was convicted of false imprisonment and of conspiring to supply ecstasy, amphetamine sulphate and cannabis. Scott Hunt, 22, was sentenced to five years for conspiring to supply ecstasy. He was also given nine months' consecutive for possessing a revolver and four bullets. James Skeets, 21, was sentenced to two years' imprisonment after being convicted of conspiring to supply cannabis. Tony Barker, 31, was jailed for three years for conspiring to supply amphetamine sulphate. Anthony Dann, 25, was sentenced to three years' imprisonment for grievous bodily harm with intent on Reggie Nunn. Jason Vella was convicted on four conspiracy charges to supply ecstasy, amphetamine sulphate and cannabis, causing grievous bodily harm with intent to Reg Nunn and actual bodily harm to Alan Bailey. He pleaded guilty to falsely imprisoning Mark Skeets and causing him actual bodily harm; falsely imprisoning Dean Power on two occasions, causing grievous bodily harm the first time, and actual bodily harm the second.

Judge Alan Simpson branded Vella the Tsar of South East Essex. He said: 'You've imposed your will on those who argued with you with torture and terror.' He sentenced Jason to 17 years' imprisonment. Jason turned to the judge and said: 'Fuck you.' He turned to the prosecutor and said: 'Fuck you, too.' Vella remained his old self to the end.

As I was talking to Wally, I felt a sharp blow to the side of my head. I spun round. Jason Draper was standing there. He hit me again. I pulled out my sheath knife and Draper backed off. He said: 'You wouldn't use that on your friend, would you?' I threw it on the floor and said: 'I don't need it for a cunt like you.' I saw his hand come up. He was wearing a knuckle duster. It struck me on the side of the face and I grabbed him. The fight dissolved into a wrestling match because the bar was so packed with people. I can remember thinking: 'I should have stuck the knife in him. The bastard used a weapon on me.' Eventually he stepped back and disappeared through the fire exit. I couldn't work out how he had got in and I wasn't going to leave the matter there.

I asked the doormen how he got in and they told me his girlfriend had gone past Liam the doorman, down the stairs, and opened the fire exit. He'd come in and he had walked back past Liam. Liam was too scared to say or do anything. The following day I got hold of Liam when he came into work. We went into the toilets to talk. I asked him if it was true about him turning a blind eye and he admitted it was. I head-butted him in the face and he fell to the floor. I hit him a few more times and told him to get out. He was bleeding from the mouth and nose. But he still asked about his wages. I told him that the £200 he was owed wasn't going to be paid. He was being fined that amount for what he did. He left the club, and I have never seen him since.

I was furious, because even if he was frightened of him, he could have at least alerted me rather than stand there and pretend that he had not seen him. This was a typical problem with the door registration scheme. You're forced to get soft people in and it causes all sorts of trouble.

The following day the whole town was poised for a battle. Rumours and speculation were rife. Everyone knew I would not let what had happened go. The only way to maintain an effective door was to be seen to take action. Messages were coming from Draper's side that he was going to kill me. I chose to say nothing and bide my time.

On the Saturday night two police officers came to see me and the manager at Raquels. They told me that they had received numerous calls about the incident on Friday, and they'd heard that something pretty serious was going to happen. I told them that it had all been sorted out, but they refused to believe me. I was told I wasn't to work for a week until the dust had settled. The police couldn't prevent me from working, but they could make it difficult for the manager. Not only was I told not to work, I was advised to go away for the week. I reluctantly agreed, because I did not want police attention focusing on the club. A couple of days later Jason and I had our homes spun. Although I had weapons, firearms in particular, nothing was found. I stayed away for a couple of days, but my paranoia began to tell me that people would think I had run from the trouble. I returned to Basildon and to work on the Wednesday. The whole town was buzzing, waiting for one side to do something. Everyone seemed to think it was Draper who would follow through.

Meanwhile, Dave rang from Liverpool. He told me he had outstayed his welcome and he had nowhere else to go. I had a friend in Edinburgh who would put him up. But Dave wanted to come back to Basildon. I sorted it out with the landlady at the pub and he returned.

Peter Clarke, the man I had gone into partnership with when I first took over Raquels from Dave Vine, said he had a gun I could have if I needed it. I thought it might prove useful for me because an unregistered gun cannot be traced back to anyone. The way things were going, I could see I might have to use it. I assumed Clarke had heard about my problems with Draper. He told me Micky Pierce had said I could have it because I had done him a favour by being a witness in his case. I should have thought it odd at the time, but I thought it was an offer of genuine help. I took the gun, because I knew in my heart it would be needed.

For a week or so, nothing happened. And then on 29 August, which was a bank holiday, I was returning from London with Dave Thomkins when I received a call on my mobile phone informing me that Draper and three of his firm had been in Pat's pub, the Owl And Pussycat. I was told they had a gun and were looking for me. I thought because it was a bank holiday, it would be difficult to raise people. It was around midday and I assumed most people would already have gone out for the day. Whatever, if someone was looking for me, I was going to find them first.

As I was driving towards Basildon, I saw Tucker driving in front in his black Porsche. I drove up next to him and beeped my horn. All he did was bang his steering wheel and accelerate away. I accelerated after him and he pulled off the main road and onto a roundabout. He stopped and was punching the wheel, going berserk. It wasn't hard to work out he wasn't in a good mood. He had fallen out with somebody and he didn't want to talk so I reckoned he wouldn't be making himself available on that day. When I arrived in Basildon, I rang around and managed to get 14 men to go and solve this problem.

I rang Pat to see if Draper was still in the pub. She told me he was on his way to The Bull. I knew the assistant manager of the pub, so I rang him and asked him if Draper was in there. He said he hadn't arrived. I didn't want to cause trouble in the pub, because I knew the people who ran it, and I also knew it was a busy family pub, so I advised him not to let Draper in when he arrived. The assistant manager said he would tell Johnny Jones, the manager. I rang 10 or 15 minutes later, and again asked if Draper had arrived. The assistant manager said he hadn't. When I carried on ringing back at regular intervals, I found the phone had been taken off the hook. We all drove to The Bull and parked in a side road.

I had the gun with me, and also a machete. I had it clear in my mind what I had to do. It was pointless beating Draper up, because he would just bide his time and attack me at a later date. I thought the only way to end this problem would be to cripple him or kill him. In the state of mind I was in at that time, I wasn't particularly bothered which one it was to be.

All the other members of the firm were armed with coshes, truncheons, industrial ammonia, knuckle dusters and knives. Two of my closest friends knew I had the gun. One, a black youth from South London, had already told me that he would murder Draper for me. And the other said that he would walk into the pub now and shoot Draper in the head as he stood at the bar. I said that it was my problem, and that I was going to sort it out. I have no doubt that both men would have done what they said they were prepared to do.

As Dave Thomkins was not known, I asked him if he would go into the pub, walk up to Draper, squirt him in the eyes with ammonia, and then push him through a set of double doors into the street outside where he'd be beaten and then left. I told the other members of the firm that once he'd been beaten, I wanted them to walk away as there was something to do that I did not want them involved in. It was my intention to shoot Draper.

Dave walked up to the pub with a large bottle of industrial ammonia secreted in his jacket. Luck wasn't on our side. It was a 'bank holiday' there were doormen on the door (who weren't there normally), it was full of families and you had to have a ticket to get in. Dave came back and explained the problem. I said to everyone that I was not going into a pub tooled up (armed) when it was full of women and children. But they insisted it had to be sorted there and then.

I knew they were right. We walked up to the door and pushed past the doormen. Draper was standing right in front of us at the bar. He was having a drink with three or four members of his firm. They all jumped over the bar and ran. I pulled out the machete, and Draper said: 'What are you doing with that, mate?' I said, 'Fucking mate,' and went to hit him with it. Dave squirted him with the ammonia and the publican started shouting. Draper ran blind through the pub and we chased him. Unfortunately the ammonia also hit several innocent bystanders. People were screaming and running everywhere.

I really wanted it to end. I had to catch him. I couldn't let it go now. We chased him out into the beer garden. People there started screaming and running. The doormen were trying to prevent us from catching him. We got him for a brief moment. He was hit across the head with a large wooden truncheon. The doormen were grabbing me because I had the machete, which made it difficult to get to him, and Draper broke free and ran through the crowds. There was blood coming from the top of his head. He ran behind the bar. I ran to the bar, leant across it, and hit him twice with the machete: once across the head and once across the back. But I couldn't get him properly. The manager ran towards me with a lump of wood. During the distraction, Draper hid in the cellar. The pub was in chaos. It was time to leave.

We got into our cars and went our separate ways. I dropped the gun off at a house in Grays. I was annoyed it hadn't gone to plan, but it was too late to think about that now. I had to make myself scarce. I had arranged to meet Debra and the children in Chelmsford, some 15 miles away. They hadn't a clue what I was up to. I drove there, changed my car for Debra's, and we went to spend the weekend in Holland. It was the only place I could think of that was easy to reach where the police in Essex would not look for me. We drove the 30 or 40 miles to Harwich but we had missed the ferry, so we had to spend the night in a hotel. I made a few phone calls and, sure enough, the police were looking for me.

The next morning we caught the ferry to Holland and spent the day there. I knew Draper wouldn't go to the police. It was more likely they were investigating the disturbance. The following day, I returned to England and went into work that night. The police came to see me and asked me about the trouble. They had heard that Draper had been looking for me and they also heard what had happened at The Bull. I was quite frank with them. I said if someone was looking for me, they would eventually run out of public houses where they might expect to find me. And if they couldn't find me, they would turn up on my doorstep. I was not going to sit in my house and wait for a gang of men to turn up on my doorstep when my children were there. Therefore if someone was looking for me, I'd go and find them. The police said Jason hadn't made a complaint. I didn't expect him to, he was not that sort of man. They said, as policemen, they had to tell me that that sort of behaviour wouldn't be tolerated, and if a complaint could be substantiated I would be charged. However, man to man, they didn't blame me.

The incident had a big impact in Basildon, because no-one had ever messed with Draper before. People were terrified of him. It changed a lot of things about how people viewed us. The troublemakers wouldn't come near the club after that.

Trade was really very good at Raquels. Every firm of troublemakers was now out of the situation. Our tough tactics were working. To celebrate our success, the promoters held a party at the Cumberland Hotel in Southend and we were all invited. It was an excellent do. Tucker and Tate were there. Tucker said Murray would be unable to start dealing in Club UK for some time because there had been a development there. He did not elaborate. We discussed the problem with Draper. He was attracting too much police attention at Raquels. Attention we didn't want.

Tucker suggested abducting him and giving him a good hiding. I tried to explain that you couldn't do that with Draper, because he would only come back and cause further trouble. I was all for shooting him, but Tucker and Tate said that would only attract more police attention. They were adamant that whatever happened, it had to be done discreetly because they didn't want anything to upset the sale of drugs in clubs or to affect their distribution. Any police involvement had to be minimal. Tucker said the best way to take him out of the situation would be to give him a contaminated tablet of ecstasy. We had friends who were friends of Draper, and people often gave him free ecstasy in nightclubs, so it wouldn't be difficult for someone to slip him a free pill as a favour. Shortly afterwards he would collapse. Nobody would get too excited about it. Tucker said it was the ideal way to dispose of somebody. Everyone was in agreement. Tucker said he would sort out the pill and we set about recruiting somebody to supply it to him. But before the plan could be put into operation, Draper was arrested and imprisoned for driving while disqualified. Our chance had been taken away, but the idea remained appealing. Disposing of a drug user with drugs was never going to cause much fuss or arouse suspicion. The idea was put on the back burner for future use.

Bernard on his release from prison in 1985

The early days at Raquels. Bernard (*left*) with David Amess, MP (*centre*) and fellow doorman Steve Giles (*right*)

ABOVE: (*Left to right*) Tony Tucker, Pat Tate, Bernard

OPPOSITE:
TOP: Nigel Benn (*left*) with Tony Tucker; BOTTOM: Bernard's brother Michael and his wife Carol (*right*) with Page 3 Girl 'Flannagan'

Detective Superintendant Brian Storey, the detective who led the Leah Betts enquiry and who took over the Rettendon murder enquiry

Spot the 'deliberate' mistake . . .

Bernard and Mick Taylor (ex Rolling Stones)

Bernard with Mark Murray

Bernard (*centre*) and wife Debra (*second from right*)

Dave Thomkins and landlady Pat with whom he stayed in Basildon

Mark Rothermel (*left*) with Bernard

(*Left to right*) Bernard, Kate Kray, Charlie Kray, Tony Lambrianou

(*Left to right*) Bernard, Reg Kray, Dave Courtney inside H M Prison Maidstone

CHAPTER 8

Dave Thomkins' problem down in Bath had to be sorted out, but it wasn't going to be easy because of the nature of the offence. Trying to persuade a man who had been shot that the person who had done it was not all that bad and didn't deserve to go to prison was going to take more than tact.

Steve Woods, the victim of the shooting, had a bit of form himself, so he knew the score. It meant our task was not impossible. I rang Billy Gillings, the man who had done the deal on Steve and Noel's car. I asked him if he would mediate and arrange a meeting between myself and Woods. Woods could bring anyone he wished, if it made him feel safer.

Woods had just come out of hospital after a month. Billy went to see him and he agreed to meet at Leigh Delamere motorway services near Bristol. Woods insisted that his brother, who was nicknamed Noddy, accompany him. A date was set and I went to the meeting on my own. We all sat down at one of the cafeteria tables. Noddy Woods started getting a bit lippy about Dave Thomkins, so I told him in no uncertain terms that we didn't have to sit there and discuss it. I was offering him and his brother a way out. I said: 'If you persist with your lip, you'll get taken out of the game like your brother. I suggest you go and get some tea for us both, while I discuss this with Steve.' It was important to let him know who was in the driving seat.

I told them both that we didn't normally do deals with people who inform on one of our number to the police, but because he had suffered over a rather trivial matter, we were making an exception. We were prepared to offer him £20,000 not to make a statement against Dave Thomkins. Woods said he had already made a statement. So I said he would be paid the money if he retracted it. Woods wanted half up-front and half on completion. I told him, 'Bollocks, our word is our bond. Do your part of the deal, and you'll get your dough.'

He agreed and we went our separate ways. We didn't have any intention of giving him a penny. As soon as he retracted his statement, he was going to be told to 'bollocks'.

A member of the firm named Mark and I went to the next meeting. Billy Gillings and Steve Woods met us at an out-of-town location near Bristol. Billy came over to our car and I asked him if Woods had retracted his statement. Billy said he wouldn't unless he got half of the money up-front. I said to Billy: 'Put Woods in your car and take him down the road. Then tell him to get out. Drive away, and don't look back.' Billy asked why. I told him that Woods was going to be shot. Billy said he didn't want any part of it. I said: 'Okay, tell Woods to get in our car, because we want to discuss payment with him.' Billy agreed, but he kept repeating he wanted no part of it.

Woods came over. I said: 'There's no problem, get in the car.' We drove away from Bath to a deserted lane. A gun was produced and Woods was told to get out of the car because we didn't want any of his 'shit or blood' messing up our vehicle. Woods was laid on a grass bank. The gun was put to his head. He was terrified. He had not yet got over the shooting six weeks previously. His whole body was shaking, and he was weeping. He was told that the firm did not pay grasses. 'Now you are going to die.'

'I don't want any money, I just don't want any trouble,' he said.

'First you break into our friend's house and rub shit over the walls, and now you come and demand £20,000,' he was told. 'It doesn't work like that.'

'I'll retract my statement, and that will be the end of it,' he said.

He was told that if he didn't, people would come back. The talking was over. Woods went away and within three hours he had retracted his statement.

We returned to Basildon and Dave contacted a solicitor. The solicitor said he would check to see if Woods had retracted his statement, and if he had, he would arrange for Dave to give himself up the following day. The solicitor thought Woods had retracted it off his own back. The following day, I took Dave to Barking station in east London and we said our goodbyes. He travelled to Bath where he gave himself up.

What we hadn't counted on was Steve Woods' wife. She had not retracted her statement, so Dave was charged with attempted murder, threats to kill and possessing a firearm with the intention of endangering life. He was 30 years old. Dave was remanded in custody to await trial. Obviously a lot of our conversation around that time was about Dave. Some liked him, some didn't. Once he was out of the situation, I was told that he had been talking behind my back about me. It was a hammer blow, really. I had done all I could to help him, and yet he had been slagging me off to promote himself. I wasn't happy at all, but our world was overflowing with such people.

I contacted Steve Woods via a third party. He was told that Thomkins' cover had been lifted, Woods and his friends could do as they wished. I travelled to Horfield prison in Bristol, where Dave was being held on remand, along with two friends who were going to see him. I said I wanted to go and see him first. I would only be five minutes. They could wait outside. I went into the visiting room and Dave held out his hand to shake my hand. He said: 'All right, mate.' I said: 'You're no fucking mate of mine. You've been slagging me off.'

A prison visiting room isn't the best place to settle one's differences. At that moment, I didn't really care. I went for Dave. The prison officers were alerted, and Dave backed off to where they were. I walked out of the visiting room. I have not seen him since. It is a shame because I considered him a good friend. Why he did what he did to me, I will never know. He was later sentenced to ten years' imprisonment for shooting Steve Woods.

I still kept in contact with the Kray brothers. Reggie used to ring me on a regular basis, and I used to go and see him a couple of times each month at Maidstone Prison in Kent.

Drugs had riddled every part of the underworld like a cancer. The unlikeliest of men had become involved.

Everyone had some connection, whether it was as enforcers for the dealers, importers or wholesale stockists. Even car dealers were used to clean drug money. Reggie, who epitomised the old school, began using drugs and looking at the money that could be made in deals.

Reggie had started using ecstasy, cocaine and cannabis. Reg was always asking what was going on in the clubs. He asked me if I could arrange a meeting with Tucker. He said he had some people, one person in particular, from Hull whom he thought we could do business with. I said I would speak to Tucker and arrange it.

Tucker said he had no interest in Reggie Kray's plans. He respected the Krays for what they were but now, he said, Reggie was a has-been. Pat Tate had met far more useful people during his time inside. The firm was moving into the import market. Tucker said we wouldn't be needing the likes of Reggie Kray. However, he did say he would meet him out of interest, but as far as business went, Kray was to be excluded.

For Reggie's birthday, the firm were going to send him in a parcel of ecstasy and cocaine to celebrate. I'd always taken bottles of Napoleon brandy for Reggie on visits. It was quite easy getting things into Maidstone, but they were tightening up. Sometimes Reggie could hardly stand, he was so drunk. I can remember one visit, his face was blood red, and his speech was slurred. He kept asking me if the screws could notice anything. It was obvious to everybody in the visiting room that Reggie was steaming. He kept saying, 'I'm going to go to the toilet.' As he stood up and staggered to the door, I couldn't stop laughing. Every last person in that room must have known that he was drunk. However, he had been in prison longer than most of the prison officers had been alive. He had never caused them problems, so they tended to turn a blind eye.

I was surprised that Reg wanted to get involved with drugs. I had always associated him with straight villainy. Not only did Reg want to get involved on the large deals, working as a middleman, he wanted to get involved in putting on large raves around the country. He put me in touch with Bryn Jones, who said he could hire out some large aircraft hangars in various parts of Wales. However, when we discussed money, he was talking '50-50' this and '50-50' that. I don't think he appreciated the way things work. By the time we had paid for security, DJs (who are very expensive), Reggie's drink and the cost of promoting the events, there wouldn't be a great deal left anyway. In the end I told Reg that we were not interested. The dealers he had put us in touch with were also amateurish. They talked big, but nothing seemed to materialise. They were wannabes going through the motions.

Being in the Krays' circle is very tedious. They had more plastic action men around them than most High Street toy shops. Their real friends called this army the fan club. Two of the biggest fools Reggie ever embraced were Lyndsey and Leighton Frayne, who came from Wales. They marketed themselves as Kray lookalikes and twins. I suppose they could have carried it off for a little while, but their biggest failing was their accent. Instead of an East End, Cockney growl, they spoke with a deep Welsh twang straight from the valleys.

After visiting Reg, they started wearing double-breasted suits, with their hair slicked back like their hero. They walked, talked and scowled just like the twins did in their heyday. They even visited the grave of Violet Kray, the twins' mother and placed flowers there. They also visited the Blind Beggar, where Ronnie murdered George Cornell. Finally they formed their own gang. Among their recruits was a 15-stone heavy who claimed to be a former SAS man. He would stuff a sawn-off double barrelled shotgun under his jacket, and always carried a knife, which he called Big Bertha. They even planned to kidnap Paul Gascoigne.

The brothers were finally arrested after a £9,820 robbery in their home town of Newbridge. They had planned to use the loot to finance their new crime empire in London. But the raid on the Halifax Building Society was badly bungled. An accomplice, Steve Cook, was sentenced to six and a half years' imprisonment after he was apprehended trying to make his getaway on a bus. At their trial, the Fraynes were sentenced to eight years' imprisonment.

Headlines in the national press ridiculed them. One headline said: 'The Krays? We called them Pinky and Perky.'

The Fraynes finally did succeed in correctly aping their heroes. They are both serving long prison sentences.

Our association with Reggie Kray was put on hold after the *News of the World* published an exposé on the drugs being smuggled into Reg. They titled the articled 'Reg "E" Kray'. They claimed Reggie had become addicted to ecstasy in jail. Underworld cronies smuggled him in a regular supply at visiting times. They said he had become a haggard shadow of his former self. Reggie was reported as saying: 'They're fucking marvellous. When I'm out of my head I ring up all of my old enemies and ask them how they are.' I don't know if it was true, but it sounded about right.

I had always kept my affairs secret from Debra. But my paranoia couldn't be hidden. She was becoming concerned about my behaviour and urged me to go and see a doctor about it. The thought of seeing a shrink horrified me. I couldn't take the suggestion seriously. But I knew I did have a problem. I now carried both a knife and a gun everywhere. My behaviour was not normal. The feelings I was experiencing scared me, I thought I'd end up killing somebody.

One evening I came home from work and thought I was being followed, so I parked my car three or four streets away, and made my way home through the alleyways. The following morning when I awoke I looked out of the window and thought my car had been stolen. For half an hour I ranted and raved waiting for a taxi to take me to the police station to report my car stolen. I suddenly remembered where I had parked it.

On another occasion I imagined that a man who lived two streets away was following me. One evening coming in from work, I stabbed all the tyres on his car because I had a meeting the following day and I was convinced he was going to follow me. Debra thought I had finally flipped.

We were due to go out one morning when I noticed a van opposite my house with blacked out windows. I closed the curtains in the house, and told Debra we could not leave, because it was the type of van used to photograph people secretly. We stayed in the whole day. Debra was not amused. The following day the van was still there. I had even called the police and told them they were wasting their time because I knew the van was there. They denied knowing anything about it. I later found out it was owned by a plumber who lived across the road.

Looking back, I can't believe how bad I was. I just knew something, somewhere, was going to give sometime. I saw danger in everything. Unless someone has experienced paranoia, they cannot begin to believe how horrifying an illness it is. It begins with fear and escalates into violence.

The whole firm was struck down by it to some degree. Tucker, Tate and Rolfe would never, ever, open the curtains in their homes. They remained closed all the time as they thought this would prevent police surveillance teams from keeping a watchful eye on their activities within. We would never use our home phones for firm's business. There were designated public phone boxes which were used to circumvent the possibility of the police studying itemised bills which could link us to people from other firms. If you were on business, or thought you were being followed, it was common practice to drive around all roundabouts two or three times to ensure that you weren't.

If a person had been involved in something and he had difficulty getting home, we would get him to change clothes with somebody who looked nothing like him. That way if he was arrested, any description given to the police would not match the one of the person who was guilty. For example, one night there was a fight in Raquels and a doorman bashed one of those fighting. The victim went to the police and gave the name and a description of the doorman involved. When the police came and arrested him he was wearing completely different clothing to that given in the description by the victim. It was impossible for any case to be mounted against him. The victim had described being assaulted by a man named Joe wearing jeans and a T-shirt. An hour or so later, when he was arrested, Joe was wearing trousers, a shirt with a collar and a smart jacket. The victim could not explain this and no charges were made.

The paranoia was not all unfounded. The police were taking a lot of interest in me and other members of the firm. The drugs in Raquels were common knowledge, as was the violence used to maintain the peace among the revellers in the club. I had been stopped and my car searched on several occasions. I didn't deal in drugs, so there were none to find. I protected those in the trade, but people assumed I was involved in dealing so these stops and searches became more frequent, which was inconvenient, but it kept one on one's toes.

One evening on the way into work I received a call from Micky Pierce, Dave Vine's ex-partner. He told me he needed a driver to take an articulated lorry loaded with stolen coffee beans to a warehouse in Liverpool. He had tried everyone, but nobody was available. He asked me if I would do it as a favour. Without giving it much thought, I said I would. I drove to his home, a nearby farm, and together we went to Manor Park in East London to pick up a lorry to pull the trailer up to Liverpool. It was a D-registered M.A.N., a right old banger. I was told that the truck belonged to Terry Edwards, brother of the infamous Buster Edwards, the Great Train Robber.

The coffee beans were in a 40-foot container which had been stolen some time earlier. The trailer had been parked on the farm for so long that it had sunk into the mud and we had great difficulty in getting it onto the road. I finally set off for Liverpool at about 10.00 p.m. I was to meet four or five men at a bonded warehouse at five o'clock the following morning. I didn't have a licence to drive an articulated lorry but it wasn't too difficult. There was no traffic about, and once on the motorway it was just a case of pointing it in the right direction and putting my foot down.

When I reached the National Exhibition Centre turn-off in Birmingham, my problems began. Within seconds the temperature gauge had gone from normal to red, and the lorry ground to a halt. I wasn't happy. I was sitting with a sure prison sentence unable to go anywhere. However, I thought I would try and sort it out rather than abandon ship. I waited about 20 minutes on the side of the motorway. I was panicking. I thought that every car that approached was a police car.

Buster had not planned this with the precision of earlier escapades. Eventually the lorry had cooled sufficiently for me to start it again, drive it up the slip road and off the motorway. I tried ringing the people in London who owned the lorry, but I couldn't get hold of them. I thought I would sit it out until it got light when I could have a look and see if I could rectify the problem myself.

The following morning I tried in vain to repair the vehicle. I couldn't reach anyone by telephone, so I rang a local mechanic who came out and finally got the lorry restarted at 3.00 p.m. that afternoon. It cost me more than £300 of my own money. I then set off for Liverpool. My destination was Kirby, which was where I had to meet the people at the warehouse. The lorry started to play up again. On hills it was reduced to crawling speed. I could not believe that I hadn't been pulled by the police. I eventually got into Kirby at 5.30 p.m. The warehouse had closed and the men I met up there said they had spoken to security at the warehouse and we would be able to park the vehicle in a compound until the morning. 'There is no way I am staying here until the morning waiting for this warehouse to open,' I said. 'I'm going to unhitch the trailer, leave it here, and get myself back to Essex.' They weren't too happy, but I wasn't giving them a choice.

I set off at about 8.00 p.m., and when I again reached Birmingham, the lorry broke down. I called the same mechanic out. He cleaned the fuel system and once more I set off. Where the M1 and the M6 join, the vehicle broke down again. It was now the early hours of Saturday morning. I had been going since Thursday. I wasn't amused. I was £500 down, tired and pissed off. I thought: 'Fuck this.' I got out of the lorry and hitch-hiked back to Essex.

I rang the people concerned that morning, told them where the lorry was, and went to bed. My money was never reimbursed and I was never paid anything for the journey. I was unhappy, to say the least.

A week or so afterwards I heard on the news that Buster Edwards had hanged himself. He had been found by his brother Terry hanging from a metal beam in his lock-up shed near his flower stall at Waterloo station. An article in the *Sunday Mirror* stated that it was the fear of going back to prison that drove Buster to hang himself.

The article went on to say that Buster was involved with a

gang who were van-dragging – stealing lorries and selling their contents. Buster's name came up after a lorry carrying stolen coffee beans was stopped by police in Kirby, Liverpool. Three men were arrested. The beans had come from a wagon stolen in Dagenham, Essex, in June. The vehicle minus its trailer was found abandoned. I considered it a far-fetched coincidence that the police would descend on a stolen container five months after it had been stolen and that the vehicle, which was abandoned 100 miles from the trailer, was linked to it. Something kept telling me that I had been especially chosen to drive that lorry, and I should have been one of those arrested. It is only because I was late and I was adamant that I was going straight home that it hadn't happened. The fact that I never got paid for the job, or my expenses returned, reinforced my fears.

Again I was in turmoil. Common sense or paranoia, which one was talking? I had known Buster through the work I had done for James Fallon. I often saw him at Waterloo, and we became quite friendly. I regret if anything I did caused him to take his own life because he was a very likeable person.

I was beginning to have serious doubts about Micky Pierce and Peter Clarke's intentions. The writing was on the wall ever since my initial partnership with Clarke at Raquels. I couldn't work out exactly what they wanted. It seemed quite obvious that, for whatever reason, they wanted me out of the way.

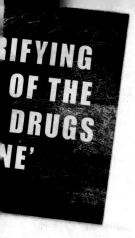
CHAPTER 9

Tucker and Tate were becoming increasingly unpredictable.
Their consumption of drugs was spiralling out of control.
Both of them used huge amounts of steroids, and they both
used cocaine, ecstasy and Special K. The real name for the
latter is Ketamine. It's an anaesthetic that is used widely in the
veterinary profession. It is exceedingly strong, and gives an
out-of-body experience.

Tucker, once level-headed, was now often totally irrational.
Tate was explosive: when they were together the mood was
always boisterous and fun, but a comment could alter it
instantly. When they were together it seemed as if each was
trying to live up to the expectations of the other. Tony could
be unusually abrupt and rude. Pat, too, became hostile.
However, when they were apart they were their old selves.
Tony was a very deep, private man. Pat was warm and
friendly. The drugs were really messing up their heads – and
their lives. I actually told Tony this one night to his face, and
he admitted it.

Occasionally he would say he was going to give up the gear
and start training again. He would disappear for a couple of
weeks. Soon he would be back – and back on the gear.

But Tony was no helpless drug addict. It was not the
desire for drugs that affected him or Pat, it was the effects
they had on their personality that was the problem. When
they were together they considered everyone to be a fool.
They took liberties with people. Although you could say to
them that what they were doing was wrong – and when they
were apart they would agree – the next time they were
together, they would laugh at your remarks as though you

were weak or not up to the competition in that league.

Tony's reputation in Basildon was far greater than in London, where he wasn't a conspicuous player. The adoration being piled on them all from the wannabes was driving them on and on. They were careering out of control. I could see through the adoring disciples that gathered in the club. And I could see how easy it was to bask in their adoration.

Tate had recruited a stable of young girls. It was rumoured in the firm that he farmed these girls out to clients in London. Tucker had taken a 17-year-old mistress named Donna Garwood. She worked at a riding school near Basildon where he and his partner Anna stabled their horses. Anna was good for Tony. When I first met him, he wouldn't have dreamed of getting involved with Donna. There was concern in the firm about the way Tucker spoke so openly in front of someone so young and impressionable.

Tony Tucker, Pat Tate and Craig Rolfe turned up at Raquels one evening with a man they introduced as 'Nipper' – because of his size, I guess. His real name was Steve Ellis. He was from Southend, and was a very likeable man. In time, I got to know him well.

Nipper was inoffensive and very funny. You couldn't help but like him. He was soon established on the scene. Everywhere the firm went, he was there. One weekend Tate, Tucker and Nipper went into a 7-Eleven store in Southend. Nipper threw a bread roll at Tate, who retaliated by throwing a cake at Nipper. They were all high spirited and soon were engaged in a food fight in the shop. The assistant kept telling them to stop, but they just got more and more carried away. Eventually the assistant said he was going to call the police. Tate ripped the phone out of the wall and told the man: 'You shouldn't say things like that.' They said they would pay for the damage, but as they were talking, the police turned up. Tucker and Tate walked off and Ellis was arrested. It was no big deal. In fact everyone thought it was rather funny.

Shortly afterwards, Donna Garwood, Tony's mistress, was trying to get in touch with him. She couldn't ring him at home in case Anna found out about their relationship, and so she rang Steve to see if she could locate him. When Garwood asked Nipper if he had seen Tony, true to form, he was sarcastic. 'He's probably at home giving his old woman one,' he said. Nipper hadn't said it maliciously. You could never get a straight answer out of him. He was always joking.

However, Garwood told Tony when she contacted him, and made it sound as though Nipper was saying it with some venom. The next time I saw Pat and Tucker, they never mentioned the phone call. But they did say that Ellis had grassed them up to the police about the 7-Eleven incident. They said they were going to make him pay.

Usually friends were allowed in the club for nothing, but Tucker said: 'When he turns up, make him pay, but make sure you let him in, because we want to get hold of him. Once he's inside the club, ring me, and we'll come down.'

The following day Tucker and Craig Rolfe turned up at Nipper's house. Tucker stuck a loaded handgun into his temple and said he was going to kill him. He was threatened with a machete and they threatened to hack off one of his hands and one of his feet. Then they looted Nipper's house. Rolfe plastered his excrement over everything that was left behind. Nipper fled. He was terrified.

On the Friday night, Tate and Rolfe came down to Raquels. We had a chat about everyday things. They said they were looking for Nipper. I said he wasn't in the club, but they wanted to check if any of his friends were in there and they had a walk around for about 15 minutes. Pat rang back later that night. He was obviously out of his head. He asked me if Nipper had turned up. I said no. I could hear him banging as if he was punching a wall. He was shouting, saying that he was going to kill Nipper. He said if he couldn't get hold of him, he would do his family. Nipper's sister, who was only 15 at the time, would be abducted, and they would cut her fingers off one by one, until Nipper was man enough to show his face. There wasn't a lot I could say to Pat. I just said okay, I'll pass the message on, and put down the phone.

Mark Murray came to see me on the Sunday of that week. He told me his partner, Bob, no longer wished to trade with him. Bob had already spoken to me. He could see the way things were going, and wisely quit. I said it was no concern of mine who he worked with or who he worked for. Murray said it would not affect trade in Raquels, he just thought I should know and pass it on to whoever needed to know.

I was going to visit Reg Kray on the Wednesday, and several times Murray had asked me if he could go. I asked Reg and he said fine. Reg had previously met Bob, as he wanted to introduce dealers he knew to dealers who worked for the firm. We arranged that I would meet Murray at his home in Pitsea on Wednesday morning. Unknown to me, officers from police HQ in Chelmsford were keeping watch outside my house on the day I was due to visit Reg. Because I wasn't doing anything untoward that day, I wasn't being particularly vigilant about my movements. They had chosen that day of all days, to nick me.

I left my home about nine in the morning as I had to take my car to have new brake shoes fitted. I drove out of Basildon towards Southend to a garage, but the mechanic hadn't shown up. This made me late. I thought sod Murray, I haven't got time to pick him up, I'll just have to make my own way there, and he can come another day.

I drove back through Basildon towards the Dartford Tunnel on the A13 – Reg was in prison at Maidstone in Kent at that time. I got about ten miles out of Basildon, and every time I braked the discs screeched. I decided it would be too dodgy to continue my journey. I pulled into a service station on the A13 and rang Mark Murray. He said if I drove back to Basildon, he would meet me and we could go down to Maidstone together.

I turned around and drove back to Basildon. The police must have found all this very promising, as they must have thought that I was either picking up or dropping off a parcel. I parked my car at Murray's and we both got into his MG sports car and drove back the way I had come. Because of the confusion, Murray hadn't bought any gear for Reggie, which was just as well. When we indicated to join the M25, Mark said: 'Don't look back now, Bernie, there's an Old Bill car behind us.'

I looked in the mirror and saw a marked police car immediately behind us. It put on its blue lights and siren and pulled us onto the side of the road. We were on an elevated section of the road and so there was nowhere we could have gone, even if we had wanted to. They had obviously chosen this spot with care.

Two uniformed policemen got out and started asking us about road tax, ownership of the vehicle, and where we had been and where we were going. They asked to search the car. It was pretty basic stuff. I knew full well that they had not stopped us for a motoring offence. This was planned. Seconds later two unmarked cars pulled up and detectives got out. To my surprise, they said they were arresting me for the theft of a vehicle. I tried to explain that the MG which Murray was driving was not my vehicle. They said: 'No, we are arresting you for the theft of a Granada,' which was the car I had been driving earlier. It was registered in my name and not stolen.

They searched me, searched Murray and searched the car thoroughly, and then they said we would both be put in separate police cars and taken to Brentwood police station.

Because of the searches visitors to prisoners undergo, I had left all my weapons at home, so I was not too concerned about the arrest. Murray was quite sheepish when we got to Brentwood police station. On the other hand, I had the right hump. I was slagging the Old Bill off, telling them I had places to go. I didn't have time for their menial games. I was quite surprised when we got to the police station and they apologised to Mark Murray and told him he could go – it was me they wanted.

These boys hadn't done their homework at all. They told me that a team of officers were at my home at that moment, searching it for drugs. I laughed and said: 'It's a fair cop. The paracetamol are in the cupboard above the sink.'

The alleged theft of my car had been engineered for the sole purpose of getting me to the police station to question me about the firm's drug distribution network. First the police had to put their paperwork in order and question me about the allegedly stolen car. I had had my Granada for about 18 months. It was not stolen. What we all used to do was get a car on finance, make a few payments and then cease further payments. By the time the finance company had located you and repossessed the vehicle, it had been run into the ground and wasn't worth much anyway. I told the Old Bill the car wasn't stolen, I had just missed a few payments. It was, basically, the truth. They told me that my car had been picked up earlier by other officers and had been taken to a compound in Chelmsford where it would be handed back to the finance company.

What did surprise me was that the police did have paperwork concerning the purchase of the vehicle. Charlie Jones, Peter Clarke's sleeping partner, had stood surety for me when we had got the car on finance. I felt the Pierce-Clarke syndrome again. From the questions I was asked in relation to the vehicle, I knew these people had played a part in the run-up to my arrest.

Pierce had put up Clarke as a suitable partner when I took over from Vine. Jones, who ran the rival door firm, had not been mentioned, but he was part of the equation. Pierce had told me the stories about Vine which caused the trouble after I took over, and it was Pierce who asked me to take the lorry to Liverpool when the people had been arrested. The reason they gave me the gun should have sounded alarm bells, but I had put that to the back of my mind.

Once the police had legitimised my arrest by conducting a brief interview about the car, they got down to the real reason I had been pulled: they wanted an informal chat about drugs. I told them I didn't know anything. They gave me a long list of people in London and Essex I was associated with and I told them I just knew them through work. I was bailed to appear at Catford police station in south-east London for a minor deception charge for applying for a credit card in a different name, and bailed to appear at Brentford for the allegation of theft concerning my car. I was then released.

When I got home I discovered those searching my house had left some paperwork for me. They had taken nine pieces of paper concerning my business, the registration document of my vehicle and a couple of bayonets and sheath knives.

I rang Murray and he was laughing at their stupidity. It should have been him they were tipping over, not me. I could tell from the police's reaction that they had found nothing. They were pissed off. When these people do pull you and find nothing, they don't think you're innocent, they just think you're a little bit cleverer than they thought you were.

The following day I had to appear in Catford. I had used a

credit card which had been obtained in a false name. I wasn't going to mess about trying to box and cox my way out of that one, it was hardly worth it, as my later Court case showed. I had obtained and used a credit card in a false name to the value of £1,000 and in return I had to pay £100 in compensation. Little wonder people turn to crime. It's all a question of what to say to the probation officer who has to prepare your report for the Courts. Everyone was doing car and credit card fraud. It was a bit of extra cash. Nobody considered it a crime.

Drug dealers would open up bank accounts in false names and put in £500 or more a week for six to eight months. Once they had a good rating, they would apply for credit cards and perhaps a loan for a car. They would then withdraw everything and close the account. It wouldn't even be recorded as a crime, just a bad debt.

When I walked out of the cell where I was being held while they sorted out the paperwork for the case, I was surprised to see two detectives from Basildon. They said they had popped down to see me for a chat. I wasn't really in the mood for it. I'd done more chatting that week than Oprah Winfrey does in a year. They said they were just passing and were going to give me a lift back to Basildon, despite the fact that it was about 30 miles out of their way.

They wanted an off-the-record chat, but I insisted I had to go home first to sort out something urgent. I armed myself with a small dictaphone tape recorder while they waited for me. Then we drove to Church Road, a few streets away from my home. It was all very amicable. They said they wanted to discuss the events of the past few days. I had lost my car, had my home searched and spent the past two days in police stations. They were indicating that the police from HQ were turning the screw on me. As the discussion went on it seemed to me that they were inferring that come what may, they had decided to nick me, whatever it took. I said: 'What are you trying to say? That if I am not caught fair and square doing something, the police from HQ at Chelmsford are going to fit me up?' They said yes, they may do.

For the benefit of the tape, I said: 'What, you can't be saying that they would fit me up?'

'It's a possibility,' one of them replied. 'Look, the Chelmsford police had plans which didn't come about. They wanted you for the people you knew, it didn't work out, so now they've got the hump.'

If I wasn't involved in the firm's crimes, they wanted me to tell them who was. I kept saying I didn't know what they were on about. They said I should assist them to keep HQ off my back. Eventually they said they were leaving, but they would keep in touch.

I went home. I had a valuable piece of ammunition: two police officers on a tape saying I was going to be fitted up. It was ammunition I hoped I would never have to use. I lodged the tape with a relative in case my home was searched and it was removed.

The following day, Friday 18 November 1994, I had arranged to visit Reg, as my attempt to visit him earlier in the week had been aborted when Murray and I had been stopped on the way there.

Tucker was meant to come with me this time. I rang his house and I rang his mobile, but I couldn't get hold of him. A person who wanted to install fruit machines and video games in their pubs and clubs had promised Reg a percentage of the takings. Reg thought Tucker might be able to help him out. I didn't think Tucker would bother, so taking him on the visit wasn't that important. I set off to visit Reggie myself.

On the way home from Maidstone Prison I heard on the radio that a man had been found dead in a ditch in Basildon. I didn't think too much about it. When I got home, I continued to try and contact Tucker, but I couldn't get him. He was having his birthday party at a snooker hall in Dagenham that Sunday. If he didn't turn up at Raquels over the weekend, I would see him then and discuss Reggie's proposition.

That weekend a few of the doormen were telling me various stories about what was happening with Nipper Ellis. They told me even Nipper's father had been threatened. Tate, they said, was going berserk. On the Sunday, I didn't fancy facing hours of listening to what they were and were not going to do to Ellis. I'd had enough grief off the Old Bill all week. I rang Tucker's house and left a message on the answering machine saying I was too ill to go. I later heard only 20 people turned up. Tony's behaviour was being noticed by more people than myself. A year earlier there had probably been nearly 200 people at his birthday party.

On Monday 21 November, I was contacted again by the Basildon detectives. They said they needed to see me quite urgently. I armed myself with a tape recorder again, and again they picked me up, and we drove to Church Road. They wanted to know if I heard anything at all about Pat Tate being shot. I said I hadn't. They also asked me if Craig Rolfe had been up to anything in the past few days and if Tony Tucker drove a black Porsche. I said he didn't, he had a BMW. They asked me if I knew anyone who had a black Porsche. I said I didn't. They said they knew I was lying as they had been watching me talking to a man in a black Porsche a few nights earlier. I wasn't being very helpful, so they said I could go and they would be back in touch.

These informal chats are engineered to break you down. Although the police cannot catch you getting up to anything, they want you to know that they are aware of your every move. By asking a seemingly trivial question, they are telling you that they are aware you are a witness or have been party to a particular incident. They want you to offer somebody up in order to save yourself.

I contacted Tucker and he was very keen to hear what the police had to say. He asked me to meet him as soon as possible. Tony said that he and Rolfe had gone to Nipper's house – again he insisted it was because he had grassed them up over the 7-Eleven incident. Nipper had confronted Tucker and Rolfe with a pump-action shotgun, and they had made themselves scarce. He said they had been trying to get him all week. He had also gone there on separate occasions with Tate.

Tucker said that on Sunday Pat had been at home getting ready for the birthday party. He was in the bathroom when somebody threw a brick through the window. Pat peered outside and Nipper opened fire from close range with a revolver. Pat put his right arm up to shield his face. The round hit him in the wrist, travelled up his arm and smashed bones in his elbow. The gunman fled and Pat was taken to hospital. Tony said: 'When Pat gets out, Nipper's going to die.'

This incident was not the firm's main problem. Kevin Whitaker, from Basildon, had been a friend of Craig Rolfe's for some time. He had introduced Kevin to Tucker and they were starting to use him as a middleman and courier for drugs.

Whitaker had been involved in a £60,000 cannabis deal with a firm from Romford. It had gone wrong, and Tucker had lost out. It was just the type of deal I had warned him about getting involved with. Dealing with unknown people was a treacherous business. But you could never tell Tony anything. Pressure was also on Rolfe, because it was he who had put Kevin up as being reliable.

As Whitaker was the go-between the debt was down to him, and Tucker wanted to know how he was going to pay. Whitaker, who knew what was coming, had tried to avoid them. On the Thursday Rolfe had spent the day trying to get hold of him. Eventually he tracked him down at his parents' house and Whitaker agreed he would meet him to sort it out.

Tucker and Rolfe turned up in Pat's cream-coloured BMW. Whitaker blamed the firm from Romford for loss of the cannabis, so Tucker and Rolfe said they would take him to the firm to confront the people. They were getting increasingly annoyed. It was dawning on them that they weren't going to get their money. They had hold of Whitaker, and they kept saying to him, 'Thieve our gear, would you? If you like drugs that much, have some more of ours.' They were forcing him to take cocaine and Special K. Like Vella's victims, Whitaker was becoming more and more terrified. Whitaker was pleading with them to let him go, but they were just laughing.

Whitaker was injected three times with huge amounts of drugs. They used a syringe and needle they'd used for injecting steroids. Tucker said Whitaker passed out. He was out of his head on the gear they had forced him to take. They left Basildon and were travelling along the A127 towards Romford. Tucker said that as they reached the Laindon/Dunton turn-off Whitaker was in and out of consciousness. They drove up the slip-road as there didn't seem much point in taking him to Romford. They turned left to go towards Laindon. Whitaker by now had completely lost

SO THIS IS ECSTASY?

consciousness. They pulled up at the Lower Dunton Road and told Whitaker to get out of the car, but they got no response. They got out and pulled Whitaker out, but he just collapsed on the side of the road. They drove off and looked back. Whitaker was motionless. Rolfe got out of the car and ran back to him. He stood over him and kept telling him to get up, but still there was no response.

'Fucking leave him,' said Tucker.

'You can't leave him here,' replied Rolfe. It was about six o'clock and everyone was coming out of work.

They drove the car back the short distance to where Whitaker lay. Tucker got out of the car, and they both put Whitaker back inside. They then drove back over the A127 to Dunton Road. Tucker said they looked at Whitaker and they knew he was dead. They pulled him out of the car and he was put in the ditch. I asked Tucker what he was going to do. He was laughing but I knew he was concerned. He said the Old Bill were not treating it as murder. They would just think that Whitaker had taken a bit too much gear at someone's house and died. That person, not wanting a body in their home, would have taken him out and dumped him anyway. He said: 'When you had that trouble with Draper, I told you the best way to get rid of someone was to give them a bit of proper gear. We certainly won't be having any more trouble with Mr Whitaker.'

I told Tony the questions the police had been asking. He did seem rather concerned that they had been linked to Whitaker so quickly. However, he kept telling me, and I think he was trying to convince himself, that they could never prove that they had killed Whitaker.

Tucker was right. Detectives could find no evidence to support any murder claims. Whitaker was written off as a junky who had overdosed. At the inquest, Coroner Dr Malcolm Weir called the death most inexplicable. Friends told how Whitaker made no secret of the fact he was heading for a rendezvous with Rolfe on the night he died. A message asking him to contact Rolfe was also logged on his radio pager. Rolfe was called as a witness at the inquest and asked to explain his contacts with Whitaker. He denied meeting Kevin, and said he only spoke to him on the phone to enquire about his baby son. Tucker also attended the inquest, but did not give evidence. An open verdict was recorded.

Pat was laid up in Basildon hospital after being shot. He had lost a lot of flesh from his upper arm, but he seemed in good spirits. The firm was making sure of that. Despite being in a hospital bed under medication, Pat was supplied with a steady stream of drugs. It was quite clear that other patients in the ward and nurses were not happy. Each evening members of the firm gathered round his bed listening to blaring house music, taking drugs, and generally having a party. Nobody would dare object.

Pat, like everyone else, suffered from paranoia. He had convinced himself that Nipper was coming back to finish him off, so he asked Tucker to give him a firearm to keep in his bed. He was at once given a handgun. Within a couple of days a nurse discovered the gun while making up Pat's bed. She contacted the police and Pat was arrested. Because he was still out on licence for his six-year robbery sentence, he was automatically returned to prison for being in possession of a firearm – which broke his parole licence conditions.

Nipper remained off the scene. Fearing a reprisal attack he had gone out and bought a Smith & Wesson for £600 and a bullet-proof vest for £400. When Nipper was finally arrested for the shooting, the case against him was never pursued because the judge ruled that the gun that he had on him at the time of the arrest was not the gun that was used to shoot Pat. Nipper served seven and a half months in jail for illegally possessing a firearm. Even while in jail death threats from the firm never ceased. Nipper said on one occasion two men came up to him in prison and told him a £10,000 contract had been put on him. A hit-man even went to his father's door looking for him when he was released. Nipper eventually fled to the West Country, where he now lives. It's unbelievable the amount of trouble a chance remark can cause.

I could see the writing was on the wall for the firm and myself. The drugs and the violence were completely out of control. As soon as somebody put a foot wrong their loyalty was questioned, and once their loyalty had been questioned their popularity quickly diminished until they were deemed an enemy. Once deemed an enemy, they became the subject of some sort of violent attack. We were all waiting for our personal tragedies to happen.

On New Year's Eve we all went to a nightclub called Ad-Lib in Southend. Everyone was buying £80-bottles of champagne. At midnight, as everyone was cheering the New Year in, Mark Murray came over to me and shook hands. He said: 'I'm glad we met, Bernard. Business is going to be good this year. We're really going to make a lot of money.' I smiled, and said: 'Of course.' I don't know what it was. I certainly wasn't sharing the firm's euphoria. I felt a sense of doom.

CHAPTER 10

I had become so paranoid that I was convinced that very soon I was going to kill somebody, or I was going to be killed myself.

Rumour, intrigue and accusations and counter accusations were resulting in a very unstable environment. The firm had a finger in every pie. As far as they were concerned, anyone or anything could be sorted. As the reputation grew, everyone wanted to be part of it. In one pub I drank in, the assistant manager used to take my money, give me my drink and twice as much in change, simply to be part of the firm in a small way. It was ludicrous. With this stupid glamour came the wannabes. They invented stories for the benefit of their friends. And stories caused concern, aroused suspicion and further police attention.

Tucker was being blamed for shooting Pat by some of Pat's female stable of half a dozen or so girls, who were like a little fan club he used to have round him and go out with. They said if he hadn't carried out the shooting himself, he had arranged it. Tucker, they said, was jealous of Tate's friendship with Nipper. It was total nonsense. They even said Tucker stoked Tate's fear and paranoia after the shooting by giving him the gun to protect himself while he was in hospital.

Murray's dealers began to shun him. They too could sense the danger. The firm was being linked to everything bad and unsavoury. Rumours about the murder of Whitaker were rife, although the police were only treating it as a suspicious death. The firm was also being linked to an attack on Darren Kerr. Kerr had been in a telephone box in Purfleet when a car had pulled up. He had acid thrown in his face. Then he was bundled into the boot and dumped in Dagenham.

Darren, who was 24, fit and handsome, suffered horrific injuries. He was blinded in one eye by the acid and the whole side of his face was a mass of angry red scars. His injuries were so bad he had to undergo surgery at the specialist burns unit at Billericay Hospital. Following the operation he was forced to wear a plastic face mask similar to that worn by ice hockey goalkeepers.

While recovering in hospital he was again paid a visit. A man turned up dressed as a clown. He had Dracula teeth, a clown's wig with a pink forehead and he was carrying a bunch of flowers. He asked the unsuspecting nurses where Darren Kerr was. The staff smiled at the clown and told him. He strolled in with his big red nose, shiny blue shell suit top and trousers tucked into his socks. When he saw Darren he whipped away the plastic flowers to reveal a shotgun. The clown opened fire and blasted a huge hole through the muscle and skin in Darren's shoulder. It missed his heart and lungs by inches. Darren staggered out of bed and saw the clown gunman walk calmly away. Nobody was laughing. Darren said later: 'I did not see him at first, because he had come in from the left, my blind side. I saw him late. He was aiming for my head. It was an instinctive reaction to twist away, and that's what saved my life.'

People blamed Pat Tate for the shooting. If Pat did do it, he must have been a good shot – he was in Whitemoor Prison at the time. Darren did have links with underworld figures and knew members of our firm quite well. But I don't think it was anyone in our firm who tried to murder him.

Debra was still urging me to go and see a doctor about my paranoia. She said if it made me feel better, she would come with me. I told her it was nonsense, but if it made her feel happier I would go, and she could come too. I went to my GP, Dr Denham. He asked me to describe what I thought was the matter with me. I told him in detail: feelings of being followed, of people talking about me. Even when I stood in front of a shop window, I had a feeling that I was going to be pushed into it. He asked Debra about my behaviour in general. She was rather more forthcoming. She told him I couldn't go anywhere without weapons and I was constantly suspicious of neighbours and friends.

Dr Denham told me that he would arrange for me to see a psychiatrist, Dr Murphy, at Basildon Hospital. In the meantime, I was prescribed Chlorpromazine, the trade name for largactil. (Chlorpromazine was the first anti-psychotic drug to be marketed. It is used to suppress aggressive and abnormal behaviour, schizophrenia and other disorders where aggressive behaviour exists. It can cause drowsiness, dizziness and muscle twitches.) Largactil is commonly known as the 'liquid cosh' because it can make you feel like a zombie. That night before I went to bed, I took three times the recommended dose, and for the first time in more than a year I slept through the night without waking. Previously I had suffered the recurring nightmare of being chased and stabbed to death. Whatever I thought of before I went to sleep, I always had the same dream. It wasn't a normal dream, either. Debra would tell me that I would actually fight in my sleep, it was so real. My exterior may have appeared tough, but my mind was paying a terrible price.

Despite the medication I was on, my paranoia did not diminish. A doorman named Ian, who had worked for me for about eight months, kept looking at me and laughing while he talked to someone else. Then he walked off. It kept preying on my mind, and in the end I convinced myself that he had been talking about me. I went upstairs and attacked him. He couldn't understand why I was doing it. I wouldn't explain, I kept hitting him and hitting him, then threw him out. When people tried to calm me down, I just got more violent. I was confused.

It was following this incident that I seriously considered for the first time getting out of the madness I was surrounded by. But it's impossible just to walk away from this situation. Incidents follow incidents – each one leads to another – and each incident you survive, the more prominent you become. Your piece of the action becomes larger. You climb the ladder in leaps and bounds, but the higher you go, the further you have to fall. With everything I knew and everything I'd done, there was no possibility of just walking away from the firm.

In January 1995 Tucker gave Mark Murray the go-ahead to

begin sorting out the gear in Club UK in South London. To make it pay, Murray would have to run a pretty slick operation. He would have to have enough dealers in there to meet the demand in order to reap the rewards his predecessors had earned.

Despite the glamour outsiders saw, within the firm it was a different story. Nathaniel, one of Murray's dealers, was working at a club in Southend. The doormen's rent was being paid at the club, but the manager had spotted Nathaniel serving up (selling drugs). He told one of the doormen to grab Nathaniel, then he'd phone the police. The doorman got Nathaniel and locked him in the manager's office. The manager phoned the police and the doorman sat on Nathaniel until they arrived. He was found with 50 ecstasy tablets and a quantity of money. He was promptly arrested and charged. At his trial he was sentenced to 18 months imprisonment.

Murray came to see me, and I said something should be done. What was the point of paying rent to the door firms if they offered no protection. They tried to say it was out of their hands because of the manager, but the doorman could easily have let Nathaniel 'escape'. The doorman was identified, and it was agreed that he would be attacked and stabbed in the car park on his way to work. Murray wanted no part of it, and it was dropped as Nathaniel was one of his people. Little wonder he couldn't recruit anyone and those who worked for him were losing confidence.

Around the same time I received a phone call from a freelance journalist. She told me that the newspaper she was currently working for had received a telephone call from a person who was saying that Raquels had people there openly selling drugs to anybody who would buy them. She knew I ran the door at Raquels, and she was warning me that someone may come to the club in order to publish an exposé.

The next time I saw Tucker, I told him. But when I did the right thing, it was thrown back in my face. Tucker wanted to know why a journalist would warn me. I said I knew lots of journalists and they were just doing me a favour.

Two years previously he would have accepted it for what it was. But now his vision was clouded by drugs and paranoia. Tucker told Murray not to tell me about Club UK, which was silly really, because it had been openly discussed and were all aware of what was going on. I had seen this scenario many times. Tucker was trying to make Murray feel like an important cog in the firm's machinery. In reality he was building him up ready to knock him down.

Without a partner, Murray found the going hard. He couldn't make Club UK work, because he couldn't recruit enough dealers. He was selling approximately 500 ecstasy pills a night in Club UK, nowhere near enough the amount needed to reap any benefit. Needless to say Tucker demanded his rent, and Murray owed me £500 every week he was there. By the time he'd paid for his stock, there wasn't anything left. He was, simply, in debt.

Those on the outside looking in were impressed by the money floating around and the power we all had, but more and more people in the know were scared because of the excessive violence. Even some doormen refused to work with us. Most of them remembered Ian and Liam being beaten up – our own sort turned on for no real reason.

A friend of mine, Bill Edwards, asked me if I could sort it out for him to work for Murray. I tried to advise him against it, but he said he needed the money and despite my warning he went to work for Murray at Club UK. Tucker, still suspicious of me, knew he was a friend of mine, and arranged for one of the doormen down there named Barry – or Baz – to pull my friend for dealing. When Barry pulled him, Bill told him that he was working for the firm. Barry didn't take any notice. He hit him in the head several times with a knuckle duster. He said: 'You shouldn't have said you were working for the firm, it's grassing.' Bill came and told me what went on. He had several stitches in his head.

I rang Tucker and asked him why Bill had been beaten up. He shrugged it off and said Barry didn't know who Bill was, and it was all a misunderstanding. I didn't believe it. I rang Bill and asked him if he wanted to do something about it. He said no, he wanted to forget it. Tucker, it seemed, was also trying to send me messages.

My best friend at that time was a man named Martin. Martin was a body-builder from Barking in East London. He had worked the door for a number of years in the London clubs. He had recently come to Raquels by word-of-mouth via a friend. We got on really well. He didn't take any shit from anybody. He was always there when it mattered. As a doorman, he was 100 per cent. As a friend, you could not want better.

One evening we were working together in the Buzz Bar. It was very busy. Everyone appeared to be having a good time. It was all regular faces, no strangers, so we weren't expecting any problems. At about 9.30 two men came into the bar. One was short and stocky. His name was Barry Chart. The other was an Irishman named Frank Kennedy. He was about six feet tall, fairly well built. Chart had worked for me previously, but was now working as a doorman for a firm from Mile End, in east London.

Both were being quite sarcastic to the staff and customers. It wasn't too bad at first, they were fairly quiet. But the less we did, the louder they got. It was as if they were trying to see how far they could go. As I walked past, Chart said to me: 'All right Bernie. Can you ask a doorman to come over?' It was a blatant insult. He was insinuating that I wasn't up to being a doorman. I grabbed hold of Chart and punched him in the face. Martin grabbed hold of Kennedy, and we led them to the double doors at the top of the stairs. As we were preparing to throw them out, I felt a sharp blow to the back of my head. Martin was also assaulted.

A fight broke out on the stairs. People we hadn't noticed previously jumped in. It was hard to say exactly what happened. I was trying to get people out of the building and defend myself at the same time. As faces appeared in the mêlée, I hit them. Somebody was holding on to my back and a man was trying to get up off the floor. I began to stamp on him. We were outnumbered. I produced a knife and our attackers began to back off. As we moved forward they ran down the stairs and through the doors into the street. The only person left was Chart. He was lying on the floor unconscious, his face a mass of blood. Because of his size I couldn't pick him up, so I pulled him down the stairs by his arm. I left him in the street.

Somebody ran forward from the crowd and kicked him in the head. I don't know who it was. An ambulance turned up and took him away. As far as we were concerned, that was the end of the matter.

When we left work at about 11.20, we went over to the burger van to buy some tea before going our separate ways. The lady serving, Chris, told us that there were two vehicles full of youths driving around saying they were looking for us. We walked across the road and a Commer van and Fiesta car pulled up at the lights. The man in the van was shouting: 'You're going to die, O'Mahoney.'

The driver of the Fiesta joined in the shouting. We were outnumbered, but it was pointless running. We didn't know who the people were, or what their problem was. We assumed they were associates of Chart and Kennedy. I ran across the road and the man in the Fiesta tried to drive away, but he stalled his vehicle. A side window of his car was smashed, and I jumped onto the bonnet. The windscreen smashed and the men in the car jumped out and ran. We gave chase. The man in the van drove off and escaped, while the men on foot were far too fast for us – they had fear on their side. We flagged down a passing cab and told him to follow the van. It went up a one-way street, and we encouraged the minicab to follow him. But the minicab driver had had enough. He slammed on his brakes, turned off the ignition, grabbed his keys and ran out of the car. The van disappeared into the distance.

Martin and I went back to our cars and drove home. There was nothing particularly unusual about this type of trouble. We thought we would hear no more about the matter.

A few days later, I was arrested by two of Basildon's finest, and taken to Rayleigh Police Station for questioning. It was the age-old story. Two doormen from a rival firm had come to Basildon to try and muscle in on our work. They had come unstuck and had run bleating to the police for help. It was alleged that I had caused injuries to Chart's torso and also broken his arm, his nose and a cheekbone. I told the police it was they who caused the trouble, and we had acted in self-defence.

During the interview, which was being taped, the two detectives produced a file. On the front of it in two-inch high letters, which had been written with a thick felt pen, were the words: 'Big, bad Bernie'. I said to one of the detectives: 'What

SO THIS IS ECSTASY?

the fuck is that meant to mean?' He said it was just a joke, following the reception their enquiries had met.

'I don't find it very funny, and I can't see how you can conduct a fair, unbiased investigation, or speak to potential witnesses after writing something like that,' I said. 'It shows what frame of mind you're in. I don't wish to talk to you any more.' There was little they could say. The interview was concluded and I was bailed to reappear at a police station for an identification parade.

I told the guy who ran the door firm from Mile End what had happened, and we were not going to forget it now that Chart and Kennedy had grassed us up. That night I received a phone call. I was told that Chart and Kennedy had not preferred charges, despite the police visiting them two or three times encouraging them to do so. The people, therefore, who would be at a planned ID parade would be the men in the Fiesta and the Commer van. We recruited witnesses in case there was a Court case. I insisted that following the incident with Chart I went straight home from the club and was totally unaware of any trouble following that.

The firm closed ranks and messages were sent out to those concerned. There wasn't going to be any Court case.

The man in the Fiesta was named Chris Green, and the man driving the Commer van was named Michael Ward, who occasionally called himself Williams. He alleged he had become involved because I punched his girlfriend while she tried to administer first aid to Barry Chart. It was total fantasy.

The very same night, Williams – or Ward – pulled up outside Raquels and shouted: 'O'Mahoney, you're going to die. I am going to shoot you.' I ran towards the van again, and he drove off. Rather typical. He wanted it all ways. He initially wanted to fight me. He lost, and then he chose to go to the police. Yet here he was again, trying to be a gangster. He had overstepped the mark. He had to learn his lesson. If he got away with it, every Tom, Dick and Harry would get ideas.

We found out Williams was staying in a place in Vange Hill Drive in Basildon. One evening after work I and another doorman went around there and banged on the door. Nobody answered. To wind him up, I wrote on the door in chalk: 'I

127

have found you, Williams. See you soon, Bernie.' Then we went home.

A short time afterwards, I read on the front page of the local newspaper that there had been a fire at Williams's flat. A 25-year-old woman had jumped for her life from a second-floor window after a blaze ripped through the building. It was reported that she was recovering in Basildon Hospital. It was believed she had fractured her back and her wrists after jumping 20 feet. Fire officers said it saved her life. Neighbours who were too scared to make their way down the smoke-filled stairway were led to safety by fire fighters. The fire started in the hallway; there was no way she would have been able to get out. The woman was believed to be alone in her flat with her Alsatian dog, which she threw from the bedroom window. It had survived the fall. Fire investigation officers and forensic scientists were at the flat to find out what caused the blaze, believed to have been started deliberately.

Two detectives came to visit me. They said they were aware of the trouble I had had with Williams, and asked me if I knew about the fire and where I had been on that night. Obviously everybody thought I had started the fire. I gave them a suitable alibi and I heard no more. Williams moved back to Manchester, his native town. However, there was still the matter of the damage to the car to be dealt with.

The first ID parade took place shortly afterwards. None of the witnesses showed up, much to the dismay of the Basildon police. My solicitor wanted to know why, but the police couldn't explain it. I was bailed to reappear for a second ID parade a week later. Obviously they too thought I was responsible for the fire.

There are two forms of ID parade. One is the traditional row of men, which the victim or witness looks up and down before indicating who he believes, if anyone, is the wrong-doer. The second form is where the suspect walks through a crowded area such as a train station or shopping centre. The witness then has to point him out to detectives. I opted for the latter, and it was arranged that I would walk through Basildon town centre, along a pre-selected stretch of the shopping mall where the witness would be with police. On the day of the ID parade, the town was deserted. My solicitor said it would be unfair for the ID parade to take place, so it was again aborted for a further week. Unknown to us, the witnesses had failed to appear again.

The police were getting agitated. They seemed to think the fire was more than coincidental. The ID parade was put back to a later date so they could contact the witnesses and get them to attend. I don't know what it was but I had a feeling that they would not be successful. The people who were screaming victim were the people who came after us in a van. These people weren't innocent victims.

My solicitor indicated to the police that if they failed to attend on this third occasion, he would apply for the matter to be dropped.

This was becoming more and more typical of our lives. As our reputation grew, so people either admired it, or wanted to pit themselves against the firm to get in on the action. The mood, from top to bottom, was getting uglier.

Chapter 11

On 27 February 1995, a new manager – Dave Simms – took over at Raquels. He was from South Wales and admitted to me he had no experience whatsoever in running a rave/house-type dance club. He was purely a 'Sharon and Tracy' disco manager.

On his first night he tried a couple of textbook management course ploys to try and impose his authority. I told him in no uncertain terms that we were all there to make this work together, and I didn't want him coming in shouting and raving and making a mess of things. He was taken aback. I told him he may be the manager, but he wasn't in charge.

His big error was when he barged into the cloakroom where the doormen and their friends went for a break. He caught one of the doormen inhaling crack cocaine from a Coca-Cola tin. Simms went berserk. I went into the office and told him he had no right to creep up on people. If the club ran smoothly, he should keep out of things. We had a furious row – the first of many.

I only ever got on with three managers: Ralph Paris, Rod Chapman and Ian Blackwell. The others had little understanding of the area. They all used to say that they wanted better clientele. I tried to explain to them that if your club was in Basildon, people on the east side would rather travel into Southend for a night out. And those on the west side would sooner travel into London. Because the only type of people we attracted were those who wouldn't get into these places, we'd done well to get the people we did. The average Raquels customer wouldn't be able to tell the difference between Liebfraumilch and Tizer.

I can't say for certain who told the police, but I had only told four or five people about the tape recording I had of the officers who said I might be fitted up. But somebody did, and the officer they alleged was going to fit me up got to hear about it. He, quite naturally, was deeply upset that two fellow policemen would tell someone from the criminal world that someone was going to be dealt with in this way. I am not privy to what happened exactly, but I was told that there was an internal police enquiry about the matter.

John Hughes, from the Chelmsford HQ, came to see me. Before talking to me, he frisked me for any hidden tape recorders. He told me he'd got to hear about the tape. Somebody I was talking to was talking to the police. Hughes asked me about the contents of the tape, and I told him. He assured me it was nonsense. I have encountered many policemen in my life. I don't trust any of them. I did believe, though, that Hughes had never had any intention of setting me up. He was a 100 per cent company man. However, the tape remained invaluable.

My appointment came around to see Dr Murphy, the psychiatrist at Basildon Hospital. I was uneasy about it. For some reason, I had imagined that Dr Murphy would be a male, but *she* wasn't. Before seeing Dr Murphy I was called into a side room, where I spoke at length to a Jamaican doctor about the feelings I was experiencing, and about my past from as far back as I could remember. I told him that I feared that I was going to kill or seriously injure somebody for a trivial matter. He took me seriously and wrote down most of what I said.

After a lengthy interview I was called in to see Dr Murphy. It may seem ludicrous, but I thought that secretly she was laughing at me and she wasn't taking me seriously. I began to get annoyed. It was weird. I couldn't work out whether it was paranoia or whether she was genuinely taking the piss. It was very confusing.

Eventually she told me that there wasn't a great deal wrong with me. I just had a violent personality. I needed to go to group discussions, she said, to talk to other people. This would be the start of my treatment: 'Hi, my name's Bernie, and I feel like killing someone.'

I said: 'I don't think so, somehow.' She told me that was all that was available. The discussion deteriorated into an argument. In the end she said I would be sent to Southend Hospital for an EEG – a test to see if you have any sort of damage to your brain. I left the hospital feeling cheated. It had taken a lot for me to admit what I was really feeling, but I had just been told that there was nothing wrong with me. How many times have I heard in the newspapers similar cases which turned to tragedy? The next time, I thought, I ought to go dressed as Lord Nelson. Perhaps then I would be noticed.

As well as my EEG, I was given an appointment to see Gary Ong, who is a community psychiatrist in Basildon. I think he, conversely, took me more seriously than my condition warranted. He asked me if I thought news readers on the TV were blaming me for the tragedies they were reporting. I left him feeling more confused than ever.

The EEG itself is rather unnerving. You have wires taped to your head, and various signals or currents are passed through. The whole process takes about an hour. I felt I was getting nowhere, so I went back to taking excessive doses of Chlorpromazine. I would be sitting there in a daze watching my limbs moving independently of me. In the morning I felt an unusual numb, wasted feeling, and I had mental blocks. It wasn't a good time for me – for both of me, in fact!

The firm's reputation, meanwhile, wasn't just growing in criminal circles. Nigel Benn's greatest moment in boxing was probably the night he fought Gerald McClellan and it was Tucker who led Nigel into the ring. He did this for most of Nigel's fights. He was very proud to be his minder. That particular fight was awesome. Both boxers traded punches toe-to-toe. Few could have survived the punishment each meted out to the other. In the dramatic finale, McClellan slumped to the canvas, then lapsed into a coma. Benn had not escaped unscathed either. He had fractured bones in his hand and cheek.

After the fight, Tucker returned to Basildon, and we all went out to a club in Southend. Mark Murray came with us. It was a memorable night. Tucker, still high after Nigel Benn's unbelievable win, was in a great mood. Drink and drugs flowed freely. Even a club manager from the area, who was supposed to be unaware of what went on in nightclubs like Raquels, was given two ecstasy tablets by Murray. He said he would try them later. Of course, all of the management and staff at Raquels were fully aware of what was going on there. You could not help but notice. They knew that it was the drug culture which was filling their club to capacity. Not only was it being filled to capacity, it was free from trouble – a first for this club. They were hardly going to root out the very thing that caused this new interest in the place. It's the same story all over the country with rave clubs: what else do people think kids do in a club for eight to ten hours where there's no alcohol on sale?

One evening, Lee, along with others who dealt for Mark Murray, came to Raquels and told me that he had been stopped by the police on his way into work. They said he had been taken to Basildon Police Station and they feared the police were going to search his flat in Laindon. Lee had a bag containing 250 ecstasy tablets there, but they were frightened to go and retrieve them in case the police arrived at the same time as they were at the flat. I told them they would have to go back quickly, as it would take the police some time to get there. I drove them to the flat and they went in and retrieved the ecstasy. We drove back to Raquels. I parked my car and went back to the club.

At the main door was a visiting senior executive. We exchanged pleasantries and shortly afterwards, Lee and the other dealers came to the door of the club. Lee told me that since getting out of the car, he had lost the bag. A frantic search began. The executive asked me what it was we were all looking for. I told him that somebody had lost some car keys and went upstairs. As Lee went to go into the club, the executive called him to one side and said: 'Are you looking for these?' He produced the bag containing his 250 ecstasy tablets. 'See me on your way out,' he said.

The executive never did say anything directly to me about the matter. But he did return the 250 ecstasy pills to Lee when he left. Dave Simms, the new manager, was visibly taken aback by events like this, and the many other instances of blind eyes being turned to the drugs trade in the club. In a vain attempt to reverse the trend, he booked a band called the

Pasadenas, a pop group who had enjoyed relative success in the charts. Another promoter of jungle music had been promised the premises for Saturday nights. In protest, the door walked out. We told Simms we were not going to work that night, and that no other door firm would take our place. In short, the club would close on Saturdays.

But the Pasadenas were booked, and he said he had to honour the booking and we should see how it went. Everyone who came to the club that night was turned away from the door for whatever reason we could think of at the time.

A few weeks later following the huge loss of custom on Saturday nights, it was agreed that the jungle promoter could start. It was an exercise to show Simms he may be manager, but it was merely a title.

One Friday night in Raquels, I was standing at the bar in the diner upstairs talking to Tony Tucker and Craig Rolfe. Rod Chapman, the assistant manager, was also with us. One of the barmaids telephoned Rod on the internal phone from downstairs and asked him to come down as she had a problem. Rod asked me to go with him to resolve whatever the difficulty was.

We went to the top bar in the main dance floor area. A barmaid called us over and said a girl was in the club who was under-age. She had refused to serve her and the girl was getting stroppy. She pointed out a girl who looked about 18: she had collar-length straight black hair. I saw the girl walking off with a friend. She went upstairs to the diner area where we had been. I said to Rod: 'We'll go up and see if she has any ID.'

I called the girl over. She seemed distressed. I asked her if she had any ID. She said she hadn't as her purse had been stolen.

'I'm sorry, if you have no ID, then you'll have to leave as the barmaid says she knows you and you are under-age,' I said.

The girl became very irate. 'I had ID on the way in,' she said. 'Why are you asking for it now?'

'You may appear 18, but the barmaid says you aren't,' I said. 'Therefore you must show the ID or leave.'

'I have had my purse stolen,' she said. 'There is £300 in it. My dad's a policeman. I'm going to get him, and you'll all be in trouble.'

'Look, any story you tell me, I've already heard,' I replied. 'If you haven't any ID, you will have to leave.'

The girl became even more upset and began shouting: 'My dad's a policeman. I've had my purse stolen.'

'I'm sorry, you will have to leave,' I repeated. 'If your dad's a policeman, he will understand that if you haven't got ID we can't let you remain here.'

Eventually she went. To be honest, I couldn't have cared less if the girl was 17 or 18. I'd always judged people on the way they behaved. Most 17-year-old girls who came in the club were trying to act older than they were anyway, so they were well behaved. It was the 30-year-old men who behaved like 12-year-olds I objected to. If the barmaid hadn't said anything, I certainly wouldn't have.

At closing time, I was putting the chains on the fire doors and waiting for the staff to leave before going home myself. I heard shouting, and went to see what the problem was. At the front doors the barmaid who had had the row said she had had a fight with the girl, because she had waited outside to have it out with her. I told her to wait inside the door until she'd gone. The barmaid said: 'Don't worry, she has already left.'

I went home and thought no more of it. It wasn't until a year later I found out the truth. Somebody who objected to the way the girl had been treated told me in confidence that what had really happened was that the barmaid had stolen the girl's purse from the toilets. The girl had her suspicions about who had taken it, and had challenged the barmaid to return it. The barmaid had then telephoned Rod to say that the girl was under-age so that we would eject her, and the accusations would cease. The girl's name was Leah Betts. She was rightfully upset.

Leah had waited outside the club and, after a confrontation with the barmaid, had been assaulted. As a result of this incident, she was barred from coming into Raquels. Obviously I didn't know at the time that she had been a victim of this theft. I knew she was 17, and she was barred because of it. But I knew lots of people in there who were only 17. If the row about the purse hadn't happened, she wouldn't have been barred. If she had been allowed in the club that

November, would the tragedy at her father's home ever have happened? Would she have avoided the peer pressure from those immersed in this culture to take a pill at her party? If this, if that. I have turned it over a million times in my mind.

The third and final identification parade was set for 17 March, two days after my birthday. I didn't expect Williams or the Fiesta driver to attend.

Reg Kray asked me to go and visit him, just in case it went wrong for me. He wanted to wish me luck. I travelled down to Maidstone to see him, and was very surprised to find that Freddie Foreman (whose wife was visiting him) was in the visiting room with Reg. Fred is the top underworld heavyweight, in my opinion. He was jailed for disposing of the body of Jack 'The Hat' McVitie whom Reggie Kray and his brother Ron had murdered. He was unsuccessfully tried for the murder of Frank Mitchell, whom the Krays sprung from prison. His body was never found. He was linked to the murder of Ginger Marks, who disappeared from a street in Bethnal Green, and he was jailed for nine years in 1990 for his part in the handling of part of a £7 million robbery from the Security Express headquarters in Shoreditch, East London. Freddie's reputation in the underworld cannot be matched. Some say the film *The Long Good Friday* is based on his life.

Reg introduced me to him. We shook hands and Fred introduced me to his wife. Fred said his daughter often went to clubs in London, and he would appreciate it if we would see her all right. I told Fred that if his daughter rang me, I would ensure she got into whichever club she was going to as a guest.

You had to have respect for these people. Fred was a really nice fellow. I went and sat down with Reg and he said he had come up with an idea for an advert. For his age Reg was very fit, and had a physique most young men would be very jealous of. He wanted me to contact any company which sold porridge. His idea was that they could use photographs of him weightlifting in an advert and use the caption, 'Look what 30 years of porridge has done for Reg Kray.' I must admit, I thought it was a very good idea, but I couldn't really see me touting it round, and I couldn't realistically see anyone taking it up.

When I got home, I rang Tucker and told him about Freddie Foreman's daughter, as she often visited one of the clubs Tucker ran. He said he would deal with it, but he didn't sound very convincing. It was typical of Tony. He had no regard for anyone, whatever their status. It took several calls to him before it was sorted out.

On the day of the ID parade I asked my brother Michael to come down to Basildon so that, if any witnesses showed up, we could find out where they were staying. The idea was that he would wait outside the police station and follow any male who left there with police officers heading towards the town centre. Then he would follow them back to the police station and see which car they got into. By taking the car registration we could have it checked and find out their address.

The same morning a reporter rang me on my mobile phone. He told me that Ronnie Kray had died of a massive heart attack. Ronnie had passed away at seven minutes past nine in the morning at Wexham Park Hospital in Slough. He was 61 years of age. Two days earlier he had collapsed in his ward at Broadmoor Hospital. He had been taken to Heatherwood Hospital in Ascot, but had been transferred to Wexham after his health had suddenly deteriorated. I was pleased that Ronnie had not died within the confines of Broadmoor.

Reg had said things weren't right when Ronnie was first admitted to hospital. He had applied to the authorities to visit his brother, but his application had been denied. I tried ringing Maidstone to offer my condolences, but the prison had been inundated with calls and none was being accepted. I felt it best to leave Reg alone and sort out my ID parade problem first.

My brother and I went into Basildon. He took up a position by the police station, and I went in to meet my solicitor. We waited for some time, but the witnesses didn't show. The charges, we were told, would be dropped.

That evening I got a call from Reg. He seemed remarkably bright. Of course he was upset about his brother, but his anguish was a private matter. He was more concerned with Ron's funeral arrangements and ensuring there were no problems. He said David Courtney (the man who had tried to set me up to be stabbed) had offered the services of his door firm/security company to guard Ron's body at English's Funeral Directors in Bethnal Green, East London. I thought it rather odd, but some people would do anything for publicity, and it seemed Courtney wanted some. Reg asked me if I would go to the parlour to do a shift watching over Ron to ensure ghouls or publicity seekers didn't pull a stunt. I said I would get in touch with Courtney and sort it out. I had no intention of doing so. Although I had a lot of respect for Ronnie and his brother, I thought this type of thing was for people who were doing it for some sort of sick glamour. I was later to be proved right.

A couple of days later, Reg asked me to visit him at Maidstone. He had been granted a special visit for 12 of his closest friends so they could have a meeting to discuss the funeral arrangements. It wouldn't take place within the confines of the normal visiting room. We were to be given a room to ourselves within the prison. I told Reg that I would be pleased to go and assist where I could.

At the prison I was searched. I was then taken by a woman prison officer to a wood-panelled room usually used for training seminars. Charlie Kray, the twins' elder brother was there. Mad Frankie Fraser, a former fellow inmate and one-time member of the notorious south London-based Richardson gang, made famous for his use of gold pliers, was also there. Frank was a real character. He had recently been shot in the head outside Turnmills nightclub in London. When the police asked him who was responsible, he refused to answer questions. When they asked him who he was, he said 'Tutankhamun'. He was referring to his bandaged head. Mummies don't speak.

Various other notorious criminals arrived in stretched limousines. Other people included prominent journalists and businessmen. Reggie thought Ronnie's death may have been suspicious. However, he had spoken to the doctor who examined his brother and was now satisfied he had died of a massive heart attack following a blood transfusion needed because of a bleeding ulcer. Reggie said Ron was quite comfortable at the time he died.

Reg asked me about the possibility of doing a deal with the

media – it was obvious that the funeral would attract a lot of attention, and there would be interest in exclusives. I said I would arrange it, no problem. I had talked to a national newspaper and a television company who were very interested in filming the church service, an interview with Reg and covering the funeral exclusively. They said the time was right to promote freedom for Reg now that his brother had died. I felt it was an opportunity that he should not miss.

The newspaper concerned asked me to ask Reg if they could have a photograph of Ronnie lying in state, as it were. Reg sounded offended and said no. I told him about the interest of the paper and the television company, but as with most things I had tried to do in the past, several other people had been given the same deal to sort out.

The media people who were keen to have the deal sealed would not wait for ever. Reg was not forthcoming and the deal was scrapped. Whatever deals Reg had, there wasn't even enough money left to pay for Ronnie's funeral. I believe to this day his expenses have still not been paid. As with the film *The Krays*, Reg in my opinion was badly advised.

Annie Allen, Geoff Allen's wife (the man I introduced to Vine for the bank job), telephoned me and suggested we attend Ronnie's funeral together. Alan Smith, a friend of mine from Edinburgh, also rang. He said he was meeting John Masterson and we could all meet up at the funeral parlour to travel together. Reggie had asked me to travel in the car behind him for Ronnie's funeral, and to remain with him throughout. However, Courtney had arranged for lots of doormen – strangers – to surround Reg, turning it into a circus. People who wanted to shake Reggie's hand were unnecessarily pushed back by these bouncers. I wanted no part of it. Annie Allen, Alan Smith, John Masterson, Tony Lambrianou, the man who had been convicted with Reg of killing Jack the Hat, and I all travelled together in a car to the funeral.

Ronnie had often talked to me about his funeral. He always said he wanted it to be a big event. He wanted the horses pulling a carriage with his coffin on it. He got just what he wanted. The whole of the East End of London turned out to see his procession. I don't think there will be another funeral like it for a criminal. I don't think there has been one before. Ronnie's death wasn't just the end of his life. When they buried Ron, they were burying one of the last subscribers to honourable crime. You either get taken out from behind in cold blood these days, or by the police via a call to *Crime Stoppers*. Ronnie's passing was the end of an era.

CHAPTER 12

When I got home from Ronnie's funeral I got washed and changed and went straight into work at the Buzz Bar with Martin. There had been a private party at Lennie McLean's pub, The Guvners in the East End, after the funeral for close family and friends. I had had quite a bit to drink then, and continued to drink while at work.

When I got home that night Debra, quite rightly, was annoyed because I hadn't been about all day and turned up drunk without getting in touch with her. We began to have a heated row and the next thing I knew there was a knock at the door. It was two police officers from Basildon. I wasn't in the mood for them and became quite abusive. They said they had had a complaint about a disturbance. I told them to go away and leave me alone. I told them there was no way they were getting into my house. They tried coming in the door, and I pushed them out. Debra was getting quite upset. She stepped outside to talk to them. Again they tried to come into the house, and I blocked their way.

'If you want to talk to them, then talk to them, but I'm going to bed,' I said to her. I slammed the door and went upstairs, but they continued to knock at the door. I went downstairs again.

'What's the problem?' I asked.

'We want to come in and talk to you.'

'Well I don't want to talk to you,' I said, and slammed the door. If someone can't say what they want to say on the pavement, then I know they're up to no good.

I had a lot of weapons, including a gun, and I began to panic. There were bayonets, knives, CS gas and ammonia around the house. The gun was hidden in the ceiling in the kitchen. I thought I had better get rid of the gun and the gas, because those were the two things I could not explain away. They'd searched my house three or four times before, and then I told them that the reason I had the bayonets was because I collected First and Second World War memorabilia, and they had to give them back to me.

I looked out the window to see if the police had gone, and it appeared they had. I removed the gun and the gas from the cupboard near the front door. I took them upstairs into the bathroom and hid them in the skylight. I was unsure what to do. They probably weren't even going to question me about the gun. Knowing their procedure, I just had it in my head I had to get the weapons out of the house. Because it was me, I thought they weren't going to go away until they were happy.

I couldn't see Debra, either. I guessed she had gone with them or to her mother's. Ten minutes later her mother rang and said that Debra had rung her from the police station. She was upset and she didn't want to go home. She was going to wait there until the police had spoken to me.

'I'm not going to speak to the police,' I said, and put the phone down.

I decided to hide the gas and the handgun in the garden. I rang a taxi, switched off all the lights and took the gun and the gas into the garden. I put them under a large plant pot. A few minutes later the taxi arrived. I said to the driver: 'Take me to Basildon Police Station.'

On our way, the driver remarked that two police cars had pulled out behind us. I had a feeling that this was far more sinister than it seemed, but I didn't have the gun on me and as far as I knew they had not seen me put it anywhere. I felt quite confident.

As we arrived at the police station a police van swung in front of the taxi and another pulled up at the side. A marked police car pulled up immediately behind us. I got out of the car and officers in blue overalls with Koch machine guns took up a position behind the van. They shouted at me: 'Put your hands in the air and kneel on the floor.'

I said: 'Fuck off, I'm paying the cab driver.'

'Put your hands in the air and kneel on the floor.'

'I've told you, I'm not a knocker,' I said. 'I'm paying the cab driver. Then I'll do what you want.'

'Don't put your hand in your pocket. Kneel on the floor!'

The police seemed more uptight and hyped up than they should have been. I didn't trust these people with truncheons, never mind guns. I put my hands in the air and an officer ran up behind me and pulled my hands behind my back. He handcuffed me and pushed me to the floor. After searching me briefly by patting my pockets and clothing, he told me to get up.

'You don't understand, I've already told you I am not going anywhere until I've paid the cab driver,' I said. 'If you want, put your hand in my pocket, take the money out and give it to him.'

He refused, so I said I wasn't getting up. Eventually he relented and took the money out of my pocket. I turned my head. I could see the cab driver. He too was on the floor with a gun to his head. It was bizarre.

I was led into the police station where I was told that they had received information that I was in possession of a gun. 'Bollocks,' I told them. The police said I would be held while a search was conducted at my house, and I was taken into the charge room. An officer explained why I was being held. I was searched again. My shoes and personal belongings were removed and I was put in a cell. I really wasn't having a good day. I decided the best thing to do was to get my head down and have a sleep and see how things were in the morning. I found it hard to sleep, though. I knew the gun was there, and if they were determined, the bastards were going to find it.

They finally came to interview me at about 3.00 p.m. the following afternoon. Two detectives introduced themselves and they began to conduct a taped interview. They gave nothing away at first.

They said: 'We would like to discuss some weapons we have found at your home.'

'If you tell me what you are talking about, then I will explain,' I replied.

The detectives told me they had searched my house. In the cupboard immediately behind the front door, they found a bayonet, approximately 18 inches long, in a sheath. They also found a rounders bat with the word 'Dentist' engraved on it. While searching the main bedroom they said they'd found an eight-inch sheath knife in a sheath bound in blue tape. Finally, they said, at the edge of the lawn at the end of the path in the garden, they had found a small aerosol can and a small leather holster which contained an automatic handgun. They left the items *in situ* for them to be photographed for the purpose of using them in evidence.

I told them there was nothing illegal about the weapons found in the house, which was true. There was nothing illegal about owning a rounders bat, either. I told them that the CS gas had been purchased while on a day-trip to France. It was for the protection of my wife who was at home most evenings alone with the children while I was at work.

As for the firearm, there were no bullets for it, I said. While up north I had purchased it from a farmer on behalf of my brother, Michael, who is himself a farmer. My intention was to give it to him for use in killing vermin.

The police could only record what I said, they couldn't really contest it. During the interview it came to light that the two original officers who came to my home had gone away when I told them to, but parked down the street, switched off all their lights and kept watch without my knowing. They had then radioed for reinforcements and approximately 12 other officers – plain-clothed, armed and uniformed – had surrounded my house and kept it under surveillance. They had actually seen me putting the weapons in the garden. When I left, some followed me and others remained at my home.

The interview was concluded. I was told the items would be sent off for forensic tests and I was bailed to reappear at the police station in a few weeks' time. I got home at about 6.00 p.m. that evening. I had been due to visit Reggie that day. However, the police had been kind enough to ring the prison to tell him that I was otherwise engaged.

I sat in the house considering my position. If I couldn't get out of this, I would get convicted and lose the door at Raquels. I began to wonder if it was such a bad thing, really. I couldn't have just walked away from the club. This was maybe the excuse that I was looking for. Then again, I had to provide for myself and my family. I really didn't know what I was going to do.

That evening I received a phone call from Peter Clarke. He told me he had seen a piece in the paper about me being arrested after going to Ronnie Kray's funeral. He asked me if the gun was the one he had given me. I said it was. He asked me if I had been charged with anything, and when I said no, he seemed quite surprised. 'Why is that then?' he asked.

It was as if he was disappointed that I hadn't been charged. I had only been bailed to reappear at the police station, pending results. When you are caught with a gun, the police are unable to charge you with possession straightaway, because it may prove later that the weapon is a replica, or it has a vital piece of the mechanism not working, such as the trigger or firing pin. This would not make it a firearm and the charge wouldn't stick. They have to have it confirmed that it's a working gun.

But I didn't tell Clarke this. He rang me the next day and told me he had a job which wanted doing in Birmingham, if I was interested. I asked him what it was, and he told me Jones, his partner, who ran a Basildon door firm, was selling a car to a man in the West Midlands. The man, an Asian, had arranged to meet him and he would have several thousand pounds in cash on him. The idea was someone else would turn up and rob him. The car would turn up later, and they would pretend to know nothing about it. He said it would be really easy. I said if it was so easy, then why weren't they doing it themselves? He said that they were very busy, otherwise they would. I taped the conversation, as I had been suspicious of these people for some time, and then I said I would give it some thought.

I rang the detective who had been named by other officers as the man who might fit me up. I told him that I had received a call from somebody who had asked me to commit a serious crime in the north of England. If information was received that I was up to no good in the next few days, they should ignore it. I was quite sure they would receive such information.

The detective asked me what it was all about. I told him briefly, without giving names and places. He told me I was being paranoid. I thought otherwise. The following day he rang me, and asked if we could meet. When we met he asked me to give my version of events. I told him that I believed Jones, Clarke and Pierce wanted me out of Raquels, or off the scene, at any cost. When I had been partners with Clarke at the club, he and Jones had held talks with the management behind my back. I told him about the trouble Pierce had stirred between myself and Vine; the numerous anonymous complaints that the licensing police and Basildon Council had received about me and other members of the door staff; the searches of my home and car for drugs; the accusation that my own car was stolen, backed by paperwork from Charlie Jones; the lorry load of coffee beans to Liverpool and the men's arrest there; the fact they had given me the very gun I was now on bail for. I told the detective I thought Jones, Clarke or Pierce was an informant. By getting me arrested, they knew I would end up losing the Raquels door.

The detective would not say whether they were or were not. He said if I believed I had been fitted up with the gun, then I should tell the truth. However, he said, if I named names, it could cause problems for me: not with the police, but other people. He said it was a matter for myself. However, he took on board what I was saying, particularly in view of the fact that I had a tape of one of them asking me to commit a robbery the day after I'd been released on bail. He couldn't help but admit that it did seem rather odd. He said he would keep abreast of the situation and I should tell him of any developments.

The very same evening, my telephone rang at home. Somebody asked if Jones was there. I would stake my life on it, that it was the detective. I have asked him a thousand times to admit it was him, but he denies it. We agree to differ. However, I now knew my fears were not unfounded concerning Pierce, Clarke and Jones. They didn't have to go to these lengths. They weren't man enough to take it direct. If they had wanted it that bad, they could have had Raquels. They only had to ask.

Whatever the outcome, they weren't going to get it now. I had the tape from the police saying I was going to be fitted up. I had the tape of Clarke trying to lure me into committing a robbery. I also knew one, if not all three, were police informants. It was all good material to get me out of this mess.

Reg Kray got in touch. He said he had heard about what had happened, and he wanted to know if there was anything he could do. He said I should go down to Maidstone to see if anything could be done to sort the problem out. I wasn't really in the mood for it. But I felt sorry for Reg after losing his brother, and so I said I would go down to see him. I felt bad about not seeing him on the day after the funeral even though I had been locked up in Basildon Police Station and there was little I could have done about it.

The newspaper which I had held talks with regarding Ronnie's funeral asked me if Reg would be willing to give an interview about Ron's death and the funeral itself. He had snubbed their earlier offer and most of the best material had been given away to various other newspapers. I spoke to Reg on the phone before visiting him, and he agreed that he would do the interview. He wanted ten grand, but I told him that would be impossible. In the end we agreed that he would do the interview and he would be paid according to the content.

I didn't like getting involved in his business. There were always too many advisers, and everything always ended in arguments. Reggie did the article and I felt it was the most sympathetic coverage he had ever had since being imprisoned. He too was pleased with it, and talks of setting up a deal with the paper for his first interview after he was freed were put in motion. It could have been quite lucrative. But his fan club were always advising him to do silly interviews with local papers. They were more interested in selling T-shirts with his picture on them than getting him out of prison and making a bit of money on the way. I'd always been of the opinion that it was these people that were keeping him in prison.

Once they had organised a 'Free The Krays' march through London. Young children had gone on the march wearing T-shirts with pictures of Ron and Reg on the front; on the back of the T-shirts they had printed 'The Krays On Tour', listing all the prisons they had been in during their 30-year sentence with dates. Little wonder those at the Home Office still considered them a threat. I'd always said they should have sat back and given just the occasional interview, talk the philosophical shit all government departments love to hear. Glorifying the events that straight people objected to was not doing them any favours, but you couldn't tell them.

Reg was paid £3,000 for the interview, and I was given £1,000 for organising it. As usual members of Reggie's fan club were up in arms, saying he should have been paid five-figure sums, which was nonsense. The most newsworthy points concerning his brother's death had been given in interviews with other papers for nothing weeks before this interview appeared in print. I thought he had had a result.

He went into one on the phone, saying he should have been given more money. I was getting a bit sick of being criticised. If he had stuck with the original agreement about the exclusive rights for the funeral we would both have had a lot of money. But as usual people interfered. As far as I know this three grand was the best payment he had had out of the whole thing.

The row blew out of all proportion a few days later. The *News of the World* published an article. The headline read: 'Ghouls snorted coke off Ronnie Kray's coffin.' It was reported that people had snorted lines of cocaine and also that they set up an Ouija board next to Ronnie's casket and tried to contact his spirit. Finally, they put a Sony Walkman on Ronnie's head and cackled with laughter, saying doesn't he look stupid with the headphones on? Reggie was outraged. Staff at the funeral parlour discovered tell-tale smudges on Ronnie's highly polished open coffin. They also found pieces of paper with letters written on them used for the Ouija session. Reggie was reported as saying he wanted Dave Courtney to explain any lapse in the watertight security he promised.

Reggie and the fan club spent most of the day ringing my house. As I knew reporters, they wanted to know who was behind these acts against Ronnie and who had spoken to the paper. They were blaming everyone. I told Reg I would try to find out, but I didn't intend doing so. I was sick to death of this pettiness. I had been told what was going on at the funeral parlour at the time it was happening. That's the main reason I didn't want to get involved in watching over Ronnie. I knew people wouldn't be doing it out of respect and things were bound to happen. When I was told, I wasn't surprised. I even knew who was involved, but it wasn't my business. If you told Reggie the truth anyway, you would be met with counter claims and it would all just get messy. I had had it a thousand times with him and Ronnie.

Lorraine, a genuine friend of Reggie's, rang me up, very upset, saying she had been blamed, and for her benefit, I spoke to Reg and told him that I knew for certain that she was not involved. However, all Reggie did was round on me, asking why I was befriending Lorraine. I was meant to be his friend, not hers. I even rang the journalist who wrote the article and told him that Lorraine was being blamed. He also offered to help her. It was bizarre. Everyone knew who was responsible, but still Reg allowed the accusations to continue.

One avid fan of Reggie's was a man named Brad Allardyce. I had met him in Maidstone Prison where he was serving a prison sentence. However, recently he had been moved to Whitemoor Prison in Cambridgeshire where Pat Tate was also serving his sentence. Reg had asked me if Pat would look after Brad, as he was rather vulnerable. I was reluctant to ask Pat, but I did so as a favour to Reg. Soon Pat and I were both regretting having anything to do with Allardyce.

Pat rang me a few times, asking who the fuck was this person I'd put on to him. Pat said he was lining something big up for the firm from inside and Allardyce was making him look like a fool. If the people he was dealing with thought he mixed with the likes of Allardyce it could blow the whole thing. All I could do was apologise.

Allardyce would ring or write to me. He seemed to think he was Reggie's right-hand man. In one letter, he wrote to me about an associate of Reg called Piper claiming he'd had Reg over on some deal: 'Gary Piper is in a lot of trouble, Bernie. He's used us and I will never let that go unpunished. Never. I'll bide my time, but when I get out, Bernie, he will be finished. Nobody crosses Reg without crossing me. I will make that cunt pay for what he's done. I am not stupid, Bernie, so I do not intend to end up back in prison down to him. But he will be sorry he ever crossed us. Reg means the world to me, Bernie. A lot of people think he has a lot of friends, but you and I know different. It's up to us to protect him. He is like a father to me, Bernie. I love him very much. Gary Piper is finished. Take it from me. Reg listens to me, Bernie, and he will always do as I ask. Because he knows I will only do what is best for him. Sometimes people take advantage of him. Well that's all stopped now because I am his right-hand man. You're a good friend, Bernie, and Reg knows that. I've seen Pat Tate, he sends his very best to you.'

In another letter he sent me a visiting order and asked me to see him. He asked if I could bring some 'birds' – slang for doves, a type of ecstasy – and maybe some 'Mickey Duff', Cockney rhyming slang for cannabis ('puff'). He said he would get phone cards and start up his own 'food boat', prison slang for wheeling and dealing inside. I don't know who this man thought he was. Censors who read the letter would hardly be fooled by somebody asking for birds and Mickey Duff. I'm surprised the police weren't kicking my door down at the same time the postman was at it. I really had to get away from these people. The wannabes were causing more trouble than the real villains.

All things happen in threes, they say. I'd been arrested for the gun, I'd fallen out with Reg and everyone who knew him, and sure enough, disaster struck again.

Roger Mellin had never been in trouble in his life. His girlfriend Tracy had a disabled child. Roger was a really nice kid. He was young and impressionable. He had often asked about selling ecstasy for Murray in Raquels as he desperately needed money. I told him to forget it. Murray, however, told Roger that he would pay him £50 a week just to store any excess drugs at his home. It sounded simple. They would be left there and picked up when required. Roger would have to do nothing for his £50. I, and others, told him he was mad. But Roger insisted he needed the money.

One morning Murray asked him if he would count out the pills for the various dealers. Roger didn't like the idea of them coming into his house, so he booked himself into a local hotel room. He sat on the bed and started sorting them out into different amounts. There was a knock at the door, and when he opened it police officers stormed into the room. On the bed there were 1,500 ecstasy tablets, quantities of cocaine and quantities of amphetamine. Roger was well and truly nicked. The police had been watching certain people and followed them to the hotel. When they had seen enough, they moved in. Roger was devastated. He knew he was going to serve a lengthy prison sentence despite the fact it was the first time he had ever been in trouble. It was a tragedy, really. Roger was a regular at Raquels. He had been lured into his nightmare for £50 a week. Somebody somewhere was determined to put our firm, which had become an insatiable monster, out of business.

Roger pleaded guilty at his trial. He never named those he was working for. For his loyalty, for £50, his girlfriend and her disabled child received nothing from the firm or Mark Murray. Roger was sentenced to five years' imprisonment. We used to say in Basildon if you wanted loyalty you should buy a dog.

When the dust had settled surrounding events at the funeral parlour with Ronnie Kray, Reg rang and asked if Debra and I would visit him. He was having an interview with Mary Riddell from the *Today* newspaper. He said he wanted us to be there. I didn't go because he asked me to. I went because I knew it would be the very last time I would see him. I didn't tell him – I didn't tell anyone except for Debra. I had had enough. I wanted out. I asked Debra not to tell anyone for the time being. Things would have to be sorted. You can't just walk away from the situation I was in. When I went, I wanted it to be for good. We started looking for a new home near Ipswich. I didn't want my children growing up surrounded by people like myself and my friends. I wanted them to have a future.

Mark Murray had been in Club UK for about seven or eight weeks by then. He hadn't paid me one penny of the £500 a week he had promised. I wrote a letter with dates and the amounts he owed me, telling him he shouldn't fuck me about. He had promised me £500 a week, and I expected it. He owed me £3,500. If he didn't come down to the club on Friday to discuss how it was going to be paid, I would be paying him a visit.

He came to the club and started making excuses. I told him I was going to America on holiday the following week. If I did not get it by the morning I was due to go I would be unable to travel and I wouldn't be very happy. I would come to look for him. He promised me it would be there.

I went to a travel agent and booked a holiday for the family. I needed to get away from everything to be able to think properly.

I was getting sick of people like Murray. Tucker was feeding him, making him think he was something. Murray had started to believe it. He tried telling me he had no money because he was losing at Club UK. He had to pay for the pills that had been lost when Roger had been arrested. I said it wasn't my problem. The money better be there. He came to my house at 6.00 a.m. on the morning we were due to leave. Our flight left Gatwick Airport at 11.00 a.m. He couldn't really have left it any later. Nevertheless, he put the money up. I told him our arrangement was now cancelled. He shouldn't make promises he didn't know he could keep. As he had paid the £3,500 I was happy with that, and that would be the end of the matter.

We flew from Gatwick to Florida, where we rented a house not far from Disneyland. We spent a week there. It was glorious. We had our own swimming pool at a luxury secluded home. We spent the day with the children in the theme parks and in the evening we would have barbecues beside the swimming pool. We went on to visit Graceland in Memphis, and then Los Angeles.

The holiday was just what I needed. In 17 days we had spent £7,500, but that short break had put my future firmly in my mind. I couldn't continue the way things were. The gun, and the conviction that went with it, would give me my way out. It was depressing flying home from America. When we landed at Gatwick it was raining and grey. Dismal. It was just how I felt.

Back home it was business as usual. Two people, Gary Murray and Richard Hearn, had left separate messages on my answering machine. Both wanted to meet me to discuss a proposition. Gary Murray (no relation to Mark) was now selling the gear for the firm on Saturdays at the jungle do because Murray already had quite a lucrative job of serving up at a club in Southend on Saturdays. He also had Club UK to worry about. Gary Murray asked me if I would put Murray out and let him take control of Fridays also. I refused.

'It's none of my business. That arrangement can't be broken because money is owed by Mark,' I said.

Richard Hearn, who had worked as a dealer for Murray, also asked me if he could take over from him. I told him to meet me at the club on Friday. I took him upstairs into a backroom and sent someone to get Mark Murray. When they were both in the room, I asked Hearn to repeat what he had asked me. He said it was all a misunderstanding, he didn't really want to take over from Mark. It was typical. Somebody wanted someone removed, but they wanted to do it behind a painted smile, rather than confront the person direct. It wasn't my style. Hearn was thrown out of the club.

It seemed people were too scared to confront others involved with the firm. This fashion of disposing of them in other ways was becoming a bigger problem. Suspicion was on everybody. Nobody was left out. Some of the dealers even accused Tony Tucker of being an informant. He wasn't. The flavour of the month depended on which circle of people you were sitting with and at what particular time.

Three more of the firm's couriers were taken out by police as they were on their way to make a drop to a London club from Basildon. Nigel Coy, 24, Richard Gilham, 29, and Jason Edwards, 25, were stopped by police in Purfleet. Each had a bag tucked inside their boxer shorts containing 100 ecstasy pills. Nigel Coy admitted to the police he had made at least eight similar drops. Coy ran a hairdressing business called Coy Cuts, and when the police searched it they found another 168 pills. Coy was also in possession of amphetamine sulphate and admitted intending to supply. At his trial he was jailed for four years. Gilham and Edwards admitted possessing ecstasy with intent to supply. They were each jailed for three years.

Club UK was going badly wrong for Mark Murray. Nobody wanted to do business with him. Roger had been arrested, so had Coy, Edwards and Gilham; Nathaniel and Lee, who had dropped the pills at Raquels when the management gave them back, had also been jailed for possession. Little wonder that Mark was forced to start dealing himself.

I went to a solicitor to discuss my prospects concerning the gun. He told me that as I had the tape and the names of those I thought had informed on me, I should call the police's bluff and threaten to expose the whole thing. Naturally the police would want none of it. I was advised not to name the people, but to threaten to do so. When it got to Court, the police would refuse to name the informants and the case against me would be dismissed. This normally happens because the police won't name informants in Court.

When I appeared at the Magistrates court in Basildon to be committed to the Crown Court, my solicitor tried to get the case thrown out early and told the Court the circumstances of how I came to be in possession of the gun. The prosecution would have none of it. So my solicitor wrote to the Crown Prosecution Service (CPS) about the 'alleged police informant' working with the Chelmsford Drug Squad – the people who had searched my house – in the hope that they would drop the case against me.

The CPS would have none of it, either. They wrote: 'These allegations are totally unfounded and completely untrue.'

The police didn't want me bringing the fit-up tape up and they also didn't want me naming informants in Court, but the CPS were preventing any deal going ahead. Another solution would have to be sought.

On 23 July I received a phone call late in the evening. I was told that a friend of mine and Tony's, Francis Martin, the head doorman at Legends nightclub in the West End, had been shot. He was 36. He had been drinking with friends at the Frog & Nightgown in the Old Kent Road, and was shot at point-blank range moments after leaving. The gunman had been lying in wait outside. Nobody had any idea why it had happened. Friends of Francis chased after the gunman, but were forced to dive for cover as he turned and fired at them. He escaped in a red Ford Orion, driven by another man.

Francis was in a stable condition, but his injuries were quite serious. He had been shot in the back. Everyone was surprised that it had happened to him, as he was well liked and not involved in the drugs trade. However, these days you didn't have to be involved in anything to qualify for being shot or wounded.

Tucker was quite upset about the shooting. But we decided to stay away from the hospital, as we didn't know what the situation was. Three weeks later, on 10 August, when we all thought he was on the road to recovery, Francis died of his injuries. It made me think more about my fate. Prison was on the horizon, but the way things were going, a grave could be round the corner.

CHAPTER 13

There was little solidarity in the firm now. The violence and the excessive use of cocaine had turned the meekest of men into explosive psychopaths.

People had turned to cocaine trying to reach the elusive high that had faded as their bodies became used to the effects of ecstasy. Cocaine is associated with gangsters and villainy and cocaine users were looked upon as if they were on a higher plain than those using ecstasy. It was a fashionable drug to be associated with.

If used over a prolonged period, cocaine destroys the septum, the partition which separates the nostrils. One member of the firm was able to put a bootlace up one nostril and bring it down the other, hold both ends and pull it up and down in a pulley-type motion – quite sick, really, but some people thought it was funny. Instead of one or two ecstasy pills per evening, some were consuming between eight and 12. They were topping that up with lines of cocaine and amphetamine sulphate.

The atmosphere of evil was like a virus. It affected everyone. Dave Simms, the Raquels manager, disapproved, but his protests were silenced. In a bid to weaken us, he had cut staff numbers, saying the club could not afford the wages bill. The door had been cut so severely, there was now little security visible in the club. When there was an incident, those involved were put down with the intention that they remained so. This cocktail amounted to madness in its purest form.

The anger, frustration and hostility were also coming out in our work. On Saturdays there were only four of us working. One evening we were downstairs at the main door talking, when we received a call on the internal telephone from the Buzz Bar. The barmaid told us there was a group of men up there causing trouble. I went up there alone and there were seven or eight soldiers, obviously home on weekend leave, drunk, making a general nuisance of themselves. I told them to leave, and one of them picked up a glass. I didn't say anything. I bent down and picked up a fire extinguisher which was by the toilet door. I swung the fire extinguisher and hit him with it. He was helped to his feet by his friends and they got him to the door. I threw the fire extinguisher again. This time it smashed the double doors. They ran down the stairs and I went after them.

When we got out into the street the other three doormen saw what was happening, and ran to assist me. One of the doormen, Jeff Balman, fell during the fight and was lying on the floor. We were greatly outnumbered so I ran into the club foyer and picked up a very heavy rectangular piece of metal. I ran into the street and went to hit the man who was standing over Jeff. I had the piece of metal in both hands, and swung it like a baseball bat. Jeff didn't see what I was doing, pushed the man off him and began to get up. The bar hit Jeff full on the side of the head and knocked him unconscious. There was blood everywhere. The men saw what had happened and ran. We had trouble getting Jeff to regain consciousness and eventually he had to be taken to hospital. He was suffering from concussion and detained. He had 13 stitches in his head and was still receiving medical attention six months after the event for pains in his head and general dizziness.

As we always had a policy of not telephoning ambulances, Jeff was put into a car and taken to hospital by another doorman. I had told him not to say he had been working. At the hospital he was told to tell staff, and if need be the police, that he had been walking through Basildon and people had set upon him and tried to mug him. That way the trouble wouldn't be associated with the club and Jeff could put in for criminal compensation.

We had no sympathy for Jeff. When he complained about his injuries, he was ridiculed. When he came into Raquels to get his wages, somebody told him that the management had got him some new safety equipment. We presented him with a child's plastic crash helmet from Toys 'R' Us. Jeff left the firm.

Two skinheads came into the Buzz Bar one Wednesday evening. One stood behind me, aping me, and laughing with his friend. I turned around and pushed him. I didn't mean to do it, but he fell backwards and his head hit the corner of a glass pillar, splitting it wide open. Martin heard the glass smash and ran from the other side of the bar with a bottle in his hand. The skinhead was on the floor, and Martin could not see the wound at the back of his head. He thought he had attacked me with a glass. Martin hit him a couple of times over the head with the bottle and we dragged him to the doors. He was thrown into one door, which smashed, cutting his upper arm. He was then beaten and thrown down the stairs. About half an hour later, people near the stairs began panicking. We looked down and the entrance was ablaze. He and his friend had returned and petrol-bombed the entrance to the bar. It was the only entrance, and all the people inside were screaming.

We told Rod Chapman to deal with the fire, and we ran out through the flames into the street. I saw the skinhead with a red petrol can in his hand. I had an Irish hurling stick in my hand. I ran across. He dropped the petrol can and said: 'It wasn't me, it wasn't me.' I hit him across the back with the stick. He fell to the ground. Martin had steel boots on, and he began stamping on him and kicking him in the head. He was begging us not to beat him any more. I hit him so hard across the back with the hurling stick it broke. He was unconscious. We picked the petrol can up and doused him in petrol. His friend, who had run a short distance away, was screaming 'Please don't burn him, please don't burn him.' We told him to come to us, as we weren't going to do anything. He wouldn't. We emptied the remainder of the petrol over his unconscious friend and said we would burn him. He became hysterical. We walked back to the bar where the fire had been put out. People said we had over-reacted, but there were 250 innocent people in the bar. If these people wanted to play with fire, then they had to be prepared to take the consequences. You couldn't allow people to take liberties like that.

With the tension that was mounting within the firm, our

actions were becoming more and more extreme. We couldn't justify everything that happened. David Arnell was probably the quietest doorman who worked with us. He wasn't a drug user. He was just surrounded by violence and acted accordingly. One evening three men, one a surgeon, were enjoying a night out at Raquels. Around 2.00 a.m., the surgeon, Dr Nwaoloko, left the club with his brother and waited for their friend outside. When their friend failed to appear Dr Nwaoloko asked me for permission to go back in, and I said go ahead. But Arnell stopped him going into the club, and an argument started. Dr Nwaoloko was pushed to the ground and kicked by Arnell several times. He lost consciousness briefly and suffered injuries to his forehead, jaw, cheek and neck. Arnell then went back to the club while Dr Nwaoloko was taken to his car by his brother. However, Arnell later went across the road and repeatedly smashed the doctor's head on his car bonnet. It was totally out of character for Dave.

I told him to plead not guilty and deny all knowledge of the attack. But when the police came he blurted out the truth, and pleaded guilty. He wasn't like us. I liked Dave. At his trial the prosecutor said Dr Nwaoloko now had a problem with his wrist resulting from the attack which prevented him doing his job as a surgeon. Because Dave had never been in trouble before in his life the judge said he would escape a prison sentence. Dave was ordered to pay £1,000 compensation and do 180 hours of community service. He quit working the same night, and has told me he will never work as a doorman again.

Tucker too was feeling vulnerable. When he used to come and see me on Friday nights to give me the invoices and the doormen's wages for the club, he would park at the top of the street in his black Porsche. I used to go up, open the door and get in. He would always have a handgun on the seat between his legs. He told me he had also applied for a firearms licence from Basildon police. He wanted to own a shotgun legally. There were plenty of arms around the firm, but as Tucker had no convictions, he might as well hold one or two legally which he could have at hand at his home without fear of being arrested. As he had no convictions, it was unlikely the police would refuse his application.

He had enjoyed a good roll in the past few months. The firm had been approached by a part-time drug dealer who had acquired £18,000-worth of cannabis to sell. Tucker told the dealer he had the right contacts and would sort out a sale for him. Tucker, Rolfe and the dealer travelled to Birmingham, where Tucker said his contact lived. While the dealer and Rolfe waited, Tucker disappeared with the cannabis. He turned up a couple of hours later and told them the police had busted them before they had got the money. He was lucky to have escaped. The dealer, had to accept the excuse Tucker gave him, or take him on. Losing 18 grand must have been a bitter pill to swallow, but it would have been less painful than calling Tucker a liar.

Everybody knew no one had been arrested. If that does occur on such a deal, the person who lost the drugs or claims to have been arrested has a duty to produce paperwork from those charged or from those who are bailed, as explained earlier. Otherwise it is considered untrue. However the dealer wasn't going to take Tucker on. But Tucker knew he couldn't get away with these scams for ever. Hence the guns, which travelled with him everywhere he dare take them.

I was going backwards and forwards to Basildon Magistrates Court waiting to be committed to Crown Court on the matter of the gun and CS gas. The police were concerned that the CPS were not allowing me to bring the question of informants into the evidence. My solicitor told me that although it was the truth, it was going to be an uphill struggle. If somebody had offered to give me a gun and I accepted it, then I was guilty. All other circumstances were mitigating at best, and did I really want to tell a judge about rival door firms involved in setting me up with guns etc. It was agreed that the best story to give the Court would be the one I had originally given to the police. That I had purchased the gun on behalf of my brother, who was going to use it to shoot vermin on the farm where he worked. That story would not involve nightclubs and doormen. It was a fairly innocent affair. The gas which had been bought to protect my wife, although illegal, was a fairly innocent act. We all agreed that a lie was more believable than the truth.

I was told by the police that if I did not mention the fit-up tape and the fact that the gun had been given to me by persons I claimed were informants then the seriousness of the charge would be played down in Court. It would go through as I was telling it. A fairly harmless affair. I gave my word I wouldn't mention the tape and I wouldn't mention the informants. A deal was struck. It was better for all concerned.

At my final appearance at Basildon Magistrates Court, the magistrate ordered that I stand trial at Chelmsford Crown Court. The prosecution despised me. I could tell by the way he looked at me and spoke about me. He handled my papers as if they were a turd or something. Court is like that. Very little of the truth comes out. Like life, they tell you, it's a game and you should play by the rules. It's true, I suppose, especially if you are in the team with all the star players. But it's a fucker when your side has all the disadvantages. What sort of game is it then?

In October Club UK in Wandsworth was raided by the police. The whole operation was televised. There were more than 1,000 people in the club. Murray's dealers threw all their pills and powders on the floor in order to escape arrest. Murray lost 800 pills in total, pills he had not yet paid Tucker for. He had lost 468 when Nigel Coy and the others had been busted. He had lost 1,500 when Roger Mellin had been busted. With this 800 he had lost 2,768 pills with a street value of £41,520. Murray was probably in debt to the tune of about 20 grand. Prison would have been salvation for him.

There are no financial advisers in the drugs world, and there are certainly no overdraft facilities. Tucker wanted his money, and he wanted it now. He came round to my house with Rolfe and asked me where Murray was. We all got into a car and went round to Murray's house. His girlfriend was there. Rolfe went in the front room and said: 'Where's Mark?' She said she didn't know. He asked if he had taken his phone with him. She said no, he had left it there. Rolfe picked it up, switched it on, and started making calls. Tucker was seated on the settee with me. He was laughing. He said to her 'Are you watching this programme?' pointing to the television. She said no. He ripped the plug from the wall, wrapped it round the telly and told Rolfe to go and load the stereo and the television into the car, which he did.

He then told Murray's girlfriend she was coming with us. She was very frightened, and said Mark would be home soon. He said: 'Don't worry about that, get in the car.' We all got into the car and drove round to another friend's house. Fortunately Tucker had forgotten why, if he ever had a reason, he had taken Murray's girlfriend round to somebody else's house. I think he just did it to ensure she didn't forewarn Murray about the fact he was looking for him. Whatever, tired of waiting, we all went home.

That night Tucker and Rolfe returned to Murray's flat. Tucker pulled out a huge bowie knife, grabbed Murray by the neck and pressed the point into his throat. He said: 'I want my money, Murray. And for every week you owe me, you pay £500 on top. If I don't get it, you're dead.'

Following the incident at the hospital after Tate had been shot, Tucker organised what he thought would be a huge party for his release. It was to be at a snooker hall in Dagenham. On Hallowe'en, the day Pat came out, Tony rang me and said he wanted me to go to the party with all the doormen. He and Pat had something they wanted to discuss with me which would be of interest to me, and an earner for us all.

I rang him back that night and said I would be unable to go because I had to go up north. It was a lie. I was trying to get out of my situation, not get more involved. I wasn't the only one who felt like this. Only 15 people attended Pat's coming-out party.

I did see him and Tony that week. They, as well as everybody else, were talking about an article which had been in the local papers. Half a million pounds' worth of cannabis had been found in a farmer's pond near a place called Rettendon. It was believed that the 336 pounds of cannabis which was wrapped in 53 different plastic parcels, about the size of video tapes, had been dropped from a low-flying aircraft. Instead of landing in the field, it had landed in a pond, and the dealers were unable to find it. A farmer named Yan Haustrup found one parcel while cutting the hedges. He didn't know what it was, and threw it on a fire. He said he then found another piece near the pond, and contacted the police. Divers recovered the haul.

Tucker and Tate were saying what a fucking idiot to throw it on the fire and then hand over £500,000-worth of gear to the Old Bill. Tate thought it was worth looking to see if any of the shipment had been missed. But it was the drugs talking. He hadn't been straight since the day he got out. Rettendon to us was only a roundabout. There wasn't anything else there. There was just a church, a post office and probably 50 or so houses. We were hardly going to scour the fields after the police had crawled all over it. Pat kept on about it. He couldn't believe that someone could be that straight and hand over anything of that much value to the police.

Pat, Tony and Craig wanted everyone to know that they were back in business. They began training together every day, filling themselves with steroids, pumping up their muscles – and their egos. They were charging about like bulldozers out of control. Pat, out of his head on cocaine and Special K, wrote Tucker's Porsche off. Despite its value, they didn't consider it a big deal and it was put into a garage for repair. Then they went down to a garage near Tucker's house, and invested in a seven-grand, F-registered metallic blue Range Rover Vogue, which was registered in Craig's name. It wouldn't be long before Tony had sorted something else out.

Pat and Tony called me and we met in the car park at Basildon Hospital, outside the Accident and Emergency entrance – a place where we often met. Pat said he wanted me to act as a back-up driver on a scam they were pulling off shortly. They had arranged to intercept a large shipment of drugs. They had done this type of thing loads of times before, but they said this was different. This was the big one. I said I would be unable to do it as the police were watching me.

I still felt something for these people. Before all this had happened, they had been my friends. They were blind to any danger. Pat was driving Tony on. I warned him to be careful, but as usual he just laughed and turned my advice into ridicule. Whatever it was they did, they had it right off. They had more money than ever. Tucker moved out of his home in Chafford Hundred into a £250,000 bungalow called Brynmount Lodge. They talked about their success, but I knew it was foolish. You could fuck about with the likes of Murray, but you had to know your limits. Not everyone would take that shit.

In an effort to get his money back from Murray, Tucker insisted that he buy all his stock directly from him. Murray had been deceiving Tucker for some time, buying weaker ecstasy pills for sale in the clubs. His reasoning was if you sold very strong ecstasy, a person would buy one and be out of his head for the whole night. That person would not need any additional pills. By selling weaker pills, the person would need three or more to get any sort of effect. However, Tucker's latest batch were a new type of ecstasy called Apples. They had been imported from Holland. They were very strong. Murray had no choice but to buy them off Tucker at an inflated rate – a) because Tucker said they were good and worth more; and b) because Murray owed him money and had little choice.

The pills caused a lot of people to be ill in Raquels. I was called up to the dance floor one Friday evening. A youth had collapsed and his friends were concerned for him. I told them to pick him up and take him downstairs where we could assess the situation in the fresh air and light because the dance floor area was dark and crowded. The kid was in a right state. I thought he was about 17 or 18. His eyes were rolling in his head. He was sweating and drifting in and out of consciousness. He got up and said to me 'I want to go.' He walked out of the door and collapsed in the street. I told his friends to take him to hospital, but they were frightened his parents were going to find out he'd been on drugs. We led him over to a bench in the town centre and sat him on it. A gang of youths were sitting nearby, watching.

I left him with his friends and went back to the club. I kept looking out of the doors to see if he was all right. I noticed his friends had left him. He was now lying across the bench. The group of youths nearby always hung about the town and were trouble. I thought that they were going to rob him as he was unconscious. I went across to him and got him to his feet. He kept saying he was all right, and started to walk off. I saw him standing near the burger van and then I saw him walking towards the cab firm. I assumed he was getting into a cab.

An hour or so later, the police arrived. They said a 15-year-old boy had been admitted to Basildon Hospital. It was thought he was suffering from a drugs overdose. As usual, the club denied all knowledge of it. The line was that these people took drugs while queueing up. We could search them, but we couldn't be held responsible for anything they did outside. As usual, it was bollocks.

Dave Simms had by now cut the door so dramatically, the club was virtually running itself. Nobody was searched going into the club and there weren't enough doormen to keep an eye on the activities of those inside, which is why we had to rely on somebody coming downstairs to tell us that there was someone lying on the dance floor unconscious.

Blame lies with the firm. Blame lies with the management. Blame lies with the police, but nobody forced anyone into that club, and nobody forced anyone to take drugs. The burden of blame and the burden of the drug culture lies with us all.

On Friday 10 November it was business as usual. I knew nearly everybody who came into the club – not by name: I knew the faces. They all said hello. As usual nobody was searched: Mark Murray was plying his trade at the top bar. Because of the police successes against his dealers, he was serving himself that night. Murray always stood near the steps at the top bar and asked people if they were sorted. He told them he had Apples, which were 'the bollocks'. Like many other people that night, whoever bought Leah's pills paid their money. They held the folded notes in their hand. Murray held the Apple ecstasy pills in his. They pretended to shake hands. It was the way all deals were done. Their hands touched, Murray taking the money, the punter taking the pills. The type of deal that would be done 100 times that night in the club. Leah Betts's fate was sealed. That deal was going to end her life, and change everybody else's.

CHAPTER 14

The story has come full circle. It was now a week after the youth had bought the pills from Murray.

Leah's death, my meeting with Packman on the garage forecourt, my arguments with Tucker, the press getting on my case, the police hassling me meant I had to get away from the intrigue. I was sick of the constant competition and life with a gun in my pocket 24 hours a day. Paranoid? I felt fucking quadraphonic. But I had no idea how I was going to support my wife and children from here on in.

I felt guilty about my close friend Martin. I knew his loyalty to me would be criticised. My leaving had to be a total departure. No occasional acquaintances from memory lane. If he were to have children of his own, I was sure he would understand my decision.

When I said to Martin let's get out of Raquels, he, Debra and I drove to Southend. The people who hired Raquels out on a Friday also hired the Ad Lib club in Southend. The music was much the same as they played at Raquels. We walked in the door and down a flight of three or four steps. Tucker and Tate were standing at the bottom with two girls. Tate smiled and put his arms around me. He patted my back, and said: 'It's great to see you, Bernie, how are you?' Tucker looked as if he had the hump.

'What's the matter?' I asked him. He shook hands with me, and said, 'Nothing.' Then he added: 'Can I have a word?'

We went out of earshot of the others, and he told me one of the doormen had grassed Donna up. Donna was constantly causing problems. In Raquels she would come downstairs and say to me that such and such a man is giving me grief such

166

and such a man is staring at me. Tony said if I had a problem, you have to throw them out.

'What's the matter with her this time?' I said to Tony.

He got annoyed and said one of the doormen grassed her up as she was in Pat's flat when the police found some whizz.

'That's bollocks, the police haven't even spoken to any doormen,' I said. He told me another doorman had confirmed it.

'Well, who's this other doorman then?' I asked. 'We'll go and see him.'

'I've got to go now,' he replied.

'Fair enough,' I said. 'Ring me up and we'll discuss what has been said.' He walked out of the door. Pat turned round and put his arm round me again.

'Don't worry about him,' he said. 'He's just got the hump.'

We shook hands, and Pat left to join Tony. I waited a minute, and I thought, 'I'm going to clear this up.' I went outside. They were sitting in their blue Range Rover. I leant against the driver's door and told Tony: 'I'm telling you no doorman's grassed Donna up. Someone's just saying it to cause trouble. And as for this doorman who confirmed it, why don't we go round and see him tomorrow, and if you think he's lying we'll bash him?'

'Fair enough, we'll fucking bash him,' Tucker said. Then they drove off.

I don't know why I said what I'd said. I had just decided to walk out of Raquels. I had told myself I wanted nothing more to do with this. I suppose the habit of the past five years was proving hard to break. The conversation had put me in a lousy mood. I was sick of these wannabes trying to get in on the act and causing trouble. The others wanted to go to another club. I wasn't really in the mood, but as it was my last night, we went.

We went to Epping Country Club and then on to a club in the East End called the Powerhouse, but I wasn't really into it. At 5.00 a.m., I shook hands with Martin and walked away. He is the best friend I have ever had. He is the most loyal friend I have ever had. Everything in this life has a price.

The following day I got a phone call. Somebody was telling me that Mark Murray's picture was on the front of the *News of the World.* Surely they had it wrong? I expected Steve Packman's picture to be in the paper, not Mark Murray's. I went out to buy a copy to see for myself. On the front page there was a picture of Murray and the heading: 'Revealed: man in ecstasy death quizzed.' The article said this was one of the men being quizzed by police investigating the death of tragic ecstasy victim Leah Betts. 'Jobless Mark Murray, 35, of Pitsea, Essex, was among six people held after Leah's death at her 18th birthday party last week. He faces further questioning after *News of the World* handed cops a secret tape containing new evidence.'

The verbal undertaking I had received about the tape remaining confidential had been ignored. I knew now that the police had the tape. Turning the page, I read the headlines: '*News of the World* tape may trap Leah's killer.'

It read: 'A secret *News of the World* tape could give police vital information in their hunt for the drug dealer whose ecstasy pill killed tragic Leah Betts. The cassette, recorded by an undercover reporter, may help cops piece together the youngster's movements before she took the fatal pill at her 18th birthday party last week.

'Last night detectives were set to quiz two men following evidence provided on the tape. The pair, Mark Murray and Steve Packman, are among six people already arrested over the lethal pill. Both were earlier released and bailed to reappear. Jobless Murray, of Pitsea, Essex, is a frequent visitor at Raquels nightclub in Basildon from where the £10 pill was supplied.

'Market trader Packman of nearby Laindon knew Leah when both attended Basildon colleges. Yesterday we handed our tape to Detective Constable Ian Shed, an officer on the case. He said: "This may be very helpful to us."

'Investigations are continuing into the chain of supply which ended in Leah's death. We want to find the main dealer.

'Leah, an A-level student, picked up the drug after finishing her Saturday job at a local store. She took the pill as soon as she returned to her home in Latchingdon, Essex, where she had invited 20 friends to celebrate her birthday. She died after begging step-mum Janet, "Help me, mum, help me."'

I hadn't seen or heard from Mark Murray since Leah's pill

was purchased. I hadn't a clue, really, what was going on. I rang Tucker, but as usual he wasn't in or wasn't answering his phone, so I sent him a fax telling him I had quit Raquels the night before, and Maurice was taking over. I said: 'There are no problems, it's safe, it's sorted.'

I heard nothing else all day. Nobody was talking to anybody that week. The following day, Monday 20 November, Tucker rang. I wasn't in. He left a message on the answering machine. He was being abusive and threatening. He said I couldn't just walk out of Raquels and he wanted an explanation. He also said I was responsible for Murray being in the paper. He said: 'I thought only that other kid was going in. You shouldn't have put Murray in. I'm going to fucking do you.'

My problems are my own. Nothing will make me involve my wife and children. I knew what may happen. I didn't need to ask Steve Ellis or his family. When the kids came out of school I booked them and Debra into a hotel near Rettendon where they spent the night.

On the news on Essex Radio, Detective Chief Inspector Brian Storey confirmed that they had received a tape but he would not discuss the contents. He told the interviewer that he wished people would talk to the police instead of the newspapers. I think he was sending me a personal message via the BBC.

I was still owed a week's money as we were paid in arrears at Raquels. I rang Martin and Maurice and told them I would be down on Friday to collect my money. Martin said: 'You had better ring me before you come, as I have heard that Tucker has got the hump.' I told him I didn't care, but I didn't want to involve him and agreed. We agreed to meet outside McDonald's (just around the corner from Raquels) and Martin said he would have my money.

I tooled myself up. I put a huge bowie knife in the back of my trousers, a bottle of squirt in my pocket, and went down to Basildon Town Centre to collect my money. Maurice and Martin met me outside McDonald's and advised me not to go round to the club.

'Tucker's there now with Tate, Rolfe and a few other people we haven't seen before,' said Martin.

'I don't give a fuck, I want my money.' I said. 'Tucker is

doing this for the benefit of the management. He's making out he's got the hump with me to please Dave Simms, because Simms doesn't like me. Simms will always warm to people who turn against me. Tucker's got nothing to worry about, the door is his. It's safe.'

'Tucker's told me he's holding your money and if you want it, you should get it yourself,' said Martin. 'But I wouldn't advise it – he's firmed up.'

I got really annoyed. I had been really loyal to the doormen at Raquels. Instead of backing me, they were all behind Tucker. Only Martin remained loyal.

'I'll give you my wages, and get yours off Tucker,' he told me. 'You can go round if you really want to. You know I'm with you. But I wouldn't advise it.'

Martin needed the work, and Tucker knew he was loyal to me. I didn't want to cause him any unnecessary problems, so I agreed. He gave me his money and went back to the club. Tucker asked Martin if he had seen me.

'I know he's your mate, but we've got a problem with him,' he said.

'Well, I've given him my money. Now I need to get paid.' Tucker said okay and gave Martin my money. As far as I was concerned, that was the end of the matter. Everyone was happy. I was out of Raquels and out of that way of life. Tucker now had complete control of Raquels. There was no need for anyone to continue with a vendetta.

The following night, Saturday 25 November, I was told that Tate and Rolfe went into the Buzz Bar, allegedly looking for me. I don't know what Pat's problem was. He and I had always got on well. I suppose he felt that because Tucker had the hump with me, he had to follow suit. It was always the way. Martin was in the Buzz Bar, and Tate asked him if he had seen me. 'Tell Bernie he can't hide forever,' he added. 'And when we see him, we are going to take lumps out of him.'

'He's my mate, I don't pass messages like that on,' Martin replied, and Tate and Rolfe left the bar.

On Monday morning, 27 November, I appeared at Chelmsford Crown Court for possessing the gun and the CS gas. I pleaded guilty to the gas, but my barrister told me to enter a plea of not guilty for possessing a firearm. It turned out the gun which Clarke and Pierce had given me was a Rhoner model SM10 self-loading pistol. The lab report stated the pistol was designed to fire eight millimetre blank or tear gas irritant cartridges so it could be used as a non-legal self-defence weapon. However it originally had a partial obstruction built into the bore of its barrel to prevent it from discharging a missile. This blockage had been removed at some point, and it was now possible for it to fire adapted cartridges. In short, it was a harmless gun that had been turned into a lethal weapon.

After discussion it was agreed I would plead guilty. However, because of the delay, the case was adjourned for two days. I was told that it would be beneficial for me if my wife and my brother also attended to give evidence to back up the story I was going to give.

On 29 November I appeared again at Chelmsford Crown Court. A detective from the Essex Police was there. He spoke to the prosecution and together with my barrister they all hammered out a deal. When my barrister returned he told me that he didn't think I would be receiving a custodial sentence, so I need not worry. I would probably get a suspended prison sentence. Nobody wanted to make waves.

The judge came in and a statement from my brother Michael was read to the Court. It said: 'I have worked as a farm hand since leaving school. I cannot recall the exact date – however, approximately 18 months ago, my elder brother Bernard came to see me at the farm. Bernard explained he had been socialising at a cattle market where he had met an old family friend. Our mother had worked for this man on his farm when we were young and we had maintained a close friendship ever since. Bernard said the man had sold him a vermin gat, which is local slang for a small handgun which is used for shooting rats etc. He had no use for it himself, but as it was offered cheaply, he had purchased it on my behalf. Assuming wrongly that I would want it, the handgun was, in short, useless. Nobody had ever seen anything like it. Even the calibre made it obsolete as you cannot purchase eight-millimetre rounds. I told Bernard the old man had had him over and we all had a good laugh at Bernard's expense. I never saw the gun again, and it was only ever mentioned again when

171

I was told Bernard had been arrested for possessing it.'

The prosecution never questioned my account. Nor did the police. The reason for possessing the gas was also accepted without question. I was sentenced to six months' imprisonment which was suspended for 12 months. The threat of prison had been lifted. I now only had to deal with the threat from Tucker and the firm.

The police were still reaping the benefits of receiving a mine of information. On the same day I was in Court, 15 addresses were raided in Basildon. Four men were charged with possessing drugs, including one also charged with theft. The police recovered 11 ecstasy tablets, half a kilo of amphetamine sulphate and herbal cannabis during the raids. They also unearthed a handgun, an electric stun gun, imitation firearms and a crossbow as well as child pornography and stolen property. A police spokesman said none of the addresses raided was directly linked to Leah's death. The spokesman added that Essex police were fully prepared to respond when this type of information was supplied.

The following day, 30 November, I received a phone call from an Essex detective. He told me that I ought to watch my back as they had received information that a firm was going to shoot me. He said Tucker was the man behind it, and I should take the threat seriously. I take all threats seriously, but life has to go on. I asked him if they had any other information, and he said no. A couple of people close to Tucker had called him. They said they had heard it being discussed. They were not prepared to give their names or any other details.

I didn't expect a gold watch when I quit the firm. But I certainly didn't expect to be shot, either.

On 1 December 1995, the funeral of Leah Betts took place in Latchingdon. Leah's natural mother had died four years previously, and following the service she was to be buried with her at a cemetery in Billericay. The Reverend Dr Don Gordon told hundreds of mourners that the teenager was not to blame. Rather the guilt lay with a society that has allowed a creeping cancer of drug abuse to destroy many lives. Dr Gordon said that in the pursuit of materialism, profit and pleasure many people had almost accepted drugs, and their dangerous effects, as a part of life. With that went a readiness to blame someone else for what was wrong. The truth is, we are all in part to blame. There was a man who knew what he was talking about.

The service began with the coffin carried into church accompanied by the hit single *Wonderwall* by Oasis, Leah's favourite band. At the close the Whitney Houston song *I Will Always Love You* was played before the cortège left for the burial service where Leah was laid to rest next to her mother Dorothy, who died from heart problems in 1992.

I sat in my car alone listening to the news bulletins about the funeral. You couldn't help but feel for her friends and family. I remembered kids in the club who had made jokes about her death. They sang the Jackson Five record, 'One bad apple doesn't spoil the whole bunch, girl.' But this was the reality. Joking about the death of an innocent girl in order to appear ruthless or hard seemed tragically sad and weak. No words, however admirable, from Paul Betts, Leah's father, or his wife Janet, Leah's stepmother, would stop this fashion. The danger they talked about gave this occupation an edge; that bit of danger made it more desirable, more daring, put 'the user' on a higher pedestal than his straight friends who didn't have the guts to do it. No officially run campaign could stop this fashion. They didn't realise it was all about rebellion.

The next day I rang Tucker. 'I hear you want to speak to me,' I said.

'I've been told you put Murray in the paper.'

'I don't care what you've been told,' I said. 'You know it isn't true. I told you Packman was going in the paper, and you said you didn't give a fuck so long as attention was taken off the firm.'

'Why didn't you tell me you were leaving Raquels when I saw you in Southend?' he asked.

'I had had enough of everything,' I explained. 'I admit I was wrong not to discuss it with you, but I just wanted to walk away. I told the manager Maurice was taking my place, and the door was safe. You've not lost out. It is still your door. In fact, you have complete control now, instead of going down the middle with me.'

'But people are talking,' he said.

'I don't give a fuck about people, Tony,' I replied. 'I'm out of it.'

He said: 'I don't believe you,' and the line went dead. I assumed he switched his mobile phone off.

Three days later, on 5 December, I was again contacted by a detective. He told me they had received information that the threats to shoot me were very real. Plans were being drawn for it to be carried out very soon. He also told me that Detective Chief Inspector Brian Storey wanted to talk to me about the Leah Betts enquiry and in particular about the comments I had made in a newspaper about the way the club had been run.

'I've moved away from Basildon now, I don't need this shit,' I said.

It was impressed upon me that I had no safe quarter. If I wanted to move away and start a new life, then I wouldn't need bad feeling from the police. I should do what they asked. It would be an informal chat. I could then go off and begin my new life, no strings attached. They also asked if Debra would be willing to talk. 'She has nothing she can tell you,' I said. 'She knows nothing.'

They said that every doorman would be spoken to, so it was in my interests to get it over and done with. I agreed that we would both attend South Woodham Ferrers Police Station the following day at about 2.00 p.m. I insisted that it be an informal chat rather than any type of official interview, otherwise I would have to bring a solicitor. They agreed.

That afternoon the snow began to fall heavily. Soon everywhere was covered with a blanket of snow. That night Pat, who had only been out of prison for six weeks, was up to his old tricks.

He was at home with his girlfriend, who called the London Pizza company in Wickford and asked for a pizza with different toppings on different sections. Roger Ryall, the manager, told the woman that they didn't do that type of pizza. Pat grabbed the phone and started swearing at him. The manager said later: 'I wasn't going to take that. So I said: "Get rid of that attitude, and I will send you a pizza."'

He obviously didn't know the type of man he was talking

to. Pat became more irate and slammed the phone down. Half an hour later he turned up at the pizza shop, picked up the till and hurled it across the room at the manager. Fearing for his life the manager backed out of the office and pushed the panic button which was linked directly to the police.

It was his second mistake of the evening. Pat, fearing arrest and returning to prison, over-reacted. He punched the manager in the face, grabbed him by the hair, and smashed his head into a glass plate on the draining board. Pat told him not to call the police, or he would come back and smash the place up and hurt his staff. However, the panic button had already been activated, and officers arrived after Pat had left. When Pat was identified and the police told Mr Ryall who he was and a bit of his history, Mr Ryall decided not to press charges after all.

Pat's call was traced to his home, but he was not arrested. Only the firm could turn ordering a pizza into an orgy of violence.

Now I had spoken to Tucker myself, I wasn't too concerned about the rumours that were flying around. It was probably just wannabes stirring it up, gloating over the fact that Tony and I had fallen out. I thought that once I had spoken to the police, my purpose would have been served; nobody would have any further business with me. I could at last see light at the end of the tunnel. I was awakening from the nightmare.

Debra and I drove to South Woodham Ferrers Police Station. We were met at the door by four detectives. Two wished to speak to Debra. DI Storey and another detective wished to speak to me.

Debra knew nothing, and therefore could say nothing, so I said I had no objection to her talking to anybody. However, if, as they had said, this was an informal chat, I would only be prepared to talk to DI Storey on his own. Storey, in my opinion, knows the score. I think he knew the pressure I was under. He agreed that we should talk alone.

Storey was well aware of the firm's involvement in just about everything. He knew what he could prove and he knew, despite knowing the facts, what was impossible to prove. Murray had been pulled, Murray had been questioned, but nobody was going to give evidence against him. I could see his task was painful, but he knew at that time the only people he could realistically prosecute were Packman and Smith.

He asked me about the tape which had been given to him – against my wishes – by the journalist. What could I say? I could hardly deny I was the person on the tape. However, he understood my predicament. He had heard that Tucker had threatened to shoot me. These were serious people. He knew it wasn't an idle threat. He asked me if I would make a statement saying I was the person on the tape. I didn't have to implicate anyone. All I had to say was 'Yes, that is me on the tape.'

Storey added that there was always the possibility that if I refused I might be subpoenaed to Court, although he made it clear he wasn't offering me an ultimatum; he was just being honest with me. I told him I understood my position. I couldn't put my family at risk for things I had done, but I wouldn't rule out the possibility of doing what he asked. I would give it some serious thought, discuss it with my family, and speak to him again in a couple of weeks. I wanted the thing with Tucker sorted out first. I didn't believe Tucker was a threat to me, I told him. It was the wannabes around him who were stirring up problems.

Storey told me that the information regarding the threats to have me shot was being treated seriously and I should be careful. The conversation lasted until about 4.00 p.m. When I came out, Debra was waiting. She said they had only kept her for half an hour, and asked about who was working on the night and other trivial matters: facts they already knew. I guess they had to speak to everyone who was in the building on the night the pill was bought. Procedure these days demands it.

I left Woodham Police Station feeling a little better about everything. Debra and I had arranged for her mother to look after the children. We left South Woodham Ferrers at about ten past four. The snow was now quite heavy. It had settled and was perhaps three or four inches deep. We arrived at Debra's mother's house at about five o'clock and stayed for a cup of tea. Then we drove on to Wickford, where we had something to eat, and headed towards the Rettendon Turnpike, the main roundabout on the A130. By now it was about 6.30. It was a miserable night. The snow was still falling and it was pitch black. Ironically at around the same time, Tucker, Tate and Rolfe were travelling along the same road.

CHAPTER 15

The following morning I'd arranged to meet my brother in London. I travelled on the train, as I didn't fancy battling through traffic in the snow. At about 11, I rang home to see if there were any messages on the answering machine. There was one. A detective was asking me to contact him a soon as I got his message. It sounded urgent.

I rang him from King's Cross station. 'We've found a Range Rover with three bodies inside,' he said. 'They've all been shot through the head. We think it's your mates.'

'What do you mean?' I asked.

'Do you recognise this registration: F424 NPE? I am sure it's them.' He told me he had seen them in the car before.

'I don't know what you're talking about,' I said. 'Tell me what's happened.' I was confused.

He repeated that they had found a Range Rover. Tucker, Tate and Rolfe were inside, but they had not been formally identified at that stage.

'Are they dead?' I asked.

He said: 'They're very dead.'

I felt relief and sadness at the same time. Who? Why? I couldn't take in what was being said. I just couldn't believe that they were actually dead. One of them, maybe. But all three in one hit. It couldn't be right. It was some sort of sick joke.

Tony, Pat, Craig. They'd all been warned, but they wouldn't listen. They should not have fucked with people in the game we were in. Any fool can pull a trigger. It doesn't take a hardman. They wouldn't listen, though. They thought nobody could touch them. I guess they were wrong.

178

The policeman wanted to know where I was. I said I would ring him later, and put the phone down. I rang Tony Tucker's mobile number. It rang and rang and rang. He wasn't going to answer. Unknown to me at that time, his mobile phone was still in his hand. The police had not yet removed it from the body. Nor had they taken the body from the Range Rover. I rang home. Debra wasn't in. I left a message on the answering machine saying I had been told that 'those three' had been found murdered. I told her not to answer the phone if anyone rang.

I walked around London in a daze. I really couldn't believe what I had been told. I even began to wonder if I had actually had the conversation.

Debra never got my message. She went straight to the school at 3.30 p.m. to pick up the children. She was met by two detectives. One walked across to her and asked: 'Are you Bernard's Debra?' When she said yes, he said: 'You and the children better come with me.' They were put in an unmarked car. Nothing was said in front of the children, but Debra was told what had happened. The police feared a revenge attack of some type might be carried out on me or my family, so they were going to remain with them until I had been located. The police – and others – obviously thought that I was connected to the murders.

The police had also driven past my house to see if I was there and saw the front door was wide open. This caused them further concern. They radioed the detectives on the case and told them what they had found. The area around my house was immediately cleared. Debra could not explain why the front door was open. She rang the house and recovered the messages from the answering machine. I had told her to meet me at Tilbury railway station in Essex, which is by the docks and would be deserted at that time of night. I would be there at about 8.30.

When I got off the train, there was no sign of Debra. I went to a phone box and rang her mother to see if she was there. I heard a loud tap on the window of the call box. A detective was standing there with Debra. I said goodbye to Debra's mother on the phone. 'You can guess what the problem is, Bernie,' said the detective. 'I hope you're not involved in this.'

179

I asked him what had happened. He told me that it was definitely Tucker, Tate and Rolfe who had been found shot through the head in their Range Rover on a deserted farm track at Rettendon. I was numb with shock. I had a bag with me. I opened it and said: 'Do you want to search it?' He said no. He told Debra to get in one car with one detective, and I got into the back of another. Two detectives sat in the front.

The detective said to me again: 'I hope you're not involved in this, Bernie.'

'I'm not, I'm not. I'm telling you I'm not,' I said. 'We fell out. What we fell out over didn't warrant that. If you're thinking I'm involved, then you've got it wrong.'

'A lot of people think it's you,' he said. 'You fell out with them. They threatened to shoot you. You didn't take the threat seriously. The next thing, they all turn up dead. What else are we meant to think?'

He told me the front door of my home was wide open. Had I left it that way? I said no. He said there was a possibility that someone was waiting for me at the house and suggested we both went there. He was armed. I said I would go in first. He wasn't going to argue.

I went in and called round all the rooms, but it was deserted. The door wasn't damaged. She had never done it in her life, but I guessed Debra must have not closed it properly when she left. It was just a coincidence. The detective told me that not only would the police think I was involved, but the firm also would think I was involved in the murders. He said it was something that I should give some careful consideration to. I kept telling him I wasn't involved.

'I am willing to go to a police station with you now,' I said. 'You can interview me or do what you want. I am not involved in their deaths.'

He put me in the car, left Debra in the house with other detectives, and drove me down the road. He stopped and asked me who could have killed Tucker, Tate and Rolfe. There were so many reasons why they could have died, it's not as though they never upset anyone. I couldn't help him.

'Your best bet is to go home and keep your head down,' he said. 'We'll be in touch.'

They left me in my house with Debra and the children. I

still couldn't believe it. It was all over the news. I don't drink that often; only when I'm on a downer. But that night I sat down and drank till I could drink no more. I rang two members of the firm: both put the phone down on me. This couldn't be happening, just when I thought everything was going to be all right. I don't think I slept at all. Every face, every horror committed and witnessed came to visit me that night.

The following day, every newspaper carried the story. Tony Tucker's father, Ronald Tucker, collapsed and died when the news was broken to him. His wife was with him at the time. It must have been terrible for her. Her husband was only 63. To lose your son and your husband on the same day must have been agonising. It has always been the families I have felt for, because they have no control over events. When you are involved, you're full of yourself, you forget about the feelings of your family.

There was a lot of speculation in the press. The trio had been found at about 8.00 a.m. the day after they had been shot. Ken Jiggins was a bricklayer and the frost had been too severe to work that day. He had arrived at Peter Theobald's door, ready to help his friend feed the 800 pheasants kept in fields at the 130-acre farm. Theobald ran a shooting range, and the birds had to be fed twice a day. They skipped tea and Theobald started up the Land Rover, scraping thick ice from its windows. They drove across a field, maybe 300 yards, and turned left into Workhouse Lane. There, in front of a locked gate leading to an angler's pond and the shooting area, was a metallic blue Range Rover. Its windows, despite the ice, were clear, and the pair could see two men in the front seats. They looked asleep, and Jiggins jumped out to ask them to move aside.

Theobald was wondering if they were poachers when Jiggins, who had tapped the driver's window, shouted out: 'There are two dead men here.'

He used his mobile phone to alert the police while Theobald went to look at the Range Rover. As well as the two in the front, he saw another man dead in the back, slumped across the seat. He looked more closely at the driver, still with his hands on the steering wheel and, he later learned, his foot on the brake. There was a round two-inch entry wound behind his ear, exiting out of his mouth. Familiar with firearms, Theobald was astonished to learn that the men had been slain by shotgun and that each had two wounds to the head. There was some blood seeping from the Range Rover, but nothing like the mess he would have expected.

Craig Rolfe, father of a seven-year-old daughter, Georgia, was the first to die, the police believe. He had been driving. The automatic gearshift was still switched to drive. The ignition was off. He looked as if he had pulled up at traffic lights. Craig was slumped to one side with blood running from his nose and mouth. His eyes were closed. In the passenger seat was Tony Tucker. He had been the second to die. He was sitting bolt-upright, his head bowed. He had blood all over his face and chest. Tate was slumped across the back seat of the car, his head lying in the broken window. He had blood around his chin which had spilled onto his chest. Each had been shot twice in the head. Tate had been shot a third time in the abdomen. None was wearing seat belts. And none had weapons, which was unbelievable for those three.

It appeared Tucker and Rolfe had known nothing. Pat had tried to react. The first shot in the abdomen had immobilised him. He had been finished off with the other two shots to the head.

Some papers claimed they had been murdered in revenge for the death of Leah Betts. They were calling it the Leah E-Wars. The *Daily Express* reported that a gangland figure was in hiding after the execution of the three drug dealers. They said the gangster allegedly ordered their assassination after he was tipped off that they were planning to kill him. The man, they said, who had links with the Krays, was accused of revealing the trio's drug dealing activities. It was nonsense, but it sounded remarkably familiar.

Some thought the three had been murdered in retaliation for the death of Kevin Whitaker, whom Tony and Craig had murdered. Others said they had been murdered by the same man who had shot Kerr – the gunman who had gone into Billericay Hospital dressed as a clown. Nipper Ellis, returned from exile, appeared in the *Sun*. He claimed they had been offered a chilling choice of how they died: blasted through the head with a shotgun, or hacked to pieces with an axe. Nipper told the *Sun* 'a very reliable source' had told him that they were going to be given two options: they could be taken apart with an axe, starting with their fingers, moving onto their hands and then their legs; or they could opt for the quick way out: shot through the back of the head. They were told: 'Either way you are going to get it. There's no escape.' Tucker and Tate, he said, messed their trousers first, then took their shots. Nipper confirmed the three were lured to the snow-covered farm track in Rettendon with the promise of another drugs deal.

'They had double-crossed too many people,' he told the *Sun*. 'They had made too many enemies. They often went to these meets, snatched the supplies and beat up the suppliers. But they did it once too often, and were set up themselves.' Nipper denied being responsible for the murders. He was a suspect because of his arrest for the earlier attempt on Tate's life.

Nipper said: 'It wasn't me who did the shooting. But I'd love to shake the hand of the man who did it. He's my hero, and I will regret to my dying day that I could not take the credit for it.'

Everyone, it seemed, regardless of their views, wanted to be linked to this dramatic murder. Donna Garwood appeared in a local paper. 'My Tony was not the villain they say he was,' ran the headline.

She said: 'They would still be alive if Pat hadn't been released from jail. If Pat was still inside this wouldn't have happened. If anything went on between the three of them, then Pat was involved, because the three of them never did anything without each other.

'I just knew it was him. It was Tony's car. And when I tried to ring him on his mobile, it was switched off. I had spoken to him that day and asked when I was going to see him again. He told me he was going to the Global Restaurant in Romford with Pat and Craig.'

Tony had two teenage children from a previous marriage, and Donna said his boy had been very ill. She said how good Tucker was, and how he spent a lot of time with him. 'It's hitting me more and more,' she said. 'I feel that a part of me has been taken away. In my eyes, Tony wasn't the drug baron or villain he has been made out to be. He used to say, "They don't know me, so who are they to judge".' It was a bit insensitive for her to appear in such a newspaper article, considering Tony lived with his partner, Anna.

The Range Rover had been covered with a tarpaulin, loaded onto a police lorry with the three bodies still inside and then taken to South Woodham Ferrers Police Station for examination. There was a tragic irony to this. Twenty-six years earlier Brian Rolfe, then only two years older than his son, Craig, had been found on Christmas Eve slumped over the steering wheel of his parked van in a lay-by near Basildon. He too had terrible head injuries. After police photographers had done their stuff, the van, with the body still in it, was loaded onto a transporter and taken to police headquarters at Chelmsford for detailed examination. So much for peace and goodwill to all men at Christmas.

When you're shocked, you do things you can't explain. I drove over to Rettendon. I didn't know the exact location where they had been found. I stopped near a phone box at Rettendon Turnpike, which overlooks all of the fields. Everywhere was covered with a blanket of snow. I looked out across the fields and thought about my friends. The men who died were not the people I had first met. The drug culture had turned them into unreasonable men. Drugs were giving them courage to do things any rational man would have thought reckless. Wannabes were boosting their egos, reinforcing the belief they couldn't be touched. The rewards cemented the notion that they were right. Regardless of what went on, I couldn't help but feel sadness for Pat, Tony, Craig and their loved ones.

The following day the police had completed all forensic tests at the site of the killing. I drove down there. To this day I can't believe they were so easily led to such a place. It is a long, unmade road, barely passable in a car. At the dead end is the gate where they died. I leant against the gate and again I was filled with sadness, thinking about them. There were half a dozen posies scattered in the snow. Notes from girls, mainly, to Pat. One read: 'Prison did this to you, Pat.' Another spoke about his problem with drugs. Others said he was a wonderful man. People had also remembered Craig and Tony.

Messages were brief. One was unsigned. Donna Garwood had left a posy with a note. She said she would love him always. I thought it was really insensitive. Hardly the type of thing Tony's partner would like to find at the spot where he died if she visited it.

At the gate there was a sign which would have been facing them as they met their deaths. It read: 'Countryside premium scheme. Farming operations must still take place, so please take special care to avoid injury. The use of guns or any other activity which disturbs people or wildlife are not allowed on this land. Enjoy your visit.' Whoever did the shooting did not pay the sign much heed.

As soon as European Leisure, the owners of Raquels, heard what had happened, Tucker's firm was sacked from running security at the club. On 12 December, Jones, the man whom I believed had set me up with the gun, was given the contract to work there. Maurice, whom I had given the club to, and considered a good friend, had agreed to stay there and work for Jones. I was really disappointed. He had no loyalty to me. How could he work for the very people who had caused me so many problems?

Two days later, on the 14th, I was having a drink in Basildon with a friend of mine. I couldn't get it out of my head that Jones had succeeded in getting Raquels. I went down to the Buzz Bar where two of his doormen were working. I began to get abusive and I was hit in the mouth. I pulled out a huge bowie knife and threatened them. They backed off. I told them it wasn't my door any more, but they had no right to come and take it. They told me they agreed. I rang Jones. I told him what I thought of him, and I told him he would never be able to keep the club. That night his doormen walked out and they never came back.

The very next day the doormen who had worked for me and Tucker were reinstated at the club. Jones had held it for two days. Basildon District Council, who run the Registered Door Staff Scheme with the Basildon Police Licensing Unit wrote to me and told me that I no longer met the criteria for registration because of the incident with the gun and the gas. To me, the incident had not taken place at my place of work, so it was not relevant to my employment.

I was asked to attend a meeting. In an ironic twist Jones had also been asked to attend a meeting as he had been involved in an incident while working at a nightclub in Canvey Island. He had assaulted a customer and been convicted. He went into the meeting first and was allowed to keep his licence.

On the face of it, I had had some CS gas in my home for the protection of my wife, and had purchased a gun for my brother for shooting vermin on his farm. But even if I'd been John the Baptist, they would have taken my licence from me. There were representatives from all political parties on the Council as well as the police. They quizzed me about the Leah Betts incident. They also made it plain that they were aware of the Rettendon murders connection.

They wanted me to sit down and talk the philosophical shit that straight people love to hear from people who want something from them. I wasn't going to play their game. I didn't need or want their licence, but this was personal. One councillor said to me: 'Give me one good reason why I should unleash you on the public?' I told her that she was talking to me as if I was some sort of caged animal. I wasn't abusive, but I wasn't going to suck up to these people, either. I wanted to say my piece. They would not give me a decision there and then. They said they would ring me.

The following day, David Britt, the Assistant Chief Environmental Health Officer who helped run the scheme, rang me. He was all apologetic, saying I had not been successful and my licence had been taken away. He said to me meekly: 'To be honest, Bernie, the reason you didn't get it is because you did not ingratiate yourself.' I told him in no uncertain terms that I wasn't going to suck up to him or anybody else. He could keep his licence. Sadly, they had managed to take it away from me long after the race had been run.

I then received a letter telling me I had been banned for at least seven years from working on the door or in any licensed premises in the Basildon District Council area. How they must have danced!

On 21 December, four days before Christmas, the first of the three funerals took place. Twenty cars followed a horse-drawn carriage containing Craig's coffin, which travelled from his mother's house in Pitsea to St Gabriel's Church. Seventy mourners attended the service at which Reverend Laurie Blaney said a few words prepared by Rolfe's partner, Donna Jaggers and his mother Lorraine. After the funeral the procession of cars, including three black hearses, drove the short distance to Pitsea Cemetery. Wreaths were laid at the burial, including one from Ms Jaggers and their daughter, Georgia, which said: 'You are not gone until you are forgotten. And we will never forget you.'

The following day the second funeral took place. Again a horse-drawn carriage led a cortège of mourners as family and friends paid their last respects to Pat Tate. Relatives dabbed their eyes to hide their grief as they left St Gabriel's Church in Pitsea. Family and friends had earlier gathered at Tate's Gordon Road house in Basildon before following the coffin to the church. Police directed traffic as a bell tolled for the 25-minute service in which Pat's brother gave a touching tribute. Four Daimler limousines carrying loved ones followed two hearses stacked with flowers. One floral tribute simply said 'Daddy'. A card attached read: 'Thanks for the good times. I will never forget you. Your baby son, Jordan.' A large tribute made out of individually lettered floral wreaths spelled 'Brother'. A card said: 'You will always be in our thoughts and never forgotten in all our lives.' As the coffin was carried into the church by six pallbearers, one heart-shaped red and white tribute rested on top. Around 60 mourners sang *All Things Bright And Beautiful* and recited the 23rd Psalm. Pat was laid in a grave next to Craig.

Later that afternoon Tony was buried in Hornchurch. There was no horse-drawn carriage. His body was carried in a limousine. More than 100 people attended. Most of them were doormen. I didn't go to any of the funerals. They weren't my friends at the end. I couldn't help feeling sad, regardless of our differences: these men were human. They had loved ones and children. Nobody, our victims included, should endure this misery.

The firm suspected at that time that I was responsible. So it wouldn't have been wise to go even if I had wanted to. I have since visited Pat and Craig's graves. All I can think of when I go there is what a terrible waste. I haven't been to visit

Tony's grave. I don't think I ever will. He was such a good friend in the beginning, I still cannot believe what he became.

After Tony had taken over Raquels exclusively from me, his pal Nigel Benn had been booked to DJ there for a night. As the club wasn't attracting customers following Leah's death, Nigel had agreed that he would DJ there on 22 December to help bring in customers. It was the night of Tony's funeral. Benn, out of respect for his friend, agreed to honour the booking. He played to a packed house. But the previous success could never again be matched. Most who went there that night would never return. The promoters knew it.

They sent a letter to all of their members. In it, they said: 'We would like to inform you we will be closing our Friday nights at Raquels. This is due to the fact that despite our efforts to keep the night up and running, it has become apparent that the recent publicity surrounding Raquels has caused the club irreparable damage. We made the decision after careful deliberation to honour the contractual commitments to both the club and our DJs. For professional reasons, and also to be loyal to our members and to not let you down, we did have every intention to carry on. But after taking time out to consider things in general, we now feel that the night has run its course. It must not be forgotten that throughout the year that passed before recent events we all had an excellent time in bringing to you a night which we felt was up there with the best in Essex. It was nice, though, to end the night on a high with the guest appearance of Nigel Benn to see it out in style. And thanks to all of you who came along to support it. He was simply gobsmacked with the reception he got from you lot. Well, as the saying goes, all good things must come to an end.'

A lot people would argue that it wasn't a good thing in the slightest that was ending.

Rumours about me continued to circulate. Sandra Lee, the sister of Dave Lee, one of my friends, rang me. She told me she had started work for a company in Basildon. Her supervisor was claiming he was a suspect in the Rettendon murders.

He told her that I had gone into a café and 'done' a man. He was referring to Mick McCarthy the man who had been gunned down in a café and been paralysed. He told her that £10,000 had been put up to have me shot. Bagleys (a nightclub in King's Cross, London) doormen and Bass Brewery doormen were going to do it that year. Members of Tucker's firm were at Bagleys on the night a doorman named Dave Anderson had been murdered, but this I guess was just another wannabe talking.

However, Mick McCarthy's shooting and Dave Anderson's murder were nothing whatsoever to do with me. I couldn't think of any connection. It sounded a bit familiar to the Leah Betts thing. Anything a bit sensational was going to attract idiots. This supervisor, I thought, was just trying to make himself sound a bit sinister. He wanted Sandra to be impressed. However, these people were dangerous. I didn't want Tucker's friends thinking I was involved in the murders.

I was a prime suspect at one stage. The police were making enquiries about my relationship with Tony in particular. They had quizzed people at the club. Some time after their deaths I applied under the Data Protection Act to have information about me on police computers released. Although I have only been allowed to have a very brief summary, police thinking early on in the investigation was clear. Print-outs I received read: 'Associate of Tucker.' 'Associate of Tate.' 'Anonymous details: O'Mahoney as possible killer.' 'Used to be partner of Tucker.' 'Previous convictions: robbery, ABH, GBH and offensive weapons.' 'Anonymous messages and newspaper clippings received. All approved.' 'O'Mahoney as possible killer.'

The police were focusing their attention on me. The firm, despite the fact I had been loyal to them, would not even acknowledge me. The atmosphere was very hostile. It was a very difficult time. Like my predecessor David Vine, I was finding out that once you fall out of favour, regardless of whether you are guilty of anything or not, you are soon deemed unfit to associate with.

When Nigel Benn honoured his promise to his friend Tony Tucker to perform at Raquels it proved to be the club's swan song. The following Friday it closed. Raquels had been open for more than 30 years. In less than two years the firm's activities had closed it.

On the same night that Raquels closed its doors, at Club UK in south London, 19-year-old Andreas Bouzis collapsed after taking an ecstasy tablet stamped with a bunny logo. Medically trained staff at the club tried in vain to revive him. A post mortem examination revealed a congenital heart defect, a constricted valve which rendered the drug fatal. Mrs Bouzis said: 'Andreas was our life, our family, our love, our reason to live. On Friday night he went to a club, just as your children may have done, now he is dead. Gone for ever. I cannot describe our feelings. Yesterday our son had a future, he had a life. Today he's dead. Families and their love are very precious. Ecstasy tablets destroy families.'

Mrs Bouzis is right. As all friends and families of my associates and those I met in clubland will tell you.

EPILOGUE

The misery, pain and death I have witnessed during our reign has left me in no doubt that I need to return to normality, whatever the cost. Images of those whose lives were ruined or lost will haunt me forever. I have left Essex in the hope my passage will be made easier. I will not be missed. Somebody will have filled my shoes and the posts left vacant by my ex-associates. I am not a drug dealer, never have been. I was a vital cog in the machine that allowed the drug dealers to ply their trade. I know how they work, I know what they fear. I know that current efforts to combat the problem are failing. Far too much rubbish has been talked about drugs since Leah's death. 'Experts' say kids need educating, so they can make an informed choice, then in the next breath, they say nobody knows the long-term effects of ecstasy.

Thousands of young girls like Leah go to nightclubs, but they are no longer pestered by a spotty kid for a dance around her handbag. They are pestered to experiment with speed, ecstasy or cocaine. Looking around the room, they see lots of others using drugs, they see chill-out areas, St John's Ambulance men, paramedics and in some instances doctors: all on standby for the benefit of those who have taken drugs. It gives the impression drug taking is a legitimate practice. The pressure to conform is immense. If the current attitude to the problem is maintained, tearful press conferences given by grieving parents will become so common they will no longer be newsworthy. And when dead kids are no longer news, we will all have reached rock bottom.

I realised that if I wanted to shed the criminal make-up I had worn for so long, the only decision that I could make which would not allow me to change my mind, would be if I agreed to co-operate with Detective Inspector Storey's request to validate the tape. I contacted him and we arranged to meet at a village police station. I will never forget sitting in that room which overlooked a quaint row of shops. Below, people were going about their everyday business and I was sitting there watching them talking about the deaths of young people. I was astride two worlds. I knew which one I wanted to inhabit. I made the statement, I validated the tape. The door to my previous life was closed firmly behind me.

After two separate, lengthy trials, neither jury could decide whether or not Steve Packman was involved in the supply of the ecstasy pill which killed Leah. The judge discharged the jury and entered a verdict of Not Guilty. Packman walked free from the Court, his name cleared, an innocent man. I had stated throughout the trial that he was not a drug dealer and he shouldn't have been in the dock. There are others however, who should have been. I had to smile when I heard the verdict, after enduring so much turmoil trying to decide whether or not I should give up my way of life and tell the truth, the jurors, all good and true, didn't believe me. Was this our man-made law at work or was it justice? It was probably the latter.